Vehicle Speeds and Operating Costs

Models for Road Planning and Management

Thawat Watanatada
Ashok M. Dhareshwar
Paulo Roberto S. Rezende Lima

in collaboration with
Patrick M. O'Keefe
Per E. Fossberg

Published for The World Bank

The Johns Hopkins University Press
Baltimore and London

The Johns Hopkins University Press
Baltimore, Maryland 21211
First printing December 1987

Library of Congress Cataloging-in-Publication Data

Watanatada, Thawat
    Vehicle speeds and operating costs : models for road planning and management / by Thawat
Watanatada, Ashok M. Dhareshwar, Paulo Roberto S. Rezende Lima ; in collaboration with Patrick M.
O'Keefe, Per E. Fossberg.
        p.   cm. — (The Highway design and maintenance standards series)

    Bibliography: p.
    1. Motor vehicles—Cost of operation—Mathematical models.
2. Motor vehicles—Speed—Mathematical models.   I. Dhareshwar,
Ashok M., 1949–   . II. Lima, Paulo Roberto S. Rezende, 1944–
III. Title.   IV. Series.
TL151.5.T48   1987   388.3'144—dc19   87–22176
ISBN 0-8018-3589-5

Foreword

An effective road transportation network is an important factor in economic and social development. It is also costly. Road construction and maintenance consume a large proportion of the national budget, while the costs borne by the road-using public for vehicle operation and depreciation are even greater. It is therefore vitally important that policies be pursed which, within financial and other constraints, minimize total transport costs for the individual road links and for the road network as a whole. To do this meaningfully, particularly when dealing with large and diverse road networks, alternatives must be compared and the tradeoffs between them carefully assessed. This in turn requires the ability to quantify and predict performance and cost functions for the desired period of analysis.

Because of the need for such quantitative functions, the World Bank initiated a study in 1969 that later became a large-scale program of collaborative research with leading research institutions and road agencies in several countries. This Highway Design and Maintenance Standards Study (HDM) has focused both on the rigorous empirical quantification of the tradeoffs between the costs of road construction, road maintenance, and vehicle operation and on the development of planning models incorporating total life-cycle cost simulation as a basis for highways decisionmaking.

This volume is one in a series that documents the results of the HDM study. The other volumes are:

Vehicle Operating Costs
Evidence from Developing Countries

Road Deterioration and Maintenance Effects
Models for Planning and Management

The Highway Design and Maintenance Standards Model
Volume 1. Description of the HDM-III Model

The Highway Design and Maintenance Standards Model
Volume 2. Users' Manual for the HDM-III Model

Road-user costs are by far the largest cost elements in road transport. Improvements in road conditions, although costly, can yet pay substantial dividends by reducing vehicle operating costs and hence generate large net benefits to the national economy as a whole. Thus, expressing vehicle operating costs in relation to road characteristics—geometry and pavement condition—is the logical approach. For certain cost components, especially fuel consumption, the required data can be obtained through controlled experiments, whereas for others, especially vehicle maintenance costs, extensive road-user surveys are needed. Both approaches were used in the HDM studies in Kenya, Brazil, and India and in the study in the Caribbean sponsored by the British Transport and Road Research Laboratory. The resulting body of knowledge on road-user costs is enormous. It covers conditions on three continents with diverse highway conditions and in radically different economic environments.

This volume takes an aggregate-mechanistic view of vehicle speed and operating costs under free flow conditions. Basing their analysis on the mechanistic principles of propulsion and motion as well as on postulated assumptions of driver behavior, the authors arrive at predictions at three levels of detail, ranging from a simulation method for use in detailed geometric design at the link level to an aggregate method for use in investment planning at the sectoral level. The models were estimated using the comprehensive data base collected in the Brazil-UNDP-World Bank highway research project and were validated along with data sets from India. One of the significant contributions to highway economics research made in this study is the probabilistic limiting velocity approach to steady-state speed prediction, which, combined with the aggregate-mechanistic methodology, will provide a possible basis for future research on the far more complex problem of operating costs under congested conditions.

This volume is to some extent a companion to *Vehicle Operating Costs: Evidence from Developing*

Countries, which is based on an aggregate-correlative methodology that considers vehicle operating costs equations in an economic context. These two approaches are complementary and elucidate different aspects and different components of the road-user cost complex.

Although the relationships described in this volume form part of the HDM-III model, they can also be used on their own. Chapter 14 provides guidelines for implementing the relationships on either mainframe or microcomputers, as well as a set of resource component tables. With the specific road characteristics provided by the user, the models predict travel speed and resource consumption in physical units for the typical vehicle classes and, when combined with prices or unit costs of the relevant resources, predict the user costs.

A guide to the approach and methodology may be obtained by reading the chapters and sections shown in the diagram below. Also, readers interested only in prediction formulas and policy applications may continue with Part III (Chapters 13 through 16) after Chapter 1.

Clell G. Harral
Principal Transport Economist

Per E. Fossberg
Highways Adviser

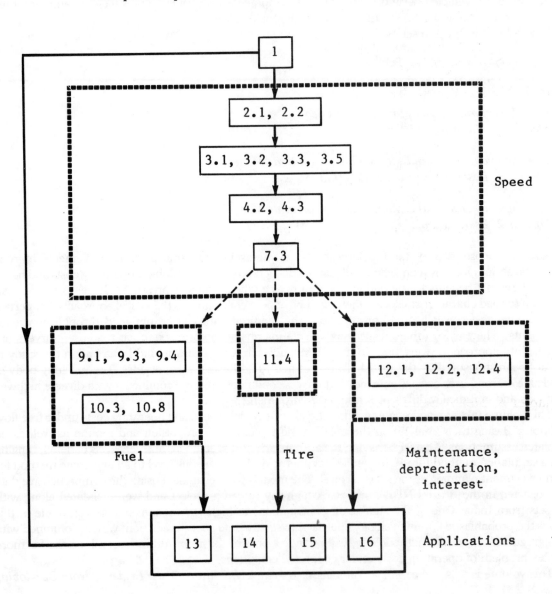

Contents

Acknowledgments

Several organizations and numerous individuals have contributed either directly or indirectly to this book.

First of all, we want to thank the Government of Brazil and the United Nations Development Programme (UNDP) for their sponsorship of the highway research project entitled "Research on the Interrelationships between Costs of Highway Construction, Maintenance and Utilization" (PICR) from which this book originated. The massive field data were collected and assembled by Empresa Brasileira de Planejamento de Transportes (GEIPOT), the project's responsible executing agency, in collaboration with the Texas Research and Development Foundation (TRDF) and the World Bank.

Of the many organizations that assisted the PICR project, particular mention should be made of the British Transport and Road Research Laboratory, the Western Australia Main Roads Department, the Massachusetts Institute of Technology, the Swedish National Road and Traffic Research Institute (VTI), the South African National Transport and Road Research Institute, and the Australian Road Research Board (ARRB).

Among the many individuals at GEIPOT, we would like to make special mention of Jose Teixeira and Teodoro Lustosa of the PICR project; Francisco Magalhaes, GEIPOT Director; and Jose Menezes Senna, GEIPOT President, for their guidance, encouragement, and provision of resources. The results here achieved would not have been possible without a solid and realistic experimental design, followed by painstaking data collection in the field, thorough experimentation and surveys. In this regard particular appreciation is due to William R. Hudson, Bertell Butler, Robert Harrison, Richard Wyatt, Russel Kaesehagen, Hugo Orellana, Stephen Linder, Stanley Buller, Pedro Moraes, John Zaniewski, Barry Moser, Leonard Moser, Douglas Plautz, and Joffre Swait of the PICR study, as well as Virgil Anderson of Purdue University and Paul Irick of the U.S. Transportation Research Board.

We further want to thank the several individuals who carefully read either the early reports on the subject or the manuscript of this book and made many useful comments and suggestions—particularly, in addition to the anonymous formal reviewers, Andrew Chesher of Bristol University, Gosta Gynnerstedt of the VTI, John Mclean and Chris Hoban of the ARRB, Thomas Gillespie of the Transportation Research Institute at the University of Michigan, Leonard Della-Moretta of the U.S. Forest Service, and Edward Sullivan of the Institute of Traffic Studies at the University of California, Berkeley.

At the World Bank, we appreciate the continued support and encouragement given by Christopher Willoughby and Louis Pouliquen, former directors, Transportation Department. Esra Bennathan and Alan Walters are acknowledged for their helpful reviews and advice and also for their intellectual challenge regarding the economic interpretations of our engineering-oriented road-user cost prediction models. Over the years many World Bank transport engineers and economists, too numerous to mention, have made suggestions about the requirements of road-user cost prediction, and we have attempted to build several features into the prediction models in response to those suggestions. We want to thank our colleagues Anil Bhandari, Bill Paterson, E. Viswanathan, and Sujiv Vurgese for their help in numerous ways, including a thorough review of the manuscript at the draft stage.

On the production side, we want to acknowledge the outstanding work of Sabine Shive as the publication coordinator. The editorial help given by Ann Petty was invaluable. Special thanks are due to Emiliana Danowski and Roberta Bensky for their great skill and unfailing patience in producing the innumerable drafts of the manuscript.

Finally, we owe our deepest gratitude to Clell Harral, who has been the single most influential and motivating force behind all these efforts. Without his total dedication, the book would not have come into being.

CHAPTER 1
Introduction

1.1 STUDY OBJECTIVES

A consensus has been growing among highway administrators, economists and engineers, in developed and developing countries alike, on using the principle of total transport cost minimization as a basis for determining road construction and maintenance policies. It has long been known that of the three main components of total life-cycle costs of a roadway, which also include those of road construction and maintenance, the road user costs of vehicle operation (including ownership) and travel time are by far the largest and can amount to more than 90 percent for two-lane highways serving a few thousand vehicles per day or more.

Therefore, it is important to quantify empirically, as accurately as practicable, how road user costs are affected by road characteristics, including geometric standards, which reflect the amount of capital investment in the road, and surfacing standards, which reflect both initial capital and subsequent maintenance expenditures. Moreover, it is important for the form of quantification, or prediction models, to be as convenient to use as possible. These issues are the main concern of this book, which, specifically, has two principal objectives:

1. To present the theory and empirical quantification of models for predicting, under free-flowing conditions, the speed, fuel consumption, tire wear and time-related components of running costs (primarily depreciation and interest charges and crew costs) of cars, utilities, buses, and a range of trucks from 6 to 40 ton gross weights. These components constitute approximately 75 percent of the total operating cost[1] of typical truck operations in Brazil (GEIPOT, 1982 Volume 5). Appendix 1A shows the classification and specifications of the vehicles employed in the Brazil study.

   The models are generally based on theories of vehicle mechanics and behavior of drivers and operators. They have been quantified almost exclusively using extensive data collected in the Brazil-UNDP-World Bank highway research

---

[1] The other components of running costs are maintenance parts and labor and lubricants; they are reported in detail in a companion volume in the series (Chesher and Harrison, forthcoming) and, for the sake of completeness, summarized in Chapter 12.

project.[2] The exceptions are the effect of narrow road widths and lubricant consumption, which are based on the data from the India Road User Cost Study (CRRI, 1982). The models are available in easy-to-use aggregate form of algebraic functions which produce predictions sensitive to major road design and maintenance variables, can reasonably be extrapolated over the likely range of policy variables and also can, in general, be adapted to suit local conditions. Although these models are useful for link-level feasibility and prefeasibility studies, they are particularly valuable for highway sector planning in which the planner searches the combination of road construction and maintenance standards that minimizes the discounted total transport cost of the road network under budget constraints.

2. To provide detailed guidelines on: first, how to use these models, along with other models reported in the companion volume (Chesher and Harrison, forthcoming) for predicting maintenance parts and labor requirements and lubricants consumption, in the prediction of total vehicle operating costs; and, second, how to adapt the model parameters to suit the conditions of a new region or country. These models have been implemented in the new version of the Highway Design and Maintenance Standards Model (HDM-III) for total transport cost prediction (Watanatada et al., forthcoming). They can also be used for predicting vehicle operating costs alone and are easily implemented on personal computers either as independent application software or via a spreadsheet package.

The important limitations of the models described in this volume may be identified as follows:

1. The models predict vehicle operating costs under the regime of unimpeded flow. Thus, the impact of vehicle interaction and congestion on vehicle operating costs is not modelled. Extension of the current results to the regime of impeded flow would be an important item in any agenda for future research on vehicle operating costs.

2. While the models predict speeds, and hence travel times, they do not address the valuation of travel time savings. The latter must be provided by the user.

---

[2] Financed by the Government of Brazil and the United Nations Development Programme (UNDP) and executed by the Empresa Brasileira de Planejamento de Transportes (GEIPOT) with the assistance of the University of Texas, Austin and the Texas Research and Development Foundation. The World Bank acted as the Executing Agency for the UNDP.

3. The models do not encompass the impact of road design and maintenance choices on road user costs through safety-related factors. For quantitative evidence of such user benefits based on the data from a study conducted in India, see CRRI (1982).

1.2   MODEL CRITERIA AND RESEARCH APPROACH

1.2.1 General Modelling Framework

The variables that affect the cost of operating a vehicle on a given route may be divided into three broad groups:

1. Road attributes, which comprise the relevant geometric and surfacing characteristics of the route, e.g., vertical and horizontal alignments, road width, and surface profile irregularity or 'roughness';

2. Vehicle attributes, which comprise the relevant physical and operating characteristics of the vehicle, e.g., the weight, payload, engine power, suspension design, and number of hours operated per year; and

3. Regional factors, which comprise the relevant economic, social, technological and institutional characteristics of the region, e.g., the region-wide speed limit, fuel prices, relative prices of new vehicles, parts and labor, stage of technological development, driver training and driving attitudes, such as lane discipline, and general attitude of vehicle drivers toward safety.

Generally speaking, vehicle operators have a tendency to adjust the operating and physical characteristics of the vehicle so as to minimize operating and travel time costs, subject to constraints imposed by the road (e.g., through vertical gradient and horizontal curvature) and the regional environment (e.g., relative resource costs, the regional speed limit and other traffic regulations). Chesher and Harrison (forthcoming) have employed a relatively simple mathematical construct to illustrate the principle of operators' cost minimization through trade-offs among major cost components. From this broad ideal, it is in principle possible to postulate a generalized mathematical model of total cost minimization which is expressed as a function of the relative prices of vehicle operating cost components, as well as the road characteristics and regional factors. Such a model would, at least in theory, be generally transferable across countries and also over time within a given country. Local adaptation would be a simple matter of providing the values of the necessary regional factors.

While the above approach has intellectual appeal, it would be extremely difficult to implement. First, a realistic mathematical form of the model would have to be very elaborate in order to capture properly all the major causal relationsips between the above three groups of variables. At the present time, our collective knowledge of vehicle operators' adaptive behavior does not seem to be sufficient to provide the necessary model specifications. Furthermore, even if such specifications were available, the task of calibrating the generalized model would still be immense. The data collection would have to be based on very large factorial designs covering multiple dimensions of relative prices, and vehicle, road and regional variables. This means that standardized data would have to be obtained from several countries of disparate characteristics. Cultural differences among countries would also have to be accounted for, which is by no means a small task.

For these reasons, it is not surprising that we have yet to see a serious pursuit of the above approach. What we have seen instead is a different, but feasible approach adopted by many previous researchers: modelling on a country- or region-specific basis physical components of vehicle operating cost, including principally speed (or its inverse, travel time per unit distance), fuel consumption, tire wear and maintenance parts and labor (Winfrey, 1963; Claffey, 1966; de Weille, 1966; Hide et al., 1975; Morosiuk and Abaynayaka, 1982; Hide, 1982). Vehicle operating costs are computed simply by multiplying the predicted quantities of physical resources consumed with their relative prices. Compared to the approach of modelling vehicle operating costs directly, the physical-component approach yields models which, if correctly specified in form, are more easily transferable to new countries, since the most direct effects of prices have been removed.

However, it is important to emphasize that the calibrated coefficients of physical-component models represent a result of operators' long-term adaptation to the regional environment and, strictly speaking, cannot be transferred to another region or country without re-calibration. In fact, our general view is that, unless there is empirical evidence or theory to indicate the contrary, the coefficients of physical-component models should be subject to at least some re-calibration when they are applied elsewhere. We return to the issue of adaptive behavior in response to changes in road characteristics below, and the issue of transferability and regional adaptation is dealt with in Chapter 14.

1.2.2 Criteria for Vehicle Operating Cost Prediction Models

Within the physical-component modelling framework stated above, the basic purpose of this study was to develop vehicle operating cost prediction models that:

1. Can be expressed in aggregate form, i.e., as algebraic functions of aggregate descriptors of road attributes, viz, average gradient, horizontal curvature and roughness, so that detailed information on road alignment is not needed (this requirement is essential for sector-level planning);

2. Are policy-sensitive, i.e., possess discriminatory power to distinguish subtle differences in vehicle physical and operating characteristics as well as among investment

alternatives involving tradeoffs between vertical and horizontal alignments and surfacing standards;

3. Have an adequate extrapolative capability, i.e., can be extrapolated over the range of vehicle and road character-istics which must be considered in an incremental economic analysis of alternatives; and

4. Have an adequate local adaptability, i.e., the model para-meters can be easily adapted to new regions or countries without having to repeat a full-scale data collection exercise.

Over the past 10 to 15 years, research efforts in developing vehicle operating cost prediction models may be categorized into two broad approaches: aggregate-correlative and micro-mechanistic. As will be elaborated below, both approaches have their own merits, and our main task was to combine them into a new approach which took advantage of the strengths of each. For discussion purposes, this new approach is called aggregate-mechanistic.

Aggregate-correlative approach

This approach, which is more extensively quantified than the micro-mechanistic one, rests on generally large data bases obtained from vehicle operator surveys as well as field experiments (e.g., measurements of fuel consumption) using specially-instrumented vehicles.[3] The models produced are expressed in relatively simple algebraic form. Although a priori reasoning has played a significant role in the development of the model form, these models still tend to rely heavily on trends indicated by the data, as opposed to mathematical forms (which are generally non-linear) that result from a more rigorous theoretical postulation. Aggregate-correlative models have been developed in the major field studies conducted in Kenya (Hide et al., 1975), the Caribbean (Hide, 1982; Morosiuk and Abaynayaka, 1982), India (CRRI, 1982) and Brazil (GEIPOT, 1982), and the earlier ones have enjoyed a wide-spread use in highway planning. The pioneering Kenya models have been implemented in the Massachusetts Institute of Technology's Road Investment Analysis Model (RIAM – Brademeyer et al., 1977), the first version of the British Transport and Road Research Laboratory's Road Transport Investment Model (RTIM – Robinson et al., 1975) and an early version of the World Bank's HDM model (Watanatada et al., 1981). The Caribbean models have been incorporated in the latest version of the RTIM model (Parsley and Robinson, 1982), and the Kenya, India and some of the Brazil models have been included in the new version of the HDM model (Watanatada et al., forthcoming).

---

[3] It proved impossible to find an appropriate term for these models. The word "correlative" is intended to imply that the mathematical forms of the models relied more heavily on a combination of observed data trends and common sense than on rigorous theory. It is not, however, intended to imply any lack of causality between the dependent and independent variables.

Judged against the above four criteria, the overall conclusion is that these aggregate-correlative models are, as a group, generally adequate with respect to the first two, although a large scope exists for possible improvement even there, and are not generally adequate with respect to the latter two criteria, i.e., extrapolation and local adaptation. The models enjoy the empirical support of large data bases, which is indeed their greatest strength. The aggregate algebraic functions are easy to use and are mostly expressed in terms of important vehicle and road descriptors. However, the model forms tend to be dictated by trends in the data which were often ambiguous (due to great variability in the data, incomplete coverage of the range of, or correlation among, the independent variables, etc.). As a result, they have a propensity to miss the more subtle interaction of the policy variables (e.g., the speed reduction effect of a steep gradient, sharp curve and rough surface acting simultaneously should be smaller than the sum of the effects of these factors acting separately). Furthermore, although they generally produce reasonable predictions over the range of policy variables covered by the data, they usually do not extrapolate well over the range of the null (or baseline) alternatives which must be postulated for incremental benefit-cost analyses, and can give unreasonable predictions (e.g., excessively low or even negative predicted speed). Finally, the model coefficients are generally difficult to interpret in physical terms (unlike parameters such as "vehicle power" for governing uphill speeds or "friction coefficient" for governing curve speeds) and, consequently, do not lend themselves to local adaptation. The types of adaptation we have found from experience with these models have generally been relatively simple, e.g., applying a multiplicative adjustment factor to bring predictions closer to locally observed values.

Micro-mechanistic approach

Employing a detailed representation of the road alignment (i.e., using data on the gradient, radius of curvature, superelevation, etc. of the generally small homogeneous subsections into which the road section can be divided), this approach draws upon theories of vehicle mechanics and driver behavior to simulate a detailed speed profile of the vehicle as it traverses the road section (see Chapter 6 for a detailed exposition).[4] Once the speed profile is known, fuel consumption and tire wear are predicted in increments at small distance intervals along the road; this is relatively straightforward since fuel consumption and tire wear can be expressed, through theories of vehicle mechanics, as analytical functions of speed. Sullivan (1976) employed this approach in the prediction of the operating costs of logging trucks, while Bester (1981) and Andersen and Gravem (1979) were specifically concerned with fuel consumption. Gynnerstedt et al. (1977), St. John and Kobett (1978) and Hoban (1983) employed mechanistic-behavioral theories to construct free speed profiles primarily as the building block for simulating traffic interaction, which in turn, led to speed prediction under impeded flow conditions.

---

[4] These models also incorporate assumptions of driver/operator behavior but for compactness of terminology they are referred to simply as "mechanistic."

The micro-mechanistic approach has a general tendency to rely less on large data bases collected in one single field study than the aggregate-correlative approach. Rather, micro-mechanistic models have tended to draw upon the results of previous work; this has been possible since the theories of vehicle mechanics and driver behavior give rise to model parameters that have readily interpretable meanings (e.g., desired speeds, acceleration/deceleration rates, maximum used power, etc.), and therefore can be transferred from one model to another. In addition, the values of unknown parameters can, as a rule, be determined from relatively small-scale experiments (e.g., to obtain coefficients of vehicle rolling resistance). Because of their generally strong theoretical basis micro-mechanistic models have an inherent tendency to transfer and extrapolate well.

However, since the micro-mechanistic models examined apparently were not developed with all the above criteria in mind, they are not in a form suitable for sector-level planning purposes. Specifically, the requirement of detailed information on road geometry is intrinsically unwieldy for quick policy analyses. In terms of empirical quantification the micro-mechanistic models tend to be less extensively developed than the aggregate-correlative counterparts. The models generally have undergone far less validation by independent data than they should have been. Finally, none of the models examined have incorporated road roughness as a major surface condition variable influencing vehicle operating costs. This has precluded the possibility of using these models at the current state of quantification to examine tradeoffs between surfacing and geometric standards even at the detailed project level.

Aggregate-mechanistic approach

Having seen the two approaches with their comparative advantages, it seemed appealing to combine their virtues, namely, aggregate form, policy-sensitivity, extrapolative ability and local adaptability into new prediction models. This was the basic approach taken in this study. It is briefly outlined in the section below. Table 1.1 provides a summary comparison of the aggregate-corrective, micro-mechanistic and aggregate-mechanistic approaches in the light of the four criteria and the state of model quantification at the completion of this study.

1.3 OUTLINE OF AGGREGATE-MECHANISTIC APPROACH

1.3.1 Scope

As mentioned earlier, in this study we are concerned with modelling speed, fuel consumption, tire wear, vehicle depreciation and interest, and crew cost. As shown in Chapter 12, vehicle depreciation and interest are inverse functions of vehicle utilization (defined as the total distance driven per vehicle per year), and the crew cost varies inversely with speed. Therefore, besides speed, fuel and tire wear, vehicle utilization also had to be modelled. The remaining components of the total operating costs—namely, maintenance parts and labor, and lubricants—are supported by well-established mechanistic-behavioral

Table 1.1: Summary comparison of aggregate-correlative micro-mechanistic and aggregate-mechanistic approaches vis-a-vis research objectives and state of model quantification

	Modelling approach		
Research objective	Aggregate-correlative	Micro-mechanistic	Aggregate mechanistic
Aggregate formulation	Yes	No	Yes
Policy sensitivity	Mostly medium[1]	Mostly high[1]	Mostly high[1]
Extrapolative ability	Mostly low	Mostly high	Mostly high
Local adaptability	Mostly low-medium	Mostly high	Mostly high
State of model quantification at completion of this study	Mostly extensive	Lacking validation and surface effects	Mostly extensive

[1] If relevant policy variables are incorporated.

Figure 1.1: Logical sequence of mechanistic modelling approach

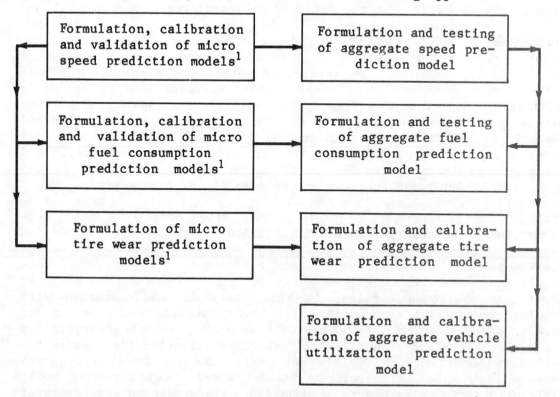

[1] Including both micro transitional and non-transitional models, as introduced in Section 1.3.4.

theories, and consequently are estimated on an aggregate-correlative basis and reported elsewhere (GEIPOT, 1982, Volume 5; Chesher and Harrison, 1987); in particular, the maintenance parts and labor models were based on the Brazil data.

1.3.2 Basic Approach

As alluded to previously, speed is functionally the most crucial variable to predict: once speed is known, it is fairly simple to predict fuel consumption, tire wear and vehicle utilization. Among these latter three variables, fuel and tires are "consumed" in an instantaneous manner and therefore can be predicted in micro increments as the vehicle traverses the road.[5] Vehicle utilization, on the other hand, represents a measure of vehicle productivity which is based on the number of round trips a given vehicle can make over a fixed route in a year, and therefore could only be modelled as an aggregate function of speed.

The basic modelling approach taken for speed and fuel consumption was first to construct micro-mechanistic models (Chapters 5, 6, 9 and 10), validate them with independent data (Chapters 8 and 10) and then transform them by means of numerical techniques into aggregate form (Chapters 7, 8 and 10).

The main advantages of this approach are not only that deep insights could be gained into the physical-behavioral phenomena at the micro level, but also that once validated to satisfaction, the micro models could be treated as a close approximation of the "truth" and consequently used as a benchmark for developing and testing aggregate-mechanistic models. Furthermore, although not intended as a prime objective of this study, the validated micro models could serve as practical prediction models in their own right for project-level studies in which the detailed response of vehicle speeds and operating costs to specific spot improvements need to be estimated. Another potentially important application of such models would be to serve as a building block for constructing models for simulating the effects of traffic flow interaction.

This approach, however, needs a large store of detailed field data for both model calibration and validation, involving the observation of actual vehicle speeds at a sample of road sites covering a full range of roughness and geometry, as well as the measurement of the speed and fuel consumption of specially instrumented vehicles traversing a sample of test sections. Moreover, since the experimental fuel consumption data were obtained from the test vehicles operated under controlled conditions in favor of fuel economy, it was necessary to adjust the experimentally-based fuel predictions to real-world conditions; this had to be done by comparison with actual fuel consumption records of vehicle operators obtained from a road user survey.

---

[5] The exception is the tire carcass which can survive through several recappings and the number of recappings to which it can be subjected affects the tire cost. This issue is dealt with separately in the "carcass life" model in Chapter 11.

Although the Brazil speed and fuel consumption data had not been collected with the mechanistic approach in mind, they were broad in scope and deep in detail (Zaniewski et al., 1980; GEIPOT, 1982, Vol. 5), and with few exceptions proved to be virtually ideal for the mechanistic approach.

On the other hand, as discussed in Chapter 11, the tire data fell short of the ideal. Because of the similarities in the physical phenomena, tire wear modelling called for the same kind of data as fuel consumption modelling, i.e., a balanced mix of detailed experimental and survey data. Unfortunately, only survey data were collected. Consequently, it was not possible to follow the same approach as taken for speed and fuel modelling, and it became necessary to calibrate the tire wear model at the aggregate level. However, as shown in Chapter 11, it was still possible to formulate a theoretical tire wear model at the micro level and then transform it into an aggregate model for calibration purposes.

As mentioned earlier, by its nature the vehicle utilization model had to be formulated at the aggregate level of a fixed route. As derived in Chapter 12, the resulting model form was expressed as a function of the average round trip speed, and aggregate data were available from the road user survey for calibrating this theoretical model.

The logical sequence of the mechanistic modelling approach followed in this study is depicted in Figure 1.1. It can be seen that speed modelling always preceded the modelling of fuel consumption, tire wear and vehicle utilization; furthermore, wherever possible micro modelling preceded aggregate modelling.

1.3.3 Steady-state Models

The basic building blocks of the mechanistic modelling approach were the models for predicting speed, fuel consumption and tire wear under steady-state conditions. Steady-state conditions arise when a homogeneous subsection is sufficiently long so that the vehicle can reach and maintain a constant speed, at which the forces acting on the vehicle and the resulting fuel consumption and tire wear remain constant.

Under steady-state conditions, the vehicle motion and associated fuel consumption and tire wear can be described in a relatively simple manner using closed form algebraic functions derived from mechanistic-behavioral theories. The steady-state models (described in detail in Chapters 3, 9 and 11) are summarized in Table 1.2 along with their underlying theories.

Strict steady-state conditions do not occur frequently in most driving situations, which are mostly transient in nature involving continual speed changes in response to variations in road alignment and surface conditions. However, the steady-state models have their appeal in their representation of the asymptotic behavior of vehicle motion. Because of this they were employed not only as the fundamental building blocks for the micro models, but also as an approximation for aggregate

Table 1.2: Summary of steady-state models for speed, fuel consumption and tire wear

Variable to be predicted	Steady-state model	Chapter(s) described	Underlying theory and origin
Speed	Steady-state speed model	3, 4	Probabilistic limiting speed theory developed in this study as an extension of deterministic limiting speed theory theory using mirror-image of probabilistic discrete choice theory.
Fuel consumption	Unit fuel consumption function	9	Empirical extension of specific fuel consumption concept to negative vehicle cle power. Principles of internal combustion engines.
Tire wear	Tread wear model	11	Generalized form of slip energy theory Synthesis of tire slip and tread wear wear theories

prediction purposes. From the test results (reported in Chapters 8, 10 and 11), it was in fact found that within the range of road severity tested, the aggregate models derived directly from the steady-state models produce satisfactorily accurate predictions relative to the micro models.

1.3.4 Micro Transitional and Non-transitional Models

Two types of micro models--transitional and non-transitional-for speed, fuel consumption and tire wear, were constructed on the foundation of the steady-state models. As noted above, vehicle motion along the road is for the most part a transient phenomenon. The main objective of the micro transitional models was to simulate the transient phenomena as closely as possible so that they could be used as the next-to-the-truth reference for testing the more simplified micro non-transitional and aggregate models.

Employing the same detailed information on road characteristics (i.e., attributes of consecutive homogeneous subsections), the micro non-transitional models differ from the micro transitional counterparts in that they completely ignore the transient or transitional effects and produce predictions only on the basis of the steady-state models applied to the individual homogeneous subsections. The micro non-transitional models were developed with two purposes in mind: first, as building blocks for the micro transitional models; and, second, as an intermediate step between the micro transitional and aggregate models in terms of micro transitional and aggregate models in terms of complexity. As elaborated in Chapters 8, 10 and 11, these intermediate models were used to compare with the micro transitional models to ascertain the effects of omitting vehicle transitional behavior, and with the aggregate models to test the accuracy of numerical approximation on the part of the latter.

In sum, the development of prediction models at naturally progressive levels of complexity proved to be useful not only in understanding the physical-behavioral phenomena associated with vehicle motion but also in providing appropriate benchmarks for testing the predictive accuracy of the models themselves.

1.4 ADAPTIVE BEHAVIOR IN RESPONSE TO CHANGES IN ROAD CHARACTERISTICS

To facilitate local adaptation and enhance flexibility, the vehicle operating cost models outlined above are expressed as functions of as many relevant vehicle attributes as possible. The user of the models must specify these attributes as inputs to the model, but he must bear in mind that the vehicle attributes could change, at least in the long run, in response to changes in road characteristics. Operators have a proclivity to adapt their vehicles and operating rules to changes in route conditions in order to maximize profit or minimize costs; they can, within constraints, vary a number of variables to minimize transport cost, e.g., the number, type and make of vehicles, the engine size, age, and tires. However, only utilization (number of kilometers driven per year) and, implicitly, fleet size (number of vehicles employed in a company) are endogenous within the vehicle operating cost relationships presented herein. Fleet size is implicitly tied to utilization in the prediction of depreciation and interest per km: when the average route speed is raised by road improvement, a vehicle can make more trips per year, thereby resulting in fewer vehicles needed to haul a given volume of transport--assuming a constant number of hours of operation per year. The treatment of utilization and fleet size as endogenous variables has arisen from their sensitivity to road improvements as well as their considerable influence on vehicle operating cost via the sizable components of depreciation and interest.

The other vehicle attributes, once exogenously specified, are regarded as constants by the model. Where the user has reason to believe that the changes in road conditions or policies being modelled will lead to other important adaptations of vehicle characteristics, he can incorporate an estimate of these changes in the input of vehicle characteristics and future traffic composition. To do this the user could either employ a subjective assessment of the likely changes or he could systematically search for the combination of vehicle attributes that yields a minimum cost for the anticipated traffic and road characteristics. To do either is clearly a larger task than the more traditional straightforward comparison of alternatives with the vehicle characteristics held fixed.

Whether it is worthwhile undertaking such a task depends on the policy question at hand. For example, the traditional approach should generally suffice for evaluating minor road improvements. On the other hand, to compare alternative schemes involving large-scale changes in the road network or such broad policies as axle load regulation and enforcement, the user should make a careful judgment on how vehicle operators are likely to respond to these schemes, in terms of the vehicle type and axle configuration, payload, etc. and incorporate these in the projections of future traffic, which can include anticipated changes in the composition of the vehicle fleet.

1.5 ORGANIZATION OF THE BOOK

The topics are divided into three parts, the first two dealing with the theoretical development and quantification of the mechanistic-behavioral models and the third with their applications.

Part I is devoted to the speed models. It begins with Chapter 2 which presents the basic definitions and relationships concerning the mechanics of vehicle motion. Chapter 2 highlights the vehicle rolling resistance-road roughness model, calibrated with Brazil experimental data. These basic physical relationships are employed in Chapters 3 and 4 which present the theoretical formulation and statistical estimation of the steady-state speed model based on the probabilistic limiting speed theory (mentioned in Table 1.2 above), for cars, utilities, buses, and light/medium, heavy and articulated trucks. The steady-state speed model provides a foundation for the formulation of the micro non-transitional and transitional speed prediction models described in Chapters 5 and 6, respectively. The micro models are then followed by the aggregate speed prediction model formulated in Chapter 7. The three speed prediction models are validated against independent data and compared with each other in Chapter 8.

As a direct follow-up application of the speed models, Part II presents the formulation and quantification of the aggregate models for predicting fuel consumption, tire wear and vehicle utilization. Chapter 9 deals with the unit fuel consumption function which provides the basic building block for the micro and aggregate fuel consumption prediction models. The formulation, calibration and validation of the latter models are presented in Chapter 10. Chapter 11 deals with tire wear while Chapter 12 describes the vehicle utilization model and also summarizes the vehicle maintenance models (including parts, labor and lubricants) reported in Chesher and Harrison, 1987.

Applications of the aggregate-mechanistic models developed above are dealt with in Part III. As several of the model parameters may need to be adapted to suit local conditions, guidelines for local adaptation are provided in Chapter 13. Chapter 14 provides a detailed step-by-step user's guide for computing total vehicle operating costs. As a reference for quick policy analysis, based on the Brazil-specific model parameters presented in Chapter 14, Chapter 15 provides tables and graphs of predicted physical resources consumed and the resulting costs of vehicle operation for a full range of road surfacing and geometric standards. These predictions are accompanied by a brief discussion on their investment policy implications. Finally, conclusions and recommendations are given in Chapter 16.

APPENDIX 1A

POPULATION AND TEST VEHICLES

Two types of vehicles were employed: those sampled from the actual vehicle population and those procured and instrumented specially for conducting controlled experiments on speed and fuel consumption[6] (GEIPOT, 1982).

The population vehicles were intended to provide actual operating data both at the detailed level through radar and stopwatch speed observations at selected road sites and at the aggregate level through operators' records of route speeds, fuel consumption, tire wear and vehicle utilization. The specially instrumented or test vehicles were to provide accurate detailed speed and fuel consumption information not obtainable from population vehicles.

For the purposes of this study, the population vehicles were categorized into ten basic classes, ranging from passenger cars to articulated trucks, as depicted in Table 1A.1 along with their principal attributes, e.g., rated gross weight. Each class is matched by a test vehicle which is considered to be representative of the class. The test vehicles comprised nine vehicles treated as representative vehicles in Table 1A.1 and two replicate vehicles, a utility (VW-Kombi) and a heavy truck (Mercedes Benz 1113 with crane). Their detailed characteristics are assembled in Table 1A.2.

---

[6] No detailed experiments on tire wear were planned in the Brazil study.

Table lA.1: Basic classes of population vehicles and principal attributes

Vehicle class	Approx-imate rated gross weight (tons)	Weight classi-fica-tion[1]	Number of tires	Number of axles	Fuel type[2]	Engine		Representative vehicle
						Maximum SAE rated power (metric hp)	Number of cylin-ders	
1. Passenger cars	1.2	L	4	2	G	49	4	Volkswagen 1300
2. Passenger cars (medium)	1.5	L	4	2	G	148	6	Opala
3. Passenger cars (large)	1.9	L	4	2	G	201	8	Dodge Dart
4. Utilities	2.1	L	4	2	G	61	4	Volkswagen Kombi
5. Large buses	11.5	H	6	2	D	149	6	Mercedes Benz 0362
6. Light trucks (gasoline)	6.1	H	6	2	G	171	8	Ford-400
7. Light trucks (diesel)	6.1	H	6	2	D	103	4	Ford-4000
8. Medium trucks	15.0	H	6	2	D	149	6	Mercedes Benz 1113[3]
9. Heavy trucks	18.5	H	10	3	D	149	6	Mercedes Benz 1113[4]
10. Articulated	40.0	H	18	5	D	289	6	Scania 110/39

Note: Figures are those of representative vehicles.

[1] L= light vehicle (rated gross weight under 3.5 tons);
    H= heavy vehicle (rated gross weight of 3.5 tons or more).
[2] G= gasoline engine; D= diesel engine.
[3] Excludes third rear axle.
[4] Includes third rear axle.

Source: Classification scheme adapted from Brazil-UNDP-World Bank highway research project data physical characteristics adapted from those of the matched representative vehicle (see table 1A.2).

Table 1A.2: Test vehicles and physical characteristics

Class	Car			Utility	Large Bus	Light Truck		Heavy Truck		Articulated Truck
Make	Volkswagen	Chevrolet	Chrysler	Volkswagen	Mercedes Benz	Ford	Ford	Mercedes Benz	Mercedes Benz	Scania
Model	1,300	Opala	Dodge Dart	Kombi[1]	O-362	F-400	F-4000	1,113[2]	1,113[2] with crane	110/39
Weight (kg)										
Tare[4]	960	1,200	1,650	1,320	8,100	3,120	3,270	6,600	6,570	14,730
Rated gross	1,160	1,466	1,915	2,155	11,500	6,060	6,060	18,500	18,500	40,000
Engine										
Fuel type	Gas	Gas	Gas	Gas	Diesel	Gas	Diesel	Diesel	Diesel	Diesel
Number of cylinders	4	6	8	4	6	8	4	6	6	6
Maximum rated torque (m-kgf)	9.1	30.9	41.5	10.3	37	33.5	29.2	37	37	79
Engine speed at maximum rated torque (rpm)	2,600	2,400	2,400	2,600	2,000	2,200	1,600	2,000	2,000	1,200
Maximum SAE rated power (metric hp)	49	148	201	61	149	171	103	149	149	289
Engine speed at maximum power (rpm)	4,600	4,000	4,400	4,600	2,800	4,400	3,000	2,800	2,800	2,200
Drive train										
Gear 1	3.80	3.07	2.71	3.80	8.02	6.40	5.90	8.02	8.02	13.51
Gear 2	2.06	1.68	1.60	2.06	4.77	3.09	2.85	4.77	4.77	10.07
Gear 3	1.32	1.00	1.00	1.32	2.75	1.69	1.56	2.75	2.75	7.55
Gear 4	0.89			0.89	1.66	1.00	1.00	1.66	1.66	5.66
Gear 5					1.00			1.00	1.00	4.24
Gear 6										3.19
Gear 7										2.38
Gear 8										1.78
Gear 9										1.34
Gear 10										1.00
Differential	4.375	3.08	3.15	4.375	4.875	5.140	4.630	4.875	4.875	4.710
No. of axles	2	2	2	2	2	2	2	3[4]	3[4]	5
Tires										
Number	4	4	4	4	6	6		10	10	18
Weight (kg)	5	15	17	19	88	43	4	88	88	92
Diameter (m)	0.645	0.626	0.649	0.654	1.016	0.808	0.80	1.016	1.016	1.080
Radius of gyration (m)	0.260	0.235	0.240	0.250	0.380	0.300	0.30	0.380	0.380	0.405
Rotational inertial mass of tires (kg)	39.0	.33.8	37.2	44.4	295.4	142.3	142.	492.4	492.4	931.5
Aerodynamic drag coefficient	0.45	0.50	0.45	0.46	0.65	0.70	0.70	0.85	0.85	0.63
Projected frontal area (m^2)	1.80	2.08	2.20	2.72	6.30	3.25	3.25	5.20	5.20	5.75

[1] Two identical vehicles were procured for this model.
[2] These are virtually identical vehicles except for slight difference in tare weight.
[3] Tare weight includes 150 kg weight of two drivers.
[4] These models were also available without the rear tandem-axle. In this case they were be classified as medium trucks.

Source: Zaniewski et al. (1982) and vehicle manufacturers.

PART I
Vehicle Speed Prediction Models

CHAPTER 2

The Force Balance Relationship

This chapter is concerned with an exposition of Newton's fundamental law governing motion as it applies in the context of a vehicle traversing a roadway. Section 2.1 briefly describes the roadway attributes and their measures used in the study. Section 2.2 presents the basic force balance equation and derives expressions for the different physical quantities brought together by the relationship. Section 2.3 gives an outline' of various concrete applications of the basic equation made in the study. As part of the study, an empirical relationship between the coefficient of rolling resistance and road roughness was established. The derivation and estimation of the relationship is presented in Appendix 2A.

2.1 ROADWAY ATTRIBUTES AND THEIR MEASURES

The attributes of the roadway at the point of contact with the vehicle, which determine vehicle operation on it, are vertical alignment, horizontal alignment, surface characteristics and cross section. These attributes are relevant for short road sections as well as for long homogeneous sections, and the way these attributes are represented in the study is outlined below. Analogous aggregate descriptors for a heterogeneous roadway are discussed in Chapter 7.

2.1.1 Vertical Alignment

Generally, the vertical alignment of a roadway consists of tangent grades, and vertical curves which are generally parabolic. In this study, the vertical alignment of a road is approximated by tangent or linear grades. At the point of contact with the vehicle, the vertical alignment of the road is represented by its gradient (also referred to as slope or grade). It is a signed dimensionless quantity defined as the sine of the angle of inclination the roadway makes with the horizontal plane, as shown in Figure 2.1. It is generally approximated by the tangent of the incline angle. Let

GR = road gradient, expressed as a fraction; and
ϕ = angle of incline of the road, in radians.

Then, we have

$$GR = \tan\phi \qquad\qquad (2.1)$$

GR is positive for traversal against gravity (uphill travel), and negative for traversal along gravity (downhill travel). Often, for ease of expression, the gradient is stated in hundredths (%), and occasionally, even in thousandths (m/km).

Figure 2.1: Gradient and vehicle motion forces

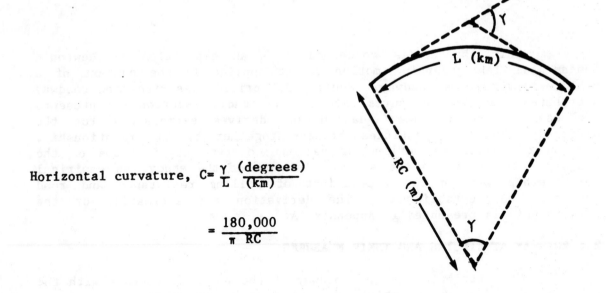

Horizontal curvature, $C = \dfrac{\gamma}{L} \dfrac{\text{(degrees)}}{\text{(km)}}$

$\qquad\qquad\qquad = \dfrac{180,000}{\pi \; RC}$

Figure 2.2: Equivalent definitions of horizontal curvature

For modelling purposes it is often convenient to characterize vertical alignment using two non-negative quantities called "rise (RS)" and "fall (FL)." These are defined as follows:

$$RS = \begin{cases} GR & \text{if } GR \geq 0 \\ 0 & \text{otherwise} \end{cases} \tag{2.2a}$$

$$FL = \begin{cases} -GR & \text{if } GR \leq 0 \\ 0 & \text{otherwise.} \end{cases} \tag{2.2b}$$

These measures are useful for treating positive and negative gradients asymmetrically, and for developing aggregate descriptors of vertical alignment.

2.1.2 Horizontal Alignment

Generally, the horizontal alignment consists of tangents, horizontal curves and banking. In this study, horizontal curves are assumed to be circular. At the point of contact with the vehicle the horizontal alignment is represented by its horizontal curvature (also called degree of curvature) and rate of superelevation.

The horizontal curvature of a curve is defined as the angle (in degrees) subtended at the center by a unit arc-length of the curve (in km). Referring to Figure 2.2, let

C = horizontal curvature, in degrees/km;
γ = central angle subtended by the curve, in degrees; and
L = arc-length of the curve, in km.

Then we have,

$$C = \gamma/L \tag{2.3}$$

It may be noted that C is an inverse function of the radius of curvature of the curve:

$$C = \frac{180,000}{\pi RC} \tag{2.4}$$

where RC = radius of curvature of the curve, in m. Further, it may be noted that the angle subtended by an arc of a circle at the center is equal to the external angle made by the tangents to the circle at the ends of the arc. Thus C also expresses the absolute angular deviation of the two tangent lines at the end-points of the curve.

For a straight road, the value of C is zero and the value of radius of curvature is taken to be infinity. For practical purposes, a road with a radius of curvature of 10,000 m or more may be assumed to be straight.

The banking of a curve is represented by the rate of superelevation, defined as the sine of the superelevation angle, that is, the
vertical distance between the heights of the inner and outer edges of the
road divided by the road width (assuming zero road camber). It is generally approximated by the tangent of the superelevation angle. It is
expressed as a fraction, and is denoted by SP. The rate of
superelevation is often referred to simply as superelevation.

2.1.3 Surface Characteristics

The surface characteristics considered in this study are the
road profile irregularity and surface type.

The unit of roughness originally used in this study is QI
(which is short for QI counts/km). It is a calibrated Maysmeter estimate
of a reference Quarter-car Index of profile measured by a dynamic
profilometer (GEIPOT, 1982; Paterson, 1987).

Since the completion of this study, roughness has come to be
defined in the now-standard International Roughness Index (m/km IRI).
This measure is a summary index of the irregularity of the road profile
in the wheelpath; it is measured as the accumulated axle-body movement
made by a simulated passenger car over a unit distance of travel (in m/km
IRI). The IRI quantifies the impact of roughness on a moving vehicle in
much the same way as vibrations induced by roughness influence vehicle
costs, and hence is considered to be the most applicable measure of
roughness for economic evaluation purposes (Sayers, Gillespie and
Paterson, 1986, and Paterson, 1987). An approximate relationship between
the two units is:

$$IRI = QI/13. \tag{2.5}$$

In this study only two types of road surface are distinguished,
paved and unpaved. The former class includes primarily asphalt concrete
and surface treatment surfacings, and the latter class includes compacted
gravel and earth roads.

2.1.4 Cross Section

Important cross sectional aspects of rural roads are effective
number of lanes or carriageway width, shoulder width, and shoulder
condition. Since most of the road sections included in the Brazil study
were more than six meters wide and had adequate shoulders, road cross
section was not considered to be an important determinant of vehicle
operation in the main study. However, the effect of carriageway width on
vehicle speeds was investigated as a part of the analysis of
transferability of the steady-state speed model based on Indian data
(Section 4.4). As a result of the analysis, roads are divided into two
width classes based on the effective number of lanes, namely, single-lane
roads and intermediate and dual-lane roads. The former class consists of
roads which are 3.5 to 4 m wide and on which vehicles in the two
directions share both wheel paths. The latter class consists of roads
which are at least 5.5 m wide; on these roads the vehicles in the two

directions either share one wheel path or have distinct wheel paths. It is common practice in India to widen single-lane roads in two stages: initially, to an intermediate width, and then into a double-lane road. It was observed in India that roads with widths between 4 m and 5.5 m were not common. The apparent reason for this is that these widths do not serve useful purposes. For example, a 5 m wide road would be too narrow for two trucks to cross, but too wide for a single-lane road. The effect of shoulder width and condition has not been modeled in the present study.

2.2 BASIC RELATIONSHIPS

The physical relationship that has the single most extensive use in this study is that of vehicle force balance. The force balance relationship has been used by a number of previous researchers in the simulation of vehicle speeds under both free and impeded traffic flows including, among others, Gynnerstedt et al. (1977), St John and Kobett (1978), Sullivan (1976), and Hoban (1983).

When a vehicle traverses a straight road that makes an incline angle ϕ radians to the horizontal, as illustrated in Figure 2.1, the force balance equation is given by :

$$m'a = DF - GF - AF - RR \qquad (2.6)$$

where   m' = the effective mass of the vehicle, in kg;

        a   = the acceleration of the vehicle in the direction of travel, in m/m^2;

       DF = the vehicle drive force delivered at the driving wheels, in newtons;

       GF = the component of the gravitational force in the direction opposite to the vehicle travel, in newtons;

       AF = the air resistance, in newtons; and

       RR = the vehicle rolling resistance, in newtons.

2.2.1 Effective Vehicle Mass

A general formula for computing the effective mass of the vehicle is given by (Taborek, 1957):

$$m' = m + m_w + m_e \qquad (2.7)$$

where   m   = the vehicle mass, in kg;

      m_w = the component of the vehicle effective mass attributable to the rotational inertia of the wheels, in kg; and

m_e = the component of the vehicle effective mass attributable to the rotational inertia of the parts that rotate at the engine speed, in kg.

The above equation ignores the relatively small contributions of the manual transmission parts, gears and shafts. The effective "rotational inertia" mass of the wheels, m_w, is given by:

$$m_w = \frac{I_w}{RRT^2} \qquad (2.8)$$

where I_w = the moment of inertia of mass of mounted wheels, in kg-m^2; and

RRT = the rolling radius of each tire, in meters.

The term I_w is given by:

$$I_w = M_w \, RWG^2 \qquad (2.9)$$

where M_w = the total mass of all mounted wheels; and

RWG = the radius of gyration of each wheel, in meters.

The term m_e is expressed as:

$$m_e = \frac{I_e \, SR^2}{RRT^2} \qquad (2.10)$$

where I_e = the total moment of inertia of mass at engine speed of all parts that rotate, in kg-m^2; and

SR = the ratio of the engine speed to the drive axle speed (i.e., the speed reduction ratio).

For a given vehicle the term m_w is constant and normally smaller than 5 percent of the vehicle mass. An average value of 4 percent is recommended by Koffman (1955). The term m_e is proportional to the gearspeed ratio. For example, when the vehicle is in a low gear (e.g., when accelerating from standstill), m_e is relatively large, but when the vehicle changes to the top gear m_e assumes its smallest possible value. Average values of the "effective mass factor," defined as the ratio m'/m, vary from about 1.1 in top gear for both cars and trucks to about 1.4 in first gear for cars and 2.5 in low gears for trucks.

2.2.2 Vehicle Drive Force

The vehicle drive force, DF, may be related to the vehicle power as:

$$DF = \frac{736 \ HP}{V} \tag{2.11}$$

where   HP = the vehicle power delivered at the driving wheels, in metric hp; and

      V = the vehicle travel speed, in m/s.

2.2.3 Gravitational Force

The gravitational resistance force is given by:

$$GF = m \ g \ \sin\phi \tag{2.12}$$

where ϕ = angle of incline in radians (see Figure 2.1); and

      g = acceleration due to gravity, in m/s^2.

This can be approximated for small ϕ by:

$$GF = m \ g \ GR \tag{2.13}$$

where   GR = tan ϕ is the road gradient introduced in Section 2.1. For 15 percent gradient, which is an extreme case, the approximate formula above (Equation 2.13) has an error of 1.1 percent.

2.2.4 Air Resistance

The air resistance is given by:

$$AF = \frac{1}{2} \ RHO \ CD \ AR \ (V + V_w)^2 \tag{2.14}$$

where   RHO = the mass density of air, in kg/m^3;

      CD = the dimensionless aerodynamic drag coefficient of the vehicle

      AR = the projected frontal area of the vehicle, in m^2; and

      Vw = the component of wind velocity in the direction opposite to the vehicle travel, in m/s.

The mass density of air, RHO, is a function of both altitude and atmospheric temperature. Atmospheric temparature is also a function of altitude but the relationship also depends on latitude. Since RHO is relatively insensitive to altitude and atmospheric temparature within the range we normally encounter, the following formula which relates RHO to altitude alone has been suggested (St. John and Kobett, 1978):

$$RHO = 1.225 \ (1 - 2.26 \ ALT \ 10^{-5})^{4.225} \qquad\qquad (2.15)$$

where   ALT = elevation of the road above the mean sea level, in meters.

The aerodynamic drag coefficient, CD, represents three sources of air resistance (Taborek, 1957; Wong, 1978):

1. Form drag, which is caused by the turbulence in the wake of the vehicle; it is a function of the shape of the vehicle body and accounts for most of air resistance;

2. Skin friction, which is caused by the shear force exerted on the vehicle exterior surfaces by the air stream; skin friction accounts for about 10 percent of total air resistance; and

3. Interior friction, which is caused by the flow of air through the raiator or vehicle interior for cooling and ventilating purposes; interior friction accounts for a small part of total air resistance.

Typical values of the aerodynamic drag coefficient for different types of vehicles are shown in Table 2.1.

Table 2.1: Aerodynamic drag coefficients

Vehicle type	CD (dimensionless)
Passenger car	0.3 – 0.6
Convertible	0.4 – 0.65
Racing cars	0.25 – 0.3
Bus	0.6 – 0.7
Truck	0.8 – 1.0

Source: Wong (1978).

2.2.5 Rolling Resistance

The following discussion is restricted in scope to vehicle rolling resistance on hard surfaces (e.g., paved roads and compacted unpaved roads). The main reason is that almost all the roads in service today fall into this category (with the rare exceptions of fair-weather-only unpaved roads which turn into a very wet, soggy state after a flood or heavy rainfall, roads after a major snow storm, unpaved roads during a spring thaw, etc). A second reason is that less is known of the more complicated relationship between vehicle rolling resistance and the deformation characteristics of soft road surfaces.

Smooth surfaces were the major focus of earlier research on vehicle rolling resistance. The single most important cause of vehicle rolling resistance was found to be the tire, which, in turn, arose primarily from the internal friction in the rubber and cord of the tire carcass resulting from tire deflection (Taborek, 1957; Wong, 1978; van Eldik Thieme and Dijks, 1981). Internal friction or hysteresis accounts for 90 - 95 percent of total tire rolling resistance. Two other causes provide secondary contributions:

1. Slippage between the surfaces of the rubber tread and the road (about 5-10 percent); and

2. Windage between the rotating tire and the surrounding air (1 - 3 percent).

In more recent research, Lu (1983) investigated the effect of rough surfaces on vehicle rolling resistance. In addition to the effect of tire hysteresis when the road is smooth, Lu identified two other important sources which turn increasingly dominant when the road becomes rougher:

1. Additional hysteresis losses in the tire due to road surface irregularities; and

2. Energy dissipation in the suspension system due to the relative motion between the sprung and unsprung masses.

Lu simulated these effects on a computer by traversing an idealized vehicle of given tire and suspension mechanical properties over longitudinal road profiles of different roughness levels. The rolling resistance of the vehicle was found to increase by an order of 100 percent from smooth to very rough. While the results from the simulation are specific to the particular characteristics of the idealized vehicle, they highlight the importance of road roughness.

Generally, the vehicle rolling resistance, RR, is expressed as:

$$RR = mg \cos\phi \ CR \qquad (2.16)$$

where $mg \cos\phi$ = the component of the vehicle gravitational force in the direction perpendicular to the road surface, in newtons; and

CR = the dimensionless coefficient of rolling resistance.

Equation 2.15 above may be simplified to:

$$RR = m \ g \ CR \qquad\qquad (2.17)$$

which introduces a 1 percent error for the extreme case of 15 percent gradient.

Tire mechanical properties which influence rolling resistance depend on a number of factors including primarily: the inflation pressure, ambient temperature, tire diameter and other geometric characteristics, and tire construction and rubber material. Taborek (1957), Wong (1978), and van Eldik Thieme and Dijks (1981) provide discussions of the effect of these factors. The suspension stiffness and damping characteristics depend primarily on the mechanical design of the suspension system, and the viscosity of the damping fluid used; the latter, in turn, is influenced by the ambient temperature (Gillespie, 1980).

Finally, the coefficient of rolling resistance is influenced by the speed of the vehicle because the energy dissipation due to tread deformation and carcass vibration increases with speed (Wong, 1981). The relationship between the coefficient of rolling resistance and speed is non-linear of degree 2.5, with the effect of speed being more significant at lower inflation pressures. For inflation pressures above 28 psi, the relationship could be divided roughly into three regimes: a fairly flat portion up to about 100 km/h, a linear portion between 100 km/h and 130 km/h and a steep non-linear portion above 130 km/h (Taborek, 1957).

Owing to the complexity of the relationship between the above factors and the coefficient of rolling resistance, it is necessary to strive for simplification by focussing on policy-relevant factors. In the Brazil study, road roughness was considered to be of primary importance because of its sensitivity to construction and maintenance standards policies. Further, because of the wide range of vehicles involved (from small cars to articulated trucks) with varying tire radii and constructions, it was considered desirable to investigate the effect of the size of the vehicle on the coefficient of rolling resistance. The effects of tire pressure and ambient temperature were minimized by conducting the test runs under standard pressure and temperature conditions. Finally, it was decided to ignore the effect of vehicle speed because the range of speeds of interest in the context of rural roads in the developing countries lies predominantly in the flat regime of the rolling resistance-speed relationship described above.

An experiment was conducted to test the roughness effect on vehicle rolling resistance with the other variables held constant. The test vehicles were coasted down in neutral over paved and unpaved road sections of different roughness levels. The time-distance data obtained from the experiment enabled the relationship between the coefficient of rolling resistance and road roughness to be estimated separately for light and heavy vehicles:

Light vehicles (cars and utilities):

$$CR = 0.0218 + 0.0000467 \ QI \qquad (2.18a)$$

Heavy vehicles (buses and trucks):

$$CR = 0.0139 + 0.0000198 \ QI \qquad (2.18b)$$

where QI is the road roughness, in QI units. The analysis procedure and interpretation of the results are given in Appendix 2A.

2.3 APPLICATIONS

As a result of the discussion in the previous section, the force balance may be written as:

$$m'a = \frac{736 \ HP}{V} - m \ g \ GR - m \ g \ CR - 1/2 \ RHO \ CD \ AR \ V^2 \qquad (2.19)$$

In this study the force balance equation has four principal applications:

1. To derive the coefficients of rolling resistance for the test vehicles. In this application the power term in Equation 2.19 is zero since the test vehicles were coasting down in neutral. By integrating Equation 2.19 over the coast-down distance, an energy balance equation is obtained. The coefficient of rolling resistance can be computed given that the other parameters and variables are known. (See details in Appendix 2A).

2. To derive the used driving power and the used braking power of vehicles under steady-state conditions. In this application, the acceleration term in Equation 2.19 is zero. When a vehicle travels up a steep hill the driver usually utilizes the maximum sustainable level of engine power. This is particularly true for loaded trucks. If the uphill speed of the vehicle is known, the force balance equation 2.19 can be used to compute the used driving power, denoted by HPDRIVE. Similarly, when a vehicle travels down a very steep hill the driver usually utilizes both the engine and the regular brakes to keep the vehicle from accelerating out of control. Again this is particularly evident for heavily loaded trucks. If the downhill speed of the vehicle is known, the magnitude of the used braking power, denoted by HPBRAKE, can be computed. The used driving and braking powers have two main uses: (i) in developing the steady-state speed model (Chapters 3 and 4) and the free-speed profile simulation model (Chapter 6); and (ii) in the adaption of the vehicle operating cost relationships developed in this study to suit local conditions (Chapter 13).

3. As a converse to the above, to compute the driving and braking constraining speeds which are the necessary components in the prediction of vehicle travel speeds. Using the force balance relationship these constraining speeds can be computed once the used driving and braking powers are known (see Chapter 3).

4. To simulate the free-speed profile of a vehicle as it traverses a given road stretch. It is necessary to first establish a set of behavioral assumptions regarding how the driver uses the vehicle driving and braking powers in controlling the vehicle's speed and acceleration/deceleration. Given these assumptions, the free-speed profile of the vehicle can be determined by successive application of the force balance relationship at discrete intervals along the road (see Chapter 6).

APPENDIX 2A

DEVELOPMENT OF RELATIONSHIP BETWEEN COEFFICIENTOF ROLLING RESISTANCE AND ROAD ROUGHNESS

This appendix presents the results of the analysis to determine the relationship of the coefficient of rolling resistance to road roughness.

2A.1 COAST-DOWN EXPERIMENT

The coast-down experiment is one of several methods available for determining vehicle rolling resistance (Van Eldik Thieme and Dijks, 1981). Basically it involves coasting down a vehicle in neutral from a relatively high speed (preferably 120 km/h or more) over a road section of known uniform geometry (usually level-tangent) and surface characteristics. Information on speed and deceleration and/or time and distance during the coast-down is recorded for subsequent calculations to arrive at an estimate of the rolling resistance coefficient.

The coast-down experiment in this study involved 9 test vehicles, one car, two replicate utilities (VW-Kombi's), one large bus, two light trucks, two replicate heavy trucks and one articulated truck. The major characteristics of these vehicles are shown in Table 1A.2. Four level-tangent road sections were selected for the experiment, two paved (smooth and rough) and two compacted unpaved (smooth and rough). The characteristics of these sites are summarized in Table 2A.1(a).

At each test site, two load levels, empty and loaded, were used on each test vehicle (see the numerical values in Table 2A.1(b)). At each load level the vehicle was coasted down 6 times in each direction. The distance travelled during the coast-down was recorded on a special instrument at 1-second intervals. Also measured during the experiment were the wind speed and direction, the ambient temperature, the rainfall, and the road surface conditions. The tire inflation pressure of each vehicle was maintained at a standard value throughout. More detailed descriptions of the coast-down experiment are given in GEIPOT (1982).

2A.2 ENERGY BALANCE EQUATION

Based on the force balance equation different alternative analytical formulas for determining the rolling resistance coefficient can be derived. For a vehicle coasting down in neutral, the drive force equals zero, so the force balance equation can be re-written as:

$$m' \frac{dV}{dt} = - m\, g\, GR - m\, g\, CR - 1/2\ RHO\ CD\ AR\ (V - V_w)^2 \qquad (2A.1)$$

where t is elapsed time and V = V(t).

Table 2A.1(a): Summary characteristics of road sections employed in coast-down experiment

Characteristics	Section			
	Paved smooth	Paved rough	Unpaved smooth	Unpaved rough
Type of surfacing material	Double surface treated	Double surface treated	Laterite gravel	Laterite gravel
Average gradient (percent)	0.2	0.2	1.5	1.0
Average horizontal curvature (degrees/km)	14	0	0	0
Average roughness (QI)	29	80	58	178
Average rut depth (mm)	7	2	6	54
Average depth of loose material (mm)	–	–	4	9
Average moisture content (percent)	–	–	1	2
Average ambient temperature (°C)	24.5	23.2	24.2	20.8
Average wind speed (m/s)	3.6	3.0	3.5	3.4
Average rainfall (mm/month)	0	0	0	0
Average spacing of corrugation (m)	–	–	0	0
Average depth of corrugation (mm)	–	–	0	0

Source: Brazil-UNDP-World Bank highway research project data.

One possible derivation is to re-state the above equation as:

$$Y = B + A X$$

where $Y = m' \dfrac{dV}{dt}$

$$B = - m g GR - m g CR$$

$$A = - 1/2 RHO CD AR$$

and $X = (V - V_w)^2$

From a vehicle coast-down, a series of data points (X, Y) can in principle be obtained which can then be used in linear regression analysis to estimate the parameters B and A. With knowledge of the road Table gradient (GR), the vehicle weight (m), the air mass density (RHO) and the vehicle projected frontal area (AR), the coefficients of rolling resistance (CR) and aerodynamic resistance (CD) can be determined (St. John and Kobett, 1978). Although relatively simple and analytically appealing, this approach was not possible in the Brazil-UNDP study. Instrumentation mitations precluded accurate time-distance profile measurement

Table 2A.1(b): Summary of loads and number of test runs employed in coast-down experiment

| Test vehicle | Load carried (kg) by load level | | Number of runs | | | | | | |
| | | | By Load level | | By section | | | | |
	Un-loaded	Loaded	Un-loaded	Loaded	Paved smooth	Paved rough	Un-paved smooth	Un-paved rough	Total
Small car	0	280	39	45	22	24	20	18	84
Utility	0	550	40	45	24	19	22	20	85
Replicate utility	0	550	17	24	20	16	4	1	41
Bus	0	2250	41	34	19	19	22	15	75
Light gasoline truck	150	3510	22	32	9	22	11	12	54
Light diesel truck	0	3325	34	23	9	19	9	29	57
Heavy truck	1730	11970	44	47	23	35	23	10	91
Heavy truck with crane	1670	12045	35	36	21	12	21	17	71
Articulated truck	0	26600	21	31	23	13	5	11	52
Total number of runs			293	317	170	179	137	124	610

Source: Brazil-UNDP-World Bank highway research project data.

at vehicle speeds greater than 80 km/h.   Therefore the test vehicles could not be coasted down from a sufficiently high speed (over 120 km/h) needed to generate a good range of data points (X, Y).   However, as aerodynamic drag coefficients of the test vehicles were available from the manufacturers, it was decided to use the energy balance approach for determining the rolling resistance coefficient.

The energy balance equation can be derived from the force balance equation as follows: first, rewrite Equation 2A.1 as :

$$m' \frac{dV}{dx} V + m\ g\ GR + m\ g\ CR + 1/2\ RHO\ CD\ AR\ (V + V_w)^2 = 0 \quad (2A.2)$$

where $x = x(t)$ = the distance travelled by the vehicle during the coast-down.

Integrating the above equation between any two distance points x_1 and x_2 during the coast-down, we obtain an energy balance equation:

$$\Delta KE_{12} + \Delta PE_{12} + \Delta RE_{12} + \Delta AR_{12} = 0 \qquad\qquad (2A.3)$$

where $$\Delta KE_{12} = \int_{x_1}^{x_2} m' \, V \, dV = 1/2 \, m' \, (V_2^2 - V_1^2)$$

$$\Delta PE_{12} = \int_{x_1}^{x_2} m \, g \, GR \, dx = m \, g \, GR \, (x_2 - x_1)$$

$$\Delta RE_{12} = \int_{x_1}^{x_2} m \, g \, CR \, dx = m \, g \, CR \, (x_2 - x_1)$$

and $$\Delta AR_{12} = \int_{x_1}^{x_2} 1/2 \, RHO \, CD \, AR \, (V - V_w)^2 \, dx$$

The terms ΔKE_{12} and ΔPE_{12} are the changes in the kinetic and potential energies, respectively, of the vehicle between points x_1 and x_2 (in J). The remaining terms ΔRE_{12} and ΔAR_{12} are the energy losses due to rolling and air resistances, respectively, in covering the distance between these points (in J). The air resistance term generally does not have a closed form solution. However, assuming constant acceleration and wind speed, the energy loss due to air resistance can be expressed in the following closed form:

$$\Delta RE_{12} = 1/2 \, RHO \, CD \, AR \, [(V_2^2 + V_1^2)/2 + V_w^2 \qquad\qquad (2A.4)$$
$$+ 2/3 \, V_w \, (V_2 + V_2 \, V_1 + V_1)^2/(V_2 + V_1)] \, (x_2 - x_1)$$

The assumption of constant acceleration is adequate if the distance between x_1 and x_2 is relatively short, or if the vehicle speed is so low that the air resistance loss becomes a small component of the total loss. The adequacy of this assumption will be discussed further subsequently.

Strictly speaking, the vehicle rolling resistance produced in the coast-down experiment does not consist entirely of tire and suspension motion resistances. It also includes small resistances due to friction in the wheel bearings and in the drive-shaft and differential. According to Taborek (1958), the efficiency of bearings is in the range 0.98 - 0.99 and the efficiency of differentials is about 0.95. For modelling purposes in this study the 1-2 percent losses in the wheel bearings were ignored. Although the differential was not so efficient as the wheel bearings, the loss in it would have been a negligible fraction of the total rolling resistance losses since the drive shaft was spinning under virtually no load. Therefore, the losses in the differential were also ignored.

To compute the effective mass, m', we set the term m_e to 0 in Equation 2.7, since the vehicle was in neutral. The term m_w is computed based on the following simplifications:

1. Using the average of the inner and outer radii of the tire, denoted by RMT (in meters), to approximate the radius of gyration of each wheel; and

2. Using the nominal radius of each tire, denoted by RNT (in m), to approximate the effective rolling radius, RRT.[1]

The resulting formula is given by:

$$m' = m + m_w = m + M_w \left[\frac{RMT}{RNT}\right]^2 \qquad (2A.5)$$

where M_w is the total mass of all mounted wheels, in kg, as defined earlier. The values of m_w computed for the test vehicles are shown in Table 1A.2.

2A.3 DETERMINATION OF ROLLING RESISTANCE COEFFICIENTS

The computational procedure employed can be described in the following steps.

1. Using linear regression analysis, the following quadratic curve was fitted to the last 15 seconds of each time distance profile:

$$x = x(t) = p_0 + p_1 t + p_2 t^2$$

where p_0, p_1 and p_2 are estimated parameters. The above quadratic curve assumes that the vehicle deceleration (equal to $-d^2x/dt^2$ or $-2p_2$) was constant. This assumption was considered to be realistic when only the last 15 seconds of the time-distance profile was used. Figure 2A.1 shows a plot of the time-distance data points and the fitted curve, for a typical vehicle run.

2. The coefficient CR for each vehicle run was computed using the energy balance equation (2A.3) with the vehicle speeds at the beginning and end of the 15-second period (denoted by subscripts 1 and 2, respectively) given by:

$$V_1 = p_1 + 2 p_2 t_1$$

$$V_2 = p_1 + 2 p_2 t_2$$

3. For each combination of vehicle, road section, load level and direction an average CR coefficient was computed from the replicate run values obtained in step 2 and compiled in Table 2A.2. Let $CR_{vs\ell d}$ denote this average, where v,

---

[1] From experimental results compiled by van Eldik Thieme and Dijks (1981) the ratio of effective radius to the radius when the tire is unloaded varies in the range 0.95 – 1.00 depending primarily on the tire construction, vehicle speed and load.

Figure 2A.1: Time distance observations from a typical coast-down run and the fitted curve

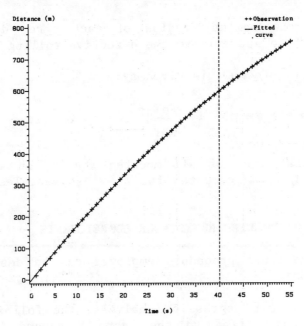

Source: Brazil-UNDP-World Bank highway research project data and
          author's analysis

Figure 2A.2: Computed rolling resistance coefficient versus roughness for all combinations of test vehicle and road section

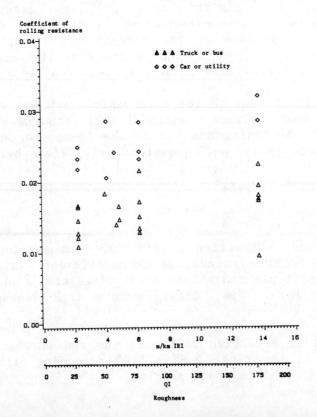

Table 2A.2: Computed coefficients of rolling resistance for each test vehicle by road section, load level and direction

Vehicle Type	LC	D	Paved Smooth			Paved Rough			Unpaved Smooth			Unpaved Rough		
			CR_{veld}	CR_{vel}	CR_{ve}	CR_{veld}	CR_{vel}	CR_{ve}	CR_{veld}	CR_{vel}	CR_{ve}	CR_{veld}	CR_{vel}	CR_{ve}
Small car	U	1	0.0242	0.0251	0.0249	0.0227	0.0219	0.0242	0.0354	0.0283	0.0285	0.0207	0.0353	0.0319
		2	0.0259			0.0210			0.0211			0.0498		
	L	1	0.0236	0.0247		0.0261	0.0266		0.0400	0.0288		0.0258	0.0286	
		2	0.0259			0.0270			0.0177			0.0314		
Utility	U	1	0.0228	0.0267	0.0218	0.0221	0.0230	0.0232	0.0254	0.0219	0.0205	0.0164	0.0293	0.0285
		2	0.0267			0.0240			0.0184			0.0422		
	L	1	0.0167	0.0188		0.0215	0.0233		0.0238	0.0192		0.0093	0.0276	
		2	0.0209			0.0250			0.0146			0.0459		
Replicate utility	U	1	0.0217	0.0221	0.0232	0.0279	0.0297	0.0284	-	-	0.0241	-	-	*
		2	0.0226			0.0315			-			-		
	L	1	0.0237	0.0243		0.0265	0.0271		0.0370	0.0241		0.0131	*	
		2	0.0249			0.0276			0.0113			-		
Bus	U	1	0.0115	0.0109	0.0108	0.0161	0.0114	0.0134	0.0164	0.0136	0.0165	0.0013	0.0193	0.0193
		2	0.0104			0.0067			0.0109			0.0374		
	L	1	0.0080	0.0107		0.0165	0.0153		0.0269	0.0194		-	*	
		2	0.0134			0.0142			0.0119			0.0361		
Light gas truck	U	1	-	-	0.0145	0.0184	0.0187	0.171	0.0223	0.0183	0.0183	-	-	0.0179
		2	-			0.189			0.0143			-		
	L	1	0.0131	0.0145		0.0151	0.0156		-	-		0.0013	0.0179	
		2	0.0159			0.0160			-			0.0346		
Light diesel truck	U	1	-	-	0.0166	0.0239	0.0215	0.0215	0.0534	*	*	0.0172	0.0232	0.0223
		2	-			0.0191			-			0.0292		
	L	1	0.0226	0.0166		-	-		0.0433	*		0.0175	0.0214	
		2	0.0106			-			-			0.0253		
Heavy truck	U	1	0.0172	0.0190	0.0164	0.0147	0.0177	0.0150	0.0192	0.0151	0.0146	0.0034	0.0094	0.0094
		2	0.0207			0.0206			0.0110			0.0154		
	L	1	0.0126	0.0138		0.0125	0.0124		0.0159	0.0141		-	-	
		2	0.0151			0.0122			0.0126			-		
Heavy truck with crane	U	1	0.0198	0.0127	0.0121	0.0136	0.0128	0.128	0.0185	0.0158	0.0139	0.0007	0.0182	0.0172
		2	0.0056			0.0121			0.0131			0.0358		
	L	1	0.0103	0.0115		-	-		0.0133	0.0121		0.0161	0.0161	
		2	0.0127			-			0.0109			0.0162		
Articulated truck	U	1	0.0128	0.0141	0.0127	-	*	0.0128	-	*	*	0.0020	0.0194	0.0174
		2	0.0153			0.0131			0.0126			0.0369		
	L	1	0.0107	0.0114		0.0137	0.0119		-	*		0.0157	0.0154	
		2	0.0120			0.0119			0.0133			0.0151		

LC = Loading condition, U = Unloaded, L = Loaded, D = Direction of travel

1 = Downhill in the case of the paved smooth and unpaved smooth sections and uphill in the case of the unpaved rough section. The paved rough section is flat.

2 = Reverse direction to the above (1).

- = Means that no usable run was available for the particular combination of vehicle, Loading condition and direction.

* = Signifies that average was not taken because the value for one of the directions was not available.

Source: Analysis of Brazil-UNDP-World Bank highway research project data.

s, ℓ and d stand for vehicle, road section, load level and direction, respectively.

4. For each combination of vehicle, road section and load level, a CR coefficient, denoted by $CR_{vs\ell}$, was computed by simple averaging over the two directions:

$$CR_{vs\ell} = \frac{1}{2} (CR_{vs\ell 1} + CR_{vs\ell 2})$$

where subscripts 1 and 2 denote the two directions. The significance of this step is to cancel out direction-dependent errors, viz., in the measurement of road gradient and wind speed. Korst and White (1973) provide an analytical rationale for the need to average out the coefficient estimates over the two directions. The values of $CR_{vs\ell}$ are tabulated in Table 2A.2.

5. For each combination of vehicle and road section, a CR coefficient, denoted by CR_{vs} was computed by averaging over the load levels:

$$CR_{vs} = \frac{1}{2} (CR_{vs1} + CR_{vs2})$$

where subscripts 1 and 2 denote the low and high load levels, respectively. Averaging over load levels was based on previous findings that the rolling resistance coefficient is independent of vehicle load (within the operating range). This finding is clearly supported by the numerical results in Table 2A.2. (For the vehicle section combinations that had useful time distance data for only one level no averaging was necessary). The values of CR_{vs} are shown in Table 2A.2.

2A.4 DETERMINATION OF RELATIONSHIP BETWEEN ROLLING RESISTANCE COEFFICIENT AND ROAD ROUGHNESS

Figure 2A.2 shows a plot of rolling resistance coefficient against road roughness for all combinations of test vehicles and road sections obtained from the data points in Table 2A.2. The test vehicles are separated into two groups:

1. Light vehicles - car or utility
2. Heavy vehicles - bus or truck.

From the data plot two trends are evident:

1. The rolling resistance of a vehicle generally increases with road roughness. This agrees with the findings by Lu

Table 2A.3: Computed rolling resistance coefficents by vehicle group and section

Section Vehicle group	Paved smooth	Paved rough	Unpaved smooth	Unpaved rough
Cars and utilities	0.02331	0.02525	0.02440	0.3020
Trucks and buses	0.01386	0.01544	0.01584	0.01727

Source: Analysis of Brazil-UNDP-World Bank highway research project data.

Figure 2A.3: Rolling resistance coefficient versus roughness by vehicle group: data points and fitted lines

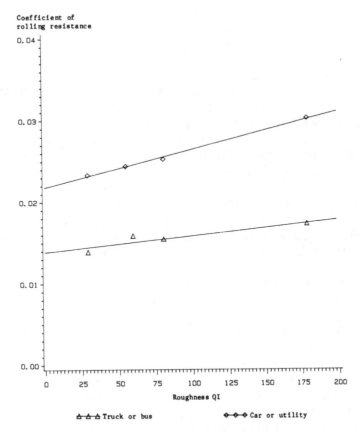

Source: Analysis of Brazil-UNDP-World Bank highway research project data.

(1983) cited in the text. Furthermore, according to Limpert (1982), the rolling resistance can increase by as much as 30 percent between a smooth and a badly potholed road.

2. As a group, the rolling resistance of the light vehicles is considerably higher than that of the heavy vehicles. From the discussion in Van Eldik Thieme and Dijks (1981), tire inflation pressures used on commercial vehicles are generally 3 − 4 times those used on passenger cars (the tires used on the VW-Kombi's are of passenger-car size). This results in a smaller hysteresis loss on commercial vehicle tires.

Since there are too few data points to estimate coefficients specific for each test vehicle, it was decided to develop separate relationships only for the light and heavy vehicle groups. This was done by first averaging out the CR values of the test vehicles by section and vehicle group, yielding results shown in Table 2A.3. Figure 2A.3 shows a plot of the vehicle-group averge of rolling resistance was then regressedagainst road roughness, resulting in the following relationships:

Light vehicle: CR = 0.0218 + 0.0000467 QI

Heavy vehicle: CR = 0.0139 + 0.0000198 QI

Figure 2A.3 also shows a graph of the fitted regression lines superimposed with the data points. It can be seen that both the intercept and the slope for the light vehicle class are greater than those for the heavy vehicle class. This observation is consistent with the early discussion on the difference between light and heavy vehicle tires. It is also consistent with Taborek's findings (1958) that the coefficient of rolling resistance tends to be more sensitive to road surface conditions as the tire diameter decreases. The coefficient values for light and heavy vehicles increase by 46 and 31 percent, respectively, as roughness increases from very smooth (QI = 20) to very rough (QI = 250). This observation is broadly consistant with the computer simulation results obtained by Lu (1983).

Two other studies investigating the relationship between the coefficient of rolling resistance and roughness have been reported in the literature from India (Kadiyali et al., 1982) and South Africa (Bester, 1984). Due to the preliminary nature of the India results, only the South Africa results are discussed below.

The South African study also used coast-down technique, and runs were made with cars (8 sections) and trucks (5 sections). The roughness of the sections was between 12 QI and 75 QI. Using the recommended value for the speed-dependent component of the coefficient of rolling resistance, and assuming the roughness effect to be entirely due to rolling resistance, the relationships estimated in the study may be written as follows:

Car: $CR = 0.0152 + 0.0000331\ QI + (6.99 + 0.049\ QI)\ 10^{-6}\ V^2$

Truck: $CR = 0.0086 + 0.0000826\ QI + 6.99\ 10^{-6}\ V^2$

where V = vehicle speed in m/s.

Ignoring the marginal contribution of the speed-dependent part to the coefficient of rolling resistance (e.g., about 0.001 at 12 m/s for trucks), it can be seen that the South Africa relationships are numerically similar to those from Brazil--with the exception of the roughness coefficient for trucks being larger in the former (0.0000826) than in the latter (0.0000198). This discrepancy may be due in part to the relatively small range of roughness used in the South Africa Study. Further, the road sections in the South African study sample were bunched over the very low end of the roughness spectrum with five of the eight sections having roughness values below 24 QI. The relative magnitude of the roughness coefficients in the Brazil relationships seem to be more plausible on a priori grounds, because the extent of pentration is less for larger tires. At any rate, both studies predict a lower value of the coefficient of rolling resistance for heavy vehicles than for light vehicles. A significant finding of the South African study is that, while concrete and asphaltic concrete pavements have a lower rolling resistance than roads with a surface treatment with the same roughness, the differences are negligible.

2A.5   CONCLUSIONS AND RECOMMENDATIONS

The main limitation of the Brazil relationships is that, due to the fact that there were only four road sections, two for each pavement type, the relationships are less robust than they should be, nor do they make a distinction between pavement types.

For highway investment planning purposes the relationships from the Brazilian study are recommended on an interim basis, with their applications restricted to paved and compacted unpaved surfaces and vehicles with relatively low speeds. Further work is recommended to strengthen these relationships by using field data from more road sections of different surface characteristics, and also by merging experimental data with quarter-car simulation models which can incorporate the effect of suspension characteristics and tire damping.

CHAPTER 3

Steady-State Speed Model: Formulation

This chapter is concerned with the theory and analytical derivation of the steady-state speed model, functionally the most important model developed in this volume. The approach to speed prediction adopted is described first (Section 3.1). It is followed by a discussion of the limiting speed model (Section 3.2) and the detailed analytical derivation of the associated "limiting" speeds (Section 3.3). This provides the basis for the probabilistic version which enables the parameters of the limiting speed model to be estimated (Section 3.4). Section 3.5 provides a summary of the steady-state speed prediction formula.

3.1 PROBLEM STATEMENT AND APPROACH

The problem of predicting free-flow speeds for a roadway may be stated as follows: given the vertical and horizontal profiles, the surface type and condition, and the width of the roadway, predict the speed profile of an unimpeded vehicle of known characteristics along the roadway.

The level and nature of the decision for which the speed predictions are required (for example, sectoral policy analysis, appraisal of a new road project, or evaluation of a proposed minor improvement) has implications both for the inputs into and the output from the prediction. On the input side, the level of detail available on the roadway may vary from just a few aggregate descriptors of the roadway to detailed information based on geometric design and condition survey. Similarly, on the output side, the accuracy and the level of detail desired of the predicted speed may range from just the space-mean speed for the round-trip travel on the roadway to nearly continuous speed profile across the roadway with statistical confidence statements.

In order to cope with the diversity of demands the speed prediction model is called upon to cope with, it is convenient, even necessary, to structure the process of speed prediction into two inter-related, but conceptually distinct, components:

1. A model to predict an appropriately defined concept of vehicle speed on a stretch of road over which the characteristics of interest do not change appreciably. We refer to such a road stretch as a homogeneous section of the roadway. The concept of speed used is that of a steady-state speed and this part of the speed prediction process may be called a <u>steady-state speed prediction model</u>.

2.   A set of procedures to apply the above for predicting the
vehicle speed profile over a heterogeneous roadway, using
the available information on the roadway and with the desired degree of accuracy for the particular application.
We may refer to these procedures as <u>roadway speed prediction methods</u>.

        The current chapter is devoted to a theoretical account of the
steady-state speed prediction model.   (The next chapter presents the
details regarding the econometric implementation of the model.) Chapters
5 through 7 describe alternative procedures for predicting roadway speeds
based on the steady-state speed predictions.

        The <u>steady-state speed</u> of an unimpeded vehicle of known
attributes traversing a homogeneous road section of known
characteristics, located in a given socioeconomic and traffic environment
may be defined as the speed the vehicle would eventually attain and
maintain if the homogeneous road section were indefinitely long.   Thus
steady-state speed in a given environment may be regarded as an inherent
property we can associate with a given combination of a homogeneous road
section and a vehicle.

        The distance covered by a vehicle before it reaches its
steady-state speed varies considerably.   For a heavily loaded truck
entering a steep uphill gradient from a long level-tangent section, the
distance would be only a few tens of meters long.   On the other hand,
when the same truck enters a level-tangent section at crawl speed, it
would need to travel several hundred meters before reaching its maximum
cruising speed.

        In the model to be described, a homogeneous road section is
assumed to be completely defined if its surface type, slope, curvature,
superelevation and surface irregularity measure are specified.[1] It may
variables under the control of the highway planner.   We occasionally
refer to these as "speed-influencing characteristics" or "road severity
factors," collectively denoted by the symbol X.   It should be noted that
the direction of travel on the homogeneous section is part of the
description of the section.   In other words, the term section stands for
the longer expression "section-direction."

        The word "vehicle" is also a short-hand for "the
operator-vehicle system" and the term operator is used to bring out the
fact that the speed decision-maker may be an individual driver or a
transport firm.   As for the characteristics of the vehicle, the
vehicle-class and loading (in the case of a truck) are supposed to be
known.   Also, a set of technical characteristics of the vehicle, such as

---

[1] Roads are assumed to be at least 5.5 m wide. As estimated initially
     using roadside speed observations made in Brazil, road width was not
     one of the independent variables, but the effect of road width on the
     steady-state speed has been incorporated based on data collected in
     India, as described in Section 4.4.

unladen weight, drag coefficient, and so on, are assumed to be known or assignable with reasonable accuracy.   We denote the technical characteristics of the vehicle by the symbol Y.

Finally, we come to a set of behavioral-technical characteristics of the vehicle, such as used power, perceived friction ratio, desired speed, and so on.   These are the estimated parameters of the steady-state speed preciction model and are collectively denoted by the symbol θ.   For a given application these parameters may be estimated afresh, calibrated on the basis of limited observations or, in some cases, judgmentally determined.

The socioeconomic and traffic environment is explicitly mentioned as given because it is not explicitly modelled.   In other words, the speed decision has not been modelled as being part of the economic decision problem of a vehicle operating firm or a private driver.   Also, features of the general traffic environment within which the particular homogeneous section is located, such as design consistency, have not been related to attained speed.   Thus, the model parameters would embody the effect of the environment in which they were estimated, and the degree of transferability of different parameter estimates may vary.

The steady-state speed, as defined above, is the appropriate speed concept to work with in the context of homogeneous sections because it represents a state of equilibrium in the driver-vehicle-roadway system so that the process of measurement on the system is well-defined.   In fact, the concept of steady-state speed is fundamental for any speed prediction model, whether or not it is explicitly recognized.   Since homogeneous road sections represent the most natural way of dividing a roadway, the steady-state speed on the homogeneous section is a theoretical starting point for further analysis.   It also represents a "base" level of detail at which speed predictions for the entire roadway could be carried out.   Relative to it, one can conceptualize predictions on a more detailed basis as well as on a more aggregate basis. Essentially, the process of incorporating more details consists in modelling transitions betwen successive steady-state speeds on adjacent homogeneous sections.   Moreover, as discussed later, the aggregate methods to predict roadway speeds entail representing the entire heterogeneous roadway as a small number of hypothetical "average" homogeneous sections; in fact, as explained in Chapter 7, the procedure of aggregate prediction basically entails treating the entire roadway as two homogeneous sections of positive and negative grades with road characteristics represented by averages.   The average journey speed over the roadway is computed on the basis of the predicted steady-state speeds on these idealized road sections.

In practical terms also, prediction of speed simply as the space mean speed of the steady-state speeds of homogeneous sections as described in Chapter 5 represents one plausible level of detail which might be adequate for some applications.   Indeed we shall study the performance of more detailed level predictions and more aggregate level predictions by comparing them with the performance of steady-state speed predictions.

3.2   LIMITING SPEED MODEL: APPROACH AND BASIC FORMULATION

Our modelling objective is to develop a functional expression which relates the steady-state speed of a given vehicle class to a set X of descriptors or variables which capture the geometric and surface characteristics of the homogeneous road section. Specifically, these descriptors are:

1. The road gradient, GR, expressed as a fraction (to represent the vertical alignment);

2. The horizontal curvature, C, in degrees/km (or the radius of curvature, RC, in m), and the curve superelevation, SP, expressed as a fraction (to represent the horizontal alignment); and

3. The road roughness, QI, in QI (or m/km IRI) units, and the surface type, ST, which may be paved or unpaved (to represent surface characteristics).

Brief descriptions of these variables were given in Section 2.1.

One approach which has been employed in several previous studies is to relate the steady-state speed directly to these road descriptors. Because of the difficulties in developing a proper mathematical expression, a linear form has generally been adopted. The most basic of such models may be stylized as:

$$VSS = q_0 + q_1\ GR + q_2\ C + q_3\ QI \qquad\qquad (3.1a)$$

where VSS denotes the steady-state speed (in m/s) and q_0 through q_3 are model parameters.

Some of the refinements over the basic model found in the literature follow. First, the model is estimated independently for different surface types. Second, vehicle characteristics, such as power-to-weight ratio and other roadway descriptors, such as rut depth, are introduced as needed as independent variables. Third, a dummy variable formulation is sometimes used to allow the positive and negative grades to have different coefficients. Briefly, this is done by using the rise (RS) and fall (FL) variables defined in Section 2.1, and specifying the model as:

$$VSS = q_0 + q_{11}\ RS + q_{12}\ FL + q_2\ C + q_3\ QI \qquad\qquad (3.1b)$$

Linear models of similar forms have been empirically estimated in several studies yielding coefficients of expected signs and reasonable magnitudes (Hide, 1975; Morosiuk and Abaynayaka, 1982; CRRI, 1982; and TRDF, 1980). The values of coefficients other than q_0 have generally been found to be negative, indicating the negative influence of road severity on vehicle speed, although the coefficient of "fall," q_{12}, is occasionally found to have a small positive value for some vehicle classes in some studies. The constant term, q_0, which has generally been found to be positive, represents various subjective (or not easily quantifiable) factors. When road severity variables are at their minimum values, e.g., when the road is flat (GR = 0), straight (C = 0) and smooth (QI approaching zero), the steady-state speed approaches q_0;   at this point the vehicle speed tends to be constrained by subjective factors.

Although the direct approach is evidently workable, its application requires care to circumvent the following inherent problems:

1. It is possible to predict unreasonably low (at times negative) steady-state speeds, especially for low standard roads where the road gradient (GR), curvature (C), and roughness (QI) simultaneously assume large values. In these cases, one has to take recourse to imposing a floor value on the predicted steady-state speeds, but such a procedure distorts benefits from road improvement projects. This is a serious limitation in the light of the fact that, more often than not, it is precisely such roads that are candidates for upgrading.

2. The partial derivative of steady-state speed with respect to each road severity variable is constant (equal to q_i); this is unrealistic, particularly when applied to low-standard roads. For example, on a very rough, steep uphill road section, vehicle speeds cannot be raised significantly simply by making the surface smoother while the gradient is still the speed-limiting factor.

The issues raised above point to the lack in the linear form of a desirable property, namely, asymptotic consistency; that is, as one road severity variable increases and the others are held constant, the steady-state speed should decrease and should approach zero at a decreasing rate and never become negative. This problem can be mitigated partly by making the mathematical form nonlinear and incorporating interaction terms to make the partial derivatives sensitive to road standard, but the approach would still be ad hoc. That is, the model would not incorporate our prior scientific and behavioral knowledge regarding vehicle dynamics and driver behavior and would consequently be of questionable reliability in extrapolation or transference to a new country.

The limiting speed approach is an alternative to the above. Instead of directly associating the steady-state speed with the speed-influencing parameters of the homogeneous section, the approach consists of first associating a set of steady-state "limiting or constraining speeds" with the speed-influencing parameters. Then the vehicle is postulated to be driven at the maximum attainable speed subject to these speed constraints. That is, the observed steady-state speed of the vehicle is regarded as the minimum of the unobservable or latent speed constraints generated by the interaction of road severity factors with relevant characteristics of the vehicle. Formally, the model may be written as

$$\text{VSS} = \min\ [\text{VDRIVE, VBRAKE, VCURVE, VROUGH, VDESIR}] \qquad (3.2)$$

where   VSS   = the attained steady-state speed;

VDRIVE = the speed limited by gradient and used driving power, i.e., power applied in the direction of motion;

VBRAKE = the speed limited by gradient and used braking power, i.e., power applied against the direction of motion;

VCURVE = the speed limited by curvature;

VROUGH = the speed limited by roughness; and

VDESIR = the desired speed in the absence of road severity factors.

All the above quantities are expressed in m/s.

As will be seen in the next section, VDRIVE and VBRAKE are primarily functions of the road gradient and the load level and secondarily a function of road roughness. VCURVE is a function of the horizontal curvature and superelevation as well as the surface type and load level. VROUGH is a function of road roughness. Finally, VDESIR, which in general should be a function of several factors, is treated as a constant for a given surface type in the original model estimated with Brazil data. However, in the later extension of the steady-state speed model using data from India, VDESIR also depends on the width class of the homogeneous section.

It should be noted that a given road descriptor or vehicle characteristic may be associated with more than one constraining speed. For example, as derived in the next section, the vehicle weight influences both VDRIVE and VBRAKE and road roughness appears as a determinant of VDRIVE, VBRAKE and VROUGH. In other words vehicle and road characteristics affect the steady-state speed through one or more constraining speeds.

Figures 3.1-3.3 provide graphical illustrations of constraining speeds and the attained speed for a loaded heavy truck, Mercedes Benz 1113.[2]   Figure 3.1 plots the steady-state and constraining speeds against the road gradient for a slightly curved, smooth paved section. In this figure three constraining speeds are binding over the ± 10 percent range of the road gradient. The maximum possible driving speed (VDRIVE) dominates over slightly negative (-0.2 percent) and

---

[2] The constraining speeds are as derived in Section 3.4, with the parameter values compiled in Chapter 14 for the Mercedes Benz 1113.

Figure 3.1:   Constraining and steady–state speeds versus gradient

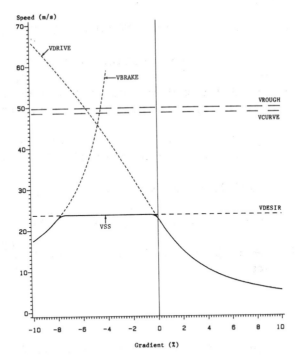

Source: Analysis of Brazil–UNDP–World Bank highway research project
          data.

Figure 3.2:   Constraining and steady–state speeds versus curvature

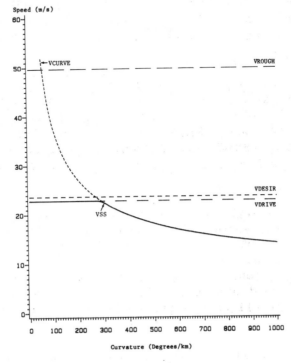

Source: Analysis of Brazil–UNDP–World Bank highway research project
          data.

Figure 3.3:   Constraining and steady–state speeds versus curvature

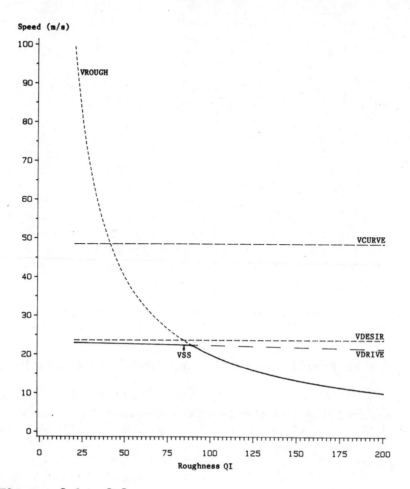

Notes for Figures 3.1 – 3.3

1. To interpret the figures, choose any value on the respective road characteristic (horizontal) axis, imagine a vertical line passing through the value, and read off various speed values.

2. The figures are for a loaded heavy truck (Mercedes Benz 1113) on a paved road. The parameter values used are the ones given in Table 14.1 and 14.2 for a heavy truck.

3. The non-varying road characteristic values are GR=0, C=57 degrees/km, and QI–40. The VBRAKE curve is not shown in Figures 3.2 and 3.3 because its value is infinity.

4. These notes also apply to Figures 3.6 – 3.8.

Source: Analysis of Brazil–UNDP–World Bank highway research project data.

positive gradients. For negative gradients of magnitude greater than 7.5 percent the maximum allowable braking speed (VBRAKE) becomes dominant. In the mid-range the steady-state speed is determined by the desired speed (VDESIR). Neither the maximum allowable curve speed (VCURVE) northe maximum ride severity speed (VROUGH) has any influence on the steady-state speed.

The plot in Figure 3.2 shows the effect of the horizontal curvature on the steady-state speed for a level smooth paved road. In this example two constraining speeds are binding. The maximum possible driving speed (VDRIVE) prevails over gentle curvature up to 300 degrees/km (approximately corresponding to a radius of curvature of 200 m) beyond which the steady-state speed is dictated by the curve speed constraint (VCURVE).

The effect of road roughness on the steady-state speed for a level-tangent paved road is shown in Figure 3.3. Two constraining speeds are binding, with the maximum possible driving speed (VDRIVE) over the smooth range (QI under about 90) and the maximum ride severity speed (VROUGH) over the rough range (QI over 90).

It should be noted that the VSS values graphed in these figures refer to a particular instance of vehicle traversal, and not to average VSS values. This point will be further clarified when the probabilistic version of the model is described in the next section.

In all three examples the steady-state speed drops monotonically but always remains positive as the road attributes—gradient, curvature and roughness—become severe. Thus the limiting speed approach satisfies the asymptotic consistency requirements discussed above. An even stronger appeal of this approach is that a considerable amount of prior scientific and engineering knowledge can be incorporated in the process of associating the constraining speeds with speed-influencing parameters. This has in fact been done by previous researchers, including Guenther (1969), Moavenzadeh et al. (1971), Sullivan (1977) and Galanis (1980). The various studies differ in the number of limiting speeds used as well as the way the limiting speeds are related to road and vehicle characteristics.

3.3 LIMITING SPEED MODEL: DERIVATION OF CONSTRAINING SPEEDS

In this section, expressions are derived for the five steady-state limiting speeds for a vehicle class in terms of the homogeneous section characteristics X, the vehicle attributes Y, and estimable parameters θ.

3.3.1 Driving Power-limited Speed, VDRIVE

The concept of driving speed constraint based on a constant used driving power has been employed in detailed vehicle speed simulation by previous researchers, including Sullivan (1977) and Gynnerstedt et al. (1977), among others. Under steady-state conditions the acceleration is zero, and the force balance introduced in Chapter 2 (Equation 2.19) may be written as:

$$\frac{736\ HP}{V} = m\ g\ GR + m\ g\ CR + 1/2\ RHO\ CD\ AR\ V^2 \qquad (3.3)$$

The variables above are as defined in Chapter 2. The value of mass density of air, RHO, may be calculated as a function of elevation of the section above the Mean Sea Level (ALT, in m), using Equation 2.15. The wind velocity, V_W, is assumed to be negligible.

The speed limited by driving power, VDRIVE, is assumed to be governed by a constant "used driving power," denoted by HPDRIVE. Substituting HPDRIVE for HP in Equation 3.3 above and simplifying, we get

$$1/2\ RHO\ CD\ AR\ V^3 + m\ g\ (GR + CR)\ V - 736\ HPDRIVE = 0 \qquad (3.4)$$

which is a cubic equation with V as the unknown. For all values of GR, the number of sign changes in the coefficients of the equation is unity. Thus, by Descartes' rule of signs, the equation always has exactly one positive root (Dickson, 1957). We define VDRIVE as the unique positive solution to Equation 3.4.

Cubic equations are generally solved by iterative methods. However, since the coefficient of the square term in Equation 3.4 is zero, the equation has a closed form solution. The solution procedure is outlined in Appendix 3B. The VDRIVE curve as a function of gradient may be seen in Figure 3.1.

The used driving power, HPDRIVE, is the model parameter to be estimated from observed speed data for this speed constraint. The vehicle attributes were obtained from other sources. The average vehicle mass (m) was obtained from actual portable-scale weighing of sample vehicles in the population at various sites (GEIPOT, 1982). The average vehicle aerodynamic drag coefficient and projected frontal area were adapted from values supplied by the manufacturers of the test vehicles (Appendix 1A).

3.3.2 Braking Power-limited Speed, VBRAKE

The concept of the braking crawl speed has been previously employed in traffic simulation modelling (Sullivan, 1977; and St. John and Kobett, 1978). When a vehicle descends a long steep grade its maximum descent speed is known to be controlled by the vehicle braking capability, which, according to informal conversations with and observations of truck drivers, results from the use of the vehicle engine retardation power or the regular brakes themselves or both. This braking capability is defined as the "used braking power," a positive quantity denoted by HPBRAKE, which is assumed to govern the braking power-limited speed constraint, VBRAKE. Substituting HPBRAKE for HP in the force balance equation for steady-state speed (Equation 3.3) results in:

$$- \frac{736 \ \text{HPBRAKE}}{V} = m \ g \ GR + m \ g \ CR - 0.5 \ RHO \ CD \ AR \ V^2 \tag{3.5}$$

Since the braking speed constraint is likely to become binding only on steep negative grades (more than 5 percent) where the steady-state speeds are relatively low, the air resistance term in Equation 3.5 becomes insignificant and may be dropped without causing a large error in the solution. Further, when the "effective gradient" (GR + CR) of a homogeneous section is non-negative, VBRAKE becomes irrelevant since braking is not needed to control the vehicle speed. This is identical to defining the value of VBRAKE to be infinity for such sections. Thus, the braking power-limited speed constraint is obtained as:

$$VBRAKE = \begin{cases} - \dfrac{736 \ \text{HPBRAKE}}{m \ g \ (GR + CR)} & \text{if } GR + CR < 0 \\[2ex] \infty & \text{if } GR + CR \geq 0 \end{cases} \tag{3.6}$$

where HPBRAKE is the model parameter to be estimated. The VBRAKE curve as a function of gradient may be seen in Figure 3.1.

3.3.3 Curvature-limited Speed Constraint, VCURVE

The optimal speed at which a vehicle can negotiate a horizontal curve has been a subject of numerous empirical studies (Gynnerstedt et al., 1977, among others).

Let RC denote the radius of the curve of the section-direction, in meters, and SP the curve's superelevation, expressed as a fraction (e.g., SP = 0.06 for 6 percent superelevation). For the vehicle travelling at a steady-state speed V, the lateral or side force on the vehicle in the direction parallel to the road surface, LF, in newtons, is given by the following kinematic relationship:

$$LF = \frac{m \ V^2}{RC} \cos SP - m \ g \ \sin SP \tag{3.7}$$

The two terms on the right hand side of Equation 3.7 are, respectively, the centrifugal and gravitational forces acting on the vehicle, both in directions parallel to the road surface.

The force on the vehicle in the direction perpendicular to the road surface, the normal force as denoted by NF, in newtons, is given by:

$$NF = m \ g \ \cos SP + \frac{m \ V^2}{RC} \sin SP \tag{3.8}$$

Since curve superelevations normally do not exceed 20 percent, we may use the following approximations:

$$\cos SP \simeq 1$$
$$\sin SP \simeq SP$$

Consequently, Equations 3.7 and 3.8 simplify to:

$$LF = \frac{m\ V^2}{RC} - m\ g\ SP \qquad\qquad (3.9)$$

and

$$NF = m\ g + \frac{m\ V^2}{RC}\ SP \qquad\qquad (3.10)$$

The curvature-limited speed constraint is assumed to be governed by the "used perceived friction ratio," denoted by FRATIO and defined as the ratio of the lateral force to the normal force:

$$FRATIO = \frac{LF}{NF} \qquad\qquad (3.11)$$

Substituting Equations 3.9 and 3.10 in the above equation yields:

$$FRATIO = \frac{\dfrac{V^2}{g\ RC} - SP}{1 + \left[\dfrac{V^2}{g\ RC}\right]\ SP} \qquad\qquad (3.12)$$

which can be simplified further by neglecting the small term $\left[\dfrac{V^2}{g\ RC}\right]\ SP$ thereby producing:

$$FRATIO = \frac{V^2}{g\ RC} - SP \qquad\qquad (3.13)$$

Solving for V, we have the curvature-limited speed constraint, VCURVE, expressed as:

$$\text{VCURVE} = \sqrt{(\text{FRATIO} + \text{SP}) \, g \, \text{RC}} \qquad\qquad (3.14)$$

where FRATIO is the parameter to be estimated in the curve speed constraint.   VCURVE as a function of horizontal curvature is shown in Figure 3.2.

As shall be seen in Section 4.2, the FRATIO parameter for a vehicle class depends on the surface type of the section and, for a truck, the net load.   For practical purposes the curvature-constrained speed need be considered only when the radius of curvature (RC) is smaller than 10,000 meters.

The adjective "perceived" in "used perceived friction ratio" is used to distinguish this ratio from the actual friction ratio, defined as TF/NF, where TF is the total force on the vehicle in the direction parallel to the road surface;   TF is equal to the vectorial sum of the lateral force, LF, as defined above, and the vehicle's drive force, DF, which is longitudinal to the vehicle's axis.

$$\text{TF} = \sqrt{\text{LF}^2 + \text{DF}^2} \qquad\qquad (3.15)$$

The use of the used actual friction ratio for determining the curvature-limited speed constraint was also attempted in regression analysis.   In terms of R-square and t-statistics the regression results were comparable to those based on the used perceived friction ratio. However, the actual friction ratio was found to be inappropriate for steep and highly banked curves where the driving speed constraint dominates but the used actual friction ratios computed are considerably higher than those obtained on flat curves of similar radii.   These high friction ratios are in fact heavily dominated by the drive force (DF) as opposed to the lateral force (LF), and are thus associated with the tendency of longitudinal wheel slipping as opposed to lateral wheel skidding.   For these reasons the used perceived friction ratio was preferred to the used actual friction ratio.

An extension of the model with the used perceived friction ratio as a function of road roughness was also attempted.   On a priori grounds, used perceived friction ratio would be related to road roughness because vehicles generally tend to lose contact with the road surface as it becomes rougher.   Thus a model form,

$$\text{FRATIO} = p_0 + p_1 \, \text{QI} \qquad\qquad (3.16)$$

where   QI = the roughness, in QI; and

p_0, p_1 = the model parameters

was attempted.   The results seemed to indicate that the coefficient p_1 was statistically insignificant.   This is probably due to part of the roughness effect being captured by the difference in the FRATIO estimates for paved and unpaved roads.   Additional research would be needed to arrive at well determined estimates of p_1 for each surface type.

3.3.4   Roughness–limited Speed Constraint, VROUGH

This speed constraint is derived from the "average rectified velocity" measure (ARV) defined in general for a given vehicle with a rigid rear-axle as the average rate of rear-axle suspension motion, which is defined more specifically as the rate of cumulative absolute displacement of the rear-axle relative to the vehicle body (in mm/s).   It is advocated as an adequate measure of ride discomfort, or severity (Gillespie et al., 1980; Gillespie, 1981).   ARV is related to the vehicle speed, V, by means of the following identity (Gillespie et al., 1980):

$$ARV = V\ ARS \tag{3.17}$$

where   ARS =   the "average rectified slope" measure, defined as the amount of rear-axle suspension motion per unit travel distance (in mm/m or m/km).   For modelling purposes the relevant ARV and ARS measures are those of the "calibrated" standard Maysmeter-equipped Opala passenger car used in the Brazil–UNDP study (GEIPOT, 1982; Paterson, 1987).

For the Opala–Maysmeter car, the ARS measure was found to be sensitive to the travel speed, through the following general relationship (Paterson and Watanatada, 1985):

$$ARS(V) = ARS80 \left[\frac{V}{22.2}\right]^{(r_0 + r_1\ \ell n\ ARS80)} \tag{3.18}$$

where   ARSO   =   the average rectified slope measured at the
                        travel speed of 22.2 m/s or 80 km/h; and

r_0, r_1 =   empirically determined parameters which vary from one
                        surface type to another, as given in the table below:

Surface type	r_0	r_1
Asphaltic concrete	0	0
Surface treated or gravel	1.31	−0.291
Earth or clay	2.27	−0.529

Source: Paterson and Watanatada (1985).

The ARS80 measure is related to QI, the standard road roughness measure used in the Brazil-UNDP study, through the following relationships:[3]

$$ARS80 = 0.0882 \ QI \qquad (3.19)$$

Substituting the above equation in Eq. 3.18 we have

$$ARS \ (V) = k_0 \ QI \ \left[\frac{V}{22.2}\right]^{[r_0 + r_1 \ \ell n \ (k_0 \ QI)]} \qquad (3.20)$$

where $k_0 = 0.0882$. Combining the above equation with Equation 3.17 results in a relationship which expresses the ARV measure for the calibrated standard Opala-Maysmeter vehicle as a function of the vehicle speed and QI roughness measure:

$$ARV \ (V) = k_0 \ QI \ V \ \left[\frac{V}{22.2}\right]^{[r_0 + r_1 \ \ell n \ (k_0 \ QI)]} \qquad (3.21)$$

For r_0 and r_1 equal to zero the above relationship reduces to a simple form in which ARV is proportional to V:

$$ARV \ (V) = k_0 \ QI \ V \qquad (3.22)$$

Gillespie (1981) argues that the ARV statistic is a measure that closely relates to vibration levels on road using vehicles which, in turn, relate to ride discomfort and perception of vehicle and cargo damage. U.S. military research has determined relationships between the vibration levels imposed on the driver, and the maximum travel speed (Lee and Pradko, 1968; Beck, 1978). While the vibration limits found from the military experiments may not correspond directly to the limits for civilian transport which is also associated with the concern for vehicle and cargo damage, these findings have suggested a methodology for formulating the ride severity speed constraint. Applying the basic methodology to a limited data set obtained from the road user cost survey Paterson (1982) found that observed vehicle speeds tended to be dominated by a limiting ARV value for travelling on rough roads.

---

[3] The conversion factor is computed as:

$$0.0882 = \frac{5.08}{0.18 \times 320}$$

where   5.08 = the rear-axle suspension motion, in mm, per unit count of the Maysmeter readout; and

0.18 = the average calibration factor for Opala-Maysmeter vehicles, which is used for conversion between the QI roughness unit and Maysmeter counts over 320 meters of standard travel distance.

In applying these findings to the ride severity speed constraint we assume that the roughness-limited speed is governed by the limiting ARV of the average population vehicle (in a given class). We assume further that the ARV of the average population vehicle is proportional to that of the "calibrated" standard Opala-Maysmeter vehicle. Thus, it is possible to use the limiting ARV for the calibrated standard Opala-Maysmeter vehicle, denoted by ARVMAX, as the surrogate for that of the average population vehicle. By substituting ARVMAX for ARV in Equation 3.21 and solving for V we obtain a closed form solution which expresses the ride severity speed constraint, VROUGH, as a function of ARVMAX:

$$\text{VROUGH} = \exp\left\{\frac{\ln[\text{ARVMAX}/(k_0\ QI)] + \ln(22.2)[r_0 + r_1\ \ln(k_0\ QI)]}{1 + r_0 + r_1\ \ln(k_0\ QI)}\right\} \quad (3.23)$$

where ARVMAX is the only parameter to be statistically estimated.

When the parameters r_0 and r_1 equal zero the above relationship reduces to:

$$\text{VROUGH} = \frac{\text{ARVMAX}}{k_0\ \ QI} \quad (3.24)$$

From a theoretical standpoint, Equation 3.23 is more desirable than Equation 3.24 since it recognizes the speed-sensitive nature of vehicle suspension systems. However, as it is relatively unwiedly to use in practice, Equation 3.24 was also attempted for all surface types in the regression analysis to see whether the results were acceptable. As it turned out the results based on Equation 3.24 were virtually the same in terms of R-square, t-statistics and goodness of fit. Therefore Equation 3.24, which is much simpler, was chosen for the final steady-state speed model. These results are reported in Chapter 4. VROUGH as a function of QI is shown in Figure 3.3.

3.3.5 Desired Speed, VDESIR

On a straight, flat and smooth road, although the driving, braking, curve and ride severity speed constraints do not exist, the vehicle still does not normally travel at the speed afforded by its own maximum or even used power. Rather, its speed is usually governed by subjective considerations of such factors as fuel economy, vehicle wear, safety or blanket speed limits (together with the driver's perception of the strictness of enforcement). Since it is not possible to separate these effects in the study data, they are combined in the parameter "desired speed," VDESIR (in m/s).

As we shall see in Section 4.2, where estimation based on observed speed data from Brazil is presented, it was found satisfactory to assume that VDESIR for a vehicle class depends only on the surface type of the homogeneous section.   However, in the extension to the steady-state speed prediction model based on Indian data, VDESIR depends also on the width class of the homogeneous section.   The details regarding the extended model are presented in Section 4.4.

3.3.6 Summary and Discussion

A stylized summary of the limiting speed specification of the steady-state speed model is as follows:

Let   X = the set of characteristics of the homogeneous road section
        = (GR, C, SP, QI, ST, CR, ALT)

      Y = the set of characteristics of a given class of vehicles
        = (m, CD, AR)

      θ = the set of parameters for the combination of driver and vehicle class, specific to the environment

        = (HPDRIVE, HPBRAKE, FRATIO, ARVMAX, VDESIR).

Then the predicted steady-state speed VSS of a vehicle of given class with characteristics Y, traversing a homogeneous road section with characteristics X in an environment with parameters θ, is

$$VSS = VSS(X, Y: \theta)$$
$$= min (VDRIVE, VBRAKE, VCURVE, VROUGH, VDESIR)$$

where VDRIVE, etc., are as described above.

We shall briefly discuss the nature of the information requirements X, Y and θ in turn.   Of the information on the homogeneous road section needed to use the model, the important variables are GR, C, R and ST which are precisely the policy variables under the control of the highway planner.   As for the other variables, while accurate values would improve the quality of the predictions, approximate values would produce acceptable results.   The superelevation values may be derived as a function of curvature based on the average design standards in the region.   The following relationships based on average Brazil standards are used as defaults in the HDM-III:

$$SP = \begin{cases} 0.00012 & C & \text{for paved sections} \\ 0.00017 & C & \text{for unpaved sections} \end{cases} \quad (3.25)$$

For the coefficient of rolling resistance, the relationship expressing it as a function of section roughness, presented in Appendix 2A may be used.Finally, the value of altitude, if not known, may be taken to be zero.

As regards the information on the vehicle needed to use the model, the values of mass of the vehicle, drag coefficient and frontal area may be taken to be the same as those for a representative make prevalent in the region, or average values may be used.   In fact, the each of the vehicle classes estimated. The mass of the vehicle may be taken to be the sum of tare weight of the representative vehicle and average payload for the vehicle class in the region. The latter are important only for trucks, and are generally available from axle load studies in the region.

We turn next to the question of estimation of model parameters θ.

3.4 LIMITING SPEED MODEL: PROBABILISTIC FORMULATION

As regards the parameter estimates needed to use the limiting speed model, the approach taken in previous studies has been to calibrate the desired parameters individually (i.e., one at a time) based either on controlled experiments using test fleet vehicles and driven by trained staff, or on a limited set of speed observations. Since the driving environment under experimental conditions is artificial, the parameter values do not reflect aspects of decision-making involved in the driving behaviour of the vehicle population. While it is tempting to interpret parameters such as used driving power as purely technical they would, nevertheless, embody behavioral aspects and, as such, the transferability of different parameter estimates are likely to be different and has to be evaluated with care.

Further, and even more important, the data obtained from controlled experiments still contain random variations in the constraining speeds and the resultant attained speeds. Such variations would still arise for a number of reasons even if the hypotheses regarding driver behavior were to hold strictly. Some of the important reasons are measurement errors, omission of characteristics of the road section and vehicle (for example, sight distance, sag curve, age and repair condition of the vehicle, trip purpose, nature of business), deviations of the section and vehicle characteristics from the values actually used, the inability of the driver to determine the binding constraint with certainty, and the inability of the modeller to completely specify the decision procedure of the vehicle operator. In sum, the limiting speeds have to be treated as random variables and the parameters have to be estimated on that basis. The explicit recognition of the stochastic (or probabilistic or random) nature of the constraining speeds is what distinguishes the probabilistic steady-state speed prediction model presented here from those of earlier studies.

The recognition of randomness mentioned above provides the link with econometrics. It may be observed that the essential arithmetic operation involved in the specification of the model is that of taking the minimum of a finite number (four, in our case) of quantities. Estimation techniques to handle specifications based on minimization (or maximization) over a set of discrete alternatives have been developed relatively recently by researchers in the field of urban travel demand, based on earlier work in fields such as psychometry, biometry and reliability. One of the well-known formulations, namely, multinomial logit, has been used with an error component structure to derive and estimate the probabilistic version of the limiting speed model described above.

It was observed that, even if the assumption of constant θ is true, the limiting speeds vary over different homogeneous sections and over different vehicles of the same class and that these variations can only be partially explained by the variation in the observed characteristics of the section (X) and vehicle (Y). That is, the limiting speeds have a systematic (or deterministic or characteristic) part and a random part (or disturbance or error). We formalize this notion by treating the limiting speeds as random variables (or variates) with means or expected values given by the expressions derived in Section 3.3. For example, denoting the driving power-limited speed variate by $V_{dr} = V_{dr}(X,Y:\theta)$, we may write:

$$V_{dr}(X,Y:\theta) = VDRIVE(X,Y:\theta)\ \xi_{dr}(X,Y:\theta)$$

where $\xi_{dr} = \xi_{dr}(X,Y:\theta)$ is the random part of V_{dr}. For notational clarity, we occasionally suppress the arguments, and use the traditional expression V_{dr} for the mean of variate V_{dr}, instead of VDRIVE. Thus, we may write the above expression as:

$$V_{dr} = VDRIVE\ \xi_{dr} = \overline{V}_{dr}\ \xi_{dr}.$$

Treating the other limiting speeds analogously, we have,

$$V_{br} = VBRAKE\ \xi_{br} = \overline{V}_{br}\ \xi_{br}$$

$$V_c\ = VCURVE\ \xi_c\ = \overline{V}_c\ \xi_c$$

$$V_r\ = VROUGH\ \xi_r\ = \overline{V}_r\ \xi_r$$

and
$$V_d\ = VDESIR\ \xi_d\ = \overline{V}_d\ \xi_d.$$

We may express the above definitions compactly as:

$$V_z = \overline{V}_z \xi_z, \text{ for } z = dr, br, c, r \text{ and } d \qquad (3.26)$$

So far, there is no loss of generality in the above, because we have not imposed any restrictions on the error term.

Now, we define the observed steady-state speed to be the random variable V given by:

$$V = V(X,Y:\theta)$$

$$= \min\ [V_{dr},\ V_{br},\ V_c,\ V_r,\ V_d]$$

Just as the speed constraint random variables, V may be expressed as:

$$V(X,Y:\theta) = VSS(X,Y:\theta)\ \xi(X,Y:\theta)$$

or,

$$V = VSS \; \xi = \bar{V} \; \xi.$$ (3.27)

These random variables may be interpreted as follows.

A vehicle which has reached a steady-state speed (say, v m/s) on a homogeneous road section is assumed to give rise to one set of particular values (or realizations) of these random variables. Following the convention of using corresponding lower case letters for realizations, we denote the realizations of random variables V_{dr}, V_{br}, V_c, V_r and V_d, by v_{dr}, v_{br}, v_c, and v_d. The realizations are latent or unobservable. The (observable) steady-state speed v and the (unobservable) realizations v_{dr}, v_{br}, v_c, v_r and v_c are related by:

$$v = \min \; [v_{dr}, \; v_{br}, \; v_c, \; v_r, \; v_d]$$

We interpret $V = V(X, Y : \theta)$ as a random variable whose realizations are the steady-state speeds (such as v) of vehicles characterized by Y on sections characterized by X for fixed θ. The VSS curves shown in Figure 3.1-3.3 may be interpreted under the probabilistic framework to be particular realizations of the random variable V.

The mean VSS = $\bar{V}(X, Y : \theta)$ of the random variable $\bar{V}(X, Y, \theta)$ may be seen as the characteristic or average steady-state speed that we can associate with the section X and vehicle Y for fixed θ. Basically, we are interested in $\bar{V}$ as a function of $\bar{V}_{dr}$, $\bar{V}_{br}$, $\bar{V}_c$, $\bar{V}_r$ and $\bar{V}_d$.

Now we come to the slightly surprising result that, in general,

$$\bar{V} \neq V'$$

where $V' = \min \; [\bar{V}_{dr}, \; \bar{V}_{br}, \; \bar{V}_c, \; \bar{V}, \; \bar{V}_d].$

In fact,

$$\bar{V} \leq V'$$

with the equality holding if and only if the random variables are perfectly postively correlated or they are degenerate, that is, the variations are all zero. In other words, the mean of the minimum is generally less than the minimum of the means. This apparently counter-intuitive result may be illustrated by means of a simple example. Suppose two fair dice are thrown. Let us define variate X_1 as the number on the first die and variate X_2 as the number on the second die. Finally, define the variate $\bar{X}$ as the minimum of X_1 and X_2. Then $\bar{X}_1 = \bar{X}_2 = 3^1/_2$. The value of $\bar{X}$ depends on the correlation between the throws. If the throws are independent, $\bar{X} = 2^{23}/_{36}$ and, if the throws are perfectly positively correlated, $\bar{X} = 3^1/_2$.

The result is illustrated for two constraining speed variates in Figure 3.4 where the distributions of V_c and V_r with means 30 m/s and 33 m/s are drawn along with the distribution of $V = \min [V_c, V_r]$. By definition, V' is 30 m/s, but the mean of V is seen to be about 26 m/s. This is further illustrated in Figure 3.5 which is the stochastic version of Figure 3.1. For each value of GR, five random realizations are generated for the variate V. The VSS curve is seen to be below the V' curve.

The relation between the means of the speed constraints and the mean steady-state speed depends on the assumptions imposed on the joint distribution of the errors of the speed constraint variates. We specify the error structure by making use of two well-known distributions (lognormal and normal), and two distributions from a class known as asymptotic extreme value distributions. These are the Weibull distribution and the Gumbel distribution. A brief account of the distributions is given in Appendix 3A. Further details may be found in Johnson and Kotz (1970) or Benjamin and Cornell (1970).

The main property of both the distributions, highlighted in the appendix, is that the minimum or maximum of a set of independent Weibull (Gumbel) variates is also Weibull (respectively, Gumbel) whose mean can be expressed as a closed form function of the means of the individual variates. This property is what makes these distributions suitable for minimization formulation. Just as normal distributions are preserved when the arithmetic operation involved is one of addition, the Weibull and the Gumbel distributions are preserved when the arithmetic operation involved is minimization (or maximization). This enables one to derive the distribution of the minimum variate as a relatively more tractable closed function.

The Weibull and the Gumbel distributions are closely related to each other. If W is a Weibull distribution with shape parameter β and scale parameter α then the variate ℓn W has a Gumbel distribution with scale parameter β and location parameter ℓn α. The relationship between them is analogous to the relation between lognormal and normal distributions. The distributional assumptions are theoretically equivalent whether they are formulated in terms of a Weibull and lognormal distributions or Gumbel and normal distributions. In the case of steady-state speed model, it is more natural to formulate the model in terms of the Weibull and lognormal distributions, because they deal with speeds rather than logarithms of speeds. However, it is more convenient to estimate the model by working with logarithms, using the Gumbel and normal distributions; this would make errors additive rather than multiplicative, thereby considerably reducing the problem of heteroskedasticity. The speed predictions are then obtained by exponentiating the log-speed predictions. It should be noted that a correction factor is needed because the antilog of the mean is not the same as the mean of the antilog. The error structure for the speed model is presented in detail below, followed by the final form of the equivalent log-speed model.

We specify the disturbances pertaining to a particular speed

Figure 3.4: Probability densities of two constraining speeds and the attained speed

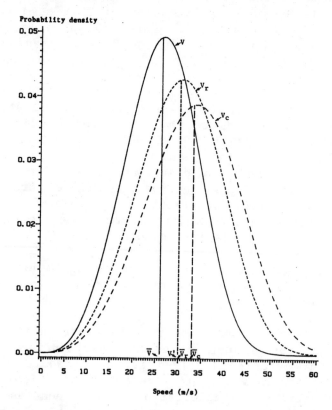

Figure 3.5: Randomly generated speed realizations, and the V' and $\overline{V}$ curves

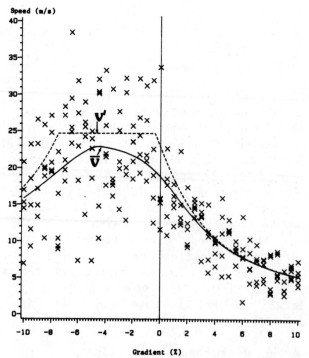

observation and the associated speed constraints using three nested
components of error. First, errors pertaining to the homogeneous section
itself. These errors encompass factors such as unmeasured characteristics of the section and of the vehicles in general at that section, as
well as speed measurement errors at that section. Second, errors
pertaining to the particular vehicle observed at that section. These
errors include unmeasured characterstics of the particular vehicle at the
section. Finally, given the above errors, there would be errors specific
to the various speed constraint variates for that speed observation. We
proceed by imposing fairly standard assumptions (lognormality) regarding
the first two components of error. We use the Weibull distribution in
respect of the third component to derive the conditional distribution of
the observed speed variate.

Thus in Equation 3.26, we regard the random part ξ_z for a
given realization v_z of a constraining speed variate V_z for vehicle Y
on section X to be the product of three mutually independent components
of error: first, error $\epsilon(X)$ specific to the particular section; second,
error $\zeta(X,Y)$ specific to the particular vehicle at the particular
section; and, third, the error $\nu_z(X,Y)$ specific to the particular speed
constraint for the particular vehicle at the particular section. That
is,

$$v_z = \overline{V}_z \; \xi_z = \overline{V}_z \; \epsilon(X) \; \zeta(X,Y) \; \nu_z(X,Y) \tag{3.28}$$

The specific distributional assumptions made on the error
components are as follows:

1. $\epsilon(X)$ are independent and have identical lognormal
     distributions with mean 1.

2. $\zeta(X,Y)$ are independent and have identical lognormal
     distributions with mean 1.

3. $\nu_z(X,Y)$ are independent and have identical Weibull
     distributions with mean 1 and shape parameter β.

Under the above assumptions, for any particular realizations of
the section and the vehicle specific errors, the speed constraint
variates V_{dr}, V_{br}, V_c, V_r and V_d have independent Weibull
distributions with the same shape parameter β. Thus, using the main
property of the Weibull distribution given in Appendix 3A, we have the
following results:

1.   Conditional on $\epsilon(X)$ and $\zeta(X,Y)$, the attained speed variate
     V has a Weibull distribution with a shape parameter β.

2.   The relationship between the mean of the attained speed
     and the means of the limiting speed variates is:

$$\overline{V} = (\overline{V}_{dr}^{-1/\beta} + \overline{V}_{br}^{-1/\beta} + \overline{V}_c^{-1/\beta} + \overline{V}_r^{-1/\beta} + \overline{V}_d^{-1/\beta})^{-\beta} \tag{3.29}$$

where

$$\bar{V}_z = \bar{V}_z(X,Y:\theta) \text{ and hence, } \bar{V} = \bar{V}(X,Y:\theta,\beta).$$

Thus, observed speed random variable, V, may be written as

$$V = \bar{V} \xi = \bar{V} \epsilon(X) \zeta(X,Y) \nu(X,Y)$$

where $\nu(X,Y)$ have independent Weibull distributions with mean 1 and shape parameter β.

The error components ζ and ν are specific to a particular speed observation. It is convenient to introduce a random variable ω which is the product of ζ and ν. We define

$$\omega(X,Y) = \zeta(X,Y) \nu(X,Y). \tag{3.30}$$

The variate ω is the product of independent lognormal and Weibull variates. Its distribution is observed to be approximately lognormal. Thus, the distribution of observed speed variate itself is approximately lognormal.

Thus, the probabilistic steady-state speed model may be written, in terms of the variables used earlier, as

$$V = VSS \ \epsilon \ \omega \tag{3.31}$$

where

$$VSS = (VDRIVE^{-1/\beta} + VBRAKE^{-1/\beta} + VCURVE^{-1/\beta} + VROUGH^{-1/\beta} + VDESIR^{-1/\beta})^{-\beta} \tag{3.32}$$

We next present the equivalent log-speed model. For this, we first define the logarithms of observed speed variate, V, and the constraining speed variates, V_z. Let

$$U = U(X,Y:\theta) = \ln V(X,Y:\theta) \tag{3.33}$$

$$U_z X,Y:\theta) = \ln V_z(X,Y:\theta), \text{ for } z = dr, \ br, \ c, \ r \text{ and } d \tag{3.34}$$

Assuming that for a given speed observation, the logarithms of the constraining speeds have independent Gumbel distributions with constant mean and scale parameter β, we can use the main property of the Gumbel distribution given in Appendix 3A to derive the expression for the mean, $\bar{U}$, of the log-speed variate U as

$$\bar{U} = -\beta \ \ln \ \{\exp(-\bar{U}_{dr}/\beta) + \exp(-\bar{U}_{br}/\beta) + \exp(-\bar{U}_c/\beta) + \exp(-\bar{U}_r/\beta) + \exp(-\bar{U}_d/\beta)\} \tag{3.35}$$

where $\bar{U}_z = \bar{U}_z(X,Y:\theta)$ are the means of the random variables U_z,

and $\bar{U} = \bar{U}(X,Y:\theta,\beta)$ is the mean of U.

This may be simplified to

$$\overline{U} = -\beta \ \ell n(VDRIVE^{-1/\beta} + VBRAKE^{-1/\beta} + VCURVE^{-1/\beta} + VROUGH^{-1/\beta} + VDESIR^{-1/\beta})$$
$$(3.36)$$

Thus, by analogy with the speed model, we may write the log-speed model as

$$U = \overline{U} + e + w \qquad\qquad (3.37)$$

In Equation 3.37, $e = e(X)$ are the logarithms of section-specific errors in the observed speed. They have independent normal distributions with constant mean and variance. The $w = w(X,Y)$ are the logarithms of errors specific to the speed observation. They are independent and identically distributed as convolutions of independent normal and Gumbel distributions with constant means. The latter are approximately normal with constant mean and variance. Thus, the distribution of log-speed variate itself is approximately normal.

β is an additional parameter introduced by the particular probabilistic approach over and above the set of other parameters θ. It has an intuitive interpretation as an indicator of the dispersion of the constraining speed random variables. More rigorously, β is related to the standard deviation of the constraining speed variates and hence that of the observed speeds, that is, the spread in the speeds of a vehicle repeatedly traversing a homogeneous section. This may readily be seen by noting the relation between the shape parameter and the variance of the Weibull distribution. The relationship is even clearer in the case of the Gumbel distribution, for which

Variance = $\beta \ \pi^2/6$, or
Standard deviation = $\beta \ \pi/\sqrt{6}$

In other words, under the assumptions of the model, the conditional standard deviation of log-speeds is approximately 1.28 β. The value of β may be expected to be well below unity.

The estimates of the variances of e and w (σ_e^2 and σ_w^2, respectively) along with the total variance σ^2 are useful in deriving the sampling distributions of predicted speeds for different applications.

As mentioned earlier, it is the log-speed model defined by Equation 3.36 and 3.37 which is used to estimate the parameters θ and β. Since the means of the error terms in this model are not zero, in order to obtain unbiased steady-state speed predictions an estimation bias correction factor has to be introduced. The choice of the correction factor depends on the application for which the speed predictions are desired. These factors are functions of the variances of the error terms in Equation 3.37. The variances are also useful in calculating the confidence intervals for the speed predictions. These issues are discussed next.

Various predicted steady-state speeds which may be computed using the estimates of model parameters are themselves random variables. Three important concepts of speed prediction are as follows:

1. Prediction of the mean of a large number (notionally, infinity) of individual steady-state speeds on a given homogeneous section;

2. Prediction of the mean of a large number (notionally, infinity) of individual steady-state speeds for a specific vehicle; and

3. Prediction of the steady-state speed of an individual vehicle of give attributes over a homogeneous section of given characteristics.

The first kind of prediction is important for general economic analysis. The second kind of prediction is useful for Monte-Carlo studies of speed behavior on specific vehicles traversing a stretch of road. The third kind of prediction is useful for evaluating the results of statistical estimation. The approximate formulas for unbiased estimates of the mean, the variance and the coefficient of variation of VSS for the above three regimes of prediction may be derived assuming normality of the error terms. When the respective variances are small, say less than 0.05, these formulas may be simplified using the following approximation:

$$\exp(x) \simeq (1 + x)$$

Both sets of formulas for the three regimes of speed prediction are given below.

Section-specific speed prediction

$$E[VSS] = (VDRIVE^{-1/\beta} + VBRAKE^{-1/\beta} + VCURVE^{-1/\beta} + VROUGH^{-1/\beta} + VDESIR^{-1/\beta})^{-\beta} \exp(\sigma_e^2/2)$$

$$Var\ [VSS] = E^2[VSS]\ (\exp(\sigma_e^2) - 1)$$

$$CV\ [VSS] = \sqrt{(\exp(\sigma_e^2) - 1)}$$

As mentioned earlier, the above formulas are relevant for speed prediction in the context of economic analysis and are used in Chapters 13 through 15. We denote the "estimation bias correction factor" for this regime of prediction, $\exp(\sigma_e^2/2)$, by $E°$.

The set of simplified formulas is as follows:

$$E[VSS] = (VDRIVE^{-1/\beta} + VBRAKE^{-1/\beta} + VCURVE^{-1/\beta} + VROUGH^{-1/\beta} + VDESIR^{-1/\beta})^{-\beta}(1 + \sigma_e^2/2)$$

$$Var\,[VSS] = E^2[VSS]\,\sigma_e^2$$

$$CV\,[VSS] = \sigma_e$$

Vehicle-specific speed prediction

$$E[VSS] = (VDRIVE^{-1/\beta} + VBRAKE^{-1/\beta} + VCURVE^{-1/\beta} + VROUGH^{-1/\beta} + VDESIR^{-1/\beta})^{-\beta}\,exp(\sigma_w^2/2)$$

$$Var\,[VSS] = E^2[VSS]\,(exp(\sigma_w^2) - 1)$$

$$CV\,[VSS] = \sqrt{(exp(\sigma_w^2) - 1)}$$

For this case, the set of simpler formulas is:

$$E[VSS] = (VDRIVE^{-1/\beta} + VBRAKE^{-1/\beta} + VCURVE^{-1/\beta} + VROUGH^{-1/\beta} + VDESIR^{-1/\beta})^{-\beta}(1 + \sigma_w^2/2)$$

$$Var\,[VSS] = E^2[VSS]\,\sigma_w^2$$

$$CV\,[VSS] = \sigma_w$$

Individual speed prediction

$$E[VSS] = (VDRIVE^{-1/\beta} + VBRAKE^{-1/\beta} + VCURVE^{-1/\beta} + VROUGH^{-1/\beta} + VDESIR^{-1/\beta})^{-\beta}exp(\sigma^2/2)$$

$$Var\,[VSS] = E^2[VSS]\,(exp(\sigma^2) - 1)$$

$$CV\,[VSS] = \sqrt{(exp(\sigma^2) - 1)}$$

The simpler formulas are:

$$E[VSS] = (VDRIVE^{-1/\beta} + VBRAKE^{-1/\beta} + VCURVE^{-1/\beta} + VROUGH^{-1/\beta} + VDESIR^{-1/\beta})^{-\beta}(1 + \sigma^2/2)$$

$$Var[VSS] = E^2[VSS]\,\sigma^2$$

$$CV[VSS] = \sigma$$

The difference between the predicted values of E[VSS] for the three cases is at most 2%, as may be seen in Table 4.3(c) where the estimates of the variances based on Brazil data are presented.

Equation 3.32, along with the expressions for VDRIVE, etc., given in the last section, constitutes a multinomial logit model which is non–linear in the parameters θ and β.   It is of interest to note the similarities and differences between the probabilistic steady–state speed model and the probabilistic discrete choice demand models.   The latter have been employed to develop models for predicting the market shares of competing alternatives (for example, travel modes, universities) as responses of utility maximizing individuals of known characteristics (Y) to policy variables (X) influencing the utilities of the alternatives (Domencich and MacFadden 1975; Ben–Akiva and Lerman, 1985).   In the the speed model, the section characteristics are regarded as policy variables under the control of highway planners which influence the alternative limiting speeds on the sections depending on the characteristics of the vehicles.   The vehicle operators are hypothesized as choosing the speed constraint with the highest speed.   The differences between the two models is that in probabilistic discrete choice theory, the alternative chosen by the individual is observable but the realized utility is not. In contrast, in the probabilistic limiting speed model, the binding speed constraint is not observable but the realized speed is.   Further, the demand models are based on the notion of utility which is an ordinal measure, and thus the β parameter cannot be identified.   However, since speed is a cardinal measure, the β parameter in the speed model can be identified.   As such, the proper analogue of the speed model in economic theory would be the qualitative response models in the theory of the firm (MacFadden, 1982).

Some of the important properties of the VSS function (Equation 3.32) are noted below.

The function is homogeneous of degree one in VDRIVE, etc.   That is, if each of the average speeds is multiplied by a constant, say, 3.6, the average steady–state speed is also multiplied by 3.6.

The partial derivatives $\partial VSS/\partial VDRIVE$, etc., are all positive; thus, as any of the average constraining speeds decreases, so does the average steady–state speed.

As noted before, the average steady–state speed is somewhat less than the minimum of the average constraining speeds.   The extent of the difference depends on β and other constraining speeds.   If β is zero, that is, if there is no variation in the constraining speeds, then the mean steady–state speed is identical to the arithmetic minimum of the means of the constraining speeds, as in Figures 3.1 – 3.3.   As β increases from zero, so does the spread around the means of the constraining speeds and, as a result, the mean of the resulting speeds falls below the minimum of the means.   This feature is illustrated in Figures 3.6 – 3.8 which show the mean steady–state speed VSS as a function, respectively of gradient, curvature and roughness for a heavy truck, with β = 0.27.   These figures are the probabilistic counterparts of Figures 3.1 – 3.3.

Figure 3.6:   Constraining and steady-state speeds versus gradient: probabilistic version

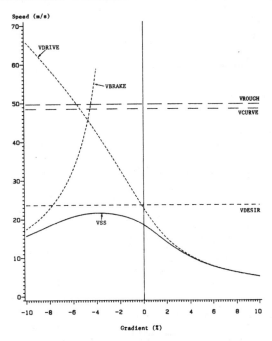

Source: Analysis of Brazil-UNDP-World Bank highway research project
data (See also notes for Figures 3.1 - 3.3).

Figure 3.7:   Constraining and steady-state speeds versus curvature: probabilistic version

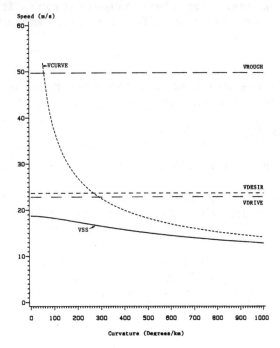

Source: Analysis of Brazil-UNDP-World Bank highway research project data
(See also notes for Figures 3.1 - 3.3).

**Figure 3.8:   Constraining and steady-state speeds versus roughness:
                probabilistic version**

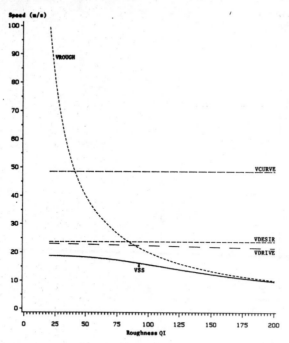

Source: Analysis of Brazil-UNDP-World Bank highway research project data
          (see also notes for Figures 3.1 - 3.3).

A better feel for the function may be obtained by examining a
series of section diagrams. For these illustrations, it is assumed that
VBRAKE is infinity; that is, the effective gradient of the section is
non-negative.

1.   Holding the means of all the constraining speeds at a
     constant value V_0, and letting only β vary, we have:

$$VSS = 4^{-\beta}V_0$$

This function is illustrated for V_0=30 m/s in Figure 3.9.

2.   Holding VDRIVE, VROUGH, and VDESIR constant at 30 m/s, the
     curve showing the VSS as a function of VCURVE is given in
     Figure 3.10, for different values of β.

3.   The contours resulting from varying two of the speed
     constraints,VCURVE and VROUGH while holding VDRIVE and
     VDESIR constant at 30 m/s, and β constant at 0.27 may be
     seen in Figure 3.11.

Finally, Figure 3.12 demonstrates the sensitivity of VSS to β.
Here the mean steady-state speed versus gradient curves are drawn for
values of β ranging from 0 to 0.5.

Figure 3.9: Mean steady-state speed as a function of β with mean constraining speeds as 30 m/s

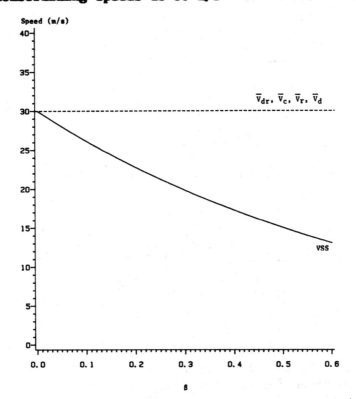

Figure 3.10: Mean steady-state speed as a function of one mean constraining speed for various values of β

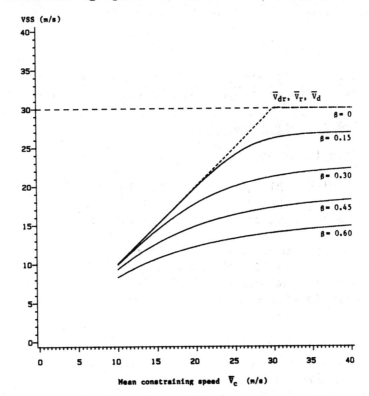

Figure 3.11: Mean steady-state speed contours as two mean constraining speeds vary, with $\beta = 0.27$

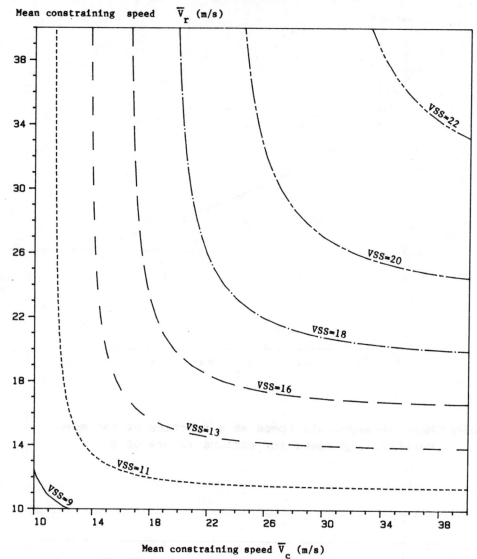

3.5   SUMMARY OF STEADY-STATE SPEED MODEL

The desired steady-state speed prediction, VSS, for a vehicle class and specific section is given by the following relationship:

$$VSS = E°(VDRIVE^{-1/\beta} + VBRAKE^{-1/\beta} + VCURVE^{-1/\beta} + VROUGH^{-1/\beta} + VDESIR^{-1/\beta})^{-\beta} \tag{3.38}$$

where $E°$ is the estimation bias correction factor, given by:

$$E° = \exp(\sigma_e^2/2) \tag{3.39}$$

VDRIVE, VBRAKE, VCURVE, VROUGH and VDESIR are the limiting speeds as derived in Section 3.3. The parameters and statistics to be estimated are HPDRIVE. HPBRAKE. FRATIO. ARVMAX. VDESIR. β and σ^2.

Figure 3.12: Sensitivity of steady-state speed to the β parameter

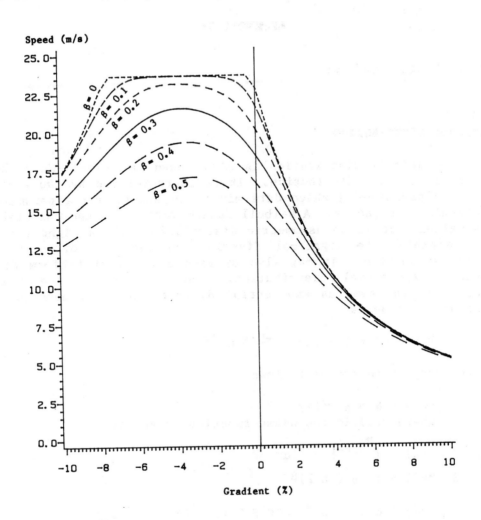

APPENDIX 3A

EXTREME VALUE DISTRIBUTIONS

3A.1 WEIBULL DISTRIBUTION

The Weibull distribution is also known as Weibull-Gnedenko or type-III extreme value distibution. It is characterized by two positive parameters: a parameter β which determines its shape, and a parameter α which determines its scale. A Weibull random variable W can only take on positive values. It is an asymmetric distribution with a right tail and somewhat resembles the lognormal distribution which is often a close alternative assumption. It may also be seen as a flexible form of the better-known exponential distribution. When β is 1, the Weibull distribution is the same as exponential distribution with mean α. Its distribution function is:

$$P[W < w] = 1 - \exp(-\alpha^{-1/\beta} w^{1/\beta})$$

Some of its properties are as follows:

1. Mean : $W = \alpha \, \Gamma(1+\beta)$
   where $\Gamma(.)$ is the Gamma function, given by

   $$\Gamma(k) = \int_0^\infty x^{k-1} e^{-x} dx$$

2. Median : $\alpha \, (\ln 2)^\beta$

3. Mode : $\alpha \, (1 - \beta)^\beta$ for $\beta < 1$, and 0 for $\beta \geq 1$

4. Variance : $\alpha^2 \, [\Gamma(1 + 2\beta) - (\Gamma(1 + \beta))^2]$

5. If W has a Weibull distribution with shape parameter β and scale parameter α then the variate aW, where a is a positive constant, has a Weibull distribution with the same shape parameter β and scale parameter $a\alpha$.

Main property

If W_1, W_2,..., W_n have independent Weibull distributions with the same shape parameter β, and with scale parameters α_1, α_2,..., α_n, respectively, then the random variable

$$W = \min [W_1, W_2, ..., W_n]$$

has a Weibull distribution with the same shape parameter β and scale parameter α, given by

$$\alpha = (\alpha_1^{-1/\beta} + \alpha_2^{-1/\beta} + ... + \alpha_n^{-1/\beta})^{-\beta}$$

The mean $\bar{W}$ is related to the means $\bar{W}_1$, $\bar{W}_2$,..., $\bar{W}_n$ by

$$\bar{W} = (\bar{W}_1^{-1/\beta} + \bar{W}_2^{-1/\beta} + \ldots + \bar{W}_n^{-1/\beta})^{-\beta}$$

3A.2   GUMBEL DISTRIBUTION

The Gumbel distribution is also known as type-I extreme value distribution or often simply as the extreme value distribution.   It is also characterized by two parameters: a scale parameter λ which is positive and a location parameter μ which may be positive or negative. The range of a Gumbel variate Z is the entire real line.   It is an asymmetric distribution with a right tale.   When λ is less than 0.5 the distribution begins to resemble a normal distribution and the resemblance is closest when λ is about 0.27.   Its cumulative distribution function is

$$P[Z < z] = 1 - \exp(-\exp((z - \mu)/\lambda))$$

Some of its properties are:

1. Mean : $\mu + \lambda \ \Gamma'(1)$ where $\Gamma'(1) = -\gamma \approx - 0.5772$, which is known as Euler's constant.

2. Median : $\mu + \lambda \ \ell n \ \ell n \ 2$

3. Mode : μ

4. Variance : $\lambda^2 \ \pi^2/6$

5. If Z has a Gumbel distribution with parameters λ and μ, then the variate $aZ + b$, where $a > 0$ and b are constants, has a Gumbel distribution with parameters $a\lambda$ and $a\mu + b$.

Main property

If Z_1, Z_2, ..., Z_n have independent Gumbel distributions with the same scale parameter λ and location parameters μ_1 μ_2...., μ_n, respectively, then the variate

$$Z = \min [Z^1, Z_2, \ldots, Z_n]$$

has a Gumbel distribution with the same scale parameter and with location parameter μ given by:

$$\mu = \ell n \ \left\{ \exp(\mu_1/\lambda) + \exp(\mu_2/\lambda) + \ldots + \exp(\mu n/\lambda) \right\}^{-\lambda}$$

The mean $\bar{Z}$ is related to the means $\bar{Z}_1$, $\bar{Z}_2$, ..., $\bar{Z}_n$ by:

$$\bar{Z} = \ell n \left\{ (\exp(\bar{Z}_1))^{-1/\lambda} + (\exp(\bar{Z}_2))^{-1/\lambda} + \ldots + (\exp(\bar{Z}_n))^{-1/\lambda} \right\}^{-\lambda}$$

APPENDIX 3B

GENERAL SOLUTION TO STEADY-STATE FORCE-BALANCE EQUATION

The formulas to compute the driving power-limited speed constraint, VDRIVE, discussed in Section 3.3.1 are presented here. Recall that VDRIVE is defined as the positive root of the force-balance equation under steady-state conditions (Equation 3.4):

$$1/2 \; RHO \; CD \; AR \; V^3 + m \; g \; (GR + CR) \; V - 736 \; HPDRIVE = 0 \qquad (3B.1)$$

Equation 3B.1 may be written as:

$$V^3 + 3c \; V - 2b = 0 \qquad\qquad\qquad (3B.2)$$

where $\qquad c = \dfrac{m \; g \; (GR + CR)}{3A}$

$$A = 1/2 \; RHO \; CD \; AR$$

$$b = \dfrac{HPDRIVE \; 736}{2 \; A}$$

The nature of the roots to Equation 3B.2 depends on a quantity D, which may be termed the discriminant of the equation, defined by:
$$D = b^2 + c^3$$

There are two important cases:

(1) $D > 0$: One real root and two complex roots.
(2) $D < 0$: Three real roots.

Case 1: $D > 0$

The solution is:

$$VDRIVE = \sqrt[3]{\sqrt{D} + b} - \sqrt[3]{\sqrt{D} - b}$$

This formula is applicable to all positive values of GR and also when GR is negative but $|GR|$ is small.

Case 2: $D \leq 0$

This case is known in the theory of equations as the "case with three real roots" or "the irreducible case". The algebraic formulas for solving a cubic equation become "circular" in this case and trigonometric formulas are required (Dickson, 1957). The formulas are derived using the following triple angle identity:

$$\cos 3z = 4 \cos^3 z - 3 \cos z \qquad (3B.3)$$

It may be shown that:

$$\cos z, \quad \cos \left(z + \frac{2\pi}{3}\right) \quad \text{and} \quad \cos \left(z + \frac{4\pi}{3}\right)$$

are the three roots of (3B.3). The method of finding the roots for the case of negative discriminant depends on transforming Equation 3B.2 into the form of Equation 3B.3 through an appropriate change of variable, as follows:

Step 1 : Compute r such that:

$$r = 2\sqrt{-c} = 2\sqrt{-\frac{mg\ (GR + CR)}{3\ A}}$$

Step 2 : Find an angle z in radians such that:

$$\cos 3z = -\frac{2b}{cr}$$

That is,

$$z = \frac{1}{3} \arccos \left[-\frac{2b}{cr}\right]$$

Step 3 : Determine the three roots of the cubic using

$$v_1 = r \cos (z)$$

$$v_2 = r \cos \left[z + \frac{2\pi}{3}\right]$$

$$v_3 = r \cos \left[z + \frac{4\pi}{3}\right]$$

In the context of positive power, two of these will be negative and the remaining positive. The positive root is taken as the desired solution.

CHAPTER 4

Steady-State Speed Model:
Parameter Estimation, Adaptation and Transferability

The main thrust of this chapter is on the statistical estimation of the steady-state speed model based on speed data from Brazil. A description of the data is given in Section 4.1 and the estimation results are presented and discussed in Section 4.2. Guidelines for adapting some of the model parameters to reflect specific vehicle characteristics are provided in Section 4.3. Section 4.4 investigates the question of transferability of model parameters to other environments based on speed data from India, and discusses the effect of road width on steady-state speed. The technical details regarding the estimation procedure are given in Appendix 4A, and the results of some auxiliary analyses are presented in Appendices 4B, 4C and 4D.

4.1 DATA

The data for the steady-state speed model were obtained from some 100,000 radar speed observations of vehicles at selected homogeneous road sections over a period of a year. Detailed description of the field instrumentation and measurement procedure are given in GEIPOT (1982, Vol. 3). Sections were distinguished by direction of travel. The unpaved sections were further distinguished by roughness intervals of 50 QI, since the roughness of these sections often vary significantly over non-consecutive observation periods. This procedure resulted in a total of 216 homogeneous sections with the gradient ranging from -9 to 11 percent, the radius of curvature of curvy sections from 20 to 2000 m, and the surface condition from paved and smooth (20 QI) to unpaved and very rough (200 QI). The summary of characteristics of the road sections is given in Table 4.1.

The observations made for each vehicle sighting were one or more spot speeds on the section, the vehicle type and load condition. The vehicle types observed were categorized into six classes. These classes are shown in Table 4.2(a) along with the adopted average vehicle characteristics. The average gross vehicle masses were obtained from a separate axle load study for Brazil. The values of aerodynamic drag coefficient and frontal area were adapted from those for typical makes and models prevalent in Brazil for each vehicle class. Because of the influence of payload on vehicle performance, a distinction is made in this classification between loaded and unloaded trucks. However, for cars, utilities and buses, no such distinction is made since these vehicles have a small payload range relative to their total weights. For the unloaded and loaded categories of the respective truck classes, the same values of projected frontal area and drag coefficient are used, although these values would be slightly different depending on the nature of loading. It should be noted that the vehicle classes used in the

Table 4.1: Statistics of test sections

Characteristics		Number of sections	Mean	Min.	Max.	Std. dev.	CV (%)
Vertical gradient (%)	Positive[1]	111	3.4	0.0	10.8	2.8	80.8
	Negative[1] (absolute values)	105	3.8	0.0	8.7	2.7	71.1
Radius of curvature (m)	Tangent sections	10	∞	∞	∞	–	–
	Curvy: paved	46	298.9	20.0	950.0	258.7	86.6
	unpaved	52	251.0	37.0	870.0	217.8	86.8
Super-elevation (%)	Tangent sections	10	0	–	–	–	–
	Curvy: paved	46	5.6	0.0	11.0	3.1	55.3
	unpaved	52	9.1	0.0	20.0	4.7	51.4
Roughness (QI)	Paved	50	51.6	20.0	122.0	25.5	49.4
	Unpaved	58	123.9	56.6	192.5	38.1	30.8

[1] Differentiated by section-direction.
Source: Brazil-UNDP-World Bank highway research project data.

Table 4.2(a): Vehicle classes and characteristics used in steady-state speed model estimation

Vehicle class	Aerodynamic drag coefficient (dimensionless)[1]	Projected frontal area, AR (m^2)[1]	Total vehicle weight (kg)
1. Car	0.50	2.00	1,200
2. Utility	0.60	3.00	2,000
3. Bus	0.65	6.30	10,400
4. Light[2]/medium truck[3]	0.70	4.5	5,400 unloaded 11,900 loaded
5. Heavy truck	0.85	5.2	7,900 unloaded 19,200 loaded
6. Articulated truck	0.65	5.8	15,900 unloaded 37,700 loaded

[1] Obtained from the vehicle manufacturers.
[2] Includes both gasoline and diesel light trucks introduced in Table 1A.1.
[3] Because of the way in which light and medium trucks were coded in speed observations it was not possible to separate these truck classes for separate model estimation.
Source: Brazil-UNDP-World Bank highway research project data.

Table 4.2(b): Statistics of observed mean speeds

Vehicle class	Loading condition	Number of mean-speed data points	Number individual speed observation			Mean speed (km/h)				
			Mean	Min.	Max.	Mean	Min.	Max.	Std. dev.	CV (%)
Car	–	216	164.1	9	825	62.5	21.4	99.6	16.8	27.0
Utility	–	216	62.6	2	239	56.1	19.8	91.2	15.0	26.8
Bus	–	216	23.7	1	76	52.4	19.0	92.0	18.3	34.9
Light/ medium truck	Unloaded	216	29.8	1	251	53.2	18.9	83.0	14.5	27.3
	Loaded	215	34.0	2	223	45.4	17.6	79.9	16.1	35.4
Heavy truck	Unloaded	187	14.9	1	102	52.5	20.0	88.3	16.4	31.2
	Loaded	194	31.9	1	216	42.8	9.0	78.6	18.5	43.3
Artic. truck	Unloaded	112	4.7	1	36	54.8	17.0	89.8	18.8	34.4
	Loaded	120	11.1	1	79	44.2	9.1	91.7	21.9	49.5

Source: Brazil-UNDP-World Bank highway research project data.

estimation are aggregate groupings of the basic vehicle classes introduced earlier in Appendix 1A. Because of this, some of the estimated model parameters would have to be adjusted for the latter classes. This issue is discussed in Section 4.3.

The sections had one, three or five observation stations. For sections with more than one station, the spot speeds for each observed vehicle were averaged after eliminating vehicles judged not to have attained a steady-state speed, on the basis of a visual examination of the speed-distance plots. Further, speed observations obtained with the radar visible to the drivers of the observed vehicles were excluded.[1] In all, about 80,000 speed observations were included. Finally, for each vehicle class, the logarithms of individual speed observations pertaining to a section were averaged, yielding the dependent variable values of the estimation data set. The summary statistics regarding the range of speeds observed and the number of individual speeds making up various mean-log data points are presented in Table 4.2(b). For ease of reference, mean speeds rather than the logarithmic values are given.

4.2 ESTIMATION RESULTS

The estimation was done in two stages.[2] In the first stage,

---

[1] This essentially eliminated all observations taken before November 1976.

[2] The technical details regarding the estimation procedure are given in Appendix 4A. The tests for normality of residuals are presented in Appendix 4B.

for each of the six vehicle classes, regression runs were made separately for paved and unpaved sections, and in the case of trucks, for unladen and laden categories. That is, the model parameters were estimated without any restrictions being placed on them. The objective in this stage was to see whether the parameter estimates were significantly different across these sub-classes. Insignificant variation of some parameters across the sub-classes would permit pooling the observations by imposing restrictions on these parameters leading to better-determined demonstrated in the next section, there is a well defined relationship between these quantities. The magnitudes of the braking power appears to increase with the gross vehicle weight. As would be expected, the estimates. The results of unrestricted estimates indicated that the used driving power (HPDRIVE), the used braking power (HPBRAKE), the limiting average rectified velocity (ARVMAX), and the β parameters did not vary significantly by surface type or load level. The friction ratio (FRATIO) and the desired speed (VDESIR) parameters were considerably different between paved and unpaved surfaces. Further, for trucks traversing paved sections the FRATIO parameter differed by loading condition.

In the second stage, regression runs were made with restrictions of equality being imposed on the corresponding parameters pertaining to different surface types and load categories. The results from these runs confirmed the indications from the first stage. The complete details regarding these runs with different combinations of pooling the observations, along with the results of χ^2 tests for model equivalence, are given in Appendix 4C.

The final results are presented in Table 4.3(a). These consist of six sets of parameter estimates, for cars, utilities, buses, light/medium trucks, heavy trucks and articulated trucks. Each set includes estimates of the following parameters:

1. β, HPDRIVE, HPBRAKE and ARVMAX parameters which are applicable for paved and unpaved surfaces, and unloaded and loaded trucks.

2. VDESIR parameter for unpaved surfaces, and the increment for paved surfaces. For ease of reference, the computed value of VDESIR for paved sections is also included.

3. FRATIO parameter for unpaved surfaces, the increment for paved surfaces, and the further increment for loaded trucks on paved surfaces. Again, for ease of reference, the computed values for the respective cases are included.

The asymptotic t-statistics associated with these parameter estimates are given in Table 4.3(b) in a similar format. A goodness-of-fit measure analogous to the R^2 value in linear models is also given. This was obtained by regressing the mean observed speeds against predicted speeds. The estimated standard errors, σ_e, σ_w, and σ, of the model error terms are given in Table 4.3(c).

There were too few observations for articulated trucks to support the determination of all the model parameters and the HPBRAKE and

Table 4.3(a): Estimation results of steady-state speed model for six vehicle classes: estimates

Vehicle class	β	HPDRIVE metric hp	HPBRAKE metric hp	ARVMAX mm/s	VDESIR (km/h) Unpaved Value	Paved Increment over unpaved value	Paved Value	FRATIO Unpaved unloaded or loaded	Paved Unloaded Increment over unpaved value	Paved Unloaded Value	Paved Loaded Increment over paved unloaded	Paved Loaded Value
	a	b	c	d	e	f	e + f	g	h	g + h	i	g + h + i
Car	0.274	36.4	21.7	259.7	82.2	16.2	98.3	0.124	0.144	0.268	–	–
Utility	0.306	44.4	32.6	239.7	78.3	16.6	94.9	0.117	0.104	0.221	–	–
Bus	0.273	112.9	213.6	212.8	69.4	24.0	93.4	0.095	0.138	0.233	–	–
Truck:												
Light/ medium	0.304	94.7	190.8	194.0	71.9	9.7	81.6	0.099	0.154	0.253	-0.083	0.170
Heavy	0.310	108.2	257.1	177.7	72.1	16.8	88.8	0.087	0.205	0.292	-0.107	0.185
Artic.	0.244	200.0	500.0[1]	130.9	49.6	34.5	84.1	0.040[1]	0.139	0.179	-0.049	0.130

[1] These parameters for the articulated truck class were exogenously assigned.

Source: Analysis of Brazil-UNDP-World Bank highway research project data as described in Section 4.2

Table 4.3 (b): Some important statistics associated with the estimation

Vehicle class	β	HPDRIVE	HPBRAKE	ARVMAX	VDESIR Unpaved	VDESIR Increment for paved surface	FRATIO Unpaved	FRATIO Increment for paved Unloaded	FRATIO Increment for paved Loaded	VARIANCES σ^2_e	VARIANCES σ^2_w	R^2	Number of observations	SSR
	a	b	c	d	e	f	g	h	i					
Car	10.9	15.2	7.9	20.3	22.8	4.9	12.4	10.3	–	0.00654	0.0224	0.92	216	1.36
Utility	10.9	19.3	7.9	17.5	17.4	4.0	9.3	7.0	–	0.00808	0.0355	0.89	216	1.68
Bus	6.8	27.3	4.6	12.0	12.0	3.8	5.3	5.3	–	0.02477	0.0276	0.83	216	5.15
Truck:														
Light/ medium	13.4	44.0	9.5	24.6	18.4	2.8	9.0	7.3	-3.7	0.01574	0.0405	0.87	431	6.64
Heavy	9.7	41.6	10.9	19.1	11.6	2.8	3.8	5.9	-3.1	0.02578	0.0369	0.85	381	9.59
Artic.	7.0	33.9	–	19.0	11.6	7.0	–	5.0	-1.5	0.03588	0.0365	0.81	232	8.07

[1] The numbers in the parameter columns are the respective asymptotic t-statistics.

[2] SSR denotes the sum of squared residuals.

[3] For explanation of variances, see Chapter 3.

Source: Analysis of Brazil-UNDP-World Bank highway research project data as described in Section 4.2

Table 4.3(c):   Estimated standard errors of model error terms

Vehicle class	Estimated standard error		
	σ_e	σ_w	σ
Car	0.081	0.150	0.170
Utility	0.090	0.188	0.209
Bus	0.157	0.166	0.229
Light/medium truck	0.125	0.201	0.237
Heavy truck	0.161	0.192	0.250
Articulated truck	0.189	0.191	0.269

Source: Analysis of Brazil-UNDP-World Bank highway research project
         data as described in Section 4.2.

FRATIO parameters were assigned the values of 500 metric hp and 0.40,
respectively, when the estimation was carried out.

All parameter estimates shown in Table 4.3 are of the expected
sign and magnitude, and all but one are significant at the 95 percent
confidence level, with values of asymptotic t-statistics as high as 44.
The range of the β estimates of 0.244 - 0.310 is well below unity, which
agrees with prior expectation discussed in Chapter 3.   Except for the
mixed class of light/medium trucks, the magnitudes of the used driving
power (HPDRIVE) are consistently smaller than the maximum rated power
values of the corresponding test vehicles (Table 1A.2).   In fact, as
greater the weight of a vehicle the more the braking capability needed to
render the vehicle operations safe.   An approximate relationship between
the braking power and the gross vehicle weight is also derived in the
next section.

The FRATIO estimates, from 0.087 to 0.292, are well below the
range of 0.6 - 0.7 found from skid-pad tests of modern high-performance
passenger cars.   This seems to indicate a large margin of safety within
which vehicles are generally operated on public roads.   This may also be
due to the tendency of the average driver to limit lateral acceleration
to an acceptable level of comfort of the driver and the passengers.   The
role of friction ratio as a dual criterion for skid and comfort has been
discussed in Good (1978) and Oglesby and Hicks (1982).   Within the total
range of FRATIO estimates, the following observations can be made:

1.   The range for unpaved roads (0.087 - 0.124) are
     significantly smaller than that for paved roads (0.130
     - 0.292).

2.   For paved road operations, loaded trucks have smaller
     FRATIO values than unloaded trucks (0.130 - 0.185
     versus 0.179 - 0.292).

3.   The FRATIO tends to vary inversely with the size of

the vehicle. For example, the FRATIO estimates for paved roads are the largest for passenger cars (0.268) and smallest for loaded articulated trucks (0.130).

The estimates of the average rectified velocity (ARVMAX) show a clear tendency to vary inversely with the vehicle size, starting with the largest value (259.7 mm/s) for cars and ending with the smallest (130.9 mm/s) for articulated trucks. This is somewhat surprising because on purely physical reasoning one would expect the smaller vehicles to be more sensitive to road roughness than larger ones. The reversal of relative magnitudes is probably explained in part by higher tire stiffness of larger vehicles, and in part by the economic response of the driver to the relatively higher cost impact of roughness on larger vehicles. As mentioned in Chapter 3, regression was also carried out for the more complicated ARV formula (speed-sensitive ARS). The results presented in Appendix 4D indicate no improvement in goodness-of-fit offered by the more elaborate formula.

The estimates for the desired speed (VDESIR) are, as expected, higher for paved roads (81.6 - 98.3 km/h) than for unpaved roads (49.6 - 82.8 km/h). Moreover, they tend to be larger for smaller vehicles, although, with the exception of the estimate for articulated trucks on unpaved roads (49.6 km/h), they are relatively constant for each surface type.

According to the interpretations made in Section 3.4, the estimated values of σ_e (0.081 - 0.189) indicate that the standard errors of model predictions associated with unmeasured vehicle and road attributes at a given road site are 8.1 - 18.9 percent of the predicted speed. Similarly, the estimated values of σ (0.170 - 0.269) imply that the standard errors of model predictions associated with the above measurement error and the random nature of individual speed observations themselves are 17.0 - 26.9 percent of the predicted speeds.

To get an idea of the goodness-of-fit of the estimated steady-state speed relationships, a plot of observed against predicted speeds is shown in Figure 4.1 for heavy trucks. Superimposed in the plot are the lines of equality and its plus and minus deviations by the σ_e and σ standard errors (narrow and wide bands, respectively). Also for heavy trucks, Table 4.4 shows average prediction errors for different groupings of the data points based on the road curvature, gradient, roughness and surface type and the vehicle load level.

It can be seen that even though the differences between observed and predicted speeds for data points aggregated at the section-direction level (Figure 4.1) are relatively large (standard error of about 1.95 m/s or 7 km/h) they are reduced to a much smaller magnitude when aggregated into groups of section-directions of similar characteristics. This indicates a good fit of the model with the data.

Figures 4.2 - 4.4 show, for unloaded and loaded heavy trucks, graphs of predicted steady-state speed plotted against the gradient, radius of curvature and roughness respectively, for both paved and

Figure 4.1:   Observed speed versus speed predicted by steady-state speed model for heavy trucks

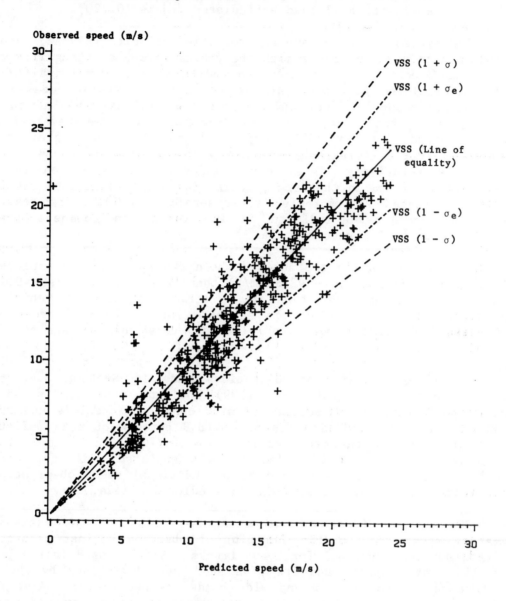

Source: Analysis of Brazil-UNDP-World Bank highway research project
          data as described in Section 4.2

Table 4.4: Average speed prediction errors for different groupings of data points (for heavy trucks)

Basis for grouping observations	Definition of group	Number of observations in group	Mean observed speed for group (km/h)	Mean predicted speed for group (km/h)	
				Predicted speed	difference (obs-pred)
Gradient (GR) in percent	GR<-4	94	54.13	54.21	-0.08
	-4<GR<3	192	53.09	53.36	-0.27
	3<GR	95	29.69	30.03	-0.34
Radius of curvature (RC) in m	RC<100	71	33.54	33.57	-0.03
	100<RC<250	121	46.03	45.90	0.13
	250<RC	189	53.71	54.26	-0.55
Surface type and roughness (QI) in QI counts	Paved: QI< 80	180	54.73	54.67	0.06
	80< QI	24	45.58	47.05	-1.47
	Unpaved: QI< 80	29	49.85	50.48	-0.63
	80<QI<130	74	43.29	43.28	0.01
	130< QI	74	33.89	34.54	-0.65
Surface type and loading condition	Paved: unloaded	101	59.14	60.41	-1.27
	loaded	103	48.27	47.27	1.00
	Unpaved: unloaded	86	44.58	44.31	0.27
	loaded	91	36.52	37.50	-0.98
All observations		381	47.51	47.75	-0.24

Source: Analysis of Brazil-UNDP-World Bank highway research project data.

unpaved surfaces. These prediction curves exhibit speed behavior which is broadly consistent with prior expectations. The predicted speed generally falls as the road becomes steeper, bendier or rougher. Other things being equal, the heavy truck is predicted to travel faster on a paved surface than on an unpaved one. As noted above, this is ascribed to the larger desired speed (VDESIR) for paved surfaces (88.8 km/h) than for unpaved surfaces (72.1 km/h). Similarly, with one exception, the truck would make a faster trip when empty than when laden with a heavy load. The one exception occurs on a long straight road of moderately negative gradient (between -2 and -4 percent) when the laden speed exceeds the unladen one by a slight margin (Figure 4.2). This is attributed to the fact that the additional gravitational force afforded by the extra weight, which aids the vehicle's own drive force, more than compensates for the extra burden it imposes on the engine and brakes.

Figure 4.2: Predicted speed versus gradient for heavy trucks

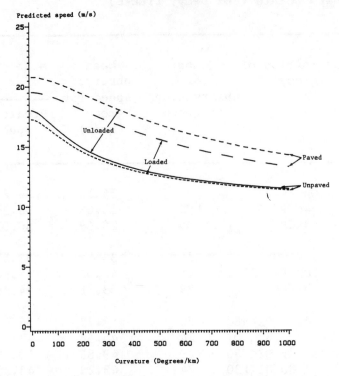

Source: Analysis of Brazil-UNDP-World Bank highway research project
          data (See also notes for Figures 3.1-3.3).

Figure 4.3: Predicted speed versus curvature for heavy trucks

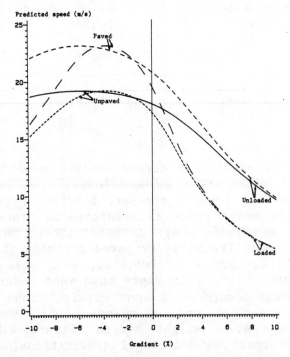

Source: Analysis of Brazil-UNDP-World Bank highway research project
          data (See also notes for Figures 3.1-3.3).

Figure 4.4: Predicted speed versus roughness for heavy trucks

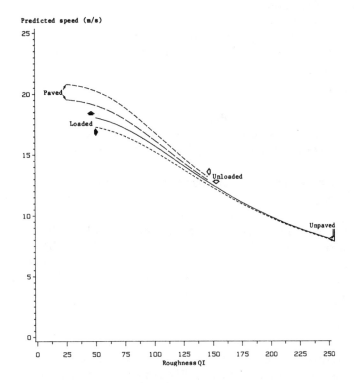

Source: Analysis of Brazil-UNDP-World Bank highway research project
          data as described in Section 4.2 (See also notes for Figures
          3.1-3.3).

Outside of the -2 to -4 percent regime, especially at the extreme values
of the road gradient (both positive and negative) the load becomes a
liability as it suppresses both the maximum possible driving speed
(VDRIVE) and the maximum allowable braking speed (VBRAKE).

        Asymptotic properties of the predicted speed can be gleaned
from the three plots. Besides being generally monotonically decreasing
with increasing road severity, predicted speeds for paved, unpaved,
loaded and unloaded conditions have a tendency to converge when one speed
constraint approaches total dominance. In Figure 4.2, owing to the
diminishing influence of the desired speed diffential, the predicted
speeds on paved and unpaved surfaces merge together as the road becomes
steeper. Although not as pronounced, the tendency to merge is also seen
in Figure 4.3 when the road curvature rises. In Figure 4.4 all four
prediction curves, for paved, unpaved, loaded and unloaded combinations
asymptotically converge when the very high roughness (QI over 200)
completely dominates the speed behavior.

4.3 ADAPTATION OF PARAMETER ESTIMATES FOR PREDICTION

        The set of parameter estimates presented in Table 4.3, along
with the vehicle class attributes given in Table 4.2(a), can be used
directly for predicting steady-state speeds of the respective vehicle
classes. However, with better information on vehicles, predictions of

the limiting velocity model can be improved by incorporating some modifications as follows:

1. By using a finer scheme of classification of vehicles and directly measured vehicle characteristics, such as tare weight, payload and frontal area, rather than imputed quantities;

2. By adapting HPDRIVE and HPBRAKE parameter values to reflect known vehicle attributes, such as rated power and carrying capacity, respectively; and

3. By using a parameterized relation between FRATIO and payload.

These modifications are based on the characteristics of the vehicles forming part of the test fleet for the Brazil study (see Appendix 1A) and the field study conducted using these vehicles for fuel consumption analysis. The details of the field study are given in Chapter 9. The modifications are described in the following subsections.

4.3.1 Redefinition of Vehicle Classes

As mentioned in Section 4.1, some of the vehicle classes in the six-fold scheme of vehicle classification used in the estimation of the steady-state speed model parameters are aggregate groupings of the basic vehicle classes listed in Appendix 1A. It can be refined to comprise 10 vehicle classes each anchored by a specific test fleet vehicle with determinate characteristics. The highlights of the new classification scheme are given below.

The relatively heterogeneous class of cars may be sub-divided into three classes, viz., small car, medium car and large car, with the corresponding test vehicles being VW-1300, Chevrolet Opala, and Dodge Dart, respectively. The actual values of tare weight, frontal area and drag coefficient of the test fleet vehicles may be associated with the respective vehicle classes. Except for the HPDRIVE and HPBRAKE parameterparameters, these three classes share the same set of parameter estimates given in Table 4.3. The determination of the horsepower parameters for these classes of cars as well for the other vehicle classes is discussed in Section 4.3.2.

A large proportion of vehicles in the light/medium truck class were light gasoline or diesel trucks comparable to Ford 400 and Ford 4000 in the test fleet. This class has been redefined to include "light gasoline truck" and "light diesel truck" classes with the physical characteristics being given by Ford 400 and Ford 4000, respectively. These two classes of light trucks share the same set of parameters as estimated in Section 4.2 for the light/medium class, with the exception of horsepower paramters. The distinction between these two classes is relatively minor so far as speed prediction is concerned; as we shall see in Chapters 9 and 10, the distinction is important for predicting fuel consumption.

The heavy truck class may be subdivided into "medium truck" and "heavy truck" classes. The main distinction between these two classes is that the latter has an additional axle making it a three-axle truck with a higher average payload. The test fleet vehicle corresponding to both the classes is Mercedes Benz 1113. The two classes share the set of parameters estimated for the erstwhile heavy truck class, again the horsepower parameters excepted. The distinction between the two classes is not very significant for the purpose of speed prediction; as we shall see in Chapter 11, it is significant for predicting tire wear.

The utility, bus and articulated truck classes remain the same as before and use most of the parameter estimates given in Table 4.3. Only the power-related parameters have been modified to reflect the rated power and load capacity of the corresponding test fleet vehicles, viz., VW-Kombi, Mercedes Benz 0-362, and Scania 110/39, respectively.

4.3.2 Determination of HPDRIVE and HPBRAKE Parameters

The data employed for this purpose were the same as those used in estimating the unit fuel consumption functions described in Chapter 9. The experiment from which the data were developed involved operating the 11 test vehicles over 1-km distance on a variety of test sections at constant speeds, in constant gears and under different loads. The uphill and downhill runs at high speeds under large loads on steep sections gave rise to extreme values of the positive (driving) and negative (braking) powers.

Used driving power

For each test vehicle, the general rule was to pick a number from roughly the 90-95 percentile range of the distribution of the positive power as HPDRIVE. The 90-95 percentile range was assumed to reflect the power used when positive gradient was the constraining road severity factor. The values of HPDRIVE estimated in this manner are shown in Table 4.5 in comparison with the manufacturer's SAE maximum rated power, HPRATED (both in metric power units).

It can be seen that HPDRIVE makes up only a fraction of HPRATED for all vehicles. Between the gasoline and diesel vehicles, the former tend to have smaller HPDRIVE/HPRATED ratios than the latter. The difference between HPRATED and HPDRIVE seems to be accounted for by the following factors:

1.   Losses in the vehicle transmission and accessories;

2.   The inability of the drivers to attain the maximum power capabilities of the vehicles because of gear ratio discreteness; and

3.   The unwillingness of the drivers to use the full power of the engine, particularly for the gasoline vehicles with high power-to-weight ratios.

Table 4.5:   Used driving power (HPDRIVE) and manufacturer's maximum rated horsepower (HPRATED) for test vehicles

Test vehicle Make/model	HPDRIVE (metric hp)	HPRATED (metric hp)	HPDRIVE/ HPRATED
Gasoline powered vehicles:			
VW-1300	30	49	0.61
Chevrolet Opala	70	148	0.47
Dodge Dart	85	201	0.42
VW-Kombi (2)[1]	40	61	0.66
Ford 400	80	171	0.47
Diesel powered vehicles:			
Mercedes Benz 0-362 Bus[2]	100	149	0.67
Ford 4000	60	103	0.58
Mercedes Benz 1113 (2)[2]	100	149	0.67
Scania 110/39	210	289	0.73

[1] The two replicate vehicles are assumed to have the same HPBRAKE.
[2] As these vehicles have the same basic specifications of their engines and drive trains, they are assumed to have the same HPBRAKE.
Source: Brazil-UNDP-World Bank highway research project data and analysis.

To quantify the relationship between HPDRIVE and HPRATED, the vehicles are divided into two groups, gasoline powered and diesel powered.

For the gasoline vehicles, we assume the following form of relationship between HPDRIVE and HPRATED:

$$HPDRIVE = p \; HPRATED^{q} \tag{4.1}$$

where p and q are coefficients to be estimated.   Taking natural logs on both sides of the above equation and running ordinary least square regression on the 5 data points in Table 4.5 yielded the following coefficient estimates:

$$\ell n \; HPDRIVE = 0.682 + 0.714 \; \ell n \; HPRATED \tag{4.2}$$
$$(3.4) \quad (16.7)$$

with R-square = 0.99 and mean square error = 0.003 (the values in parentheses are t-statistics).   The above estimated equations can be rewritten as:

$$HPDRIVE = 1.98 \; HPRATED^{0.714} \tag{4.3}$$

which is shown graphically in Figure 4.5 along with the data points to

Figure 4.5:   HPDRIVE versus HPRATED

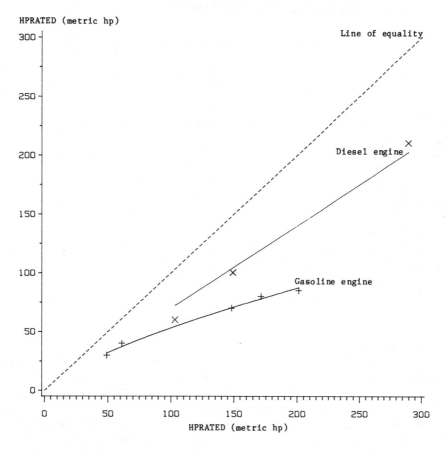

Source: Brazil—UNDP—World Bank highway research project data and
          analysis.

which the curve was fitted. The estimated exponent 0.714 is smaller than
1.0 which is consistent with our expectation that the more powerful the
vehicle (for relatively constant weight), the less willing the driver is
to use its full power. Rounding off the coefficients gives:

$$\text{HPDRIVE} = 2.0 \ \text{HPRATED}^{0.7} \qquad\qquad (4.4)$$

which is recommended as an approximation of the used driving power for
gasoline powered vehicles.

For the diesel vehicles, the ratios HPDRIVE/HPRATED are not
very different and the differences show no clear trend. Therefore, an
average ratio of 0.66 rounded to 0.7 yielding the following relationship
recommended as an approximation:

$$\text{HPDRIVE} = 0.7 \ \text{HPRATED} \qquad\qquad (4.5)$$

It should be emphasized that it is a broad empirical trend
based on the test fleet vehicles used in the Brazil study. In regions
where it is a common practice to overload trucks a coefficient higher
than 0.7 may be appropriate.

Table 4.6: Used braking power (HPBRAKE) and manufacturer's rated gross weight (GVW) for test vehicles

Vehicle Make/model	HPBRAKE (metric hp)	GVW (tons)	HPBRAKE GVW
VW-Kombi (2)[1]	30	2.1	14.3
Ford 400	100	6.1	16.4
Ford 4000	100	6.1	16.4
Mercedes Benz 1113 (2)[1]	250	18.5	13.5
Scania 110/39	500	40.0	12.5

[1] These replicate vehicles are assumed to have the same HPBRAKE.
Source: Brazil-UNDP-World Bank highway research project data and
analysis results as described in Section 4.2.

Used braking power

For each test vehicle, the general rule was to pick roughly the largest magnitude of the negative power values. The results are shown in Table 4.6 along with the manufacturer's rated gross vehicle weights (GVW). The three passenger cars and the bus are excluded from Table 4.6 as apparently their braking capabilities were not fully utilized during the experiment. The HPBRAKE values in Table 4.6 appear to be resulting from the dual use of the engine and brake pedal for braking. According to the test drivers, this was necessary in order to maintain a relatively high speed when the test vehicles were running down a steep hill. It seems reasonable for safety reasons that the vehicle's total braking capability should somehow be related to its total design weight, namely the rated gross vehicle weight, GVW, in tons. As shown in Table 4.6, the ratios HPBRAKE/GVW appear to be similar across the test vehicles. The maximum variations from the average ratio of 14.6 metric horsepower per ton are approximately + 14 percent. The similarity of the ratios is probably due to vehicle designers generally attempting to match the braking capability of the vehicle with its design weight.

Thus, it may be recommended that the used braking power for a given vehicle be computed from the following simple formula:

$$HPBRAKE = 14 \ GVW \quad or \quad 15 \ GVW \tag{4.6}$$

The estimates of HPBRAKE for the remaining test vehicles become:

VW-1300 $1.2 \times 14 = 16.8 \simeq 17$
Chevrolet Opala $1.5 \times 14 = 21$
Dodge Dart $1.9 \times 14 = 26.6 \simeq 27$
Mercedes Benz 0-362 Bus $11.5 \times 14 = 161.0 \simeq 160$

4.3.3 Parameterization of Perceived Friction Ratio for Partially Loaded Trucks

In the formulation of the steady-state speed model (Chapter 3), the maximum allowable curve speed is derived using the perceived friction ratio parameter (FRATIO). As seen in Section 4.2, the estimated value of FRATIO depends on the surface type traversed. In addition, the value of FRATIO for trucks also depends on whether the vehicle is empty or loaded.

The relationship between perceived friction ratio and payload is complex and depends on the nature of loading, such as, density of the cargo, the center of gravity, and load shift considerations. However, in the Brazil speed experiment only the loading condition of the trucks was observed. Thus, in order to determine the value of FRATIO to be used when a truck is under an arbitrary load, one has to interpolate. Since there is no known a priori functional form, and there are only two data points available for each truck class, it was decided to use linear interpolation. A linear approach to interpolation between closely spaced values is not expected to introduce a significant error. This approach may be described as follows. Let,

FRATIO_E = the value of the friction ratio for an empty truck of a given size;

FRATIO_F = the value of the friction ratio for a loaded truck of the same size traversing the same type of surface;

STDLOAD   = the average payload for the loaded truck (in kg) as assumed in the estimation (Table 4.1);

LOAD   = the payload carried by the vehicle (in kg); and

FRATIO(LOAD) = the value of friction ratio for LOAD. This is the parameter we wish to determine.

Then, by linear interpolation, we have:

$$\frac{\text{FRATIO}_F - \text{FRATIO}_E}{\text{STDLOAD} - 0} = \frac{\text{FRATIO(LOAD)} - \text{FRATIO}_E}{\text{LOAD} - 0} \qquad (4.7)$$

This transforms into:

$$FRATIO(LOAD) = FRATIO_E + LOAD \left\{ \frac{FRATIO_F - FRATIO_E}{STDLOAD} \right\} \qquad (4.7a)$$

$$= FRATIO_0 - LOAD\ FRATIO_1 \qquad (4.7b)$$

$$\text{where} \qquad FRATIO_0 = FRATIO_E \qquad\qquad\qquad\qquad (4.8)$$

$$\text{and} \qquad FRATIO_1 = -\frac{FRATIO_F - FRATIO_E}{STDLOAD} \qquad\qquad (4.9)$$

The values of all the parameters for the five classes of trucks and for both paved and unpaved surfaces are given in Table 4.7.

Table 4.7: Results of parameterization of perceived friction ratio

Truck class	Surface type	$FRATIO_E$	$FRATIO_F$	STDLOAD (kg)	$FRATIO_0$	$FRATIO_1$
Light gasoline	Paved	0.251	0.170	6500	0.251	0.00001246
	Unpaved	0.097	0.097		0.097	0
Light diesel	Paved	0.251	0.170	6500	0.251	
	Unpaved	0.097	0.097		0.097	0
Medium	Paved	0.289	0.184	11300	0.289	0.00000929
	Unpaved	0.081	0.081		0.081	0
Heavy	Paved	0.289	0.184	11300	0.289	0.00000929
	Unpaved	0.081	0.081		0.081	0
Articulated	Paved	0.175	0.124	21800	0.175	0.00000234
	Unpaved	0.040	0.040		0.040	0

Source: Brazil-UNDP-World Bank highway research project data and analysis results as described in Section 4.2

4.4 TRANSFERABILITY OF THE LIMITING SPEED MODEL: A CASE STUDY OF INDIA

The transferability of the limiting speed approach for predicting steady-state speeds on homogeneous sections may be investigated using data from a different environment. This section presents the results of the analysis based on the speed data collected in India in connection with the Road User Cost Study (RUCS). Full details of the study are given in CRRI (1982).

Since the Indian data were collected for a full-fledged project of estimating a free speed prediction model, a suitable benchmark level of predictive ability already exists, which can be used to test the performance of the limiting velocity approach. In addition to being a suitable test of the tranferability of the limiting speed approach, the application of the methodology described in Chapter 3 to Indian data has two by-products of importance in their own right. First, the effort would serve as a substantial case study of adaptation of the parameters of the speed model in a radically different socioeconomic and technological environment; and, a such, would assist in clarifying the steps involved in such an adaptation and in pointing out the limitations of adaptation of model form and model parameters. Hence, it would be possible to arrive at a rating (or taxonomy) of model parameters in terms of the degree of necessity of calibration. Second, since the factorial matrix of the speed study in India included road width as a dimension, the calibration study would enable us to add an important highway policy variable, viz., road width, to the list of options modelled.

The organization of the remainder of the section is as follows. The Indian speed data are described briefly and the results of the linear speed model are presented in Section 4.4.1. The approach taken to investigate the transferability of the limiting speed model form and model parameters is described next (Section 4.4.2). The results of the analysis are presented and discussed in Section 4.4.3, along with the recommended treatment of width effect on steady-state speeds.

4.4.1 Data

The speed data collected in India for the Road User Costs Study comprise about 14,000 speed measurements of free-flowing vehicles at 38 selected road sites. Distinguishing speed observations at a road-site by the direction of travel, there are 76 section-directions covering gradient values from −9 to +9 percent, radii of curvature from 200 m to 2000 m and roughness values from 37 QI to 277 QI. Only paved sections were included in the Indian study. A further dimension of road characteristics in the Indian study is road width, and the sample sections are grouped into three width categories, as follows:

Table 4.8 provides a summary of the section characteristics.

Double lane roads: width above 6.5 m
Intermediate roads: width around 5.5 m
Single lane roads: width below 4 m

The observations may be classified into three vehicle classes, namely, cars, buses, and trucks. The average physical characteristics of these classes of vehicles in India are given in Table 4.9(a). Since the range of makes and models of vehicles in India is much smaller than that in Brazil, there would be little variation from the assumed average values. On the other hand, as regards the unmodelled vehicle characteristics, such as age and maintenance condition, their range in the vehicle population in India is much greater than that found in Brazil.

With respect to each vehicle class, the individual speeds observed at a given section-direction were averaged. Table 4.9(b) gives the summary statistics of the mean speed values for each vehicle class. Many different linear equations were tried out by CRRI, and the equations finally selected are as follows:

Cars: V = 16.83 − 53.33 RS − 51.11 FL − 0.00217 C − 0.055 QI + 0.29 W

Buses: V = 15.27 − 83.61 RS − 63.33 FL − 0.00214 C − 0.034 QI + 0.17 W

Trucks: V = 13.14 − 74.72 RS − 73.61 FL − 0.00275 C − 0.029 QI + 0.29 W

where   V = vehicle speed in m/s;

and   W = road width in m.

The other variables are as defined in Section 2.1. The R^2 values are 0.71, 0.78, and 0.70, respectively.

4.4.2 Approach

The parameters needed to use the limiting velocity-based speed prediction method are: HPDRIVE, HPBRAKE, FRATIO, ARVMAX, VDESIR, and β. In addition, we need a new parameter to model the effect of pavement width. Of these parameters, FRATIO and ARVMAX are expected to be relatively insensitive to a change in location. As regards HPDRIVE and BRAKE, as described in Section 4.3.2, these parameters have a technological determination in that they are expected to be much more sensitive to rated horsepower and gross vehicle weight than to features of the socioeconomic environment.

On a priori grounds, the desired speed parameters may be expected to be the most sensitive to a change in the environment within which the vehicle operates. The shape parameter β of the distribution of the underlying constraining speeds is closely associated with the dispersion of these speeds, and, as such, it is not possible to predict on a priori grounds whether the Brazil values would hold for India.

Because of the foregoing discussion, it was decided to use the Brazil values for FRATIO and ARVMAX parameters; to use the approximate relationships derived in the previous section to determine exogenously the HPDRIVE and HPBRAKE parameters; and to use the Indian observed speed data to arrive at estimates of VDESIR and β parameters by means of non-linear least squares. The power parameter values assigned before the regression are given in Table 4.10, along with the HPRATED and GVW values for the Indian vehicles.

The following paragraphs give an account of the way the effect of pavement width on the free-flow speeds of vehicles was modelled. Table 4.11 gives the frequency distribution of the width values in the sample of test section. It may be observed that width values are not evenly distributed over the range of 3.5-7.0 m. In fact, three clusters of width values may be identified. In the terminology used in the Indian

Table 4.8: Statistics of test sections in the Indian study

Characteristic	Mean	Minimum	Maximum	Std. Dev.
Gradient (dimensionless)	0.01	0.0	0.09	0.02
Curvature (degrees/km)	274.0	1.0	1243.0	347.2
Roughness (QI)	81.6	37.3	277.3	32.8

Source: India Road User Costs Study Data.

Table 4.9(a): Vehicle classes and characteristics for Indian vehicles

Vehicle class	Aerodynamic drag coefficient;[1] C_D	Projected frontal area, AR[2] (m^2)	Total vehicle weight[3] (kg)
Small car	0.50	2.05	1,200
Bus	0.65	5.37	8,415
Medium truck	0.85	5.37	10,665

[1] The C_D values are taken to be the same as those for corresponding Brazilian vehicles.
[2] The AR values are for typical vehicles in India, taken from CRRI (1982).
[3] The values for vehicle weights are from CRRI (1982). For buses and trucks, 0.75 of maximum net load is taken as the average payload.
Source: India Road User Costs Study Data.

Table 4.9(b): Statistics of Indian observed mean speeds

Vehicle class	Number of mean-speed data points	Mean speed (m/s)				
		Mean	Min.	Max.	Std.dev.	CV(%)
Small car	76	12.20	6.66	18.59	2.77	23
Bus	76	11.28	4.53	17.78	3.16	28
Medium truck	76	10.31	3.42	15.83	2.86	28

Source: India Road User Costs Study Data.

Table 4.10: Exogenously assigned horsepower parameter values

Vehicle class	HPDRIVE (metric hp)	HPBRAKE (metric hp)	HPRATED (metric hp)	GVW (ton)
Small car	31	18	49.4	1.37
Bus	79	129	113.5	9.18
Medium truck	79	171	113.5	12.18

Note: The HPRATED and GVW values for cars are averages of the values
          for Ambassador and Padmini makes (CRRI, 1982).
Source: Analysis of India Road User Costs Study Data.

study, the three width classes are "single-lane sections," "intermediate
sections," and "double-lane sections." This phenomenon of discrete
values for width was also observed in the TRRL-Kenya study (TRRL 1975).
Thus, it is more appropriate to treat width as a qualitative or
classification variable than as a continuous variable. The modelling
implication of the above conclusion is that width will be treated
analogously as surface type and not as, say, road gradient. It may be
recalled from Section 4.2 that it was necessary to distinguish two
parameters, viz., FRATIO and VDESIR, by surface type for a given vehicle
class. A convenient way to incorporate the effect of width in the speed
model is to distinguish the VDESIR parameter by the width class of the
pavement for each vehicle class and this was the approach that was
followed.

Figure 4.6 plots averages of mean section speeds for each
vehicle class for the three width classes. For cars, there is a small
reduction in average speed for intermediate sections relative to the
double-lane sections, and a somewhat larger reduction in going from the
intermediate sections to the single-lane sections. However, for buses
and trucks, the average speed on intermediate-lane sections is higher
than that on double-lane sections. This anamaly is probably due to the
fact that it is relatively more difficult to maintain strict
free-flow. As for cars, preliminary results indicated that the difference
in the desired speeds for cars between the intermediate and the
double-lane sections was small and not well-determined in terms of
asymptotic t-statistics. Thus, it was decided to distinguish only two
classes of sections by width for all the vehicles: single lane sections,
and intermediate and dual lane sections.

Preliminary estimation runs indicated that for each vehicle
class, the desired speed over the single-lane sections were proportional
to the desired speed over the wider sections. Hence the width effect was
modelled by introducing a multiplicative free-flow "width effect
parameter," BW, which may be defined as follows. Let

    VDESIR = desired speed without incorporating width effect, in
             m/s;
           = desired speed for intermediate and dual-lane sections;

Table 4.11:   Frequency distribution of width values of Indian test sections

Width class	Width (m)	Frequency
Single-lane	3.5	1
	3.7	10
	3.8	15
Intermediate	5.5	22
	5.6	2
Double-lane	6.5	2
	6.6	6
	6.8	4
	7.0	14

Source: India Road User Costs Study Data.

Figure 4.6:   Observed speed for the three width classes for Indian vehicles

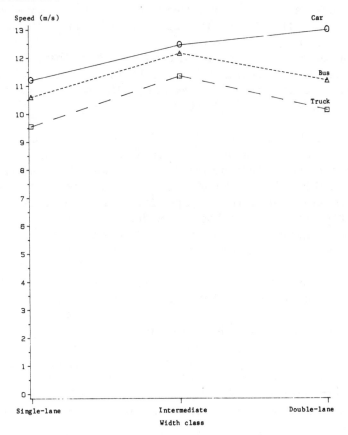

Source: India Road User Costs Study Data.

VDESIR' = desired speed incorporating width effect, in m/s;

= desired speed for single-lane sections.

Then the dimensionless width effect parameter, BW, for the single-lane sections, is defined as:

BW = VDESIR'/VDESIR   (4.10)

For each vehicle class, VDESIR and BW parameters were estimated, in addition to the β parameter. The desired speed for single-lane sections may then be computed as:

VDESIR' = BW VDESIR   (4.11)

4.4.3 Results

Table 4.12 presents the estimation results. For each vehicle class, the estimates for VDESIR, BW and β are presented. The computed values of VDESIR' are also included. The asymptotic t-statistics are given in parentheses, and the sum of squared residuals (SSR) and the R^2 values are appended along-side.

The VDESIR values for all vehicle and width classes are of the expected order of magnitude, but somewhat larger than expected. (The possible reason for the somewhat large values of VDESIR parameter for India is discussed later following the discussion of the β estimates.) In terms of the asymptotic t-statistics, the β and VDESIR parameters for wide sections are well-determined for all vehicle classes. However, the estimates of the width effect parameter, BW, for buses and trucks have relatively low values of t-statistic.

More significant is the magnitude of the β parameter in relation to the Brazilian values, the estimates for the Indian data being nearly twice those for Brazilian data. It may be recalled that the β parameter is functionally related to the dispersion of the underlying distributions of the constraining speeds. Given the error structure of the probabilistic limiting velocity model, it means that for a given vehicle unit on a given road over repeated runs, the variances of the constraining speeds are higher for India than for Brazil. The reasons for this are not clear but may plausibly have to do with the more congested traffic environment. The most striking characteristic of Indian traffic is the ever-present possibility of traffic impediments such as pedestrians, bicyclists and animal-driven vehicles. It is possible that this factor may have caused the subjective response of the vehicle operators to road severity factors to be less consistent. It would be useful in the future to test this hypothesis by means of data from, for example, the Caribbean and Kenya where rural traffic is relatively congestion-free. If the hypothesis turns out to be true, then the Brazil-calibrated β parameter may be considered to be generally applicable.

The analytical implication of a higher value of the β estimate

Table 4.12: Estimation results of transferability study based on Indian speed data

Vehicle class	β	VDESIR (m/s) Intermediate and dual-lane sections	Width effect parameter, BW (dimensionless)	VDESIR'	SSR	R^2
Small car	0.675 (20.0)	28.51 (8.0)	0.75 (3.1)	21.25	2.3	0.71
Bus	0.609 (18.4)	29.91 (6.8)	0.78 (2.3)	23.18	1.9	0.81
Medium truck	0.585 (13.0)	26.41 (4.9)	0.73 (2.0)	19.31	2.7	0.68

Note: The asymptotic t-statistics associated with the estimates are given in parentheses.

Source: Analysis of India Road User Costs Study Data.

is that the partial derivatives of predicted speed with respect to road severity factors is higher in magnitude. In other words, as highways deteriorate, the decrease in speeds is larger. It probably explains the relatively high values of VDESIR estimates on wide sections because VDESIR reflects speeds on an idealized near-perfect pavement.

The R^2 values for the limiting speed model are slightly higher than those for the linear model for cars and buses and slightly lower for trucks. It should be noted that the number of parameters estimated is three in the case of the limiting speed model and six in the case of the linear model. The mean of residuals was lower for the limiting speed model in a majority of groupings of observations by levels of road severity factors. Thus, the models have comparable explanatory power.

Figures 4.7 - 4.9 contrast the steady-state speed predictions of the two models in the case of a medium truck as functions of gradient, curvature, and roughness, respectively. In each case, speed curves are plotted for both wide (7 m) and narrow (3.5 m) sections. It may be seen from these curves that, relative to the limiting speed model, the linear model over-predicts speeds for the lower range of road severity factors, and under-predicts for the upper range. The limiting speed model shows a consistently asymptotic behavior as road severity factors worsen. The linear model exhibits a constant width effect over the entire range of the other variables, as expected from the functional form. The limiting speed model predicts a width effect which is largest when the road conditions are very good, and diminishes when the road conditions deteriorate becoming insignificant under extreme conditions. This may be seen most clearly in Figure 4.7.

It is also clear from these figures that despite the large VDESIR values, the predicted steady-state speeds are of the same order as observed speeds. Further, care should be taken not to interpret the quantity 1/BW as representing the speed increase that would result on widening the section. The predicted increase in speed due to widening a section would depend on the values of other road severity factors.

The following conclusions may be drawn from the results of the application of the limiting speed approach to Indian speed data:

1. The limiting speed approach to predicting steady-state speeds on homogeneous sections is applicable in such different socioeconomic and traffic environments as Brazil and India and produces more consistent and intuitively appealing predictions than the linear model.

2. The desired speed parameter needs to be calibrated on the basis of observed speeds. While it is ideal to have speed observations covering a wide range of section characteristics, our experience with the Indian data has indicated that the calibrations based on a limited field study should be adequate. The procedures for calibrating VDESIR as well as other speed model parameters using a non-random sampling technique are described in Chapter 13.

3. It is necessary to choose the β parameter value with care. Since the parameter encompasses all the road severity factors, at least a medium-size field study would be required for obtaining a reliable estimate of β. It is expected that for most regional applications the estimates of β derived in the Brazil study would be appropriate. For environments, such as India, which have congested rural roads and low level of traffic discipline, somewhat higher values of the β parameter may be used.

4. The width of rural roads in India were found to be clustered around three values, viz., 3.75 m, 5.5 m, and 6.75 m. Thus, it seems more appropriate to conceive ofroad width as a qualitative variable characterizing thewidth class of the road section rather than as a continuous variable ranging from, say, 3.5 m to 7 m.

5. There does not appear to be a significant width effect on the free-flow steady-state speed of vehicles, and the slight effect is manifest only for single-lane sections, less than 4 m wide. Within the framework of the limiting velocity model, the effect of width class on the desired speeds was found to be multiplicative in nature.

6. The Indian study did not include unpaved sections. Also, the effect of road width on utilities, and light andarticulated trucks needs to be examined in future studies. Since the width effect on desired speeds was

found to be multiplicative, it appears reasonable to use the same width effect parameter values for unpaved sections as well, pending further studies. It is also tentatively recommended that the width effect on utilities may be taken to be the same as that on cars, and the width effect on all categories of trucks to be the same as that on medium trucks.

7. Finally, some limitations of the transferability study for India are noted below:

    a. Individual speed observations were not available during the analysis, with the result that estimation was done with mean speed, rather than mean log speed, as the dependent variable. As noted earlier (Section 3.4), this leads to a fairly severe problem of heteroskedasticity.

    b. A more general formulation of the effect of road cross section on steady-state speeds would encompass the width and condition of road shoulders. While these data were collected for the Indian study, they were not available in coded form for the analysis.

    c. A more general formulation of the effect of road cross section on steady-state speeds would encompass the width and condition of road shoulders. While these data were collected for the Indian study, they were not available in coded form for the analysis.

Figure 4.7: Predicted speed versus gradient for narrow and wide sections for Indian trucks: limiting speed and linear models

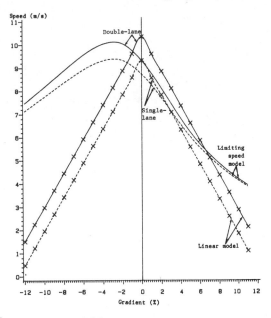

Note: C = 500 deg/km; QI = 120
Source: Analysis of India Road User Costs Study Data (See also notes for Figures 3.1 - 3.3).

**Figure 4.8: Predicted speed versus curvature for narrow and wide
sections for Indian trucks: limiting speed and linear
models**

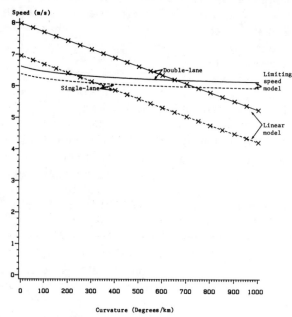

Note: Gradient = 5%;   QI = 120

Source: Analysis of India Road User Costs Study Data (See also notes for
Figures 3.1 - 3.3).

**Figure 4.9: Predicted speed versus roughness for narrow and wide sections
for Indian trucks: limiting speed and linear models**

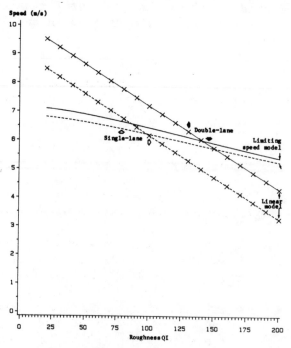

Source: Analysis of India Road User Costs Study Data (See also notes for
Figure 3.1 - 3.3).

APPENDIX 4A

STEADY STATE SPEED MODEL: ESTIMATION PROCEDURE

The data set for estimating θ and β in the steady-state speed model presented in Section 3.4 for a particular vehicle class, say a heavy truck, consists of sample observations:

$$(v_{ij}, X_i, Y_{ij}) \qquad i = 1,2,..,I \text{ and } j = 1,2,..,J_i$$

where X_i are the observed characteristics of a sample of homogeneous sections, Y_{ij} are the observed characteristics of a sample of heavy trucks in the respective sections, v_{ij} are the observed steady-state speeds of these heavy trucks, I is the number of sections in the sample and J_i is the number of heavy trucks observed in section i. Let,

$$u_{ij} = \ell n \ v_{ij} \tag{4A.1}$$

Then the speed model may be written as:

$$v_{ij} = \overline{V}(X_i, Y_{ij} : \theta, \beta) \ \varepsilon_i \ \omega_{ij} \tag{4A.2}$$

where ε_i are independent lognormal distributions with mean 1, and ω_{ij} have independent approximately lognormal distributions with mean 1. Similarly, the log-speed model may be written as:

$$u_{ij} = \overline{U}(X_i, Y_{ij} : \theta, \beta) + e_i + w_{ij} \tag{4A.3}$$

where e_i have independent normal distributions with constant mean and w_{ij} have independent approximately normal distributions with constant means.

The estimation problem then is to find estimates of θ and β which satisfy a suitable criterion. The two most commonly used criteria for estimating a logit model are maximum likelihood and least squares. The criterion chosen in the Brazil study was least squares, and the considerations governing the choice are summarized below.

1. One of the two main reasons for preferring the maximum likelihood method is that least squares cannot be applied straightforwardly when the dependent variable logically has a limited range, for example, when it stands for probability and thus has to lie between 0 and 1. This does not apply to the speed model because the dependent variable here is speed or its logarithm.

2. The second reason for preferring the maximum likelihood
method is that it is relatively more efficient in terms of
low variance of the estimates. However, the likelihood
function is very sensitive to distributional assumptions
and consequently, the maximum likelihood estimators are
not robust. But, the regression function is not sensitive
to distribution of the error and the least squares
estimators are robust.

3. The data set for estimation may be considered as a sample
of homogeneous sections with repeated speed observations
for a vehicle of given class and load condition, and the
predicted expected speeds would be the same for a
particular homogeneous section. This feature of the data
was exploited by working with the means of observed log
speeds for each homogeneous section. The savings in
computational costs are significant considering that the
number of speed observations for a vehicle class is more
than 15,000 over about 200 sections.

However, the mean of a sample of Weibull (Gumbel) random
variables is not Weibull (Gumbel) and maximum likelihood
technique by its nature, is not robust with respect to
relaxing the distributional assumptions leading to
inconsistent estimators. On the other hand, least squares
estimators are known to be robust with respect to
distribution of errors (Williams, 1978). Moreover, as
pointed out in Chesher and Harrison (1987), non-linear
least squares estimators are analogous to pseudo-maximum
likelihood estimators discussed in Gourieroux et al.,
(1984).

4. Finally, least squares technique is much simpler to use
because of the availability of a versatile statistical
routine (the NLIN procedure of SAS.) Thus the task of
reprogramming for trying out different formulations of
steady-state speeds and different levels of pooling of the
data (across load classes and surface types) was not
prohibitive.

Between the Weibull or speed model (Equation 4A.1) and the
Gumbel or log-speed model (Equation 4A.3), while the two are equivalent
theoretically, once the least squares approach is chosen, it is
computationally much more convenient to work with the Gumbel model,
because of its additive error structure. In order to use the Weibull
model, one has to write, for example,

$$v_{ij} = \overline{V}(X_i, Y_{ij}: \theta, \beta) + \delta_{ij}$$

where $\delta_{ij} = (V - 1) \varepsilon_i \omega_{ij}$. Thus, the variance of each error
would involve $\overline{V}^2$; that is, the model would be heteroscedastic. This
necessitates weighted least squares with weights depending on θ and β.
Further, the Gamma function and its derivative have to be evaluated while

solving the normal equations.   It is much simpler to use the Gumbel
formulation, noting that for unbiased predictions, a correction factor is
needed after exponentiation as discussed in Section 3.4.

The structure of the data described in (3) above, was utilized
as follows. The only attribute of a vehicle unit observed in the field
was its vehicle class, and in the case of a truck, its load class. The
other characteristics were determined on an average basis for the entire
data set relating to a vehicle class, treating empty and loaded trucks as
separate classes of vehicles for each category of trucks. Thus, the set
of vehicle characteristics, Y_{ij}, is the same for all observations of
the same vehicle and load class, and we can write Y for Y_{ij}. Thus,

$$\overline{U}(X_i, Y_{ij} : \theta, \beta) = \overline{U}(X_i, Y : \theta, \beta), \quad \text{for } j = 1, 2, \ldots, J_i$$

Defining for each section, i:

$$u_i = \sum_{j=1}^{J_i} u_{ij} / J_i \tag{4A.4}$$

and

$$w_i = \sum_{j=1}^{J_i} w_{ij} / J_i \tag{4A.5}$$

we can write the log-speed model as:

$$u_i = \overline{U}(X_i, Y : \theta, \beta) + e_i + w_i \tag{4A.6}$$

By central limit theorem, the w_i would be very nearly normal
with constant mean, but with variances inversely proportional to the
sample sizes J_i at section i. The resulting heteroscedasticity may be
easily taken care of by means of iteratively weighted non-linear least
squares. The weights γ_i for an iteration were determined using the
ratio of the sum of squared residuals from the previous iteration and the
variance of log speeds at the respective sections, with the iterations
being started with uniform weighting. Thus we can write the sum of
squared residuals to be minimized as:

$$SSQ(\theta, \beta) = \sum_{i=1}^{I} \gamma_i \, (u_i - \overline{U}(X_i, Y : \theta, \beta))^2 \tag{4A.7}$$

At convergence, the estimates of θ and β would be identical to
the respective maximum likelihood estimates if the errors are normal
(Malinvaud, 1980). The results of the tests for normality of error terms
is presented in Appendix 4B.

APPENDIX 4B

THE TEST FOR NORMALITY OF RESIDUALS OF THE FINAL STEADY-STATE SPEED MODEL

In this appendix, the results of the significance tests for the normality of the residuals of the final steady-state speed model are reported for all vehicle classes. The test uses the Kolmogorov-Smirnov D statistic. The values of the D statistic for each model estimated are given in the respective tables. The values for the final model are given in Table 4B.1 along with the probability of obtaining a higher value of the D-statistic by chance, which depends on the sample size.

From Table 4B.1 it may be seen that the null hypothesis that residuals of the final model are normal, is:

1. Rejected at 1 percent level of significance for light and medium trucks and heavy trucks;

2. Rejected at 5 percent level of significance, but not at 1 percent for cars; and

3. Not rejected for utilities, buses and articulated trucks.

It is known that the D-test overemphasizes tail values (Cox and Hinkley, 1974) and that the critical values are overly sensitive to sample-size (Krishniah, 1980; and Conover, 1980). It may be observed that significant rejection of the null hypothesis takes place in the two truck classes where the sample size is about twice that for other classes. Thus, it was decided to accept the estimates presented in Table 4.3.

Table 4B.1   Results of tests for normality of residuals

Vehicle class	Sample size	Value of Kolmogorov-Smirnov D-statistic	Prob (• > D) due to chance
Car	216	0.062	0.04
Utility	216	0.039	0.15
Bus	216	0.060	0.06
Truck:			
Light/medium	431	0.058	Less than 0.01
Heavy	381	0.075	Less than 0.01
Articulated	232	0.059	0.05

Source: Analysis of Brazil-UNDP-World Bank highway research project data.

APPENDIX 4C

ESTIMATION RESULTS FOR SEPARATE REGRESSIONS BY LOAD LEVEL AND BY PAVED AND UNPAVED GROUPING

This appendix reports on different models estimated during the exploratory phase of the steady-state model estimation process. Basically, different models arise because of the multiplicity of ways in which observations for a given vehicle class may be pooled. In the case of cars, utilities and buses the choice was between independent estimation by surface type and pooled estimation. In the case of the three truck classes, the choice was between four combinations of pooling or not pooling the observations in respect of different surface types and loading conditions. In addition to presenting the estimates under different conditions of pooling the observations, a discussion of the statistical significance of different sets of estimates, based on the log-likelihood ratio test, is included.

In making the final choice between different possible models, the following considerations were taken into account.

1. A model which pools observations is to be preferred because of its inherent simplicity and low data requirements for applications in different environments. Further, if the parameters to be estimated may be classified on a priori grounds between those that are sensitive to the basis of pooling (viz. surface type and loading condition) and those that are expected to be invariant, the pooled model would utilize the information more efficiently.

2. The selected model should have significant estimates as judged by the asymptotic t-statistic values.

3. The relative magnitudes and signs of the estimates should be in conformity with theoretical expectations.

4. Ideally, the selected model should not be statistically different from the other models.

On a priori grounds, we would expect the desired speed (VDESIR) parameter to be different for unpaved and paved surfaces. In addition, we would expect the perceived friction ratio (FRATIO) parameter to differ by surface traversed as well as by the loading condition for trucks. Since the value of FRATIO would already be low for unpaved surfaces, it was decided to separate the data on the basis of loading condition only in the case of trucks travelling on paved surfaces in intermediate levels of pooling.

The following tabulation lists the parameters estimated for each model. Note that the β, HPDRIVE, HPBRAKE, and ARVMAX parameters are estimated for all the models. Only the additional parameters are listed for each model:

Vehicle class	Model name	Parameters estimated
Cars, Utilities, Buses	Unpooled	VDESIR for the relevant surface FRATIO for the relevant surface
	Pooled	VDESIR for unpaved surfaces ∇DESIR or increment to above for paved surfaces FRATIO for unpaved surfaces ∇FRATIO or increment to above for paved surfaces
Trucks: light, medium, heavy and articulated	Unpooled	VDESIR for the relevant surface and loading FRATIO for the relevant surface and loading
	Loads Pooled	VDESIR for the relevant surface FRATIO for the relevant surface and empty vehicle ∇FRATIO or increment to the above for a loaded vehicle (applicable for paved surfaces only)
	Surfaces pooled	VDESIR for unpaved surfaces and relevant loading ∇DESIR or increment to above for paved surfaces FRATIO for unpaved surfaces and relevant loading ∇FRATIO or increment to above for paved surfaces
	Loads and surfaces pooled	VDESIR for unpaved surfaces and either loading ∇DESIR or increment to above for paved surfaces FRATIO for unpaved surfaces and either loading ∇FRATIO or increment to above for paved surfaces and empty vehicle ∇∇FRATIO or further increment for paved surfaces and loaded vehicle

A study of Tables 4.3, 4C.1 and 4C.2 reveals the following:

1. The parameter HPDRIVE changes very little between different models for the same vehicle class. The maximum difference is 14 percent for heavy trucks. The asymptotic t-statistics are uniformly significant.

2. The same is true of the parameter HPBRAKE except for articulated trucks and for the cases where the value was very high. Some t-statistics are poor.

3. ARVMAX and β parameters vary between models by about 25-30 percent. The t-statistics are uniformly significant.

Table 4C.1(a): Estimation results with surface type unpooled for cars, utilities and buses: estimates

Vehicle class	Model name	Surface	β	HPDRIVE	HPBRAKE	ARVMAX	VDESIR	FRATIO
Car	Unpooled	Unpaved	0.317	34.5	18.4	289.7	89.4	0.136
		Paved	0.212	34.3	19.2	204.0	93.0	0.250
Utility	Unpooled	Unpaved	0.346	44.1	28.9	263.8	84.5	0.129
		Paved	0.257	43.1	30.1	192.8	89.4	0.210
Bus	Unpooled	Unpaved	0.266	95.6	∞ [1]	215.7	70.0	0.096
		Paved	0.179	121.7	165.6	184.7	82.9	0.214

[1] The value was very large, nearly infinity.

Source: Analysis of Brazil-UNDP-World Bank highway research project data.

Table 4C.1(b): Some important statistics associated with the estimation

Vehicle class	Model	Surface	β	HP DRIVE	HP BRAKE	ARVMAX	VDESIR	FRATIO	σ_w^2	R^2	No. of obs.	SSR	D
Car	Unpooled	Unpaved	7.9	10.0	6.4	12.4	13.1	8.6	0.006812	0.86	112	0.72	0.064
		Paved	7.6	15.6	8.8	17.0	32.7	20.8	0.005503	0.92	104	0.54	0.054
Utility	Unpooled	Unpaved	6.9	11.0	5.6	10.6	9.9	6.1	0.008970	0.79	112	0.95	0.049
		Paved	8.6	18.7	7.8	13.0	21.8	17.5	0.006822	0.91	104	0.67	0.075
Bus	Unpooled	Unpaved	4.5	18.7	∞ [1]	9.9	9.7	4.6	0.026826	0.70	112	2.87	0.049
		Paved	3.9	31.0	7.3	10.7	20.9	12.6	0.016585	0.87	104	1.63	0.100

[1] The value was very large, nearly infinity.

Notes: a) The numbers in the parameter columns are the respective asymptotic t-statistics.

b) SSR denotes the sum of squared residuals.

c) D denotes the Kolmogorov-Smirnov D_2 statistic (see Appendix 4B).

d) For explanation of the variance, σ_w^2, see Chapter 3.

Source: Analysis of Brazil-UNDP-World Bank highway reseach project data.

Table 4C.2(a): Estimation results at various levels of pooling by surface type and loading condition for trucks: estimates

Class	Model	Loading condition	Surface	β	HPDRIVE	HPBRAKE	ARVMAX	VDESIR		FRATIO			
								Unpaved	Paved	Empty unpaved	Empty paved	Loaded unpaved	Loaded paved
Light and medium	Unpooled	Empty	Unpaved	0.314	84.1	131.3	206.0	78.8		0.116			
			Paved	0.213	82.0	∞ [1]	169.7		75.9		0.231		
		Loaded	Unpaved	0.332	95.9	257.1	192.7	68.9				0.094	
			Paved	0.234	97.7	170.9	160.5		75.4				0.158
	Loads Pooled	Both	Unpaved	0.350	94.0	174.6	206.9	78.8		0.115		0.115	
			Paved	0.262	95.3	180.3	174.3		78.0		0.241		0.162
	Surfaces pooled	Empty	Both	0.265	83.7	[1]	192.9	72.3	79.2	0.102	0.246		
		Loaded		0.298	97.1	203.2	183.3	65.9	80.4			0.086	0.168
Heavy	Unpooled	Empty	Unpaved	0.346	94.9	194.8	186.4	97.5		0.092			
			Paved	0.288	107.6	297.9	177.6		84.3		0.286		
		Loaded	Unpaved	0.363	107.9	268.7	193.9	64.4				0.166	
			Paved	0.215	111.2	231.0	147.1		78.7				0.166
	Loads pooled	Both	Unpaved	0.405	106.8	241.2	196.7	87.6		0.152		0.152	
			Paved	0.256	109.9	244.4	163.0		81.8		0.274		0.173
	Surfaces pooled	Empty	Both	0.322	104.7	290.8	182.1	87.6	89.7	0.073	0.302		
		Loaded		0.275	108.9	251.1	170.7	58.0	85.2			0.103	0.176
Articulated	Unpooled	Empty	Paved	0.207	185.5	265.6	148.9		82.3		0.175		
		Loaded	Paved	0.165	210.2	594.2	125.6		74.2				0.106
	Loads pooled	Both	Paved	0.220	203.9	616.3	141.3		80.1		0.169		0.112
	Surface pooled	Empty	Both	0.222	184.0	302.2	134.7	75.3	84.9	0.010	0.183		
		Loaded		0.236	205.4	847.1	123.4	42.9	79.7			0.028	0.116

[1] The value was very large, nearly infinity.
Source: Analysis of Brazil-UNDP-World Bank highway research project data.

Table 4C.2(b) Some important statistics associated with the estimation

Class	Model	Loading condition	Surface	β	HP-DRIVE	HP-BRAKE	ARVMAX	VDESIR Unpaved	VDESIR Paved	FRATIO Empty unpaved	FRATIO Empty paved	FRATIO Loaded unpaved	FRATIO Loaded paved	σ^2_w	σ^2_e	R^2	No. of obs.	SSR	D
Light and medium	Un-pooled	Empty	Unpaved	5.6	11.3	1.9	13.5	8.8		5.0				0.01407	0.03659	0.743	112	1.49	0.064
			Paved	6.8	28.3	= [1]/	15.5		36.2	-	17.7	-	-	0.00721	0.02304	0.893	104	0.71	0.087
		Loaded	Unpaved	6.1	20.8	2.0	11.8	8.8				4.3		0.01716	0.06128	0.793	111	1.80	0.058
			Paved	4.7	29.1	6.4	8.6		16.4				9.9	0.02184	0.03890	0.869	104	2.14	0.112
	Loads Pooled	Both	Unpaved	8.8	25.4	6.9	16.8	11.1		6.4				0.01613	0.04980	0.774	223	3.50	0.045
			Paved	9.4	38.1	8.2	13.8		30.0		13.0		-4.0	0.01423	0.03149	0.881	208	2.86	0.085
	Surfaces pooled	Empty	Both	9.1	24.3	[1]	23.0	17.2	1.9	7.8	7.8			0.01090	0.02969	0.867	216	2.28	0.070
		Loaded		8.3	34.7	6.4	15.1	12.0	2.8			5.0	4.1	0.01938	0.04995	0.863	215	4.01	0.083
Heavy	Un-pooled	Empty	Unpaved	3.9	10.3	1.7	11.1	3.7		2.1				0.01841	0.04150	0.729	86	1.47	0.089
			Paved	8.1	27.7	1.1	12.9		21.0		15.1			0.00736	0.01799	0.892	101	0.70	0.058
		Loaded	Unpaved	3.3	17.3	4.2	6.5	5.5				1.4		0.02727	0.05673	0.761	91	2.32	0.067
			Paved	3.2	24.2	7.5	6.8		9.8				6.9	0.04535	0.03757	0.835	103	4.40	0.111
	Loads pooled	Both	Unpaved	5.7	21.4	7.1	11.6	5.7		2.5				0.02314	0.04921	0.761	177	3.96	0.057
			Paved	6.7	35.4	10.2	11.5		18.8		9.8		-3.3	0.02518	0.03285	0.863	204	4.96	0.110
	Surfaces pooled	Empty	Both	8.7	23.9	1.4	19.4	8.2	0.2	4.1	8.8			0.01295	0.02744	0.863	187	2.32	0.070
		Loaded		5.5	32.1	8.0	10.3	9.7	3.3			1.9	1.3	0.03808	0.04100	0.828	194	7.08	0.083
Articulated	Un-pooled	Empty	Paved	4.5	26.5	5.9	15.3		19.2		8.8			0.01451	0.02439	0.814	84	1.13	0.08
		Loaded	Paved	2.3	23.8	2.3	9.7		13.6				4.8	0.04600	0.03748	0.829	85	3.63	0.10
	Loads pooled	Both	Paved	5.1	31.9	3.9	14.1		20.0		6.8		-2.0	0.03085	0.03424	0.824	169	5.00	0.090
	Surfaces pooled	Empty	Both	7.0	31.9	5.1	28.1	5.0	0.7	3.3	10.2			0.01093	0.02896	0.814	112	1.14	0.057
		Loaded		3.5	23.9	1.0	9.8	8.0	4.7			1.1	2.6	0.05030	0.03910	0.819	120	5.64	0.073

[1] The value was very large, nearly infinity.

Notes: a) the numbers in the parameter columns are the respective asymptotic t-statistics.

b) SSR denotes the sum of squared residuals.

c) D denotes the Kolmogorov-Smirnov D statistic (see Appendix 4B).

d) For explanation of the variances see Chapter 3.

Source: Analysis of Brazil-UNDP-World Bank highway research project data.

4. There are two anomalous results for the VDESIR parameter. In the case of light/medium and heavy trucks, the unpaved values are higher than paved values. This is contrary to theoretical expectations. However, three of the t-statistics are very low for the unpooled models.

5. The t-statistics are low for heavy and articulated truck FRATIO parameters in the unpooled cases.

6. As mentioned in the text of Chapter 4, for the pooled models, the signs and relative magnitudes of the estimates are in conformity with theoretical expectations. All the t-statistics are significant with a single exception.

Tests were performed to judge the statistical significance of the differences between different models. The appropriate statistical methodology to judge the significance of the difference between the pooled and unpooled runs for each vehicle class is the log-likelihood ratio test. This ratio is defined as follows:

$$\chi = 2 \ln (\text{likelihood ratio}) = n\left(\frac{\text{SSR of pooled run}}{\text{Sum of SSRs of unpooled runs}} - 1\right)$$

where   n = total sample size, and

SSR = sum of squared residuals for the appropriate regression.

The random variable χ as defined above is distributed as χ_f^2 with degrees of freedom, f, equal to the number of restricted parameters in the more constrained model. The SSR values are shown in Tables 4.3(b) and 4C.1(b) and 4C.2(b), and the critical values for the relevant χ_f^2 distributions are given below:

Degrees of freedom, f		4	5	6	7	9
Significance level	1%	9.49	11.07	12.59	14.07	16.92
	5%	13.28	15.09	16.81	18.48	21.67

In choosing the level of significance of the test two considerations were taken into account.

1. For practical reasons, the simplicity of the pooled model is strongly preferred.

2. Due to the large sample size at our disposal, the power of the significance test is high even when the level of significance chosen is stronger than the 5 or 1 percent level commonly used for small and intermediate sample sizes.

The test results are shown in Table 4C.3. From this table it is evident that the differences between unpooled and intermediate-pooled models are not significant. However, the difference between intermediate-pooled and pooled models are generally significant at traditional critical levels. Nonetheless, on grounds stated in the foregoing discussion, it is reasonable to accept models estimated by pooling observations by surface types as well as loading condition.

Table 4C.3:   Log-likelihood ratio tests

Vehicle class	Models compared			Number of restrictions	Value of log likelihood ratio
	Relatively unrestricted model	Restricted model	Case		
Car	Unpooled	Pooled		4	17.14
Utility	Unpooled	Pooled		4	8.00
Bus	Unpooled	Pooled		4	31.20
Truck:					
Light/ medium	Unpooled	Loads pooled	Unpaved	6	14.23
			Paved	5	0.73
		Surfaces pooled	Empty	4	7.85
			Loaded	4	3.82
	Loads pooled	Pooled		4	18.97
	Surfaces pooled	Pooled		7	23.98
Heavy	Unpooled	Loads pooled	Unpaved	6	7.94
			Paved	5	0.00
		Surfaces pooled	Empty	4	12.93
			Loaded	4	10.39
	Loads pooled	Pooled		4	28.62
	Surfaces pooled			7	7.70
Artic.	Unpooled	Loads pooled	Paved	5	8.52
	Surfaces pooled	Pooled		9	44.14

Source: Analysis of Brazil-UNDP-World Bank highway research project data.

APPENDIX 4D

ESTIMATION RESULTS BASED ON SPEED–SENSITIVE AVERAGE RECTIFIED SLOPE

This appendix is devoted to discussion of the results of the estimation of the steady-state speed model which uses the more complicated ARV formula (i.e., the speed-sensitive average rectified slope formulation). The principles underlying this formulation were discussed in Section 3.3.4. While computationally trivial, the additional effort needed to use the speed-sensitive version in practical applications is considerable in terms of data requirements. Specifically, the material type of the road surface has to be input which is not required elsewhere in the model. Thus it is of interest to investigate how the simpler version, of which the parameter estimates are presented in the main text of this chapter, compares with the speed-sensitive version. The comparison consists of three aspects. The first was to find out whether the two formulations of the ARVMAX parameter give rise to markedly different numerical estimates of parameters other than ARVMAX. The second was to compare explanatory power of the two versions in terms of the regression statistics. The final aspect was to compare speed predictions arrived at using the two versions for different groupings of speed observations by various speed-influencing factors for a heavy truck.

The estimation results of the speed-sensitive formulation are presented in Table 4D.1. This table is formatted identically as Table 4.3, with parameter estimates in part a of the table and the associated regression statistics in part b. A comparison of Tables 4.3(a) and 4D.1(a) reveals that the estimates of parameters other than ARVMAX do not change significantly in absolute magnitude, and their relative magnitude across the vehicle classes is preserved. In fact, the change in absolute magnitude is five percent or less. Turning next to a comparison of the explanatory power of the two versions of the speed model, it may be seen from Tables 4.3(b) and 4D.1(b) that the R^2 values and the standard errors of residuals of the two estimations are almost identical and that the simpler version is marginally better.

Finally, Table 4D.2 presents, for a heavy truck, the observed speeds, and the speed predictions using the different ARVMAX formulations, averaged over different groupings of the data points based on the road curvature, gradient, roughness and surface type, and vehicle load level. The differences between the two predictions are less than one percent in almost all the groupings. Further, there is no systematic trend in the relative magnitudes of the two predictions. Thus it may be concluded that the speed prediction model using the simple ARV formulation is the version to be preferred.

Table 4D.1(a): Estimation results of steady-state speed model for six vehicle classes: estimates

Vehicle class	β a	HPDRIVE metric hp b	HPBRAKE metric hp c	ARVMAX mm/s d	VDESIR (km/h) Unpaved Value e	VDESIR Paved Increment over unpaved value f	VDESIR Paved Value e + f	FRATIO Paved Unpaved unloaded or loaded g	FRATIO Paved Unloaded Increment over unpaved value h	FRATIO Paved Unloaded Value g + h	FRATIO Paved Loaded Increment over paved unloaded i	FRATIO Paved Loaded Value g+h+i
Car	0.288	37.3	22.8	283.8	80.7	18.5	99.3	0.128	0.143	0.271	–	–
Utility	0.322	45.2	34.2	269.6	76.3	19.9	96.2	0.122	0.103	0.225	–	–
Bus	0.290	113.9	222.6	243.1	68.1	26.6	94.7	0.100	0.137	0.237	–	–
Truck:												
Light/medium	0.321	95.6	196.6	227.8	69.1	13.2	82.4	0.106	0.153	0.259	-0.085	0.174
Heavy	0.338	109.3	265.8	214.6	68.7	22.7	91.4	0.103	0.199	0.302	-0.110	0.192
Artic.	0.264	201.9	500.0[1]	154.0	50.2	34.6	84.8	0.040[1]	0.141	0.181	-0.046	0.135

[1] These parameters were exogenously determined.
Source: Analysis of Brazil-UNDP-World Bank highway research project data.

Table 4D.1(b): Some important statistics associated with the estimation

Vehicle class	β a	HPDRIVE b	HPBRAKE c	ARVMAX d	VDESIR Unpaved e	VDESIR Increment for paved surface f	FRATIO Unpaved g	FRATIO Increment for paved Unloaded h	FRATIO Increment for paved Loaded i	σ^2_e	σ^2_w	R^2	Number of observations	SSR	D
Car	11.1	14.3	7.1	25.3	23.7	5.8	11.6	9.5	–	0.00683	0.0224	0.911	216	1.42	0.059
Utility	11.3	18.5	7.3	21.9	18.3	5.0	8.7	6.5	–	0.00838	0.0355	0.885	216	1.74	0.037
Bus	6.9	26.5	4.4	15.2	12.8	4.2	5.3	5.1	–	0.02504	0.0276	0.828	216	5.21	0.048
Truck:															
Light/medium	13.9	42.3	9.2	31.2	20.8	4.4	8.4	6.9	-3.6	0.01604	0.0405	0.861	431	6.77	0.055
Heavy	10.2	39.6	10.5	23.4	13.5	4.0	3.7	5.3	-3.0	0.02635	0.0369	0.846	381	9.80	0.069
Artic.	6.9	33.1	–	24.1	12.2	6.9	–	5.0	-1.4	0.03552	0.0365	0.811	231	7.99	0.070

[1] The numbers in the parameter columns are the respective asymptotic t-statistics.
[2] SSR denotes the sum of squared residuals.
[3] For explanation of variances, see Chapter 3.
Source: Analysis of Brazil-UNDP-World Bank highway research project data.

Table 4D.2: Average speed predictions for different groupings of data points (for heavy trucks)

Basis for grouping observations	Definition of group	Number of observations in group	Mean observed speed for group (km/h)	Mean predicted speed for group (km/h)	
				With simple ARV formulation	With speed-sensitive ARV formulation
Gradient (GR) in percent	GR < −4	94	54.13	54.21	54.06
	−4 ≤ GR < 3	192	53.09	53.36	53.54
	3 ≤ GR	95	29.69	30.03	29.89
Radius of curvature (RC) in m.	RC ≤ 100	71	33.54	33.57	33.43
	100 < RC < 250	121	46.03	45.90	45.85
	250 < RC	189	53.71	54.26	54.39
Surface type and roughness (QI) in QI counts	Paved: QI ≤ 80	180	54.73	54.67	54.49
	80 < QI	24	45.58	47.05	49.21
	Unpaved: QI ≤ 80	29	49.85	50.48	49.80
	80 < QI ≤ 130	74	43.29	43.28	43.59
	130 < QI	74	33.89	34.54	34.36
Surface type and loading condition	Paved : unloaded	101	59.14	60.41	60.54
	loaded	103	48.27	47.27	47.32
	Unpaved: unloaded	86	44.58	44.31	44.21
	loaded	91	36.52	37.50	37.47
All observations		381	47.51	47.75	47.77

Source: Analysis of Brazil–UNDP–World Bank highway research project data.

CHAPTER 5
Micro Non-Transitional Speed Prediction Model

As alluded to in Chapter 1, three speed prediction models were investigated in this study: the micro transitional and nontransitional models and the aggregate model. The micro models are based on detailed information on the road geometry, whereas the aggregate model is based on a representation of the actual road by two idealized road segments of positive and negative gradients (as described in detail in Chapter 7).

In comparing the two micro models, the latter relies on steady-state speed behavior alone, while the former also simulates transitional speed behavior involving vehicle acceleration and deceleration. While the micro non-transitional and aggregate models differ markedly in the level of detail of geometric information, both deal with steady-state speed prediction only. Therefore, of these three models the micro non-transitional may be regarded as the intermediate one with respect to both level of detail of input data and degree of accuracy.

Besides being a speed prediction method in its own right, the micro non-transitional model serves two other main purposes:

1. As a building block for the micro transitional model; and

2. As a reference for assessing the accuracy of the aggregate model.

For these reasons, the micro non-transitional model is presented before the other two models. The prediction procedure employed by the model is presented in Section 5.1, followed by a discussion in Section 5.2, in which steady-state conditions are compared with actual driver behavior which is transitional in nature.

5.1 PREDICTION PROCEDURE

Let L denote the length of a given road stretch, in meters. The micro non-transitional model proceeds by first dividing the road stretch into a number of subsections. Each subsection, denoted by s, has a length L_s (in meters) and is assumed to have uniform characteristics, i.e., constant slope (GR_s), radius of horizontal curvature (RC_s), superelevation (SP_s), and roughness (QI_s). Letting X_s denote the vector of road characteristics for subsection s, from Equation 3.43 in Chapter 3 the steady-state speed prediction for subsection s, VSS_s, is computed as a function of X_s:

$$VSS_s = VSS(X_s) \qquad (5.1)$$

The prediction of average journey speed or space-mean speed over the road stretch in the designated direction, denoted by SMS, is computed on the basis of the travel time the vehicle takes to traverse each subsection at the steady-state speed, VSS_s:

$$SMS = \frac{L}{\sum_s \frac{L_s}{VSS_s}} \qquad (5.2)$$

where the summation above is over all subsections. The schematic illustration in Figure 5.1 shows that the micro non-transitional model produces a speed profile which consists of "steps" corresponding to the steady-state speeds for the individual subsections.

The expression for SMS in Equation 5.2 above is a harmonic mean, which on some occasions is inconvenient to use. For clarity of expression, we shall often use the concept of "time per distance," which is the inverse of space-mean speed. The time per distance, τ_s, of the vehicle over the subsection s is thus the inverse of VSS_s, that is,

$$\tau_s = \frac{1}{VSS_s} \quad (s/m)$$

The time per distance, τ, of the vehicle over the roadway, is simply the weighted arithmetic mean of these times per distance. That is,

$$\tau = \frac{\sum_s \tau_s L_s}{L} \quad (s/m)$$

Since the space-mean speed for the roadway involves a harmonic mean and the time per distance for the roadway involves the simpler operation of arithmetic mean, some of the properties of aggregation procedures may be expressed more simply using the time per distance notion.

Further, the method to compute average time per distance over the roadway using the constant time per distance values of the homogenous subsections illustrates the general method of computing average consumption over the roadway of other resources which are directly proportional to the distance, for example, fuel consumption (Chapter 10) and tire wear (Chapter 11). However, since the concept of speed is more widely prevalent than that of "time per distance" we shall alternate between these two concepts depending on the context.

5.2 STEADY-STATE VERSUS TRANSITIONAL SPEED BEHAVIOR

If the homogeneous subsections were infinitely long, their steady-state speeds would closely approximate the actual speeds since the time the vehicle spends on making speed transitions from one subsection to the next is a negligible portion of the total journey time. However, in reality, the geometric characteristics of many roads do change over relatively short distances, so that the homogeneous subsections into

Figure 5.1: Illustration of micro non-transitional speed prediction model

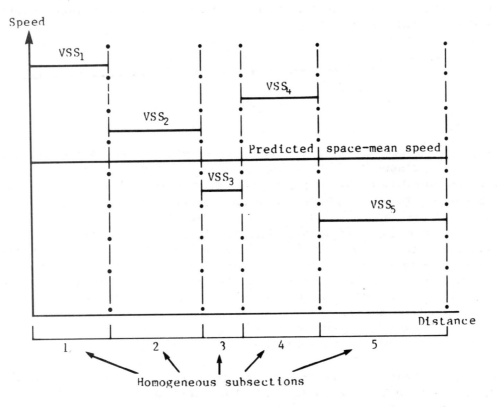

which the roads are divided become correspondingly short. In these instances, a relatively large portion of the vehicle journey is devoted to acceleration and deceleration and a relatively small portion to constant speed travel. In extreme cases, in which the homogeneous subsections are very short and road characteristics change dramatically from one subsection to the next (as commonly found in mountainous terrain) the vehicle may operate at the steady-state speed for a very small portion of the travel time.

Several previous investigators have employed steady-state speeds as a building block for simulating actual speed profiles.[1] However, with the exception of Sullivan (1976), the main emphasis of these studies has been placed on the simulation of traffic flow interaction effects, and relatively little effort has been devoted to capturing the fects of road geometric characteristics on transitional speed behavior. This latter point is the primary objective of the micro transitional speed prediction model. Before developing the transitional model, it is essential to understand the differences between the transitional and steady-state speed behavior which exist in a number of driving situations.

---

[1] Although nomenclature for steady-state speeds varies among researchers, the basic idea is essentially the same (Sullivan, 1977; Gynnerstedt, 1977; St. John and Kobett, 1978; Hoban, 1983; among others).

The steady-state speed profile assumes that: first, the vehicle can accelerate or decelerate at an infinite rate; and, second, the driver does not adjust the speed in anticipation of changes in the road characteristics ahead. In reality, however, drivers do see the road conditions that lie ahead and react to them. They may accelerate or decelerate within the engine power and braking capabilities of the vehicle so as to render the journey safe and economical (with respect to fuel consumption, wear and tear of tires and parts, etc.). Driver anticipation is discussed in more detail by means of typical examples in the following paragraphs.

Figure 5.2 shows a situation in which a vehicle makes a transition from a steep downhill grade to a steep uphill one (i.e., when there is a sag curve). The steady-state speeds for these subsections (VSS_s and VSS_{s+1}) are relatively low since they are dominated by the low maximum allowable downhill and maximum possible uphill speeds ($VBRAKE_s$ for subsection s and $VDRIVE_{s+1}$ for subsection s+1, respectively). However, before getting to the end of the negative-gradient subsection, the vehicle accelerates with the help of gravity so that when it arrives at the bottom of the negative slope, its speed approaches a maximum "safe" level. This high speed is carried into the positive-gradient subsection and attenuates toward the subsection's steady-state speed (VSS_{s+1}). This is a typical situation in which the driver achieves a savings in travel time as well as in fuel consumption by means of vehicle momentum.

Figure 5.3 illustrates the behavior of a vehicle negotiating a bend. The vehicle traverses three subsections: level-tangent (s-1), level-curved (s), and then level-tangent (s+1). As the vehicle moves from the tangent to curved subsection, its finite braking capability causes the vehicle to decelerate gradually (from VSS_{s-1} to VSS_s). Similarly, after leaving the curved subsection, its finite driving power enables the vehicle to gradually accelerate to the steady-state speed of the new tangent subsection (VSS_{s+1}).

A situation where the steady-state of a subsection is not reached is shown in Figure 5.4. The vehicle travels on a tangent road stretch where there is a steep uphill subsection (s) between two level subsections(s-1 and s+1). After maintaining a steady-state speed throughout subsection s-1 the vehicle slows down as it climbs uphill on subsection s. However, the length of the climb is not enough for the speed to drop to the steady-state value (VSS_s) when the vehicle enters the level subsection (s+1) and accelerates to a higher steady-state speed (VSS_{s+1}).

Another situation where a vehicle does not reach a steady-state speed of a subsection is illustrated in Figure 5.5 in which the vehicle climbs up a steep hill on a tangent subsection (s-1) at a slow speed and then accelerates as it enters a level-tangent subsection (s). Since this subsection is short, the vehicle does not have enough time to attain the steady-state speed (VSS_s) before it begins decelerating in anticipation of a sharp curve (subsection s+1).

Figure 5.2: Transitional speed situation 1: use of vehicle momentum on sag curve

(a) Vehicle speed profile

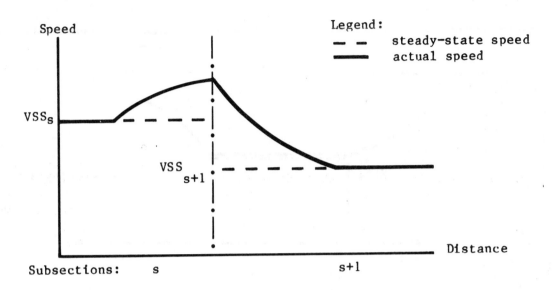

(b) Vertical road profile

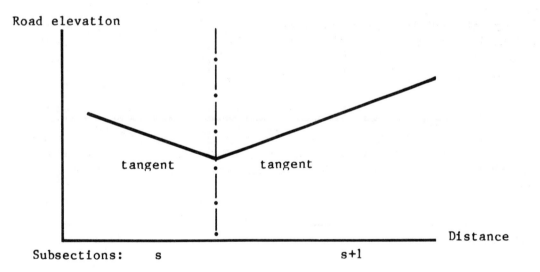

Figure 5.3: Transitional speed situation 2: negotiating a curve

(a) Vertical speed profile

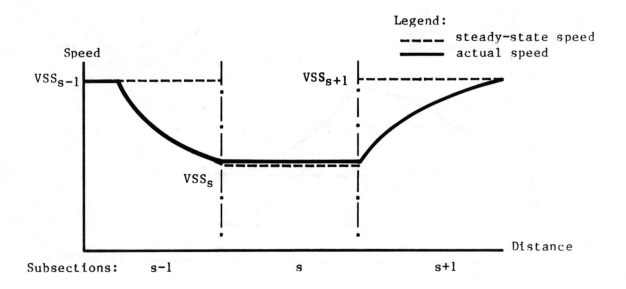

(b) Vertical road profile

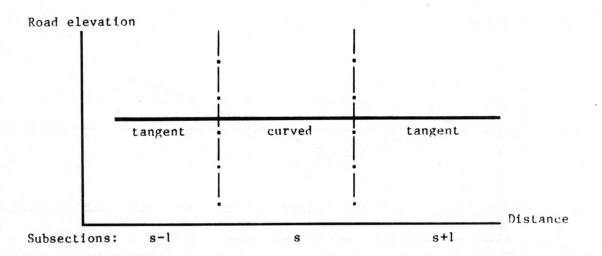

Figure 5.4: Transitional speed situation 3: climbing a short steep hill

(a) Vertical road profile

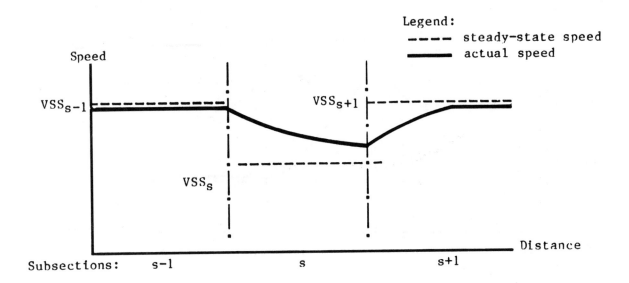

(b) Vertical road profile

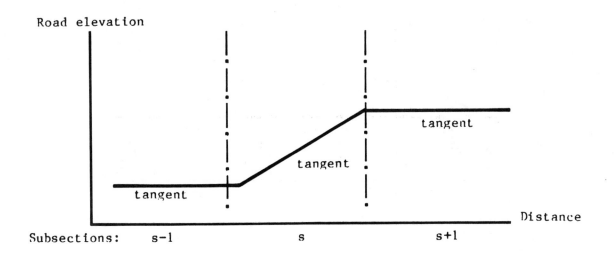

Figure 5.5: Transitional speed situation 4: anticipating curve while travelling at low speed

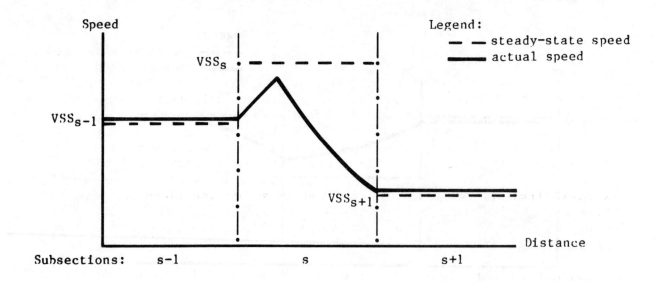

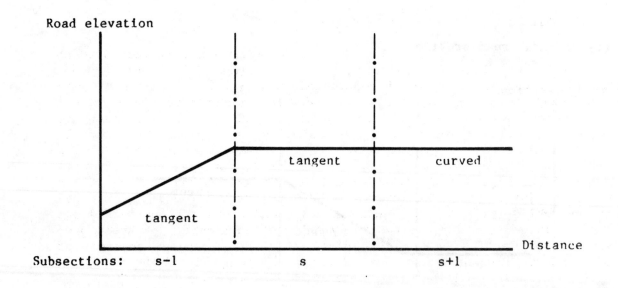

CHAPTER 6

Micro Transitional Speed Prediction Model

Although the micro transitional model employs the same detailed geometric information as the micro non-transitional counterpart, its logic is much more elaborate, since, from the discussion in the preceding chapter, transitional speed behavior is a complex phenomenon. While it is a method for predicting free speeds in its own right, the micro transitional model also serves in this study as a reference for assessing the accuracy of the other, less precise models. As a research contribution, the micro transitional model can be used as a building block for future work in simulating traffic flow interaction under congestion; it can also be used in future simulation of the wear of vehicle tires and parts.

This chapter is organized into four sections. The first section provides an overview of the simulation logic (6.1), then followed by a detailed exposition of the logic consisting of the backward and forward recursions (6.2 and 6.3). The final section (6.4) deals briefly with the empirical verification of the major driver-behavior assumptions employed.

6.1 OVERVIEW OF SPEED PROFILE SIMULATION

In reality, the speed profile of a vehicle along a road stretch is a continuous function of distance: for any given point along the road there is a well-defined speed associated with it. For practical purposes, however, it is not necessary to develop a continuous mathematical function for representing the speed profile. Rather, it is sufficient to predict speeds at closely-spaced points along the road. The intervals between these discrete points are called "simulation intervals." The speed at anyother point can then be predicted by interpolation. The accuracy of the speed profile simulated this way depends on the size of the simulation intervals. The interval of 100 meters was found to be satisfactory, while the 250-meter interval was found to be too coarse and the 50-meter interval did not appreciably improve the accuracy of speed prediction. In practice, the set of distance points generated consists of the standard 100-meter intervals and the boundary points of the homogeneous subsections, as illustrated schematically in Figure 6.1. Since the subsection boundary points need not coincide with the standard points, simulation intervals can be smaller than 100 meters. Also shown in Figure 6.1 is the "step" profile of the steady-state speeds for the homogeneous subsections (constructed in the manner described in Chapter 5). Each simulation interval is treated as a unit of analysis for which the entry and exit speeds are predicted.

The micro transitional model proceeds in two phases:

First, construct the "maximum allowable speed profile" which comprises the maximum allowable speeds at the discrete points. Besides

Figure 6.1: Simulation intervals and steady-state speeds

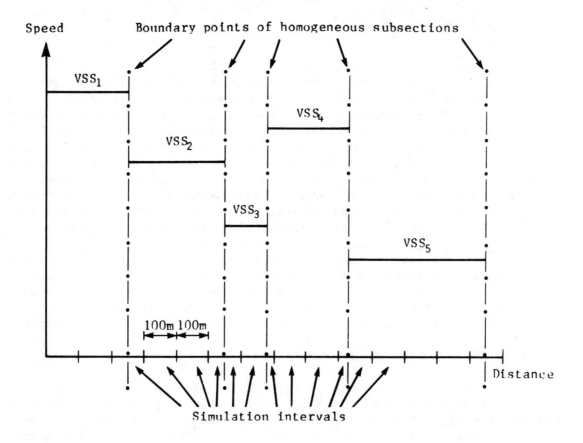

taking into account the speed constraints under steady-state conditions, this step involves making behavioral assumptions on the power usage and rates of acceleration and deceleration of the vehicle when the driver anticipates conditions of the road ahead. Driver anticipation includes braking while approaching a sharp horizontal curve, building vehicle momentum on a sag curve (i.e., downhill and then uphill), and so on (as discussed earlier in Chapter 5). Since the maximum allowable speed at any discrete point depends only on the oncoming road characteristics, this step proceeds from the downstream end to the upstream end of the road. Thus, it may be called "backward recursion."

Second, simulate the actual vehicle speed profile. This is performed by "forward recursion," i.e., proceeding from the upstream to the downstream end. The major behavioral assumption is that the driver employs the vehicle power according to a well-defined rule to travel as fast as possible subject to the constraint of the maximum allowable speed profile. The rule of power usage is given in Section 6.3.2.

As an illustration, Figure 6.2 shows the profiles of the road gradient and the steady-state, maximum allowable, and simulated speeds for a given road section, along with the profile of the observed speed of a test heavy truck in the Brazil study.

Figure 6.2: Profiles of vertical road gradient and steady-state, maximum allowable, simulated and observed speed for loaded Mercedes Benz 1113 heavy truck on hilly paved road

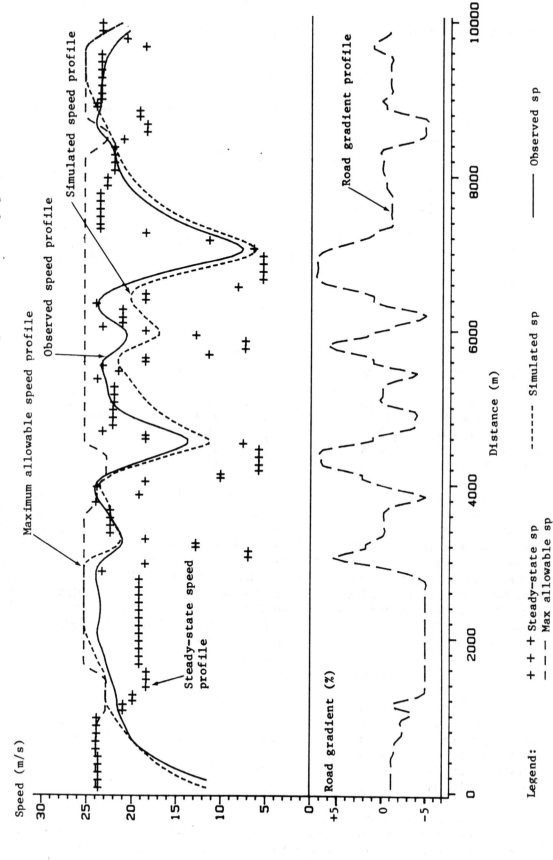

Legend: + + + Steady-state sp   ----- Simulated sp

           - - Max allowable sp   ——— Observed sp

Source: Analysis of Brazil-UNDP-World Bank highway research project data.

This simulation logic has the following desirable properties:

1. When the subsections become infinitely long, the simulated
    speed profile approaches the shape of the underlying "step"
    steady-state speed profile (as noted in Chapter 5). In
    other words, the speed predictions produced by the micro
    transitional and non-transitional models becomes closer as
    the subsection lengths get large.

2. Provided that the simulation intervals are relatively
    small, the simulated speed profile is not significantly
    affected by the size of the simulation intervals. The
    predicted journey speed over the road stretch approaches a
    constant value as the simulation intervals approach zero.
    This convergence property is analogous to Simpson's rule of
    numerical integration.

3. The assumptions of vehicle power usage are within the
    driving and braking power capabilities of the vehicle.

These properties become more apparent in the following sections
which provide a detailed description of the simulation logic.[1]

6.2 DETERMINATION OF MAXIMUM ALLOWABLE SPEED PROFILE: BACKWARD RECURSION

6.2.1 Maximum Allowable Entry Speed

Consider a simulation interval j, j = 1 to J, of length ΔL_j
in meters) as an analysis unit, as shown in Figure 6.3, along with its
adjacent intervals and the corresponding maximum allowable entry and exit
speeds. The objective of backward recursion is to determine the maximum
allowable entry speed for the interval, denoted by $VENMAX_j$ (in m/s), as
a function of the maximum allowable exit speed for the interval, denoted
by $VEXMAX_j$ (in m/s). By virtue of continuity of speed profiles, the
latter is equal to the maximum allowable entry speed of the next interval
downstream, j+1. Consequently, except for interval J at the downstream

---

[1] This logic draws upon the one developed by Sullivan (1977) with the
following improvements made:
a. Comprehensive validation of the simulation results based on an inte-
    grated set of experiments.
b. Detailed comparison of simulated and observed speed profiles to en-
    sure that all behavioral assumptions agree with actual driver
    behavior.
c. Incorporation of ride severity and desired speed constraints.
d. Explicit use of the steady-state speed as the foundation of the
    logic.
e. Use of small simulation intervals and simpler, but more generally
    applicable, driving rules to improve accuracy and facilitate under-
    standing and computation.

Figure 6.3:   Simulation intervals and maximum allowable entry and exit speeds

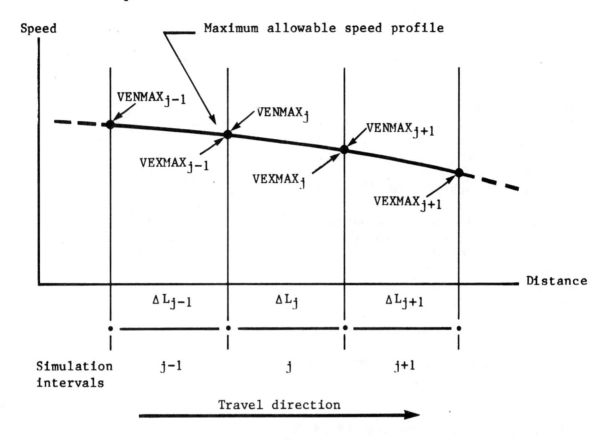

end, backward recursion proceeds from interval j+1 to interval j by setting:

$$VEXMAX_j = VENMAX_{j+1} \tag{6.1}$$

The maximum allowable exit speed at the downstream-end interval J, $VEXMAX_j$ must be given exogenously as a boundary condition.[2]

While the simulation logic provides for the vehicle's tendency to converge toward the steady-state speed, the latter may be exceeded in

---

[2] In general, this may be set to the interval's control speed, to be defined below.

transitional situations. However, the vehicle is not permitted at all times to exceed the control speed of the simulation interval, denoted by $VCTL_j$ (in m/s), and defined as:

$$VCTL_j = \exp(\sigma^2/2) \left[(VCURVE_j)^{-\frac{1}{\beta}} + (VROUGH_j)^{-\frac{1}{\beta}} + (VDESIR_j)^{-\frac{1}{\beta}} \right]^{-\beta} \quad (6.2)$$

where the term σ^2 and the constraining speeds $VCURVE_j$, $VROUGH_j$ and $VDESIR_j$ are as defined in Chapter 3, with the subscript j denoting simulation interval. As an additional constraint, the vehicle is not allowed to travel faster than the maximum speed from which it can safely decelerate before reaching a sharp curve or a location where speed restrictions apply. Finally, when the vehicle travels downhill it may not exceed the steady-state speed of the simulation interval (VSS_j), except where a momentum situation permits.

According to the speed restrictions outlined above, the maximum allowable entry speed for the simulation interval ($VENMAX_j$) can be defined as follows:

Positive effective gradient ($GR_j + CR_j \geq 0$) :

$$VENMAX_j = \min \left[VCTL_j; \; VDECEL_j \right] \quad (6.3a)$$

Negative effective gradient ($GR_j + CR_j < 0$):

$$VENMAX_j = \min \left[VCTL_j; \; VDECEL_j; \; \max (VSS_j; \; VMOMEN_j) \right] \quad (6.3b)$$

where $VDECEL_j$ = the maximum allowable speed at the beginning of the simulation interval from which it is possible to decelerate (at a given rate) to the maximum allowable exit speed ($VEXMAX_j$), in m/s; and

$VMOMEN_j$ = the maximum allowable speed at the beginning of the interval from which it is possible to accelerate under control to the maximum allowable exit speed, in m/s.

The maximum allowable "deceleration" speed, $VDECEL_j$ is computed as a kinematic function of the maximum allowable exit speed, $VEXMAX_j$ and a given constant deceleration rate, $DECEL_j$ (in m/s^2):

$$VDECEL_j = \max \left[(VEXMAX_j^2 + 2 \; DECEL_j \; \Delta L_j); \; 1 \right]^{0.5} \quad (6.4)$$

where $DECEL_j$ is defined in Section 6.2.2 as a behavioral function of the vehicle driving power and braking capabilities. In Equation 6.4, the minimum limit of 1 is imposed to insure that $VDECEL_j$ does not become too small. Similarly, the maximum allowable "momentum" speed, $VMOMEN_j$ is given by:

$$VMOMEN_j = \max \left[(VEXMAX_j^2 - 2\ AMOMEN_j\ \Delta L_j);\ 1 \right]^{0.5} \tag{6.5}$$

where $AMOMEN_j$, the acceleration rate governed by the vehicle braking capability, in m/s, is defined in Section 6.2.3 below. Like $DECEL_j$, $AMOMEN_j$ is assumed to be constant for the simulation interval.

It is useful to mention an asymptotic property of the maximum allowable entry speed, VENMAX. For a relatively long subsection which contains a number of identical simulation intervals, repeated application of Equation 6.3 will cause $VENMAX_j$ to converge to a constant value. For positive effective gradient ($GR_j + CR_j \geq 0$) $VENMAX_j$ converges to the control speed ($VCTL_j$) whereas for negative effective gradient ($GR_j + CR_j < 0$) it converges to the steady-state speed (VSS_j). An illustration of the convergence of the maximum allowable speed profile for both positive and negative effective gradients is given in Figure 6.4. For positive effective gradient, it is reasonable to regard the control speed as the "maximum allowable safe speed" rather than the steady-state speed. On a steep positive grade (say, more than 6 percent), the steady-state speed can be much lower than the control speed; this occurs when the vehicle does not have the necessary engine power to attain the latter speed. For negative gradient, however, it is reasonable to regard the steady-state speed as the "maximum allowable safe speed." On a subsection of steep negative grade, the braking power-limited speed, VBRAKE, tends to dominate so that the control speed converges to the steady-state speed.

6.2.2 Deceleration

The deceleration logic basically assumes that the driver employs a "desired" deceleration rate when the vehicle is unencumbered by its driving and braking capabilities; otherwise the deceleration rate is determined on the basis of the used driving or braking power (HPDRIVE or HPBRAKE), whichever is applicable. Graphs of the deceleration rate ($DECEL_j$) and vehicle power (HP_j) plotted against the effective gradient ($GR_j + CR_j$) in Figure 6.5 illustrates the deceleration logic. Mathematically, the deceleration rate is expressed as:

$$DECEL_j = \min \left[\max (\ DDESIR_j;\ DDRIVE_j);\ DBRAKE_j \right] \tag{6.6}$$

where $DDESIR_j$ = the "desired" deceleration rate, in m/s^2;

           $DDRIVE_j$ = the deceleration rate governed by the used driving power (HPDRIVE), in m/s^2; and

           $DBRAKE_j$ = the deceleration rate governed by the used braking power (HPBRAKE), in m/s^2.

Figure 6.4:   Convergence of maximum allowable speed profile

(a)   Subsection with gentle positive gradient(s) followed by a sharp
      curve   (s+1)

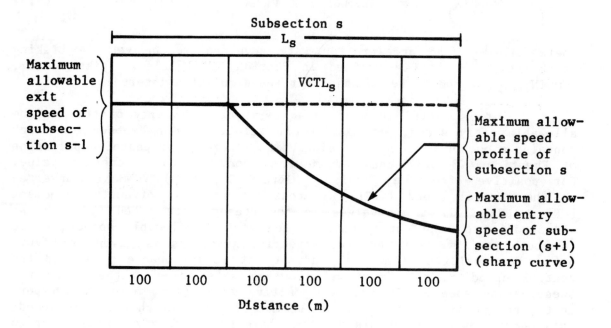

(b)   Subsection with steep negative gradient(s) followed by a tangent
      positive grade (s+1)

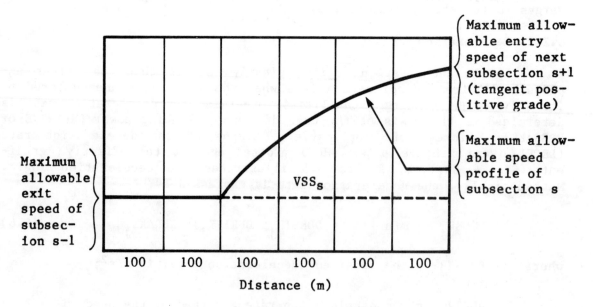

Travel direction

Figure 6.5: **Relationships between acceleration and deceleration rates, power and adjusted gradient**

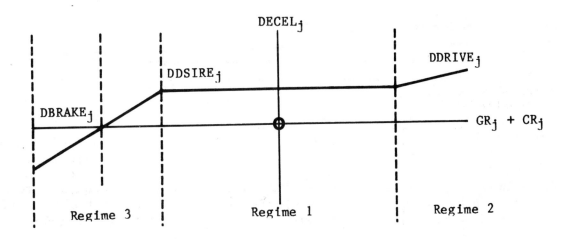

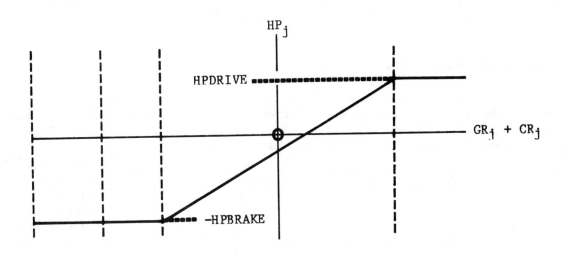

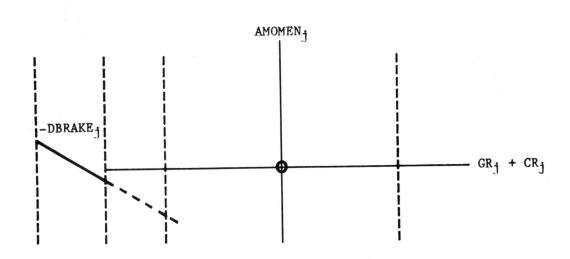

The deceleration rates, $DDESIR_j$, $DDRIVE_j$ and $DBRAKE_j$, are further elaborated in terms of three regimes of road gradient, as follows.

Regime 1: moderate grade (positive and negative)

In this regime, the vehicle power employed at the desired deceleration rate, HP_j, falls within the vehicle driving and braking capabilities, i.e.,

$$-HPBRAKE < HP_j < HPDRIVE$$

For simplicity, the desired deceleration rate, $DDESIR_j$ is assumed to be constant for a given vehicle class; values obtained from a field experiment in the Brazil study (Zaniewski et al., 1980) are given below (in m/s^2):

Car	0.6
Utility or bus	0.5
Truck	0.4

Regime 2: steep positive grade

The desired deceleration rate, $DDESIR_j$, could not be used, since the required power would exceed the maximum used driving power, HPDRIVE (i.e., $HP_j > HPDRIVE$). Therefore, the deceleration rate that can be used is that determined by HPDRIVE, as follows:

$$DDRIVE_j = -\frac{736\ HPDRIVE}{m'\ VAVG_j} + \frac{m}{m'}(GR_j + CR_j) + \frac{A\ VAVG2_j}{m'} \qquad (6.7)$$

where[3] $VAVG_j = 0.5\ (VENMAX_j + VEXMAX_j)$

$VAVG2_j = 0.5\ (VENMAX_j^2 + VEXMAX_j^2)$

and the other terms are defined before. For simplicity, the values of the effective vehicle mass (m') used in determining the rolling resistance coefficients (Appendix 2A) are also employed in the simulation logic, even though they should be higher when the vehicle is in low gear (as discussed in Chapter 2). The values of the effective vehicle mass are compiled in Table 1A.2. In this regime, we have $DDRIVE_j > DDESIR_j$, meaning that the full driving force of the engine is being exerted but the vehicle is still losing speed at a rate faster than would be desirable to the driver.

---

[3] Since $VENMAX_j$ is unknown but needed to compute $VAVG_j$, it is necessary to employ an iteration procedure for determining $VENMAX_j$, as described in Section 6.2.4.

Regime 3: steep negative grade

Like regime 2, the desired deceleration rate, $DDESIR_j$, could not be used, but for a different reason: the required power would violate the vehicle braking capacity constraint (i.e., $HP_j < -HPBRAKE$). Consequently, the feasible deceleration rate is determined by HPBRAKE:

$$DBRAKE_j = \frac{736 \text{ HPBRAKE}}{m' \text{ VAVG}_j} + \frac{m}{m'}(GR_j + CR_j) + \frac{A \text{ VAVG2}_j}{m'} \qquad (6.8)$$

As shown in Figure 6.5, in this regime the driver is applying the used braking power (HPBRAKE), although the vehicle is still decelerating at a rate slower than desirable.

6.2.3 Downhill Momentum Acceleration

As discussed in Chapter 5, when the vehicle approaches the bottom of a steep negative grade, the driver can save both fuel and travel time by building up the vehicle momentum to the highest feasible level at the bottom of the hill. In building the momentum, we assume that the driver utilizes the used braking power, HPBRAKE. This permits acceleration to begin the earliest.[4] A smaller braking power would result in a delayed onset of acceleration, and, hence, longer travel time. The downhill momentum acceleration, AMOMEN, is given by:

$$AMOMEN_j = \max\left[0; -\frac{736 \text{ HPBRAKE}}{m \text{ VAVG}_j} - \frac{m}{m'}(GR_j + CR_j) + \frac{A \text{ VAVG2}_j}{m'}\right] \qquad (6.9)$$

where the limit of zero is imposed to indicate that negative $AMOMEN_j$ is irrelevant to downhill momentum situations. Comparing the above equation with Equation 6.8, it can be seen that $DBRAKE_j = -AMOMEN_j$ when $AMOMEN_j$ is positive. This means that whenever a downhill momentum situation occurs, we have $DECEL_j = DBRAKE_j = -AMOMEN_j$, and, consequently, the maximum allowable "deceleration" and "momentum" speeds become equal ($VDECEL_j = VMOMEN_j$).

6.2.4 Iteration Procedure

As mentioned above, the maximum allowable exit speed of the simulation interval ($VENMAX_j$) is the sought after unknown quantity that is also used in computing the acceleration and deceleration rates. Thus, an iteration procedure is employed in determining VENMAX, as shown schematically in Figure 6.6. First, a trial value of $VENMAX_j$ is set equal

---

[4] This assumption was verified in comparison between simulated and observed profiles of speed and vehicle power, as presented in Section 6.4.

Figure 6.6:   **Iteration procedure for determining maximum allowable exit speed, VENMAX$_j$**

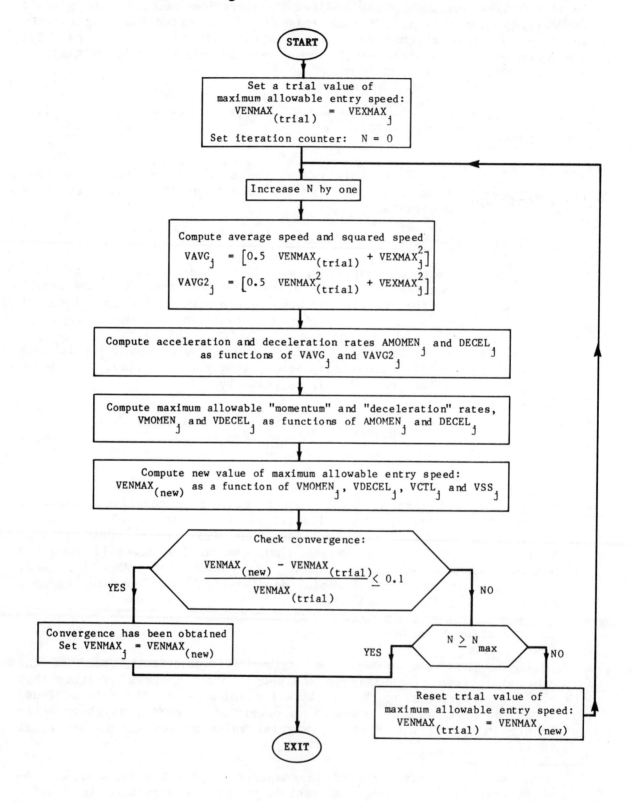

to $VEXMAX_j$. From this trial value, denoted by VENMAX(trial), a series of speed, acceleration and deceleration quantities are computed leading to a new value of VENMAX. This new value, denoted by VENMAX(new), is compared with the existing trial value. If the difference is less than 10 percent, convergence is considered to be obtained and VENMAX(new) is taken as the solution. Otherwise, the process is repeated with the new trial value of VENMAX set equal to VENMAX(new). Based on 100-meter simulation intervals, it was found from numerical testing that convergence could be obtained within few iterations. However, a limit of N_{max} is imposed to prevent the possibility of looping. Values of 4 or 5 for N_{max} was found to be adequate.

6.3 SIMULATION OF ACTUAL SPEED PROFILE: FORWARD RECURSION

6.3.1 Exit Speed

In the actual speed profile simulation, the general behavioral assumption is that the driver uses the vehicle power according to a well-defined rule and proceeds as fast as possible provided that the maximum allowable speed is not exceeded. Again, consider the simulation interval j, j = 2 to J, its adjacent intervals, and the corresponding entry and exit speeds as depicted schematically in Figure 6.7. The objective of the forward recursion is to determine the exit speed, denoted by VEX_j (in m/s) as a function of the entry speed, denoted by VEN_j (in m/s), for interval j. The entry speed for the current simulation interval, VEN_j, is equal to the exit speed of the preceding interval

Figure 6.7: Simulation intervals and entry and exit speeds

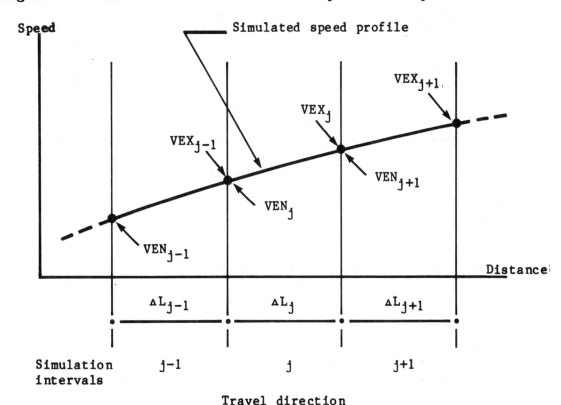

upstream, VEX_{j-1}. The forward recursion proceeds from interval $j-1$ to j by setting:

$$VEN_j = VEX_{j-1} \qquad (6.10)$$

The entry speed for the first simulation interval, however, must be specified exogenously as a boundary condition.[5]

The formulas for computing the exit speed for simulation interval j (VEX_j) are given separately for positive and negative adjusted gradients below.

Case I: negative effective gradient ($GR_j + CR_j < 0$)

In this relatively straightforward case, the formula is:

$$VEX_j = \min \left[VEXMAX_j; \; VPOWER_j \right] \qquad (6.11)$$

where $VEXMAX_j$ = the maximum allowable exit speed for the simulation interval (as determined in the backward recursion phase); and

$VPOWER_j$ = the speed at the end of the interval based on a constant acceleration rate $APOWER_j$, in m/s, as given below:

$$VPOWER_j = \max \left[(VEN^2_j + 2 \; APOWER_j \; \Delta L_j); \; 1 \right]^{0.5} \qquad (6.12)$$

where VEN_j = the entry speed for the interval, in m/s; and

$APOWER_j$ = the acceleration rate resulting from vehicle power $HPRULE_j$ defined in Section 6.3.2, in m/s^2.

As before, the limit of 1 m/s is imposed in the above formula to ensure that $VPOWER_j$ does not become too low. Examples of various possible speed profiles involving negative effective gradient are illustrated with annotations in Figure 6.8.

Case II: positive effective gradient ($GR_j + CR_j \geq 0$)

Separate formulas are provided for subcases of positive effective gradient.

---

[5] In the absence of information on the road conditions upstream, the steady state speed for the interval, VSS_1, could be used.

Figure 6.8: Examples of possible speed profiles for negative effective gradient

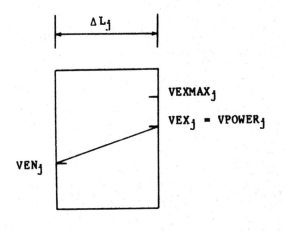

(a) Gentle grade, high $VEXMAX_j$. The vehicle accelerates to end of the simulation interval under $HPRULE_j$ unrestricted by $VEXMAX_j$

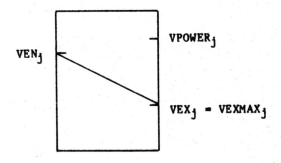

(b) Gentle grade, low $VEXMAX_j$. The vehicle has sufficient power to accelerate, but is forced to decelerate to $VEXMAX_j$.

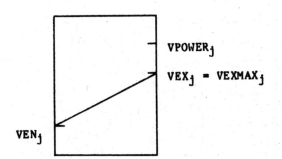

(c) Steep grade, moderate $VEXMAX_j$. The vehicle is accelerating but its rate of acceleration is restricted by $VEXMAX_j$.

Case II.A: $VEXMAX_j < VSS_j$

The formula for this case is the same as for Case I:

$$VEX_j = \min \left[VEXMAX_j; \; VPOWER_j \right] \tag{6.13}$$

Examples of possible speed profiles arising in this case provided in Figure 6.9.

Case II.B: $VEXMAX_j \geq VSS_j$

This case is more complicated than cases I and II.A since provisions must be made to insure convergence toward the steady-state speed, VSS_j. Formulas are provided separately for convergence from above ($VEN_j \geq VSS_j$) and below ($VEN_j < VSS_j$). For $VEN_j \geq VSS_j$, the formula is:

$$VEX_j = \min \left[VEXMAX_j; \; \max (VSS_j; \; VPOWER_j) \right] \tag{6.14}$$

and examples of possible speed profiles are given in Figure 6.10. For $VEN_j < VSS_j$, we have the following formula:

$$VEX_j = \min \left[\; VSS_j; \; VPOWER_j \right] \tag{6.15}$$

and examples of possible speed profiles shown in Figure 6.11.

6.3.2 Power Usage

This section provides the definition of $HPRULE_j$, the vehicle power used in computing $VPOWER_j$. The rule of vehicle power usage may be described briefly as follows. If the vehicle enters the simulation interval at a speed higher than the steady-state speed (i.e., $VEN_j \geq VSS_j$) it is assumed to decelerate toward the latter under the power equal to that needed to maintain the steady-state speed itself. Conversely, if the vehicle enters the interval at a speed lower than the steady-state (i.e., $VEN_j < VSS_j$) it is assumed to accelerate toward the latter under a power which is dependent on the road gradient but always within the bounds imposed by the maximum driving and braking powers. In the following paragraphs, formulas are provided for the cases with $VEN_j \geq VSS_j$ and $VEN_j < VSS_j$.

Case of $VEN_j \geq VSS_j$

This case applies only to positive effective gradient ($GR_j + CR_j \geq 0$) since VEN_j is always smaller than or equal to VSS_j when the effective gradient is negative. When VEN_j is greater than VSS_j.

Figure 6.9: Examples of possible speed profiles for positive effective gradient (with VERMAX$_j$ $\geq$ VSS$_j$)

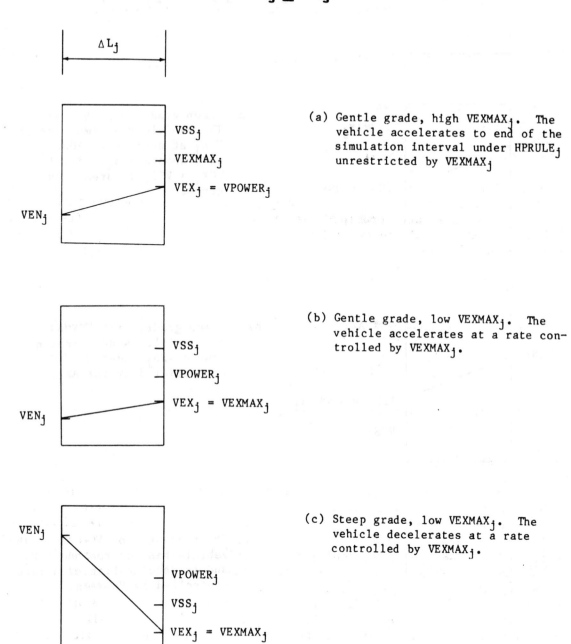

(a) Gentle grade, high VEXMAX$_j$. The vehicle accelerates to end of the simulation interval under HPRULE$_j$ unrestricted by VEXMAX$_j$

(b) Gentle grade, low VEXMAX$_j$. The vehicle accelerates at a rate controlled by VEXMAX$_j$.

(c) Steep grade, low VEXMAX$_j$. The vehicle decelerates at a rate controlled by VEXMAX$_j$.

Figure 6.10: Examples of possible speed profiles for positive effective gradient (with $VEXMAX_j > VSS_j$ and $VEN_j > VSS_j$)

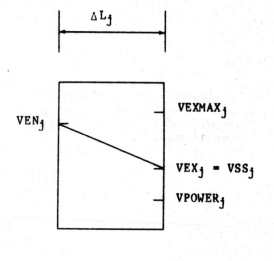

(a) Steep grade, high $VEXMAX_j$. The vehicle has almost reached VSS_j at entry but $VPOWER_j$ undershoots VSS_j. Setting $VEX_j = VSS_j$ insures convergence.

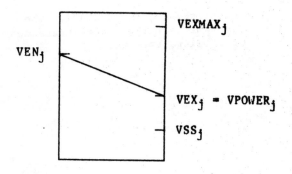

b) Steep grade, high $VEXMAX_j$. The vehicle is decelerating toward VSS_j under $HPRULE_j$ unrestricted by $VEXMAX_j$.

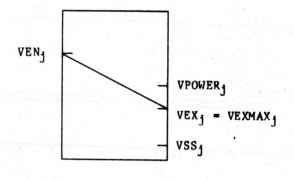

(c) Steep grade, low $VEXMAX_j$. The vehicle has not reached VSS_j and is decelerating at a rate controlled by $VEXMAX_j$.

Figure 6.11: Examples of possible speed profiles for positive effective gradient (with VEXMAX$_j$ > VSS$_j$ and VEN$_j$ < VSS$_j$)

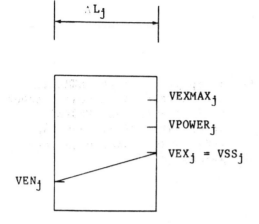

(a) Gentle grade, high VEXMAX$_j$. The vehicle has almost converged to VSS$_j$ at entry but overshoots VSS$_j$. Setting VEX$_j$ = VSS$_j$ insures convergence.

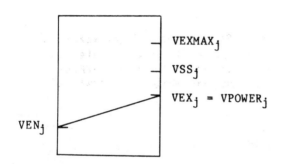

(b) Gentle grade, high VEXMAX$_j$. The vehicle is accelerating under HPRULE$_j$ toward VSS$_j$, unrestricted by VEXMAX$_j$.

the vehicle has a tendency to decelerate toward VSS$_j$, and the vehicle power is given by:

$$HPRULE_j = HPSS_j \tag{6.16}$$

where   HPSS$_j$ = the driving power required to sustain the steady-state speed of the simulation interval, given by:

$$HPSS_j = \frac{1}{736} \left[m \ g \ (GR_j + CR_j) \ VSS_j + A \ VSS_j^3 \right] \tag{6.17}$$

The above equation provides the largest possible driving power the driver can use while still guaranteeing deceleration toward the steady-state speed (when the subsection is infinitely long). The maximum used driving power, HPDRIVE does not guarantee convergence, since it is greater than $HPSS_j$ by virtue of the inequality $VDRIVE_j > VSS_j$.

Case of $VEN_j < VSS_j$

In this case, the vehicle has a tendency to accelerate toward the steady-state speed. The power usage is defined as follows:

$$HPRULE_j = \min \left[HPDRIVE; \max (HPGRAD - HPBRAKE) \right] \qquad (6.18)$$

where $HPGRAD_j$ = the used driving power modified for the effect of the effective gradient, given by:

$$HPGRAD_j = HPDRIVE + \frac{m\ g\ (GR_j + CR_j)\ VAVG_j}{736} \qquad (6.19)$$

The graphs of $HPRULE_j$ plotted against the effective gradient are shown schematically in Figure 6.12 for both $VEN_j \geq VSS_j$ and $VEN_j < VSS_j$ cases. In these graphs, the road characteristics other than the gradient (GR_j) are held constant. For the case $VEN_j \geq VSS_j$, the vehicle power ($HPRULE_j = HPSS_j$) increases with the effective gradient and asymptotically approaches the used driving power, HPDRIVE, when the effective gradient becomes large.

For the case $VEN_j < VSS_j$, the driver is assumed to apply the used driving power ($HPRULE_j = HPDRIVE$) when the effective gradient is positive ($GR_j + CR_j \geq 0$). When the effective gradient is negative, the driver is assumed to apply smaller driving power than HPDRIVE (but not smaller than -HPBRAKE). The power reduction (equal to HPDRIVE - $HPGRAD_j$) is such that, for moderately steep negative grades with $HPGRAD_j > -HPBRAKE$, the acceleration rate would equal the rate under full power HPDRIVE when the effective gradient is zero. However, for steep negative grades with $HPGRAD_j < -HPBRAKE$, this acceleration rate cannot be sustained and a higher rate must be used as the driver is constrained by the used braking power, HPBRAKE.

6.4 VERIFICATION OF ACCELERATION, DECELERATION AND POWER USAGE LOGIC

The relationships for computing the vehicle deceleration rate ($DECEL_j$), downhill momentum acceleration rate ($AMOMEN_j$), and power ($HPRULE_j$) were developed broadly in the following manner. First, preliminary relationships were constructed based on the results of a review of literature (Sullivan, 1977; Gynnerstedt, et al., 1977; St. John and Kobett, 1978; among others), and conversations with truck drivers. Second, profiles of the vehicle speed, acceleration, and power produced

Figure 6.12: Vehicle power versus effective gradient

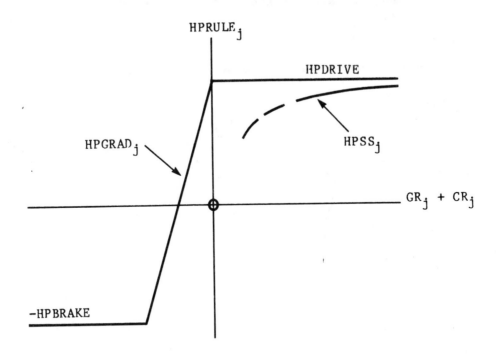

and the simulation logic were compared with those derived from observation of the test vehicles traversing several 10-km road sections. Third, modifications were made to the behavioral assumptions after major discrepancies between the simulation and observation were found. A major modification worth mentioning involved the initial assumption on extensive use of coasting in neutral (i.e., $HPRULE_j$ = 0) in both uphill and downhill travel, as employed by Sullivan (1976). However, the test vehicle data revealed that the drivers generally employed: (i) the used braking power, HPBRAKE, when accelerating in a downhill momentum situation, and (ii) the used driving power, HPDRIVE, when decelerating toward the the steady-state speed on a steep uphill grade. To get an idea of how well the acceleration, deceleration and power usage assumptions approximate reality, Figure 6.13 compares profiles of simulated and observed acceleration and power for one of the test vehicles (Mercedes Benz 1113 heavy truck) traversing a hilly paved road section. The profile of the gradient of the road is also shown in the figure.

Figure 6.13:   Profiles of road gradient and observed and simulated power and acceleration for a loaded heavy truck on a paved hilly road

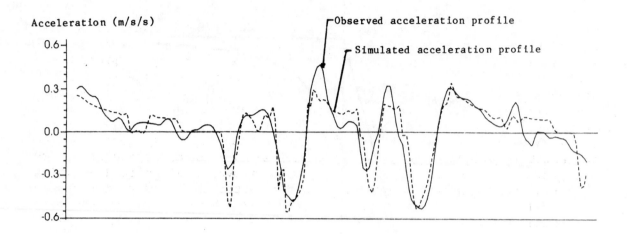

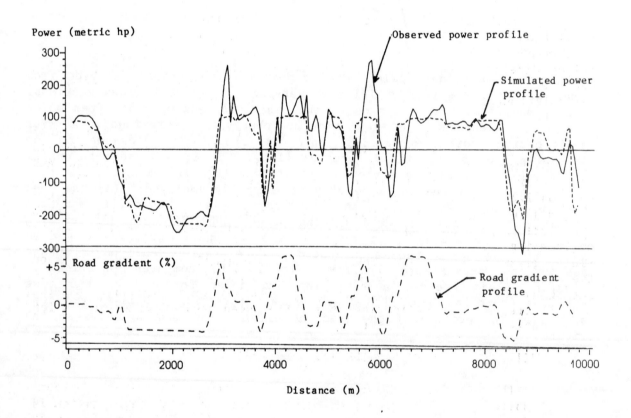

Source: Analysis of Brazil–UNDP–World Bank highway research project data.

Aggregate Prediction Model

The two micro models for predicting speeds discussed so far need detailed information regarding geometric alignment and surface condition, and in turn they can provide a whole array of speed predictions across the length of the section under consideration. While such a rich set of predictions is appropriate for handling minor geometric improvements (for example, to eliminate severely sharp bends), it would be not only superfluous but also unwieldy for policy-level decisions where the emphasis is placed on sensitivity of the average speed to broad changes in geometric alignment and surfacing standards. Hence, we sought a simpler model for predicting the average speed over a given roadway which requires only aggregate information on road attributes, while at the same time, retains as much as possible the desirable properties of the more elaborate models, namely, predictive accuracy, policy-sensitivity, extrapolative ability, and local adaptability.

The "aggregation issue" arises from the fact that the micro prediction models represent a non-linear function of road attributes. This means that the required aggregate speed prediction cannot be obtained directly from the average attributes of the roadway in question[1] but must be derived from a method that properly accounts for the mathematical properties of the prediction models themselves.

A discussion of some of the important approaches to the aggregation issue is taken up in the next section. The discussion motivates the selection, on a priori grounds, of the "integration" approach, and the various aggregation methods under this approach are described in Section 7.2. Finally, a detailed description of the recommended aggregation method is given in Section 7.3. Appendix 7A gives a step-by-step procedure to compute aggregate geometric descriptors starting from the engineering profile of a roadway, along with an illustrative example. Since, as will become apparent, the chosen aggregation method relies on the micro non-transitional prediction model, the discussion of issues relating to validation of the aggregation method is incorporated in the overall treatment of validation of all the speed prediction models, which constitutes the subject matter of Chapter 8.

7.1 REVIEW OF ALTERNATIVE AGGREGATION METHODS

The importance of aggregation was discussed above in the context of speed and travel time prediction. More generally, aggregation is equally important in the context of prediction of various components of vehicle operating costs, especially fuel consumption and tire wear.

---

[1] This is the "naive" method as discussed in Section 7.2.

Figure 7.1: Schematic display of alternative aggregation approaches and methods

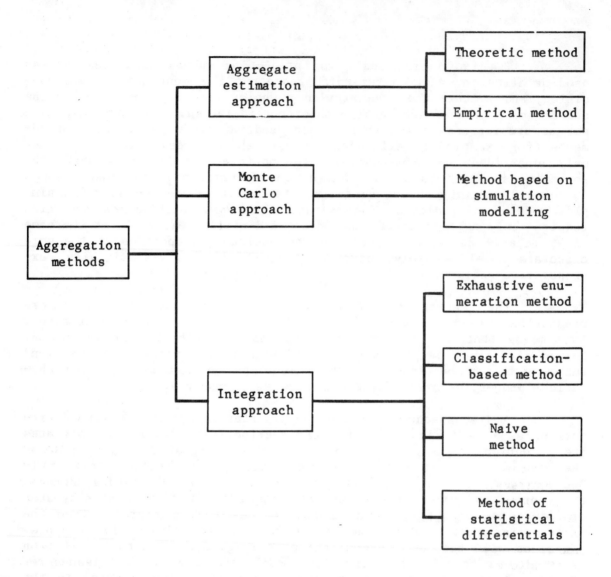

Because of its pervasive importance, some methodological issues regarding aggregation will be discussed at some length. For excellent discussions of the aggregation issue, see Fisher (1969) and Koppelman (1975).

As shown in Figure 7.1, there are three major approaches to aggregate prediction. First, one can estimate a prediction equation directly at the level of aggregation desired. This approach may be termed the aggregate estimation approach. Second, one can employ Monte Carlo simulation to generate predictions from the micro transitional model; the predictions can then be used to estimate an aggregate model. Finally, one may use the corresponding estimation equations derived at a more disaggregate level to arrive at disaggregate predictions and aggregate them explicitly. This approach may be referred to as the integration approach. We shall discuss some of the important methods which fall under these three groupings, in turn.

The ideal method under the aggregate estimation approach would be an "aggregate theoretical" one. Analogies for such a method from other disciplines are general properties of matter in physics and macro-economics. In the context of speed prediction, such a method would entail direct specification of a theoretical model of average speed as a function of average and more detailed information of geometric and surface attributes of a roadway. Given the complex and dynamic nature of vehicle motion it is unlikely that such a model can be specified in a manageable aggregate form.

A second method under the aggregate estimation approach is a purely empirical procedure where a simple, generally linear, equation relating average speed to various speed-influencing factors is estimated. This method has been followed in the TRRL Kenya study (Hide et al., 1975), and in the RUCS India study (CRRI, 1982). The method is easy to use and gives satisfactory predictions within the range of observed variation of selected factors, but is subject to the criticisms made in the context of steady-state speed modelling in Chapter 3.

The Monte Carlo approach, which entails a method based on simulation modelling, involves three steps. First, one starts with a large sample of detailed road or network profiles; these could be profiles of real roads or artificially generated. For each of these profiles, various aggregate indices that characterize the average alignments and surface conditions would be computed. Second, the micro transitional prediction model would be used to obtain detailed speed predictions from which average space-mean speeds would be computed for each road profile. The final step would be to estimate a model specification with the roadway indices as independent variables and the average space-mean speed as the dependent variable.

This approach has considerable appeal. In fact, it was the basis of an aggregation procedure developed during the earlier phase of the Brazil-UNDP-World Bank research project. However, it was not adopted because the underlying disaggregate speed prediction models were found to be unsatisfactory. (For details regarding this phase of the research project, see GEIPOT (1982, Volume 4)).

The difficulties associated with this approach relate to the sampling and the estimation steps. Since the sampling units are entire road profiles, generating a wide-ranging sample of the population of road profiles is an overwhelming task. More important, in the estimation step, it is not easy to specify a model form that possesses the desirable properties of the micro models mentioned above. Thus, it was decided first to explore the simpler methods belonging to the integration approach. Since, as will be described shortly, a satisfactory method was found in that approach, the Monte Carlo approach was not followed through. However, as part of the overall validation strategy, this approach was used to examine the structure of numerical errors introduced by various integration methods.

The third approach to aggregation, the integration approach, conceptually treats road attributes as if they were random variables of known distribution. The required space-mean speed is predicted as the inverse of the average time per distance over the roadway. The latter, in turn, is predicted as the expectation of the time distance function over the distribution of the road attributes. The name of this approach derives from the fact that taking expectation of a function over the distribution of its arguments amounts to mathematical integration. However, as will be seen, "mathematical integration" has only a conceptual connotation; this is because exact integration which produces a closed form solution can usually be accomplished only under highly restricted assumptions and is therefore rarely feasible in practice. The integration methods that will be discussed subsequently are generally approximate methods of taking expectation.

7.2 AGGREGATE SPEED PREDICTION BASED ON INTEGRATION APPROACH

Because of certain mathematical restrictions that will be elaborated below, the integration approach has found its natural applications in the prediction of consumer demand (Theil, 1955; Green, 1964; Gupta, 1969; and Koppelman, 1975). For purposes of aggregate speed prediction, the integration approach has two main advantages. First, alternative methods are available which can be tailored to suit the needs of individual applications (Koppelman, 1975). And, second, since the structure of the original detailed model can be preserved, the resulting aggregate prediction model tends to retain the desirable properties of predictive accuracy, policy sensitivity, extrapolative ability, and local adaptability.

The major disadvantage of the integration approach, however, is that it poses certain restrictions on the detailed prediction model. Specifically, the approach requires that:

1. The entity for which the aggregate prediction is made can be divided into a number of mutually exclusive units; and

2. The prediction made for each unit is dependent only on the attributes of the unit.

In the case of aggregate consumer demand prediction, these requirements are generally satisfied. The population of consumers of interest may be divided into different market segments or even into units as small as households. The demand for each unit is normally affected only by the attributes of the consumers within the unit. (This restriction is violated when the demand of, say, a consumer is affected by that of another consumer as in the proverbial case of "keeping up with the Joneses.")

In the case of **aggregate speed prediction**, the entity of interest, the roadway, may be divided into a number of homogeneous subsections. However, the second of the requirements above can only be satisfied by the micro non-transitional model, not the micro transitional one. The transitional effects in the latter method make the prediction of speed over a given subsection dependent not only on the attributes of the subsection but also on those of the adjacent subsections. In the micro non-transitional model, with the transitional effects removed, the prediction of speed is dependent only on the attributes of the subsection. Therefore, the micro non-transitional model must be used as the benchmark for testing the accuracy of candidate aggregation methods. This means that the prediction errors involved are entirely due to the numerical approximation in the aggregation methods, and have nothing to do with errors arising from ignoring the transitional effects. The latter errors have to be dealt with separately, as is done in Chapter 8.

Koppelman (op. cit.) identified four main alternative integration methods:

1. Exhaustive enumeration method;
2. Classification-based method;
3. Naive method; and
4. Method of statistical differentials.

For purposes of aggregate speed prediction, only the first two methods are directly relevant and are dealt with in this section in some detail. The latter two methods are discussed only briefly at the end of the section.

Applying the schematic used by Koppelman (op. cit.), each method involves three ingredients, as shown in Figure 7.2:

1. The distribution of road attributes, as represented by an array of vectors X_s, where X_s is the vector of road attributes for homogeneous subsection s (as used in Chapter 5);

2. The steady-state speed model, denoted by VSS; and

3. The aggregation procedure, which operates on the first two ingredients to produce the required space-mean speed prediction.

The exhaustive enumeration method uses all information given in the array of vectors X_s and amounts to the micro non-transitional model described in Chapter 5. That is, the time per distance over the roadway (τ) is a weighted average by road length of the time per distance predictions for the individual homogeneous subsections, $\tau_s = 1/\text{VSS}(X_s)$:

$$\tau = \frac{\sum_s \tau_s L_s}{L}$$

Figure 7.2: Schematic display of integration approach

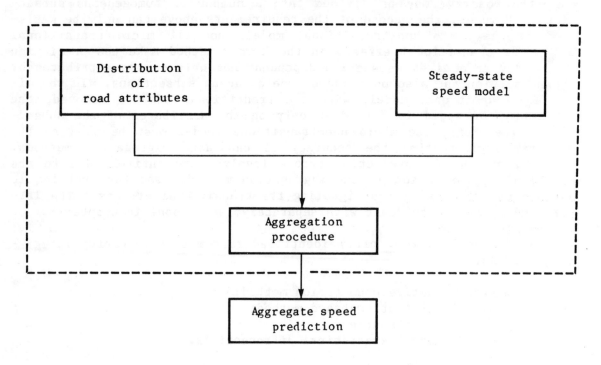

where L_s and L denote the lengths of homogeneous subsection s and the entire roadway, respectively (as given in Chapter 5).

In travel demand prediction, Koppelman (<u>op. cit.</u>) found from numerical testing that use of full information on road attributes in aggregate prediction, as implied by the exhaustive enumeration method above, was generally not necessary. In fact, he found that use of limit information, if carried out judiciously, could produce aggregate predictions almost as accurate as predictions based on full information.

The <u>classification-based method</u> was found to be the one that made the most efficient use of limited information. For this reason and also because of its simplicity, the method was chosen as the basis for developing the aggregate speed prediction model (presented in detail in the next section). The method may be briefly summarized by the following steps:

1. Classify the subsection into two or more relatively homogeneous classes (e.g., of similar gradients, curvatures, etc.).

2. Compute the time per distance for each class on the basis of the average road attributes, weighted by road length, for the class.

3. Compute the time per distance for the entire roadway as a weighted average by length over all classes.

Generally, the more classes employed, the more accurate would be the aggregate prediction but also the more unwieldy. Thus, the choice between the different classification schemes is a tradeoff between a gain in accuracy on the one hand and simplicity of the model and minimality of information requirements on the other. The classification scheme adopted was one that struck a reasonable balance between these opposing criteria.

The starting point for exploring alternative classification schemes was to note the following salient properties of the steady-state speed model and their implications on classification:

1. The model is discontinuous with respect to surface type, as evident from Chapter 4, in that the estimated desired speeds and perceived friction ratios are markedly different between paved and unpaved surfaces. This suggested that separate classes were needed for the surface types.

2. When plotted against gradient (Figure 3.1), the speed curve is not a monotonically increasing or decreasing one, but is bell-shaped with the top of the bell to the left of the zero gradient. This suggested that a relatively large number of classes might be needed for road gradient.

3. When plotted against curvature and roughness (Figures 3.2 and 3.4), speed is monotonically decreasing with respect to these variables. This suggested that a relatively small number of classes might be needed for curvature and roughness. (The behavior of speed with respect to superelevation was not examined as the latter was considered to be well correlated with curvature.)

The above considerations led to a numerical test of several candidate classification schemes using 10 actual road sections. The test yielded two major findings:

1. For a given surface type and two classes of road gradient, there was little gain in accuracy from classification by curvature and roughness.

2. The optimal number of classes for gradient was two. Very little gain in accuracy was obtained from four classes of gradient.

The above numerical results led to the final classification scheme embedded in the aggregate speed prediction model described in the next section. This scheme may be summarized in physical terms as one of converting a heterogeneous roadway of given surface type into two idealized subsections of uniform positive and negative gradients, each having the same curvature, superelevation and roughness which equal average attributes of the actual roadway.

The other integration methods alluded to earlier, the "naive" method and the method of "statistical differentials," are worth a brief discussion. The naive method is the same as the classification-based method in every respect except that the entire roadway is treated as one class of homogeneous subsections, as opposed to two or more. This method is linear. While it may be useful in applications where the detailed prediction models approximate a linear function, the naive method was found to be unsuited to the structure of the steady-state speed model. Specifically, the naive method involves averaging across positive and negative gradients whereas the steady-state model, as mentioned earlier, treats positive and negative gradients differently. In the case of predicting a round trip speed, the mean gradient would be zero by definition irrespective of the individual gradients of the subsections. Therefore, the naive method was rejected on a priori grounds.

The method of statistical differentials could be regarded as an extension of the classification-based method in that, in addition to using the means of road attributes, higher moments including the standard deviation and covariances of the attributes are also employed in aggregate prediction through Taylor's series expansion of the steady-state model (Koppelman, op. cit.). Compared to both the naive and classification-based methods, the method of statistical differentials is much more complicated and requires considerably more information if greater accuracy is sought. Since classification using first moments was already found to be satisfactory, the method of statistical differentials was not pursued.

The aggregation procedure adopted above is also applicable to other resources consumed in vehicle operation than "time per distance," in particular, fuel consumption and tire wear per distance, as described in Chapters 10 and 11, respectively.

7.3 THE AGGREGATE SPEED PREDICTION MODEL

It is assumed that the roadway is of a uniform surface type. If necessary, it may be treated as two distinct roadways and predictions of aggregate speed may be obtained separately for the paved and unpaved portions of the roadway. In other words, classification with respect to surface type is taken for granted in the following discussion. A brief note towards the end indicates the procedure to follow if the only information available regarding the surface type is the proportion of paved road.

It should be noted that there is a distinction between a given physical roadway and a traversed roadway. Depending on the direction of travel, three distinct traversed roadways can be identified for a given physical roadway. The distinction is important in defining the aggregate vertical geometric attributes for a traversed roadway. Specifically, given a stretch of road between two points, say, A and B, the three traversed roadways are:

1. The roadway traversed in travelling from A to B,

2. The roadway traversed in travelling from B to A, and

3. The roadway traversed in making the round-trip journey between A and B in either order.

Homogeneous subsections of the roadway between A and B which would have a positive grade in (1) will have a negative grade in (2), and vice versa. The roadway traversed in (3) is conceptually identical to a roadway which is twice in length and has the homogeneous subsections of both (1) and (2). A level subsection poses a slight problem in classification as a positive or negative grade and requires a special treatment, as will be dealt with below.

The aggregation procedure to be described first is applicable to travel in direction A to B. It will be seen that the aggregated information on road attributes obtained for the A-to-B journey is all that is needed for the B-to-A journey as well as for the round trip. Further, the aggregation procedure for the round trip employs data on road attributes at the same level of detail as that used in the HDM model. Considerable simplification results when predictions are desired for a round trip journey, as described below.

Let L be the length of the traversed roadway;

ST be the surface type of the roadway; and

The roadway be divided into n homogenous subsections indexed by subscript s;

For subsection (s), let

GR_s be the grade expressed as a fraction;
C_s be the curvature, in degrees/km;
SP_s be the superelevation, expressed as a fraction;
QI_s be the roughness, in QI counts; and
L_s be the length of the subsection, in m.

Define the following five attributes for the traversed roadway:

1. Let "PG_{ab}" be the weighted average of positive grades.

That is:

$$PG_{ab} = \frac{\sum\limits_{s} GR_s L_s}{\sum\limits_{s} L_s} = \frac{\sum\limits_{s} GR_s \ell_s}{LP_{ab}}$$

where the summation is over all the subsections with positive gradient in the direction of travel (i.e., with $GR_s \geq 0$), LP_{ab} is the proportion of uphill travel, and $\ell_s = L_s/L$.

2. Let "NG_{ab}" be the weighted average of the absolute values of negative grades. That is,

$$NG_{ab} = \frac{\sum\limits_{s} |GR_s| L_s}{\sum\limits_{s} L_s} = \frac{\sum\limits_{s} |GR_s| \ell_s}{LN_{ab}} = \frac{\sum\limits_{s} |GR_s| \ell_s}{1 - LP_{ab}}$$

where the summation is over all the subsections with a negative gradient in the direction of travel (i.e., with $GR_s < 0$) and LN_{ab} is the proportion of downhill travel. It should be noted that NG_{ab} is a non-negative quantity.

3. Let "C" (average curvature) be the weighted arithmetic mean of the curvatures. That is,

$$C = \frac{\sum\limits_{s} C_s L_s}{L} = \sum\limits_{s} C_s \ell_s$$

where the summation is over all the subsections. Since straight subsections have a curvature value of 0 degree/km, the summation is effectively over the curvy subsections.

4. Let "SP" (average superelevation) be the weighted average of superelevations. That is,

$$SP = \frac{\sum\limits_{s} SP_s L_s}{L} = \sum\limits_{s} SP_s L_s$$

where the summation is, as above, over the curvy subsections.

5. Let "QI" be the weighted average of roughnesses. That is,

$$QI = \frac{\sum\limits_{s} QI_s L_s}{L} = \sum\limits_{s} QI_s \ell_s$$

where the summation is over all subsections.

Now use the micro non-transitional speed prediction model as described in Chapter 5, for a hypothetical roadway consisting of two homogeneous subsections as defined in the following array:

A-to-B journey						
Homogenous subsection	Length	Surface type	Gradient	Curvature	Super-elevation	Roughness
"Uphill"	LP_{ab}	ST	PG_{ab}	C	SP	QI
"Downhill"	$1-LP_{ab}$	ST	$-NG_{ab}$	C	SP	QI

To predict the space-mean speed for the journey in the reverse direction (B-to-A), we adopt a slight change in the way level subsections are treated. For the A-to-B journey, a level subsection ($GR_s = 0$) has been classified as having a positive gradient. For the B-to-A journey we now classify it as having a negative gradient. With this convention adopted it is easy to see that the average positive and negative gradients as well as the proportion of uphill travel which have been evaluated above for the A-to-B journey are exactly reversed for the opposite travel direction, i.e.,

	A-to-B journey	B-to-A journey
Average positive gradient	PG_{ab}	$PB_{ba} = NG_{ab}$
Average negative gradient	NG_{ab}	$NG_{ba} = PG_{ab}$
Proportion of uphill travel	LP_{ab}	$LP_{ba} = 1-LP_{ab}$

and the B-to-A journey speed would be computed based on the array of information shown below:

B-to-A journey						
Homogenous subsection	Length	Surface type	Gradient	Curvature	Super-elevation	Roughness
"Uphill"	$1-LP_{ab}$	ST	NG_{ab}	C	SP	QI
"Downhill"	LP_{ab}	ST	$-PG_{ab}$	C	SP	QI

As for the round trip, by way of symmetry it can be easily shown that:

1. The proportion of the uphill travel is always equal to one-half; and

2. The average positive and negative gradients are both equal to one-half of the sum of the corresponding quantities for the A-to-B journey.

Letting,

$$PNG = [PG_{ab} + NG_{ab}]/2$$

the space-mean speed for the round trip can be computed for the information array below:

Round trip						
Homogenous subsection	Length	Surface type	Gradient	Curvature	Super-elevation	Roughness
"Uphill"	1/2	ST	PNG	C	SP	QI
"Downhill"	1/2	ST	-PNG	C	SP	QI

We next discuss the way to handle the case where the roadway is a combination of paved and unpaved surface types and the other attributes are known for the roadway as a whole and not separately for the two portions. Let PP be proportion of paved portion of the roadway. For this case, set up the summary aggregate descriptor array consisting of four imaginary homogeneous subsections as follows:

Homogenous subsection	Length	Surface type	Gradient	Curvature	Super-elevation	Rough-ness
Paved uphill	PP/2	Paved	PGN	C	SP	QI
Paved downhill	PP/2	Paved	−PGN	C	SP	QI
Unpaved uphill	(1−PP)/2	Unpaved	PGN	C	SP	QI
Unpaved downhill	(1−PP)/2	Unpaved	−PGN	C	SP	QI

Now apply the micro non-transitional prediction model to an hypothetical roadway with the above four homogenous subsections.

The aggregate descriptors of vertical and horizontal geometry for the round-trip travel, viz., PNG and C, respectively, are closely related to average rise plus fall, RF, and average horizontal curvature, which are the aggregate descriptors of the roadway used in the HDM-III. The following paragraphs define these concepts and indicate their interrelationship.

The average rise plus fall, RF, for a round-trip travel on a roadway is defined as the sum of the absolute values, in meters, of all ascents and all descents along the roadway divided by the length of the roadway, in kilometers. The concept is illustrated in Figure 7.3(a).

The average horizontal curvature of a roadway is defined as the sum of the absolute values of angular deviations (in degrees) of successive tangent lines of the horizontal alignment along the roadway, divided by the length of the roadway (in kilometers). This concept is illustrated in Figure 7.3(b).

The average rise plus fall is identical to PNG, defined above, but for a factor of 1000. While PNG is a dimensionless quantity, RF is expressed in m/km. Thus,

PGN = RF/1000

It was pointed out in Section 3.1 that for a homogeneous curve, the horizontal curve expresses both the angle subtended by it at the center as well as the angular deviation of the tangent lines bounding the curve. By extending the argument to all the curvy subsections of the roadway, it may be seen that the average curvature, C, as defined earlier and the average horizontal curvature as defined above are identical.

Figure 7.3: Illustration of road rise plus fall and horizontal curvature

a. Vertical profile of the road section

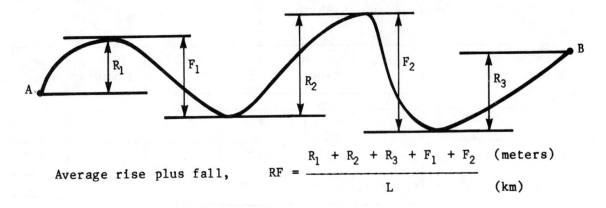

Average rise plus fall, $RF = \dfrac{R_1 + R_2 + R_3 + F_1 + F_2 \quad \text{(meters)}}{L \qquad\qquad \text{(km)}}$

b. Horizontal profile of the road section

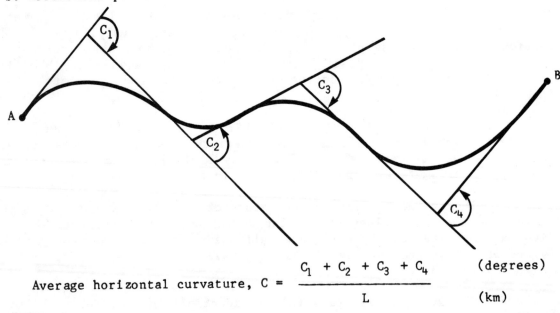

Average horizontal curvature, $C = \dfrac{C_1 + C_2 + C_3 + C_4 \quad \text{(degrees)}}{L \qquad\qquad \text{(km)}}$

APPENDIX 7A

PROCEDURE FOR COMPUTING AVERAGE ROADWAY CHARACTERISTICS FROM DETAILED GEOMETRIC PROFILE

It is assumed in the following discussion that the user starts with detailed vertical and horizontal geometric profiles of the roadway as typified by Figures 7A.1(a) and (b), respectively.

Step I. Computation of vertical geometric aggregates

Divide the roadway into subsections with crests and troughs as boundary points. Determine the lengths and average gradients (with signs retained) of the subsections and form the tabular profile of vertical geometry as shown in columns a, b and c below. The next five columns form a working table:

(a)	(b)	(c)	(d)	(e)	(f)	(g)	(h)
Sub-section s	Length (meters) ℓ_s	Gradient with sign (as a fraction) g_s	Positive gradient (as a fraction) $pg_s = 0$ or $pg_s = g_s$	Negative gradient (as a fraction) $ng_s = 0$ or $ng_s = g_s$	$p\ell_s =$ $pg_s\ell_s$	$n\ell_s =$ $ng_s\ell_s$	$p_s = 0$ or $p_s = \ell_s$
1 2 . . . . m							
Total	L				PL	NL	P

The working table (defined by column) is used as follows:

Column d   Determine the "positive gradient" pg_s of subsection s:
If the gradient of subsection s is positive, i.e., $g_s \geq 0$, then $pg_s = g_s$.

If the gradient of the subsection is negative, i.e., $g_s < 0$, then $pg_s = 0$.

Figure 7A.1: Vertical and horizontal geometric profiles

(a) Vertical geometric profile

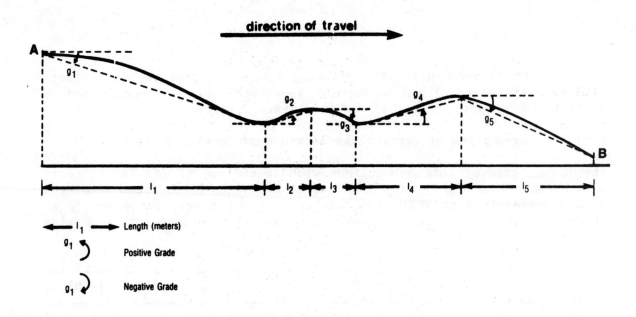

(b) Horizontal geometric profile

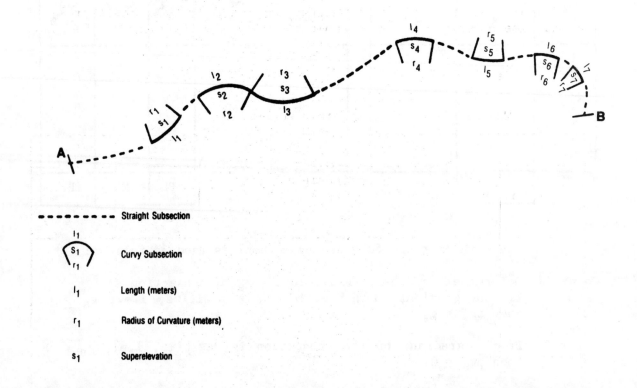

Column e Determine the "negative gradient" ng_s of the subsection s:
If the gradient of subsection s is positive, then $ng_s = 0$.

If the gradient of the subsection is negative, then $ng_s = \left| g_s \right|$, where $\left| g_s \right|$ is the absolute value of g_s.

Hence, both pg_s and ng_s are non-negative quantities, and one of them is necessarily zero for each subsection.

Column f Multiply columns b and d to get $p\ell_s$: $p\ell_s = pg_s \, \ell_s$

Column g Multiply columns b and e to get $n\ell_s$: $n\ell_s = ng_s \, \ell_s$

Column h This column chooses lengths of subsections with positive gradients. Enter the length ℓ_s of the subsection if the subsection has a positive gradient; enter zero if the subsection has a negative gradient. That is,

$$P_s = \begin{cases} \ell_s & \text{if } g_s \geq 0 \\ 0 & \text{if } g_s < 0 \end{cases}$$

Note that this column is not needed for round trip predictions.

Finally, form the totals of columns b, f, g and h as L, PL, NL and P, respectively, where L is the length of the roadway in meters.

Step II. Computation of horizontal geometric aggregates

Divide the roadway into subsections with uniform curvature using the end points of curves as boundary points. Determine the lengths, curvatures and superelevations (if known) of the curvy subsections and form the tabular profile of horizontal geometry as shown in columns i through l below. The curvature of curvy subsection is given by (from Section 3.2):

$$c_s = \frac{180,000}{\pi \, r_s}$$

The next two columns form a working table:

(i) Curvy subsection s	(j) Length (meters) ℓ_s	(k) Curvature (deg/km) c_s	(l) Superelevation (as a fraction) s_s	(m) $c\ell_s = c_s \, \ell_s$	(n) $s\ell_s = s_s \, \ell_s$
1					
2					
.					
.					
.					
.					
Total				K	S

The working table (defined by column) is used as follows:

Column m Multiply columns j and k to get $c\ell_s$: $c\ell_s = c_s\,\ell_s$

Column n Multiply columns j and l to get $s\ell_s$: $s\ell_s = s_s\,\ell_s$

Finally, form the totals of columns m and n as K and S respectively.

Step III. Computation of the average geometric characteristics

Average geometric characteristics	Symbol	Formula		Round trip
		One-way trip		
		Forward direction	Reverse direction	
Average positive gradient	PG	$\dfrac{PL}{P}$	$\dfrac{NL}{L - P}$	$\dfrac{PL + NL}{L}$
Average negative gradient	NG	$\dfrac{NL}{L - P}$	$\dfrac{PL}{P}$	$\dfrac{PL + NL}{L}$
Proportion of uphill travel	LP	$\dfrac{P}{L}$	$\dfrac{L - P}{L}$	0.5
Average curvature	C	$\dfrac{K}{L}$	$\dfrac{K}{L}$	$\dfrac{K}{L}$
Average superelevation	SP	$\dfrac{S}{L}$	$\dfrac{S}{L}$	$\dfrac{S}{L}$

Note: The proportion of uphill travel, LP, is exactly 0.5 for a round trip because of symmetry (see Section 7.3).

Illustrative example

The example roadway is about 3.5 km long and has fairly extreme geometry. Aggregate geometric attributes are desired for a one-way trip, starting from point A and ending at point B.

The vertical and horizontal geometric profiles of the roadway are shown on Figure 7A.2(a) and (b), respectively. In terms of vertical geometry, the roadway may be divided into five subsections of which three subsections have negative gradients and two subsections have positive gradients for the specified direction of travel. The lengths and gradients of the subsections are shown in Figure 7A.2(a) and summarized

Figure 7A.2: Vertical and horizontal geometric profiles: example

(a) Vertical Geometric Profile

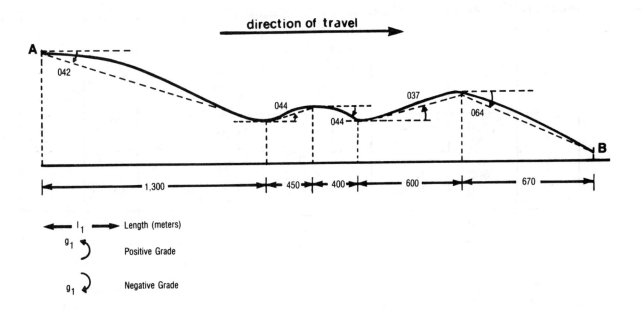

(b) Horizontal Geometric Profile

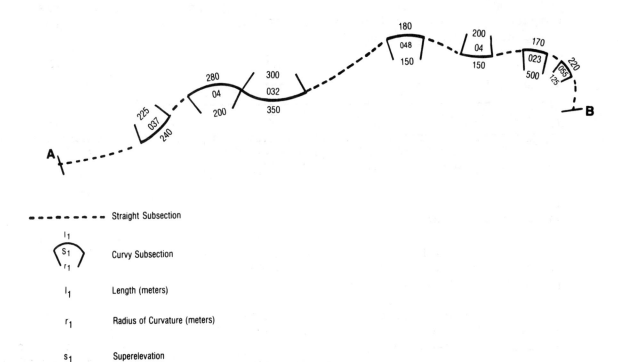

Table 7A.1: Working table for vertical geometry

(a)	(b)	(c)	(d)	(e)	(f)	(g)	(h)
Sub-section s	Length (meters) ℓ_s	Gradient with sign g_s	Positive gradient $pg_s = 0$ or $pg_s = g_s$	Negative gradient $ng_s = 0$ or $ng_s = g_s$	$p\ell_s = pg_s\,\ell_s$	$n\ell_s = ng_s\,\ell_s$	$p_s = 0$ or $p_s = \ell_s$
1	1,300	−0.042	0	0.042	0	54.60	0
2	450	0.044	0.044	0	19.80	0	450
3	400	−0.044	0	0.044	0	17.60	0
4	600	0.037	0.037	0	22.20	0	600
5	670	−0.064	0	0.064	0	42.88	0
Total	3,420				42.00	115.08	1,050

in Table 7A.1.   In terms of horizontal geometry, the roadway may be divided into 14 subsections of which seven are curved.   The lengths, curvatures and superelevations of the curvy subsections are shown in figure 7A.2(b) and summarized in Table 7A.2.

The working tables (see Tables 7A.1 and 7A.2) are then formed following the instructions, and the average geometric characteristics, computed.   Since predictions for a one-way trip are desired, the computations are as follows:

Table 7A.2: Working table for horizontal geometry

(i)	(j)	(k)	(l)	(m)	(n)
Curvy subsection s	Length (meters) ℓ_s	Curvature (deg/km) c_s	Superelevation (as a fraction) s_s	$c\ell_s = c_s\,\ell_s$	$s\ell_s = s_s\,\ell_s$
1	240	254.78	0.037	61,147	8.93
2	280	286.62	0.040	80,254	11.20
3	350	191.08	0.032	66,878	11.08
4	180	382.17	0.048	68,791	8.70
5	150	286.62	0.040	42,993	6.00
6	170	95.54	0.023	16,242	3.97
7	220	458.60	0.055	100,892	12.10
Total				437,197	61.98

Average positive gradient, PG $= \dfrac{42.00}{1050} = 0.040$

Average negative gradient, NG $= \dfrac{115.08}{2370} = 0.049$

Proportion of uphill travel, LP $= \dfrac{1050}{3420} = 0.307$

Average curvature, C $= \dfrac{437197}{3420} = 127.835$

Average superelevation, SP $= \dfrac{61.98}{3420} = 0.018$

CHAPTER 8

Validation of Speed Prediction Models

The development of a range of speed prediction models at different levels of complexity has the advantage that the prediction errors introduced in these models, defined as the difference between observed and predicted speeds, can be traced through various steps of simplification. This permits the different sources of errors to be examined separately, thereby forming a basis for conducting the validation exercise of the speed prediction model reported herein.

Section 8.1 discusses the nature of the sources of errors, followed by Section 8.2 which gives an overview of the experimental and user survey data employed in the validation. The main validation results are presented in Sections 8.3 - 8.5, with Section 8.3 dealing with the micro models, and Sections 8.4 and 8.5 with the aggregate model.

8.1 SOURCES OF PREDICTION ERRORS

As depicted in Figure 8.1, the three steps of model simplification introduce four sources of errors relating to random sampling, model specifications, transitional effects and numerical approximation.

1. <u>Micro transitional model.</u> The most elaborate of the three, the micro transitional model is considered on <u>a priori</u> grounds to be the most accurate or closest to the "truth." Its accuracy can be assessed by comparison with validation data, i.e., speed observations obtained independently from those used in developing or "calibrating" the prediction models. Granted that the validation data were from the same population of vehicles and roads as the calibration data, would expect prediction errors to arise primarily from two sources: random sampling and model mis-specifications.

   <u>Random sampling of speed observations</u> is the only source of prediction error that has nothing to do with the accuracy of the prediction models themselves, but rather with our inability to observe the "truth." If observable, the "truth" would clearly be the ideal absolute reference for measuring the prediction accuracy. For a given vehicle class and road characteristics, we define the "truth," in the sense of classical statistics, as the mean of the means of speed observations at road sites of the same characteristics. According to this definition, the "truth" is not observable, for to do so would take an infinitely large number of sites. Therefore, we must be content with something less than ideal to serve as the

175

Figure 8.1:   Sources of speed prediction errors

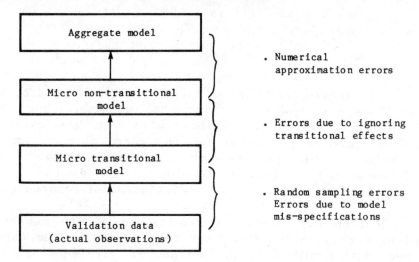

reference.   The definition of the "truth" stated above suggests that our second-best reference should be the average of averages of individual speeds at as many sites as possible.

This argument may be pursued further by examining the results of the estimation steady-state speed model in Chapter 4.   As illustrated in Table 4.4, for heavy trucks the average prediction errors for various groups of roads of similar characteristics are extremely small -- in the range of 0.03 - 1.5 km/h in magnitude.   If the steady-state speed model were perfect, in the sense that it could exactly replicate the "truth" without introducing any systematic bias, then this magnitude of error would be entirely attributable to random sampling.

As the model is not perfect, the magnitude of random sampling error is even smaller than the values computed. The range of 24-192 section-directions in these groups demonstrates that, given a sufficiently large sample size within a practical limit, it is possible to reduce the random sampling error to an acceptable level.

The above example is contrasted with Figure 4.1, also for heavy trucks, in which observed and predicted speeds are plotted and the regression between these speeds is shown to have a standard error of 7.0 km/h.

The standard error of prediction due to random sampling of sites equasl 16.1 percent of the predicted speed (from $\sigma_z = 0.161$).   For a typical predicted speed of 50 km/h, this standard error becomes 0.161 x 50 = 8.05 km/h, which, as expected, is similar to the above standard error of regression residuals.   If we use say, 25 sites for developing validation data, the random sampling standard error would be reduced to 8.0 $\div \sqrt{100}$ = 0.80 km/h.   These standard errors are similar in magnitude to the average prediction errors for groups of roads shown in Table 4.4. Following the results in Chapters 3 and 4, if an observed speed is taken at random from a heavy truck arriving at a randomly selected site, the standard error of prediction due to this random sampling process is equal to 25.0 percent (from $\sigma = 0.250$) or $0.250 \times 50 = 12.5$ km/h for 50 km/h prediction. One hundred random vehicles sampled in this manner would reduce the standard error to $25.0 \div \sqrt{100} = 2.5$ percent.

The upshot of the above discussion is that, since the "truth" is not observable, our ability to validate the prediction models depends crucially on our ability to obtain a sufficiently large amount of independent data. It is not possible to do validation simply on the basis either of individual speed observations at a site or of averages of observations at a few sites. Systematic prediction biases can be gleaned only by comparing the model predictions with observed speeds obtained from a sufficiently large number of vehicles and sites.

The second source of prediction erors, model mis-specifications, arise if the micro transitional model has not been properly specified so that the effects of vehicle and road characteristics are not captured fully in the steady-state speed relationship and the transitional speed logic. Although the micro transitional model is quite comprehensive in its attempt to simulate a highly complex real-world phenomenon, like most other behavioral models, it still is to some degree an idealization of reality. Thus, the question is not whether it has been correctly specified but really how close it is in approximating reality. Therefore, a good validation test would be to see how good the predictions are over a wide range of road and vehicle conditions.

2.   Micro non-transitional model. The next step of simplification, from the micro transition to micro non-transition model, introduces a clearly identifiable source of error: the omission of transitional effects. The magnitude of this type of error can be determined by comparing the predictions produced by the two models.

3.   Aggregate model. The last step of simplification, from the micro non-transitional to the aggregate model, involves no change in the treatment of transitional effects since neither model makes any attempt to simulate vehicle speed transitions. The only source of discrepancy between these models lies in the degree of numerical approximation of the geometric alignment of the road: the micro non-transitional model employs a large number of short, relatively homogeneous subsections whereas the

aggregate model employs only two "average" subsections. In fact, the aggregate model as defined in Chapter 7 represents only one level of aggregation --- a rather extreme one. Other levels of aggregation are possible. For example, an intermediate one in which four or more "average" sub- sections are used to distinguish between gentle and sharp curves. At any level of aggregation the associated errors can be assessed by comparing aggregate predictions with predictions produced by the micro non-transitional model.

8.2 VALIDATION DATA

Two validation exercises were conducted, one primary and one supplementary. The primary exercise employed average speeds by vehicle classes observed at a range of test sections; the supplementary exercise employed speed data obtained from the user cost survey (GEIPOT, 1982, Volume 5).

The primary exercise tested all three prediction models and used speed data from two paved and four unpaved sections (of 2-4 km lengths). Detailed information on the vertical and horizontal alignment of the road stretches was obtained from an engineering survey and the road roughness was measured using the standard Opala-Maysmeter vehicle (as alluded to earlier in Chapter 3). The average gradient of these sections varied in the range 1-5 percent and surface characteristics in the range smooth paved to medium-rough unpaved (QI = 26 - 111). The minimum radius of curvature surveyed was 100 meters. Table 8.1 provides summary characteristics of these test sections. The space-mean speeds of vehicles traversing each section were obtained from stopwatch readings at several designated stations along the stretch. Predictions were obtained using the same vehicle characteristics as for the speed model estimation (Table 4.2a), and parameter values as originally estimated (Table 4.3).

Because of the large number and variety of vehicles and also the wide range of speeds observed, the data set for the primary validation exercise is considered to be fairly encompassing. However, there are two main drawbacks. First, because the sections are relatively few in number and also short in length, the resulting random sampling errors are considered to be larger than desirable. Second, although some of the sections tested contain steep hills, none can be considered to be very rough or of severe geometric alignment, especially with respect to horizontal curvature.

Besides the six test sections listed in Table 8.1, five more actual road sections of 10 km length were selected for testing the micro non-transitional and aggregate models. Summary characteristics of these sections are compiled in Table 8.2. The addition of these sections extended the range of geometric alignment for testing purposes. Although an engineering survey was used to obtain detailed information on road geometry, no speed observations of population vehicles were made. Therefore, these additional sections were used only for comparison

Table 8.1: Summary characteristics of test sections (with speed observations) used in primary validation of speed prediction models

| General description | S E C T I O N   N U M B E R | | | | | |
	1 514	2 558	3 564	4 565	5 566	6 584
One-way length (km)	2.00	4.20	2.87	3.13	3.30	2.90
Number of homogenous subsections	4	9	22	15	15	6
Gradients (%)						
Maximum absolute	0.2	1.7	6.0	6.0	6.9	3.6
Average of positive	0.10	0.65	1.55	3.36	2.71	1.21
Average of negative	0.13	0.45	3.04	1.92	2.36	1.63
Length of positive	35.0	50.0	44.4	60.4	50.0	50.3
RF (m/km)	1.2	5.5	24.6	27.9	25.3	14.2
Number of curvy subsections	2	0	10	2	3	0
Minimum radius of curvature (m)	2929.0	∞	101.0	603.0	1130.0	∞
Maximum superelevation (%)	3.0	0.0	11.2	3.0	3.0	0.0
Radius of curvature (m)	5230.4	∞	353.9	2773.3	7488.0	∞
Superelevation (%)	16.8	0.0	5.35	0.65	0.45	0.0
Horizontal curvature (degrees/km)	11.0	0.0	162.0	20.7	0.0	5.7
Surface type	double-treated	gravel	gravel	gravel	double-treated	gravel
Roughness (QI)	26.0	110.9	103.4	76.0	73.0	80.8

Note: The aggregate descriptors of vertical geometry are for a one-way travel in an arbitrarily chosen direction.

Source: The Brazil-UNDP-World Bank highway research project data.

between the speed prediction models.[1]

    The supplementary validation exercise used speed data obtained from tachographs of individual journeys of interstate buses. Altogether, tachographs were obtained from 11 companies operating over 41 routes with characteristics as summarized in Table 8.3, along with average observed speeds. Relative to the primary validation data set, this data set has the advantage that the bus routes are relatively long (averaging 116 km one-way), and some are very rough (up to 200 QI roughness). However, as

---

[1] In fact, these sections were used mainly in the fuel consumption experiments for calibration and validation for the fuel prediction methods. This is dealt with in Chapter 10.

Table 8.2: Summary characteristics of test sections (without speed observations) used in primary validation of speed prediction models

	SECTION NUMBER				
General description	1	2	3	4	5
	559	560	561	562	563
	Paved/ rolling/ straight	Paved/ flat/ straight	Unpaved/ flat/ straight	Unpaved/ hilly	Unpaved/ rolling
One-way length (km)	10.0	10.0	10.0	10.0	10.0
Number of homogenous subsections	52	27	40	58	72
Gradients (%)					
Maximum absolute	6.0	2.0	6.6	6.5	6.8
Average of positive	0.79	0.86	0.60	4.86	8.40
Average of negative	2.61	3.00	6.30	0.38	2.42
Length of positive	25.3	68.9	41.0	89.0	38.5
RF (m/km)	22.2	6.5	6.2	42.9	19.1
Number of curvy subsections	7	2	1	23	37
Minimum radius of curvature (m)	491.0	80.0	702.0	72.0	185.0
Maximum superelevation (%)	4.0	3.0	2.0	12.0	4.6
Radius of curvature (m)	3637.0	4311.2	10000.0	535.7	565.0
Superelevation (%)	0.54	0.08	0.0	2.50	2.41
Horizontal curvature (degrees/km)	15.8	13.3	3.1	107.0	101.5
Surface type	double-treated	double-treated	gravel	gravel	gravel
Roughness (QI)	26.0	30.0	86.4	63.7	124.9

Note: The aggregate descriptors of vertical geometry are for a
        one-way travel in an arbitrarily chosen direction.
Source: Brazil-UNDP-World Bank highway research project data.

in the primary data set, these routes are only of gentle to moderate geometric alignment.   Another shortcoming is that although most bus routes had a number of stops to pick up and drop off passengers, the average stop time was not known and had to be estimated in order to compute the total driving time.   This proved to be a major source of discrepancy between the observed and predicted speeds, as reported in Section 8.5 below.

Table 8.3: Summary characteristics of interstate bus routes used in validation of aggregate speed prediction model

Characteristics	Mean	Minimum	Maximum	Standard dev.	CV (%)
Rise plus fall (m/km)	26.76	14.00	43.00	6.24	23.32
Horizontal curvature (degrees/km)	46.12	9.00	189.00	43.32	93.92
Roughness (QI)	67.07	24.00	196.00	46.69	69.61
Proportion of the route that is paved (%)	67.59	0.00	100.00	44.64	66.04
Round trip route length (km)	231.88	44.00	705.00	153.83	66.34
Number of stops	7.49	2	57	11.92	68.18
Number of stops per 100 km	12.16	0.85	103.64	16.87	138.75
Observed space-mean speed (km/h)	55.88	33.00	73.00	10.46	18.79

Source: Brazil-UNDP-World Bank highway research project data.

For road lengths of several hundred kilometers, as in the case of many of the above bus routes, the amount of data preparation and computation involved in using the micro speed prediction models is extremely large. Therefore, these tachograph bus speeds were used to test only the aggregate model.

8.3 VALIDATION OF MICRO MODELS

For the micro transitional model the observed speeds were taken as the benchmark for comparison. For each vehicle class, travel direction and, for trucks only, load level, the average observed space-mean speeds were regressed against the predicted space-mean speeds obtained from the speed profile simulation over the test sections presented in Table 8.1. Using ordinary least-squares analysis, performed with and without an intercept, the regressions yielded results as summarized in Table 8.4, along with the results based on all data points pooled together. Figure 8.2 plots the observed against predicted speeds with the data points distinguishable by vehicle class.

Table 8.4:   Regression of observed space-mean speeds (m/s) versus those predicted by the micro transitional model

Vehicle class	Number of observations	Intercept	Slope	R^2	Standard error of residuals
Car	12	4.98 (1.5)	0.76 (4.9)	0.70	1.30
		–	0.99 (53.1)	0.64	1.37
Utility	12	2.33 (0.6)	0.88 (4.7)	0.68	1.36
		–	1.01 (49.9)	0.67	1.33
Bus	11	8.17 (2.1)	0.63 (2.8)	0.47	2.08
		–	1.09 (26.5)	0.22	2.40
Light/medium truck	24	1.53 (0.8)	0.89 (7.7)	0.73	1.55
		–	0.98 (51.4)	0.72	1.53
Heavy truck	16	0.23 (0.1)	0.96 (8.3)	0.83	1.66
		–	0.98 (37.4)	0.83	1.61
Articulated truck	5	4.34 (0.8)	0.76 (0.46)	0.48	3.30
		–	1.11	0.47	3.13
All vehicle classes combined	80	1.94 (2.1)	0.899 (16.6)	0.78	1.81
		–	1.008 (84.9)	0.77	1.84

Source: Analysis of Brazil-UNDP-World Bank highway research project data.

The R^2 values in Table 8.4 and also in subsequent tables should be interpreted with care. In cases where observations are few and very similar the R^2 values could be quite low. In Table 8.4, the with-intercept regression has R^2 values above 68 percent for a majority of the vehicle classes. The pooled regression has an R^2 value of 78 percent. The R^2 values for two of the vehicle classes, namely, buses and articulated trucks, are somewhat lower. For articulated trucks, the low R^2 value (48 percent) is explained by there being very few (five) observations. For buses the reasons are unclear but the relatively narrow range of the observed speeds could have been a contributing factor.

Because of the relatively small number of data points (5 to 24) for each regression by vehicle class, the with-intercept regressions have relatively large, although generally insignificant, intercepts and slopes which markedly differ from unity, the value that would indicate bias-free predictions. The with-intercept regression in which all vehicle classes were combined into 80 data points, produced a low intercept (1.94 m/s or 7 km/h) and a slope close to one. The standard errors of residuals of these regressions fall within a 4-12 km/h range which is broadly comparable to standard errors of typical speed predictions at the section-direction level using the steady-state speed models estimated in Chapter 4. Following the discussion in Section 8.1 above, we may ascribe the departure of these intercepts and slopes from their ideal (zero and one, respectively), as well as most of the standard errors of regression, to errors resulting from random sampling and model mis-specifications.

With the intercept removed, the slopes of all regressions by vehicle class in Table 8.4 are much closer to one (0.98 to 1.11). Most noteworthy is the slope of the pooled regression (1.008) which, according to a t-test, is not significantly different from unity at the 95 percent confidence level. In fact, the relatively tight confidence interval of the estimated slope of [0.984, 1.031] suggests that on average the simulation logic mimics reality very well.

For the micro non-transitional model, two comparisons were made employing the simulation-predicted speeds and observed speeds as the benchmarks, respectively. The first comparison was to assess the nature and magnitude of the prediction errors resulting from ignoring the transitional effects and the second to evaluate the overall predictive performance of the model. The procedure used was basically the same as that for the micro transitional model, i.e., regression of the benchmark speeds against speeds predicted by the micro non-transitional model (for the six test sections presented in Table 8.1), with and without the intercept.

The results of the first comparison are compiled in Table 8.5 and Figure 8.3. Judging from the regression statistics it can be seen that the predictions produced under the steady-state speed assumption are remarkably close to those produced from full-fledged simulation. All without-intercept regressions yielded slopes slightly greater than one (1.02-1.04). In particular, the slope of 1.03 from the regression with all data points is significantly different from one, suggesting that the

Figure 8.2:   The plot of observed space-mean speeds versus those predicted by micro transitional model

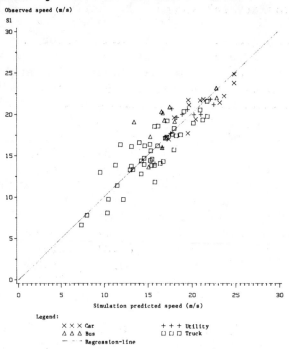

Source: Analysis of Brazil-UNDP-World Bank highway research project data.

Figure 8.3: The plot of space-mean speeds predicted by micro transitional model versus those by micro non-transitional model

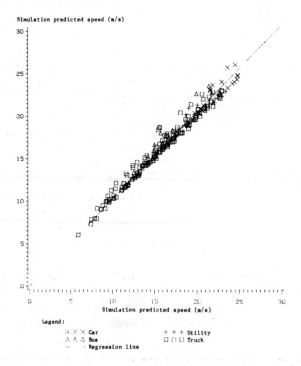

Source: Analysis of Brazil-UNDP-World Bank highway research project data.

Table 8.5: **Regression of simulated space-mean speeds (m/s) computed by by the micro transitional model, versus those by the micro non-transitional model**

Vehicle class	Number of observations	Intercept	Slope	R^2	Standard error of residuals
Car	26	−0.03 (−0.0)	1.02 (17.8)	0.93	0.73
		−	1.02 (155.1)	0.93	0.72
Utility	29	1.47 (1.8)	0.94 (21.5)	0.94	0.58
		−	1.02 (173.0)	0.94	0.60
Bus	31	0.78 (1.1)	0.99 (24.2)	0.95	0.76
		−	1.04 (127.2)	0.95	0.76
Light/medium truck	40	0.96 (1.9)	0.98 (32.5)	0.96	0.63
		−	1.03 (185.6)	0.95	0.64
Heavy truck	54	1.12 (2.7)	0.97 (35.6)	0.96	0.73
		−	1.04 (149.2)	0.96	0.77
Articulated truck	41	0.45 (1.6)	0.99 (48.3)	0.98	0.61
		−	1.02 (148.8)	0.98	0.62
All vehicle clases combined	230	0.73 (4.1)	0.986 (92.3)	0.97	0.68
		−	1.029 (374.7)	0.97	0.70

Source: Analysis of Brazil-UNDP-World Bank highway research project data.

suppression of transitional effects resulted in a slight downward bias of 3 percent on average.

Table 8.6 and Figure 8.4 present the results of the second comparison. Except for the steeper regression slopes, these results are very similar to those in Table 8.4 and Figure 8.2 for the observed versus micro transitional comparison. This indicates that barring the small downward bias the non-transitional model predicts almost as well as the transitional counterpart over the range of geometric alignment tested.

8.4 VALIDATION OF AGGREGATE MODEL BASED ON TEST SECTIONS

This section presents results of validating the aggregate model against three benchmarks: the micro non-transitional and transitional models and the observed speeds. The comparisons employed the same regression procedure as for the micro models, i.e., benchmark values versus to-be-tested predictions. In this exercise all three models were used to predict speeds for each direction of the 11 test sections shown in Tables 8.1 and 8.2 by vehicle class and, for trucks, load level. As speed observations were obtained from the first six sections (Table 8.1), only these sections were employed in the third comparison.

The results of the first comparison, aggregate versus non-transitional, are compiled in Table 8.7 and Figure 8.5. From the regression statistics it can be seen that predictions by the two models are very close. The without-intercept regression slopes of 0.92 - 0.97 indicate the tendency of the aggregate model to produce an upward bias, with an average value of 2 percent based on the slope of 0.982 from the pooled regression. Comparing the standard errors of residuals in Tables 8.7 and 8.5 we can see that, with the exception of cars and utilities, the "random" errors in numerical approximation arising from the aggregate procedure are somewhat larger in magnitude than those resulting from omitting transitional speed effects. It is worth noting that the biases due to these sources of errors are in opposite directions.

The second comparison, aggregate vs. micro transitional, yielded results compiled in Table 8.8 and Figure 8.6 The slopes of the regressions in Table 8.8 (0.95-1.05) are higher than those of the regressions in Table 8.7 (0.92-0.97). This is apparently owing to cancellation between the upward bias caused by the aggregation procedure and the downward bias caused by ignoring transitional effects. The net effect is that, within the range of road alignment in the sample of test sections, the aggregate model produces an average underprediction of about 1 percent relative to the micro transitional model (based on the slope of 1.01 from the without-intercept regression including all data points). Another point worth mentioning is that the statistics in Table 8.8 indicate even a better regression fit than those in Table 8.7. This implies that the cancellation effect of the two error sources even extends into the "random" errors.

Table 8.9 and Figure 8.7 present results from the third and final comparison: aggregate versus observed. Comparing these results

Table 8.6: Regression of observed space-mean speeds (m/s) versus those computed by the micro non-transitional model

Vehicle class	Number of observations	Intercept	Slope	R^2	Standard error of residuals
Car	12	3.49 (1.1)	0.85 (5.7)	0.77	1.15
		–	1.02 (62.5)	0.74	1.17
Utility	12	2.79 (0.8)	0.89 (4.5)	0.67	1.39
		–	1.04 (48.4)	0.65	1.37
Bus	11	9.30 (2.7)	0.59 (3.0)	0.49	2.04
		–	1.14 (24.2)	0.07	2.62
Light/medium truck	24	3.28 (1.9)	0.81 (7.3)	0.71	1.60
		–	1.02 (46.8)	0.66	1.68
Heavy truck	16	1.77 (1.0)	0.90 (7.2)	0.79	1.87
		–	1.02 (32.3)	0.77	1.86
Articulated truck	5	3.41 (0.6)	0.87 (1.8)	0.52	3.16
		–	1.15 (10.4)	0.46	2.90
All vehicle combined	80	2.89 (3.2)	0.875 (16.2)	0.77	1.84
		–	1.042 (80.3)	0.74	1.95

Source: Analysis of Brazil-UNDP-World Bank highway research project data.

Table 8.7: Regression of the space-mean speeds (m/s) predicted by the micro non-transitional model versus those by the aggregate model

Vehicle class	Number of observations	Intercept	Slope	R^2	Standard error of residuals
Car	26	−0.09 (−0.1)	0.98 (21.0)	0.95	0.56
		−	0.98 (188.2)	0.95	0.58
Utility	29	0.63 (1.0	0.94 (29.6)	0.97	0.44
		−	0.97 (232.6)	0.97	0.44
Bus	31	0.85 (1.2)	0.97 (23.3)	0.95	0.78
		−	1.02 (119.4)	0.95	0.79
Light/medium truck	49	0.64 (0.8)	0.95 (19.5)	0.89	1.01
		−	0.99 (115.0)	0.89	1.00
Heavy truck	54	0.25 (.03)	0.95 (15.0)	0.81	1.62
		−	0.97 (68.7)	0.81	1.60
Articulated truck	41	0.10 (0.1)	0.97 (15.6)	0.86	1.78
		−	0.98 (51.5)	0.86	1.75
All vehicle classes combined	230	0.35 (1.0)	0.962 (48.5)	0.91	1.25
		−	0.982 (203.7)	0.91	1.25

Source: Analysis of Brazil-UNDP-World Bank highway research project data.

Figure 8.4: The plot of observed space—mean speeds versus those predicted by micro non—transitional model

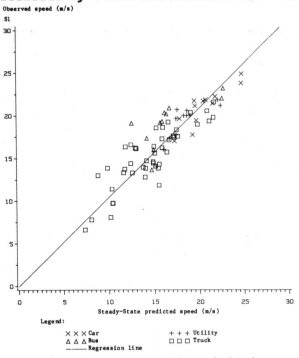

Source: Analysis of Brazil—UNDP—World Bank highway research project data.

Figure 8.5: The plot of space—mean speeds predicted by micro non—transitional model versus those by aggregate model

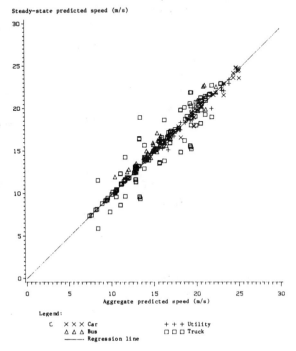

Source: Analysis of Brazil—UNDP—World Bank highway research project data.

Table 8.8: Results of regression of space–mean speeds (m/s) predicted by the micro transitional model versus those by the aggregate model

Vehicle class	Number of observations	Intercept	Slope	R^2	Standard error of residuals
Car	26	−0.74 (−0.6)	1.03 (18.2)	0.93	0.72
		−	1.00 (157.2)	0.93	0.71
Utility	29	1.90 (2.2)	0.89 (19.7)	0.94	0.62
		−	0.99 (156.0)	0.92	0.66
Bus	31	1.55 (1.7)	0.96 (17.3)	0.91	1.04
		−	1.05 (90.4)	0.90	1.07
Light/medium truck	49	1.23 (1.5)	0.95 (19.7)	0.89	0.99
		−	1.02 (118.3)	0.89	1.01
Heavy truck	54	1.24 (1.2)	0.93 (14.1)	0.79	1.67
		−	1.01 (68.2)	0.79	1.68
Articulated truck	41	0.50 (0.6)	0.97 (15.2)	0.86	1.81
		−	1.00 (51.3)	0.86	1.80
All vehicle classes combined	230	0.97 (2.7)	0.955 (45.2)	0.90	1.33
		−	1.010 (194.2)	0.90	1.35

Source: Analysis of Brazil–UNDP–World Bank highway research project data.

Table 8.9: Regression of observed space-mean speeds (m/s) versus those predicted by the aggregate model

Vehicle class	Number of observations	Intercept	Slope	R^2	Standard error of residuals
Small car	12	3.88 (1.2)	0.83 (5.1)	0.72	1.26
		–	1.01 (57.2)	0.69	1.28
Utility	12	3.58 (1.0)	0.82 (4.5)	0.67	1.40
		–	1.01 (47.1)	0.63	1.41
Large bus	11	8.74 (2.3)	0.66 (2.8)	0.47	2.08
		–	1.20 (25.4)	0.15	2.51
Light/medium truck	24	3.05 (1.8)	0.82 (7.5)	0.72	1.57
		–	1.01 (48.0)	0.68	1.64
Heavy truck	16	1.65 (0.9)	0.90 (6.9)	0.77	1.92
		–	1.01 (31.5)	0.76	1.91
Articulated truck	5	3.80 (0.7)	0.83 (1.7)	0.50	3.24
		–	1.14 (10.0)	0.42	3.01
All vehicle classes combined	80	3.27 (3.3)	0.848 (14.6)	0.73	1.99
		–	1.037	0.69	2.12

Source: Analysis of Brazil–UNDP–World Bank highway research project data.

Figure 8.6: The plot of space—mean speeds predicted by micro transitional model versus those by aggregate model

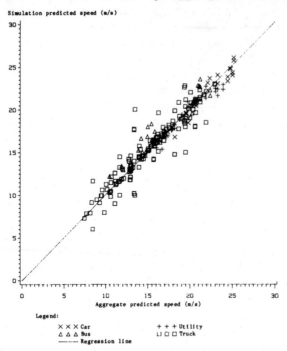

Source: Analysis of Brazil—UNDP—World Bank highway research project data.

Figures 8.7: The plot of observed space—mean speeds versus those predicted by aggregate model

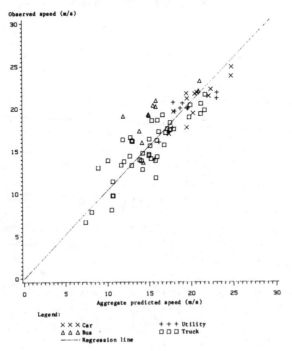

Source: Analysis of Brazil—UNDP—World Bank highway research project data.

with those in Table 8.4 we can see that for the road sections tested the much simpler aggregate model performs almost as well as the full-fledged speed profile simulation. The average overprediction of the aggregate model is less than 3 percent (based on the slope of 0.975 for the pooled regression, without the intercept) compared to the virtually bias-free predictions generated by the micro transitional model. The standard errors of residuals for the aggregate model are slightly larger than those for the micro transitional counterpart.

8.5 VALIDATION OF AGGREGATE MODEL BASED ON USER COST SURVEY

The observed speed of each of the 41 bus routes was computed as the average of the round trip space-mean speeds obtained from one or more tachographs available for the route. Each tachograph provided a time-distance log of a complete bus tour. A difficulty encountered was that the 5-minute divisions on the tachographs did not provide information on the amount of time buses spent at stops which was generally well below 5 minutes. Therefore, the latter had to be estimated and the value of 40 seconds per stop was adopted.

The predicted speeds were computed based on the aggregate procedure described in Chapter 7. The values of the total vehicle weight (10,400 kg), aerodynamic drag coefficient (0.65) and projected frontal area (6.30 m^2) are the same as those used in the steady-state speed model for buses (Table 4.1). These values are considered to be fairly representative of the Brazilian interstate bus population. For each route that had both paved and unpaved portions, speeds were first computed separately for those portions, and then the weighted harmonic mean of these speeds was taken as the predicted speed for the entire route.

The predicted and observed speeds and prediction errors are presented in Table 8.10 along with the characteristics of the routes. It is seen than the predicted speeds are higher than the observed speeds on 31 of the 41 routes. No effect of road geometry, surface type or roughness was found in the error trends. However, a further examination revealed that the number of stops per unit distance had a strong influence on the prediction errors. Table 8.11 shows mean prediction errors for 6 groupings of the routes by the number of stops per 100 km. It is evident that the magnitude of overprediction increases sharply with the number of stops per unit distance. For the two groups of routes with fewer than 10 stops per 100 km, the average amount of overprediction is smaller than 2 km/h. Figure 8.8 presents a plot of the observed against predicted speeds for these groups of routes. It can be seen that the predicted speeds track the trend of the actual speeds closely. Ordinary least-squares regression of the observed against the predicted speed with the intercept constrained to zero produced a slope of 0.97 as plotted in Figure 8.8. The standard error of residual of 4.8 km/h is about half the standard error of 8.6 km/h for 55 km/h prediction using the steady-state model for buses. This difference could be attributable to the fact that the steady-state model was estimated on the basis of spot speeds measured at short sections, whereas the observed bus speeds were made over long routes, most of which were over 100 km in round trip length (Table 8.10).

Table 8.10: Route characteristics and observed and predicted speeds

	RF (m/km)	C (deg/km)	Roughness (QI)	Paved proportion of the route (%)	No.of stops	Round-trip route length(km)	No.of stops per 100km	Speed (km/h) Observed	Predicted	Difference observed/ predicted
1	32	24	25	100	5	44	11	52	64.38	-12.38
2	33	13	41	100	27	184	15	63	63.43	-0.43
3	34	22	85	4	30	150	20	47	53.90	-6.90
4	22	21	58	88	57	55	104	56	67.27	-11.27
5	24	11	29	100	16	196	8	68	69.00	-1.00
6	22	10	37	100	6	50	12	52	69.82	-17.82
7	28	10	31	100	8	57	14	69	66.70	2.30
8	24	12	24	100	11	115	10	67	69.11	-2.11
9	27	9	32	100	20	197	10	66	67.25	-1.25
10	30	74	39	100	12	262	5	60	64.39	-4.39
11	34	58	35	100	2	170	1	60	62.51	-2.51
12	25	109	41	100	14	455	3	63	66.14	-3.14
13	18	155	47	100	8	190	4	59	67.63	-8.63
14	14	189	45	100	14	133	11	53	67.90	-14.90
15	29	16	44	88	12	415	3	61	64.55	-3.55
16	29	16	44	88	14	415	3	62	64.55	-2.55
17	31	25	37	92	16	512	3	71	63.95	7.05
18	31	78	40	100	34	444	8	58	63.71	-5.86
19	31	29	42	90	18	348	5	65	63.56	1.27
20	29	28	37	91	20	407	5	58	64.95	-6.75
21	30	27	41	92	19	457	4	66	64.36	1.20
22	43	130	40	100	20	140	14	50	55.86	-5.05
23	29	60	38	100	14	124	11	48	65.27	-17.27
24	34	93	38	100	10	309	3	59	61.75	-2.75
25	24	26	196	0	20	250	8	37	41.20	-4.20
26	31	30	142	0	7	144	5	45	48.19	-3.19
27	18	23	41	100	23	90	26	57	71.52	14.52
28	25	55	104	0	23	192	12	40	54.28	-14.28
29	29	50	127	0	29	95	31	37	50.48	-13.48
30	26	52	116	0	18	140	13	37	52.66	-15.66
31	22	52	148	0	18	128	14	49	48.86	0.14
32	18	11	101	14	30	481	6	54	58.18	-4.18
33	26	9	27	100	6	705	1	73	67.95	5.05
34	27	11	36	100	24	91	26	47	67.12	-20.12
35	21	29	106	11	4	181	2	66	56.29	9.71
36	14	25	136	4	11	142	8	56	52.63	3.37
37	14	14	123	0	50	129	39	40	54.86	-14.86
38	24	23	122	9	7	206	3	53	53.22	-0.22
39	28	50	39	100	33	235	14	71	65.98	5.02
40	34	93	38	100	3	330	1	55	61.75	-6.75
41	33	119	178	0	4	139	3	33	41.84	-8.84

Source: Analysis of Brazil-UNDP-World Bank highway research project data.

Source: Analysis of Brazil-UNDP-World Bank highway research project data.

**Table 8.11: Effect of number of stops per unit distance on prediction
errors**

Number of stops per 100 km	Number of routes	Mean error of prediction (km/h)
Fewer than 5	16	−1.84
6 − 10	7	−1.77
11 − 15	12	−7.70
16 − 26	2	−10.71
31 − 39	3	−16.15
104	1	−11.23

Source: Analysis of Brazil−UNDP−World Bank highway research project data.

**Figure 8.8: Observed speeds versus speeds predicted by the aggregate
model for bus routes with fewer than 10 stops per 100 km**

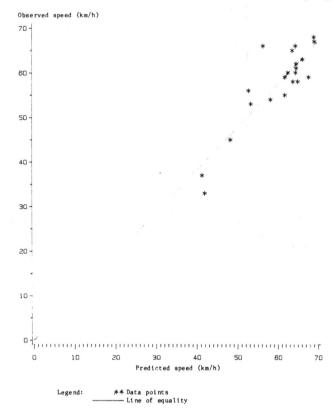

Source: Analysis of Brazil−UNDP−World Bank highway research project data.

PART II
Vehicle Operating Cost Prediction Models

CHAPTER 9

Unit Fuel Consumption Function

Once the vehicle speed has been predicted using either one of the micro models or the aggregate model, to predict fuel consumption is a relatively straightforward matter. This is done through the "unit fuel consumption function," the formulation of which is first presented (Section 9.1), followed by a short description of the data and the experiment from which the data were obtained (Section 9.2). Finally, the results of model estimation are presented and discussed in Section 9.3.

9.1 MODEL FORMULATION

Under ideal environmental conditions, i.e., constant ambient temperature, atmospheric pressure and humidity, the basic principles of internal combustion engines suggest that the rate of fuel consumption per unit time of a vehicle engine may be expressed as a function of two variables, namely the power output and the engine speed (Taylor, 1966, Volume 1). Letting UFC denote the unit fuel consumption (in ml/s) we have:

$$UFC = UFC(HP, RPM) \qquad (9.1)$$

where   HP = the vehicle power delivered at the driving wheels, in metric hp (as defined in Chapter 2); and

RPM = the engine speed, in revolutions per minute (rpm).

Although the theory of internal combustion engines is generally concerned with positive values of vehicle power, both positive and negative power must be dealt with in this study. As discussed earlier, when HP is positive, the engine is being used to provide propulsive power for the vehicle. When HP is negative, the engine is being used as a brake, either by itself or in conjunction with the regular brakes. This can occur when the vehicle is decelerating on approaching a curve or travelling downhill since negative power is needed to keep the speed under control.

For the purposes of this study, instead of using the actual engine speed, the variable RPM is computed from the following "nominal" formula which ignores tire deflection and slip:

$$RPM = \frac{60 \ V \ DRT \ GRT}{\pi \ TD} \qquad (9.2)$$

where   DRT = the differential speed ratio;

GRT = the gear speed ratio; and

TD = the nominal tire diameter, in meters; and

V   = the vehicle travelling speed, in m/s.

The values of DRT, GRT and TD for the test vehicles are listed in Table 1A.2.

9.2 ESTIMATION DATA

The data for estimating the unit fuel consumption function were obtained from an experiment using all 11 test vehicles. The experiment basically involved running the vehicles over a 1-km length in both directions on 51 selected test sections of constant slope under different loads. Of these sections, 36 were paved and 15 were unpaved. Their characteristics are compiled in Table 9.1. In each run, the vehicle travel and gear speeds were kept constant. Across runs, the vehicle speeds were varied in the range 10-120 km/h by 10 km/h increments. For each vehicle speed, all feasible gear speeds were employed. In each run, the amounts of fuel consumed and time taken to traverse the 1-km stretch were recorded. Generally six replicate runs were made for each combination of test vehicle, load level, section, direction, travel speed and gear. In all, about 60,000 runs were conducted.

For each run, the unit fuel consumption (UFC), engine speed (RPM) and vehicle power (HP) were computed. The unit fuel consumption was computed as the amount of fuel consumed over the 1-km stretch divided by the travel time; the engine speed as a function of the measured vehicle speed and gear speed ratio, according to Equation 9.2; and the vehicle power as given by Equation 2.19, with a = 0 for steady-state speed conditions:

$$HP = \frac{1}{736} \left[m\ g(GR + CR)\ V + 0.5\ RHO\ CD\ AR\ V^3 \right] \qquad (9.3)$$

where   GR = the gradient of the test section (positive or negative depending on the direction of travel) as summarized in Table 9.1;

CR = the rolling resistance coefficient, computed as a function of the roughness of the test section (summarized in Table 9.1) according to Equation 2.13;

and the mass (m), aerodynamic drag coefficient (CD) and frontal area (AR) of each test vehicle are listed in Table 1A.2.

For each set of replicate runs for a particular combination of test vehicle, load level, section, direction, travel speed and gear, average values of the variables UFC, HP and RPM were computed and treated

Table 9.1: Characteristics of test sections used in experiments to determine unit fuel consumption function

	Mean	Min.	Max.	Std. dev.	C.V. (%)
Absolute value of gradient (%)	3.2	0.0	13.0	2.7	85.8
Curvature (degrees/km)	18.9	0.0	340.0	52.4	277.8
Roughness (QI)	84.6	26.7	212.5	58.5	69.1

Surface type	Number of sections
Asphaltic concrete	16
Surface treatment	19
Other	1
Total paved	36
Laterite	10
Quartzite	5
Total unpaved	15
Total number of sections	51

Source: Brazil–UNDP–World Bank highway research project data.

as one observation in the statistical estimation. Summary statistics of the experiment, including the UFC, HP and RPM variables, are compiled in Table 9.2.

9.3 STATISTICAL ESTIMATION

From a preliminary analysis described in Appendix 9A, a general form of the UFC function was obtained for all test vehicles:

$$
UFC = \begin{cases}
UFC_0 + (a_3 + a_4\, RPM)\, HP + a_5\, HP^2 & \text{for } 0 \le HP \\
UFC_0 + a_6\, HP + a_7\, HP^2 & \text{for } NH_0 \le HP < 0 \\
UFC_0 + a_6\, NH_0 + a_7\, NH_0 & \text{for } HP < NH_0
\end{cases}
\qquad (9.4)
$$

where
$$ UFC_0 = a_0 + a_1\, RPM + a_2\, RPM^2 \qquad (9.5) $$

NH_0 = lower limit on negative power (see Appendix 9A); and

$a_0 - a_7$ = model parameters to be estimated from regression analysis.

Table 9.2: Summary statistics of experiment to determine unit fuel consumption function

Vehicle	No. of mean fuel observa- tions	Range of speed (km/h)	Payload (kg)		Power (metric hp)			Engine speed (rpm)			Unit fuel consumption (ml/s)		
			Semi- loaded	Fully loaded	Mean	Min.	Max.	Mean	Min.	Max.	Mean	Min.	Max.
Small car	1224	20–120	–	200	5.8	–14.4	34.6	2356.3	959	4096	1.04	0.13	3.30
Medium car	398	30–120	–	350	13.7	–10.3	82.5	2384.7	781	4001	3.06	0.33	8.77
Large car	421	20–120	–	350	16.5	–15.5	98.6	2385.4	1028	4525	3.14	0.33	10.36
Utility	1007	10–120	280	550	7.9	–20.1	46.4	2220.3	630	4040	1.53	0.18	4.73
Large bus	784	10–100	1010	2250	–0.46	–134.7	93.5	1877.6	1016	2796	1.71	0.01	6.62
Truck:													
Light gas	1142	10–120	1730	3510	3.8	–110.4	89.3	2412.5	1011	4165	3.40	0.37	13.71
Light & diesel	1020	10–100	1540	3325	0.00	–108.1	61.0	1918.2	865	3035	1.33	0.01	4.97
Heavy	798	8–100	5985	11970	–17.2	–268.6	113.3	1600.0	1016	2541	1.75	0.01	8.45
Articulated	811	10–70	13300	26600	–16.7	–529.9	231.1	1447.1	1155	1649	3.17	0.01	13.61
Replicate utility	1043	20–120	280	550	7.6	–36.6	46.8	2219.1	935	3784	1.52	0.19	4.76
Heavy with with crane	774	8–90	6060	12045	–18.8	–269.9	109.5	1598.4	970	2425	1.60	0.01	8.03

Source: Brazil–UNDP–World Bank highway research project data.

The estimation results based on ordinary least-squares regression, are shown in Table 9.3,[1] along with the manually determined value of NH_0 for each test vehicle. Except for the intercept term,[2] a_0, all estimated coefficients are significant at the 95 percent confidence level or greater, with t-statistics running from 2.0 to as high as 90.7 and R^2 in the range 0.92-0.98. For the Mercedes Benz 1113 as an example, a graph of the estimated UFC function plotted against HP for different values of RPM is shown in Figure 9.1.

The estimated UFC function[3] is a continuous function of HP and RPM and for a fixed RPM it increases monotonically with HP. This means that when the vehicle is called upon to exert more power, fuel consumption rises. When HP = 0, we have $UFC = UFC_0$. At idling speed, UFC_0 approaches the idling fuel consumption. Table 9.4 presents the values of idling fuel consumption for the test vehicles as approximated by UFC_0, along with the corresponding idling engine speeds. When HP is smaller than the threshold value NH_0, Equation 9.4 above states that the fuel consumption stays constant. While is it true that when the engine is being used as a brake, it does not really need any fuel so that, ideally, the fuel consumption should be zero, the engine, when it is running, always uses some fuel, for instance, the idling fuel consumption. Such relatively small amount of fuel flow is probably due to imperfections in the fuel delivery system.

The concave shape of the UFC function as illustrated in Figure 9.1 — constant UFC for HP < NH_0 and rising UFC with HP for HP > NH_0 — has an important implication in studies to determine the effect of speed change cycles on fuel consumption. Contrary to what many may believe, speed change cycles are not themselves the cause of excess fuel consumption. The excess consumption is in fact caused by operating the vehicle in such a way that the power alternates between the positive and negative regimes. While positive power always requires a substantial amount of fuel, negative power dissipates into heat the potential and kinetic energies built up previously by positive power with no compensation. When a vehicle is operated with speed changes but the power still remains within the positive regime, the potential and kinetic energies are not wasted.

Another property of the estimated UFC worth mentioning is that given the same HP, fuel consumption increases with the engine speed. This agrees with the general findings in Taylor (1966, Volume 1) and Wong (1978) that for the same power output it is always more economical to operate the internal combustion engine at low speed and high torque than vice versa.

---

[1] For regression purposes, the model form in Equation 9.4 are expressed as shown in Equation 9A.4.

[2] There is no strong a priori reason to expect a_0 to be non-zero.

[3] Combinations of negative HP and unrealistically low values of RPM can cause the value of UFC computed from the estimated coefficients to be negative. When this occurs, the value should be set to zero.

Table 9.3: Results of regression to estimate unit fuel consumption function (ml/s)

Test vehicle	Number of observations	Standard error of residuals	R^2	Intercept a_0	RPM a_1 (10^{-4})	RPM^2 a_2 (10^{-7})	PH a_3 (10^{-2})	PH RPM a_4 (10^{-6})	PH^2 a_5 (10^{-5})	NH_0	NHX a_6 (10^{-2})	NHX^2 a_7 (10^{-4})
1 Opala	398	0.1473	0.98	0.23453 (3.2)	4.06 (6.1)	1.214 (9.1)	7.775 (89.0)	–	–	–12	6.552 (11.9)	–
2 Mercedes Benz 1113 with crane	774	0.5635	0.96	–0.41555 (–6.2)	10.36 (27.1)	–	3.858 (19.9)	–	16.02 (7.1)	–85	2.764 (15.3)	1.530 (8.9)
3 Mercedes Benz 1113	798	0.6746	0.96	–0.22955 (–3.2)	9.50 (23.0)	–	3.758 (19.1)	–	19.12 (8.9)	–85	2.394 (12.6)	1.376 (7.6)
4 Mercedes Bus O–362	784	0.3261	0.97	–0.07276 (–1.3)	6.35 (24.7)	–	4.323 (24.6)	–	8.64 (3.9)	–50	2.479 (8.3)	1.150 (2.0)
5 Scania 110/39	810	0.9480	0.98	–0.30559 (–1.8)	15.61 (13.9)	–	4.002 (29.7)	–	4.41 (6.3)	–85	4.435 (15.4)	2.608 (10.1)
6 Ford 400	1142	2.0396	0.92	–0.48381 (–5.9)	12.71 (38.6)	–	5.867 (17.5)	–	43.70 (8.6)	–50	3.843 (24.3)	–
7 Ford 4000	1020	0.3413	0.94	–0.41803 (–10.2)	7.16 (34.5)	–	5.129 (72.8)	–	–	–30	2.653 (30.1)	–
8 Dodge Dart	421	0.2478	0.98	–0.23705 (–4.2)	10.08 (41.0)	–	2.784 (8.4)	9.38 (8.5)	13.91 (4.0)	–15	4.590 (9.2)	–
9 VW–Kombi 1	1043	0.1915	0.96	0.06014 (1.8)	3.76 (25.4)	–	3.846 (13.4)	13.98 (12.8)	–	–12	3.604 (16.4)	–
10 VW–Kombi 2	1007	0.2071	0.95	–0.05173 (–1.5)	4.69 (30.2)	–	2.963 (9.7)	14.66 (12.5)	–	–12	4.867 (18.9)	–
11 VW–1300	1224	0.0839	0.96	–0.08201 (–5.8)	3.34 (55.3)	–	5.630 (90.7)	–	–	–10	4.460 (22.7)	–

Notes: 1. Parentheses ( ) denote t-statistics.
2. A dash (–) indicates that the corresponding coefficient has been constrained to zero.
3. The variables PH and NHX are defined in Appendix 9A.

Source: Analysis of Brazil-UNDP-World Bank highway research project data.

Figure 9.1: Predicted unit fuel consumption versus vehicle power for different nominal engine speeds – for Mercedes Benz 1113 heavy truck

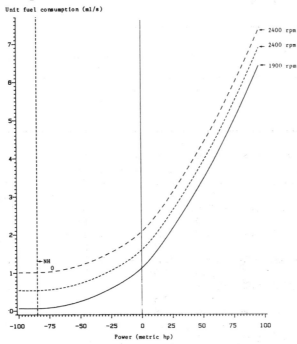

Source: Analysis of Brazil–UNDP–World Bank highway research project data.

Table 9.4: Idling fuel consumption for test vehicles based on estimated unit fuel consumption function

Vehicle	Idling fuel consumption (ml/s)	Typical engine speed while idling (rpm)
Small car	0.239	960
Medium car	0.625	780
Large car	0.772	1000
Utility	0.323	700
Large bus	0.562	1000
Light gasoline truck	0.787	1000
Light diesel truck	0.205	870
Heavy truck	0.701	980
Articulated truck	1.568	1200

Source: Analysis of Brazil–UNDP–World Bank highway research project data.

By virtue of Equations 9.3 and 9.4 and assuming a constant "normal average" engine speed, the fuel consumption per unit travel distance of each test vehicle can be computed, via the estimated UFC, as a function of the vehicle speed and vehicle and road characteristics.

An example of this is presented in Figures 9.2 (a) and (b) for the Mercedes Benz 1113 heavy truck travelling on a level road. These figures show how the vehicle power and fuel consumption per unit distance are affected by the vehicle speed, load level and road roughness and their interaction. At a given load level and roughness, as the speed increases, the power rises, partly due to increased air resistance and partly due to the need to overcome resistance forces at a faster rate; however, the fuel consumption per unit distance drops initially to a minimum before rising.

This U-shaped curve is to be expected, since the engine is relatively inefficient at low power. The analogous model developed by Bester (1981) also exhibits this feature. The empirical studies conducted by Hide et al. (1975), Morosiuk and Abaynayaka (1982), and CRRI (1982) developed fuel consumption relationships directly as a U-shape function of speed, without using the unit fuel consumption function as an intermediate step.

At given speed and roughness, both vehicle power and fuel consumption increase considerably with the load level (from unloaded to loaded). This is attributable purely to the fact that the rolling resistance is a function of vehicle weight. Similarly, at given speed and load level, increasing roughness (from very smooth paved to very rough unpaved) causes the vehicle power and fuel consumption to go up via an increase in the rolling resistance coefficient. Finally, by the combination of the above factors the effect of roughness on fuel consumption is stronger for the loaded than the unloaded truck.

As expected, the amount of the extra fuel goes up with the load level and speed, other things remaining equal. Note that the effect of roughness on fuel consumption is stronger for the loaded than the unloaded truck.

A commonly quoted characteristic of internal combustion engines is the specific fuel consumption. For the test vehicles we define the specific fuel consumption, denoted by SFC (in ml/metric hp.s), as the ratio of the fuel consumption rate to the power output:

$$\text{SFC} = \text{SFC (HP, RPM)} = \frac{\text{UFC}}{\text{HP}} \qquad \text{for HP} > 0 \qquad (9.6)$$

For each test vehicle operating at a "nominal average" engine speed, the values of SFC corresponding to value of HP equal to 25, 50, 75 and 100 percent of the vehicles' maximum used driving power (HPDRIVE) are compiled in Table 9.5. The determination of the "nominal average" engine speeds and the maximum used driving powers of the test vehicles is described in Chapter 10. Figures 9.3 (a) and (b) show specific fuel

Figure 9.2: The effect of vehicle speed, load and road surface on vehicle power and fuel consumption for a heavy truck on a level tangent road

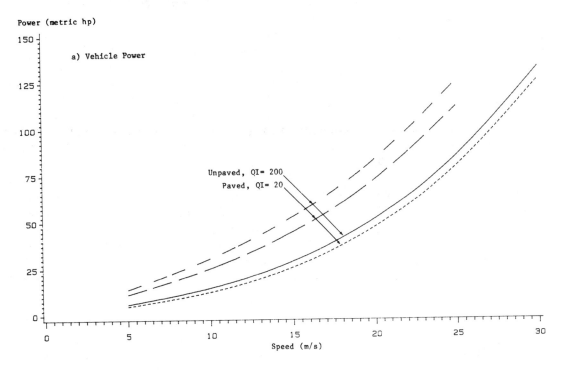

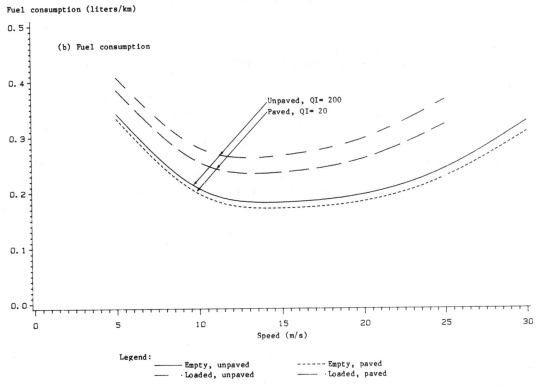

Source: Analysis of Brazil-UNDP-World Bank highway research project data.

consumption as a function of power for different values of engine speed for typical gasoline and diesel engines, respectively.

Table 9.5: Specific fuel consumption for test vehicles at nominal average engine speed for different values of power

Test vehicle	Nominal average engine speed (rpm)	HPDRIVE (metric hp)	Specific fuel consumption (ml/metric hp-s)			
			25% of HPDRIVE	50% of HPDRIVE	75% of HPDRIVE	HPDRIVE
VW-1300	3500	30	0.20	0.13	0.10	0.09
Opala	3000	70	0.22	0.15	0.13	0.11
Dodge Dart	3300	85	0.18	0.11	0.09	0.08
VW-Kombi 1	3300	40	0.17	0.10	0.08	0.07
VW-Kombi 2	3300	40	0.18	0.10	0.08	0.07
Ford 400	3300	80	0.25	0.17	0.15	0.14
Ford 4000	2500	60	0.14	0.10	0.08	0.07
Mercedes 1113	2000	100	0.11	0.08	0.07	0.07
Mercedes 1113 Replica	2000	100	0.11	0.08	0.07	0.07
Mercedes Bus 0-326	1900	100	0.09	0.07	0.06	0.06
Scania 110/39	1600	210	0.08	0.07	0.06	0.06

9.4 TRANSFERABILITY OF THE UFC FUNCTION

The question of transferability of the estimated unit fuel consumption function revolves around two issues. The simpler of the two is the extent to which the estimated function is representative of the particular make and model of the test vehicle used. This issue may be answered in the affirmative based on the evidence of the two replicate vehicles (the VW/Kombi utility and the Mercedes Benz-1113 truck). The coefficients estimated for the two sets of replicate vehicles are close to each other, and the predictions produced by the replicate sets of coefficients are even closer.

The second and larger issue is the extent to which the estimated function is representative of the vehicle class. Although we expect that the estimated UFC will be adequately representative of the respective vehicle classes in many cases, it is possible that some makes and models have a different UFC function, owing to improvements or changes in vehicle technology over time (e.g., with respect to engine design (e.g., turbocharged engine with intercooler) or fuel type (e.g., gasohol or alcohol). Thus, it is important to guard against indiscriminate use of the fuel consumption model presented here. The sample of test vehicles for the Brazil study was chosen before the two major oil crises, in the early and the late seventies, stimulated an

**Figure 9.3:   Specific fuel consumption curves for (a) a typical gasoline
engine (Chevrolet Opala) and (b) a typical diesel engine
(Mercedes 1113)**

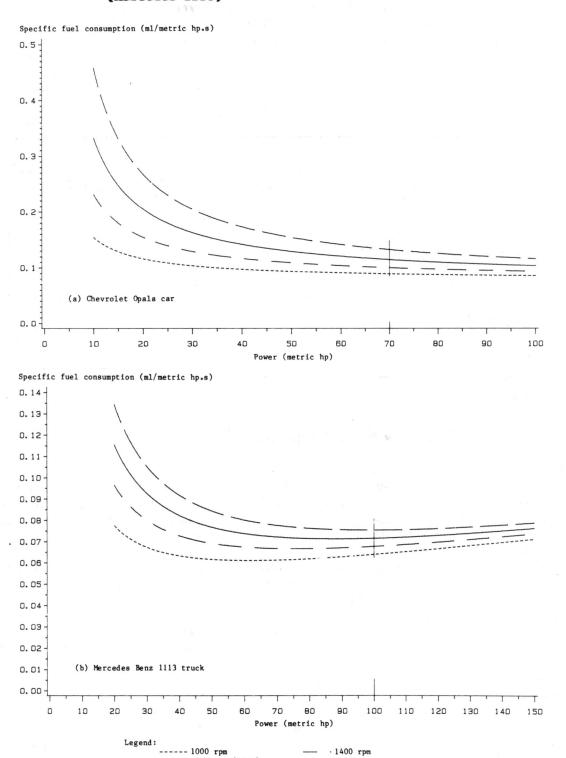

Source: Analysis of Brazil-UNDP-World Bank highway research project data.

unprecedented change in vehicle technology to improve fuel economy. The problem of representativeness is likely to be particularly serious for cars and the articulated truck. While popular in the sixties and greater part of the seventies, the VW1300 is no longer considered a good representation of the class of small cars. The Chevrolet Opala vehicle in the Brazil study test fleet had six cylinders whereas the most popular configuration for a typical medium car is a four cylinder engine. Similarly, the 8-cylinder Dodge is expected to have relatively few counterparts in most developing countries. Finally, the particular unit of Scania chosen as representative of the class of articulated trucks had a somewhat non-standard transmission which could have resulted in a relatively high fuel consumption.

The ideal course of action for obtaining reliable estimates of the UFC function for a particular vehicle would be a re-calibration. However, this would entail a major data collection and analysis effort. A crude but relatively simple alternative would be to employ a multiplicative adjustment factor, α_1, loosely termed "relative energy-efficiency factor." This factor is specific to a given vehicle class, and has a value of 1 for the particular makes and models used in the estimation of the unit fuel consumption function in the Brazilian study. For a different vehicle of the same class, which is expected to be more efficient than the test vehicle, a value of α_1, smaller than 1 may be used. Possible ranges of values of α_1 for different vehicle classes are given in Table 9.6 along with recommended values.

Table 9.6: Relative energy—efficiency factors

Vehicle class	Test vehicle	Relative energy efficiency factor α_1		
		Comparable design	Modern design	Possible range
Small car	VW-1300	1.00	0.85	0.70-1.00
Medium car	Chevrolet Opala	1.00	0.85	0.70-1.00
Large car	Dodge Dart	1.00	0.95	0.80-1.00
Utility	VW-Kombi	1.00	0.95	0.80-1.00
Bus	Mercedes 0-326	1.00	0.95	0.80-1.00
Light gasoline truck	Ford 400	1.00	0.95	0.80-1.00
Light diesel truck	Ford 4000	1.00	0.95	0.80-1.00
Medium truck	Mercedes 1113 (2 axles)	1.00	0.95	0.80-1.00
Heavy truck	Mercedes 1113 (3 axles)	1.00	0.95	0.80-1.00
Articulated truck	Scania 110/39	1.00	0.80	0.65-1.00

Source: Author's recommendation.

APPENDIX 9A

DETERMINATION OF THE FORM OF UNIT FUEL CONSUMPTION FUNCTION

The procedure followed to determine the form of the unit fuel consumption function, UFC(HP, RPM) for the test vehicles is described below, first in general terms, followed by illustration of the procedure for the Mercedes Benz 1113 heavy truck.

First, the contours of the observed unit fuel consumption (UFC) values against vehicle power (HP) were obtained for each available nomina engine speed (RPM). Visual examination of the plots led to the following model form relating the UFC to HP for any given value of RPM, say RPM_0:

$$UFC(HP, RPM_0) = \begin{cases} b_0(RPM_0) + b_1(RPM_0)\,HP + b_2(RPM_0)\,HP^2 & \text{for } HP \geq 0 \\ b_0(RPM_0) + b_3(RPM_0)\,HP + b_4(RPM_0)\,HP^2 & \text{for } HP < 0 \end{cases} \qquad (9A.1)$$

where $b_0(RPM_0)$ through $b_4(RPM_0)$ are parametric functions to be estimated for each tested value of RPM. The notation may be simplified by defining "positive power" (PH) and "negative power" (NH) as follows:

$$PH = \text{Max } [0; HP]$$
$$NH = \text{Min } [HP; 0]$$

Further, it was found desirable to impose a lower limit on negative power to simplify the functional form. The limiting value, denoted by NH_0, was determined for each test vehicle by inspecting the contour plots. Denoting the bounded negative power by NHX, we may write

$$NHX = \text{Max } [NH; NH_0]$$

Equation 9A.1 may now be written as:

$$UFC = b_0 + b_1\,PH + b_2\,PH^2 + b_3\,NHX + b_4\,NHX^2 \qquad (9A.2)$$

where the arguments of UFC and the b's are suppressed for simplicity. In the first stage of the data analysis regression runs were made using Equation 9A.2 for each test vehicle and for each nominal engine speed tested.

The next step was to determine the form of the parametric functions $b_0(RPM)$ through $b_4(RPM)$ for each test vehicle. The most general form used was a quadratic equation:

$$b_i = c_i + d_i \text{ RPM} + e_i \text{ RPM}^2, \quad i = 0\ldots.4 \qquad (9A.3)$$

where c_i, d_i and e_i are constant parameters. For any particular test vehicle a number of these constant parameters were found not to be significantly different from zero. Combining Equations 9A.2 and 9A.3, and retaining the significant parameters only, the following general form of the UFC function was arrived at:

$$\text{UFC(HP, RPM)} = (c_0 + d_0 \text{ RPM} + e_0 \text{ RPM}^2) + (c_1 + d_1 \text{ RPM}) \text{ PH} + c_2 \text{ PH}^2$$
$$+ c_3 \text{ NHX} + c_4 \text{ NHX}^2$$

or, using a_0 through a_7 to denote the parameters for convenience, we may write:

$$\text{UFC} = a_0 + a_1 \text{ RPM} + a_2 \text{ RPM}^2 + a_3 \text{PH} + a_4 \text{ RPM PH} + a_5 \text{ PH}^2 + a_6 \text{ NHX} + a_7 \text{ NHX}^2$$
$$(9A.4)$$

Table 9.3 may be consulted for details regarding the parameters judged to be significant for each test vehicle, noting, as stated above, that for a given test vehicle some of the parameters may be zero.

The final step was to derive the "single-stage" estimates of the parameters a_0 through a_7. The results are shown in Table 9.3.

Figure 9A.1 shows the contour plot for the Mercedes Benz 1113 heavy truck, using a random sample of the dataset. The value of the lower limit on negative power, NH_0, was determined to be -85 metric hp.

To illustrate the second step, the plots of b_0 and b_1 against engine speed are shown in Figures 9A.2 (a) and (b), respectively. It may be seen from Figure 9A.2 (a) that b_0 as a function of RPM has a significant linear trend but only a slight curvature. Thus, for the heavy truck,

$$b_0(\text{RPM}) = c_0 + d_0 \text{ RPM}.$$

Figure 9A.2 (b) shows that b_1 is nearly constant over the range of RPM values tested, yielding:

$$b_1(\text{RPM}) = c_1$$

Similarly, it was found that b_2 through b_4 were also nearly constant over the RPM values tested. Thus, the UFC as a function of HP and RPM for the heavy truck was:

$$\text{UFC(HP, RPM)} = (c_0 + d_0 \text{ RPM}) + c_1 \text{ PH} + c_2 \text{ PH}^2 + c_3 \text{ NHX} + c_4 \text{ NHX}^2$$

In other words, for the heavy truck the equation 9A.4 was estimated with the parameters a_2 and a_4 constrained to zero.

Figure 9A.1: Observed unit fuel consumption versus vehicle power with contours for nominal engine speed for heavy truck

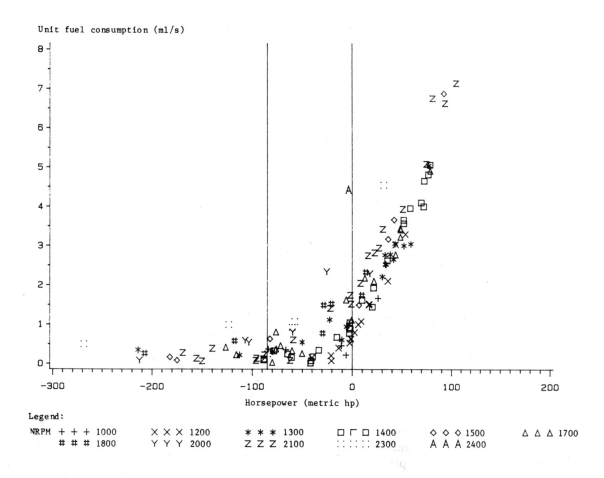

Unit fuel consumption (ml/s)

Legend:

NRPM	+ + + 1000	X X X 1200	* * * 1300	□ ⌐ □ 1400	◇ ◇ ◇ 1500	△ △ △ 1700
	# # # 1800	Y Y Y 2000	Z Z Z 2100	:::::: 2300	A A A 2400	

Source: Analysis of Brazil–UNDP–World Bank highway research project data.

Figure 9A.2: b_0 and b_1 versus nominal engine speed for heavy truck

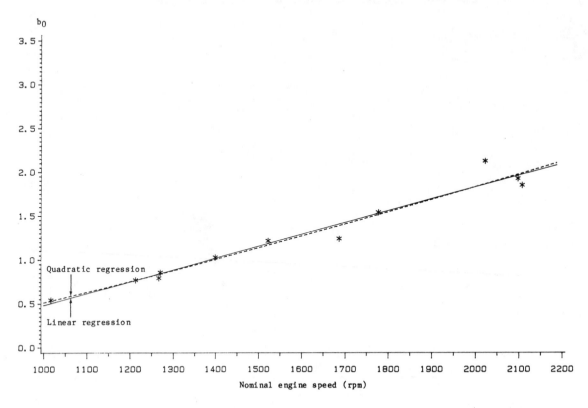

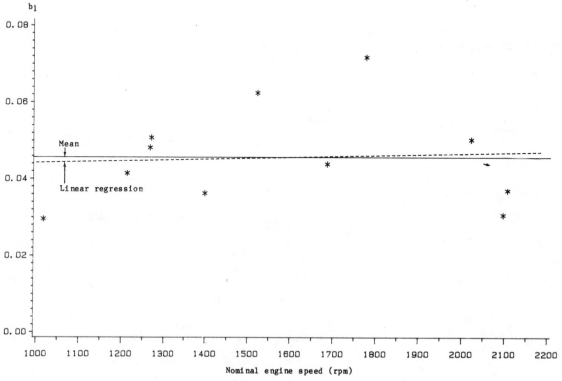

Source: Analysis of Brazil–UNDP–World Bank highway research project data.

CHAPTER 10

Fuel Consumption Prediction Models

Once speed information is known, be it in detailed or aggregate form, fuel consumption can be computed through the unit fuel consumption function presented in Chapter 9. This is the concern of this chapter, which presents specifically:

1. The fuel consumption prediction procedures based on the micro and aggregate models of speed prediction dealt with in Chapters 5-7 (Sections 10.1-10.3);

2. The calibration and validation of these models using independent fuel data (Sections 10.4-10.7); and

3. The development of adjustment factors to bring the fuel consumption predicted by these models closer to real-world operating conditions (Section 10.8).

10.1 MICRO TRANSITIONAL MODEL

This model is presented first since it is the most general. Let L denote the total distance travelled by a vehicle. Our objective is to predict the amount of fuel consumed by the vehicle per unit distance travelled, denoted by FC (in ml/m, or equivalently, liters/km). The prediction formula is:

$$FC = \frac{\sum_j \Delta F_j}{L} \qquad (10.1)$$

where the summation above is over all simulation intervals; and ΔF_j is the predicted amount over fuel consumed over simulation interval j, in ml, given by:

$$\Delta F_j = UFC\ (HP_j,\ RPM_j)\ \frac{\Delta L_j}{V_j} \qquad (10.2)$$

where HP_j, RPM_j and V_j are, respectively, the average values of vehicle power, engine speed and travel speed over simulation interval j; and ΔL_j is the length of simulation interval j, in meters (as defined in Chapter 6). The vehicle travel speed and power are computed from the following formulas:

$$V_j = \frac{1}{2} \left[VEN_j + VEX_j \right] \qquad (10.3)$$

where VEN_j and VEX_j are the entry and exit speeds determined from the speed profile simulation described in Chapter 6; and

$$HP_j = \frac{1}{736} \left\{ [m' \, a_j + m \, g \, (GR_j + CR_j)] \, V_j + A \, V_j^3 \right\} \qquad (10.4)$$

where a_j = the vehicle acceleration over the simulation interval, given by:

$$a_j = \frac{VEX_j^2 - VEN_j^2}{2 \, \Delta L_j} \qquad (10.5)$$

and the other variables are as defined previously, with subscript j denoting those that are specific to the simulation interval. The engine speed, RPM_j, is treated as a model parameter to be calibrated, as described in Section 10.6.

The general procedure for predicting fuel consumption on the basis of vehicle mechanics described above is not new and has been used in previous studies including Sullivan (1977) and Andersen and Gravem (1979). With respect to the unit fuel consumption function derived herein, simplifying assumptions have been made in these studies. One is that for positive power fuel consumption is taken to be proportional to the power. Another is that for negative power fuel consumption is set constant.

10.2 MICRO NON-TRANSITIONAL MODEL

As discussed before, the micro non-transitional model differs from its micro transitional counterpart in two major respects. First, the smaller unit of the road section for which fuel consumption is computed is the subsection (cf. Figure 5.1) as opposed to the simulation interval (cf. Figures 6.1 and 6.3). And second, within each subsection, the vehicle acceleration is zero. By adapting the relationships provided for the micro transitional model, we arrive at the following prediction formula:

$$FC = \frac{\sum\limits_s F_s}{L} \qquad (10.6)$$

where the summation above is over all homogeneous subsections; and F_s is the predicted amount of fuel consumed over subsection s, in ml, given by:

$$F_s = UFC \, (HP_s, \, RPM_s) \, \frac{L_s}{VSS_s} \qquad (10.7)$$

where HP_s, RPM_s and VSS_s are, respectively, the vehicle power, engine speed and steady-state speed over subsection s; and L_s is the length of the subsection, in meters (as defined in Chapter 5). For the engine speed RPM_s, the calibrated value obtained in Section 10.6 is used. The vehicle power, HP_s, is given by:

$$HP_s = \frac{1}{736} \left[m \ g \ (GR_s + CR_s) \ VSS_s + A \ VSS_s^3 \right] \qquad (10.8)$$

where the variables on the right-hand side of the above equation are as defined earler, with subscript s denoting those that are specific to the subsection.

10.3 AGGREGATE MODEL

As a special case of the micro non-transitional model in which there are only two subsections, uphill and downhill, the prediction formula for the aggregate method is as follows:

$$FC = \frac{F_u + F_d}{L} \qquad (10.9)$$

where F_u and F_d are the predicted amounts of fuel consumption over the uphill and downhill subsections, respectively, in ml, given by:

$$F_u = UFC \ (HP_u, \ RPM_u) \ \frac{L_u}{VSS_u} \qquad (10.10a)$$

$$F_d = UFC \ (HP_d, \ RPM_d) \ \frac{L_d}{VSS_d} \qquad (10.10b)$$

where $\qquad HP_u = \frac{1}{736} \left[m \ g \ (GR_u + CR) \ VSS_u + A \ VSS_u^3 \right] \qquad (10.11a)$

$$HP_d = \frac{1}{736} \left[m \ g \ (GR_d + CR) \ VSS_d + A \ VSS_d^3 \right] \qquad (10.11b)$$

and the other variables are as defined previously, with subscripts u and d denoting those that are specific to the uphill and downhill subsections, respectively.

10.4   DATA FOR CALIBRATION AND VALIDATION

The data used in calibrating and validating the fuel consumption prediction models described above were obtained from a field experiment. The experiment involved running nine test vehicles[1] over five 10-km test sections in each direction, loaded and unloaded. Two of the sections were paved and three were unpaved. The individual grades vary in steepness and have a maximum value of 9.3 percent. The sharpest curve has a 72-meter radius. Summary statistics of these sections are compiled in Table 8.2.[2]

During the experiment, the drivers were instructed to drive in a natural manner as if they were in a normal operating situation. During each vehicle run, the amount of fuel consumed was recorded at every 500-meter interval as well as the detailed profile of the elapsed travel time. Using finite differences, the latter was used to derive the profiles of observed speed and acceleration for the run. An illustrative example of profiles of elapsed time, vehicle speed and acceleration is presented in Figure 10.1 for a loaded heavy truck travelling on an unpaved section of moderately severe geometry.

Typically, for each combination of the test vehicle, load level, section and direction, six replicate vehicle runs were made. For analysis purposes, profiles of the vehicle speed, acceleration and power for each combination were computed as averages of the profiles obtained from the individual replicate runs. In all, a total of 535 vehicle runs were made. Summary statistics of the runs are compiled in Table 10.1.

10.5   ADAPTATION OF STEADY-STATE SPEED MODEL PARAMETERS FOR TEST VEHICLES

In the estimation of the steady-state speed relationships in Chapter 4, the vehicle classes employed generally do not exactly correspond to the test vehicles in terms of weight, load and power. The model parameters considered to be sensitive to the vehicle size, power and load are the used driving and braking powers (HPDRIVE and HPBRAKE, respectively) and the perceived friction ratio (FRATIO) for trucks on paved roads. Therefore, the values of these parameters were revised to make them more specific to the test vehicles following the guidelines given in Chapter 4. The new values of these parameters are compiled in Table 10.2 along with the originally estimated values for the closest vehicle classes.

10.6   CALIBRATION OF NOMINAL ENGINE SPEEDS

As mentioned earlier, in order to use the three fuel consumption prediction models described in Sections 10.1-10.3, we must know the engine speed (RPM). If the gear speed is known, RPM can be easily computed (using Equation 9.2). The problem is that for a given

---

[1] Excluding the Dodge and the Opala for logistical reasons.

[2] As presented in Chapter 8, these sections were also used in the validation of the micro non-transitional and aggregate speed prediction models.

Figure 10.1: Typical profiles of elapsed travel time, speed and acceleration: loaded Mercedes Benz 1113 travelling on unpaved section of relatively severe geometry

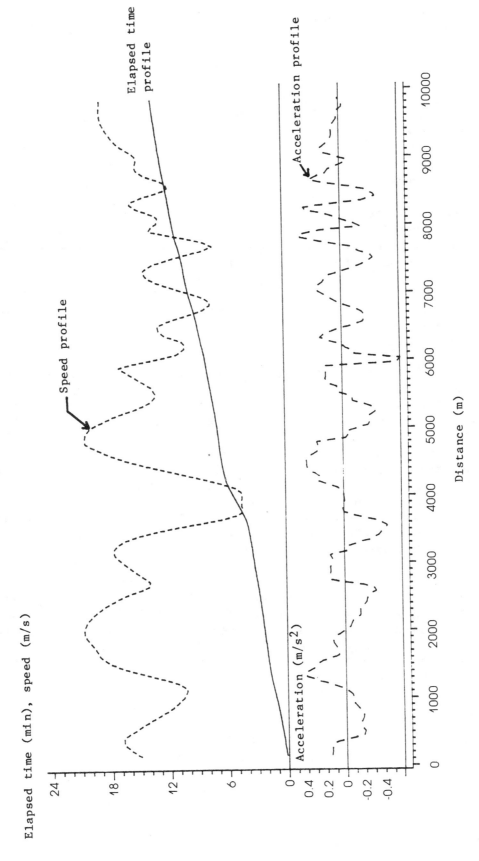

Source: Analysis of Brazil-UNDP-World Bank highway research program

Table 10.1: Summary statistics of fuel calibration/validation experiment

Vehicle	Payload when loaded (kg)	Number of runs	
		Unloaded	Loaded
Small car	280	13	28
Utility (2 vehicles)	550	24	31
Large bus	2,250	37	57
Light gasoline truck	3,510	13	12
Light diesel truck	3,325	36	42
Heavy truck	11,970	30	40
Heavy truck replicate	13,715	48	32
Articulated truck	26,600	50	42

Source: Brazil–UNDP–World Bank highway research project data.

combination of vehicle speed and power there can be more than one feasible gear and the choice of gear depends on the behavior of individual drivers. Thus, to predict used engine speed on a rigorous basis, one needs to formulate plausible hypotheses regarding gear change behavior as a function of vehicle speed, acceleration, power used and other factors and to test and calibrate the relationships based on observed data. However, engine-speed profiles were not observed in the fuel consumption validation experiments and recourse had to be taken to simpler approaches. Two approaches were tried out to predict the engine speed. The first was based on an assumption of rational driver behavior: from among the feasible gears the driver chooses the one that minimizes the fuel consumption given the power. The second approach was to make the simple assumption of constant or nominal engine speed and to determine or "calibrate" it using the fuel consumption data. These two approaches yielded comparable accuracy. Since the second approach is much simpler, it was selected for use in all three prediction models.

The nominal engine speed or the calibrated RPM value for a test vehicle was obtained simply by varying the value of RPM over the feasible range until the averages of observed fuel consumption and corresponding predictions agreed. The observed speed profiles were all available combinations of test vehicle, load level section and direction were employed as the basis for fuel consumption prediction. The calibrated RPM values for eight test vehicles are shown in Table 10.3 along with the manufacturers' RPM values at the maximum rated power. It is seen that on average, these calibrated values are about 75 percent of the rated values. Thus, for the three test vehicles for which no RPM calibration was actually carried out[3], the calibrated RPM values were assumed to equal 75 percent of the rated values (as shown in Table 10.3).

To get an idea of the goodness of fit for each test vehicle calibrated, the observed fuel consumption (by load level, section and

---

[3] As mentioned earlier, the validation experiments did not include the Dodge and the Opala. The Ford-400 was included in the experiment, but the fuel measurements were found to be erroneous.

Table 10.2: Steady-state speed model parameter adjusted for test vehicles

Test vehicle	Used driving power HPDRIVE (metric hp)		Used braking power HPBRAKE (metric hp)		PERCEIVED FRICTION RATIO					
	Original	Adjusted	Original	Adjusted	Original FRATIO		Parameterized			
							Paved		Unpaved	
					Paved unload/loaded	Unpaved	$FRATIO_0$	$FRATIO_1$	$FRATIO_0$	$FRATIO_1$
Small car	36.36	30	21.72	17	0.2674	0.1235	0.2674	0.0	0.1235	0.0
Utility	44.37	40	32.64	30	0.2217	0.1173	0.2217	0.0	0.1173	0.0
Large bus	112.95	100	213.58	160	0.2333	0.0949	0.2333	0.0	0.0949	0.0
Light gas truck	94.74	80	190.80	100	0.2535 / 0.1705	0.0994	0.2535	1.28×10^{-6}	0.0994	0.0
Light diesel truck	94.74	60	190.80	100	0.2535 / 0.1705	0.0994	0.2535	1.28×10^{-6}	0.0994	0.0
Heavy truck	108.19	100	257.10	250	0.2926 / 0.1858	0.0873	0.2926	0.94×10^{-6}	0.0873	0.0
Articulated truck	199.98	210	500.00	500	0.1789 / 0.1295	0.0400	0.1789	0.23×10^{-6}	0.0400	0.0

Source: Adapted from analysis of Brazil–UNDP–World Bank Highway research project data.

221

Table 10.3:   Calibrated engine speeds

Vehicle	CRPM Calibrated engine speed (rpm)	MRPM Maximum rated	Ratio of CRPM to MRPM
Small car	3500	4600	0.7
Medium car[1]	3000	4000	0.75
Large car[1]	3300	4400	0.75
Utility[1]	3300	4600	0.72
Large bus	2300	2800	0.82
Light gasoline truck[1]	3300	4400	0.75
Light diesel truck	2600	3000	0.87
Heavy truck	1800	2800	0.64
Articulated truck	1700	2200	0.77

[1]   As no validation data were available for these vehicles their calibrated engine speeds were determined judgementally.

Source: Adapted from analysis of Brazil-UNDP-World Bank highway research project data.

direction) was regressed against the fuel consumption predicted using observed speeds, with and without the intercept as in the speed model validation presented in Chapter 8.   The regression results compiled in Table 10.4 indicate an excellent agreement between the observed and predicted fuel consumption especially in the case of the heavy vehicles which, it may be noted, are all diesel-driven.   The fit is somewhat lower for the light gasoline-driven vehicles.   The poorest fit is in the case of the small car (VW-1300), with an R_2 value of 57 percent.   Figure 10.2 shows in graphical form the regression results with the calibrated test vehicles pooled together (into two groups, trucks and non-trucks). Again, an excellent fit is evident.   Also shown in Figure 10.2 are regression lines obtained from fuel predictions with RPM varied by $\pm$ 30 percent of the calibrated values.   The small deviations of the slopes of these lines from unity indicate the relative insensitivity of fuel predictions to the engine speed.

10.7   VALIDATION

10.7.1   Micro Transitional Model

For each calibrated test vehicle, the micro transitional method was applied to each combination of load level, section and direction for which fuel consumption was recorded.   This was accomplished by first constructing a simulated speed profile (following the procedure in Chapter 6) and then applying the relationships described in Section 10.2 (using the calibrated RPM values in Table 10.3) to the speed profile to arrive at the desired prediction.

Table 10.4: Regression results: observed fuel consumption versus fuel consumption predicted with observed speed profiles

Vehicle	Number of observations	Intercept	Slope	R^2	Standard error of residuals
Small car	8	-0.04 (-0.4)	1.448 (38)	0.57	0.017
		-	1.010 (14.1)	0.51	0.017
Utility	12	0.06 (2.8)	0.588 (4.2)	0.63	0.010
		-	0.987 (39.9)	0.34	0.013
Large bus	19	0.00 (0.1)	1.009 (38.5)	0.99	0.015
		-	1.010 (88.1)	0.99	0.015
Light diesel truck	18	0.01 (1.7)	0.933 (24.7)	0.97	0.013
		-	0.990 (62.6)	0.97	0.014
Heavy truck	15	0.02 (1.1)	0.926 (16.6)	0.96	0.032
		-	0.982 (45.3)	0.96	0.032
Articulated truck	17	0.06 (2.6)	0.930 (33.9)	0.99	0.054
		-	0.988 (52.2)	0.98	0.063
All vehicles combined	86	0.01 (2.5)	0.969 (86.3)	0.99	0.031
		-	0.989 (123.8)	0.99	0.032

Source: Analysis of Brazil-UNDP-World Bank highway research project data.

Figure 10.2: Plots of observed fuel consumption versus fuel consumption predicted with observed speed

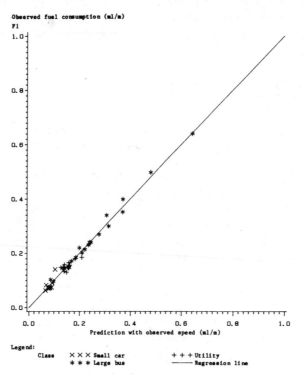

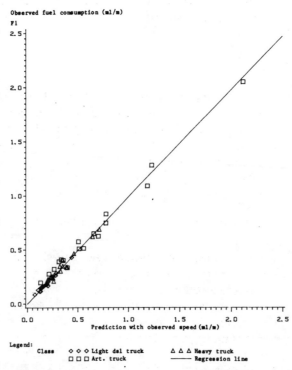

Source: Analysis of Brazil-UNDP-World Bank highway research project data.

The results of comparison between the predicted and observed the form of regression statistics similar to those in Tables 10.4 and Figure 10.2. It can be seen that as indicated by the standard errors of regression and regression slopes the prediction accuracy obtained from simulated speed profiles is uniformly high and comparable to the accuracy obtained from the observed profiles.

10.7.2 Micro Non-transitional Model

The procedure used for validating this model paralleled that of the micro transitional counterpart. The main difference was that the "step" steady-state speed profiles were used as the basis for prediction.

The predictions produced were first compared with those obtained by the micro transitional model. The results are in the form of regressiostatistics as shown in Table 10.6 and Figure 10.4. The slopes of the without-intercept regression lines virtually equal unity. This implies that the omission of transitional speed behavior introduces virtually no bias in the predictions for the road sections tested.

Similarly to the above comparison, the predictions were next compared with the corresponding observed values as shown in Table 10.7 and Figure 10.5. It is evident from the regression slopes and standard errors of regression that the non-transitional model is almost as accurate as thetransitional counterpart.

These results indicate that the accuracy of the non-transitional model is adequate for most purposes, especially within the range of road geometry tested.

10.7.3 Aggregate Model

This model was tested against the micro models as well as the observed fuel consumption, using the same procedure for comparison as those used for the micro methods, i.e., regression analysis. The results of the comparison are shown in Tables 10.8–10.10 and Figures 10.6–10.8. It can be seen that aggregate predictions closely approximate predictions by both micro models, as indicated by the slopes of the fitted lines being close to one and the small standard errors of regression.

10.8 ADJUSTMENT FACTORS FOR ACTUAL OPERATING CONDITIONS

The fuel consumption data employed in the development and validation of the foregoing fuel consumption prediction models were obtained under rather idealized controlled conditions in favor of fuel efficiency. Predictions by these models were found to be generally lower than values experienced by vehicle operators in the same geographic region but under actual conditions. Therefore, adjustment factors, denoted by α_2 were developed to bring the predictions closer to vehicle operators' values, as reported in this section.

Table 10.5: Regression results: observed fuel consumption versus fuel consumption predicted using micro transitional model

Vehicle	Number of observations	Intercept	Slope	R^2	Standard error of residuals
Small car	8	−0.04 (−0.8)	1.436 (2.6)	0.53	0.018
		−	1.010 (13.6)	0.48	0.018
Utility	12	0.05 (2.4)	0.681 (5.2)	0.73	0.001
		−	0.998 (49.6)	0.57	0.011
Large bus	19	−0.02 (−1.9)	1.017 (33.0)	0.98	0.017
		−	1.014 (68.5)	0.98	0.019
Light diesel truck	15	0.01 (1.3)	0.953 (25.6)	0.98	0.012
		−	0.999 (64.5)	0.98	0.012
Heavy truck	15	0.02 (0.9)	0.944 (16.5)	0.95	0.032
		−	0.994 (45.5)	0.95	0.032
Articulated truck	17	0.03 (1.3)	0.961 (38.6)	0.99	0.050
		−	0.988 (64.5)	0.99	0.051
All vehicles combined	86	0.01 (1.5)	0.981 (94.6)	0.99	0.028
		−	0.992 (138.5)	0.99	0.028

Source: Analysis of Brazil-UNDP-World Bank highway research project data.

**Table 10.6: Regression results: micro transitional versus micro non-
transitional steady-state speed fuel consumption prediction**

Vehicle	Number of observations	Intercept	Slope	R^2	Standard error of residuals
Small car	8	0.00 (0.8)	0.979 (27.5)	0.99	0.001
		–	1.006 (205.4)	0.99	0.001
Utility	12	0.01 (2.1)	0.954 (35.3)	0.99	0.002
		–	1.009 (243.2)	0.99	0.002
Large bus	19	0.01 (2.0)	0.976 (49.8)	0.99	0.011
		–	1.012 (108.3)	0.99	0.012
Light diesel truck	15	0.01 (2.3)	0.957 (50.1)	0.99	0.006
		–	0.997 (109.3)	0.93	0.007
Heavy truck	15	0.03 (1.8)	0.938 (24.4)	0.98	0.023
		–	1.000 (59.9)	0.97	0.024
Articulated truck	17	0.03 (1.8)	0.960 (46.4)	0.99	0.041
		–	0.990 (75.9)	0.99	0.044
All vehicles combined	86	0.01 (3.1)	0.977 (126.5)	0.99	0.021
		–	0.994 (176.1)	0.99	0.022

Source: Analysis of Brazil-UNDP-World Bank highway research project
data.

Figure 10.3: Plots of observed fuel consumption versus fuel consumption predicted using micro transitional model

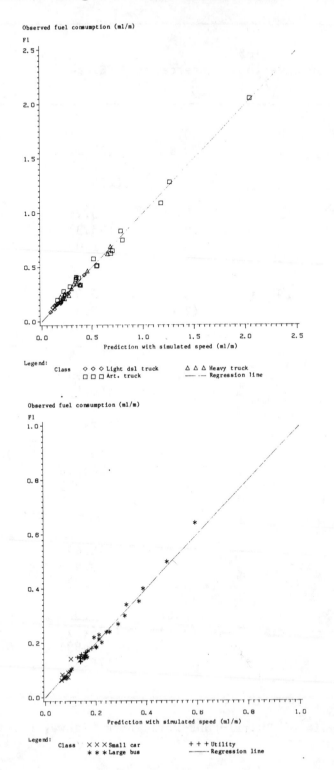

Figure 10.4: Plots of fuel consumption prediction using micro-transional model versus predictions with steady-state speed model

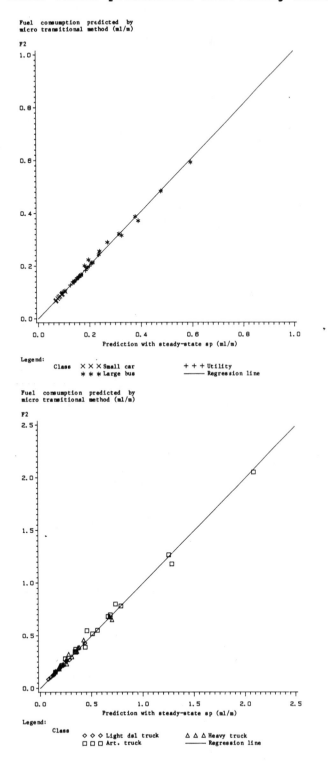

Source: Analysis of Brazil-UNDP-World Bank highway research project data.

Table 10.7: Regression results: observed fuel consumption versus fuel consumption predicted using micro non—transitional steady-state speed model

Vehicle	Number of observations	Intercept	Slope	R^2	Standard error of residuals
Small car	8	−0.04 (−0.9)	0.504 (2.9)	0.59	0.017
		–	1.018 (14.3)	0.53	0.017
Utility	12	0.05 (2.9)	0.657 (5.3)	0.74	0.009
		–	1.007 (47.3)	0.53	0.011
Large bus	19	−0.01 (−0.6)	1.047 (29.4)	0.98	0.020
		–	1.027 (66.8)	0.98	0.020
Light diesel truck	15	0.02 (2.2)	0.911 (21.4)	0.97	0.014
		–	0.995 (49.4)	0.96	0.016
Heavy truck	15	0.05 (1.8)	0.882 (12.8)	0.93	0.041
		–	0.993 (33.2)	0.91	0.043
Articulated truck	17	0.06 (2.1)	0.922 (27.4)	0.98	0.066
		–	0.978 (44.9)	0.97	0.073
All vehicles combined	86	0.02 (2.9)	0.958 (71.3)	0.98	0.037
		–	0.986 (100.9)	0.98	0.039

Source: Analysis of Brazil—UNDP—World Bank highway research project data.

Figure 10.5: Plots of observed fuel consumption versus that predicted with steady-state speed model

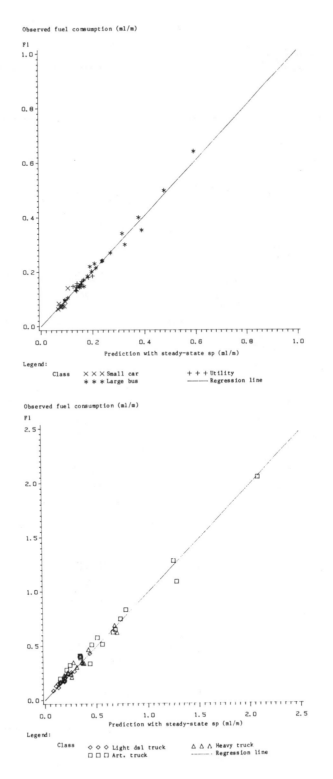

Source: Analysis of Brazil-UNDP-World Bank highway research project
          data.

Table 10.8: Regression results: steady-state consumption prediction versus fuel consumption predicted using aggregate model

Vehicle	Number of observations	Intercept	Slope	R^2	Standard error of residuals
Small car	8	0.00 (-0.2)	1.007 (118.3)	1.00	0.0
		-	1.006 (898.2)	1.00	0.0
Utility		0.00 (-2.3)	1.015 (227.7)	1.00	0.0
	12	-	1.005 (1432.1)	1.00	0.0
Large bus	19	0.00 (1.5)	0.993 (676.6)	1.00	0.0
		-	0.995 (1487.4)	1.00	0.0
Light diesel truck	15	0.00 (-2.3)	1.020 (312.7)	1.00	0.001
		-	1.013 (654.0)	1.00	0.001
Heavy truck	15	0.01 (3.5)	0.960 (254.4)	1.00	0.002
		-	0.972 (468.6)	1.00	0.003
Articulated truck	17	0.00 (4.2)	0.987 (850.0)	1.00	0.002
		-	0.991 (1011.0)	1.00	0.003
All vehicles combined	86	0.00 (3.1)	0.986 (686.9)	1.00	0.004
		-	0.990 (939.9)	1.00	0.004

Source: Analysis of Brazil-UNDP-World Bank highway research project data.

Figure 10.6 : Plots of steady-state fuel consumption prediction versus fuel consumption predicted using aggregate model

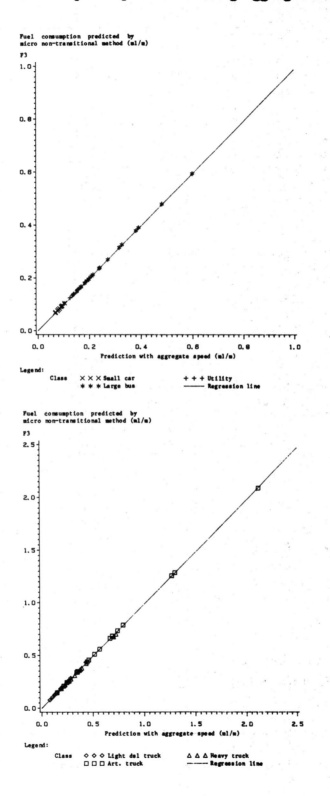

Source: Analysis of Brazil-UNDP-World Bank highway research project data.

Table 10.9: Regression results: fuel consumption predicted using micro transitional model versus fuel consumption predicted using aggregate model

Vehicle	Number of observations	Intercept	Slope	R^2	Standard error of residuals
Small car	8	0.00 (0.8)	0.987 (31.3)	0.99	0.001
		–	1.012 (232.3)	0.99	0.001
Utility	12	0.00	0.968	0.99	0.002
		–	1.014 (260.7)	0.99	0.002
Large bus	19	0.01 (2.2)	0.969 (52.0)	0.99	0.010
		–	1.007 (111.0)	0.99	0.011
Light diesel truck	15	0.01 (2.0)	0.977 (54.9)	1.00	0.006
		–	1.010 (122.9)	1.00	0.006
Heavy truck	15	0.03 (2.1)	0.900 (23.6)	0.98	0.023
		–	0.972 (56.1)	0.98	0.026
Articulated truck	17	0.03 (2.0)	0.947 (45.7)	0.99	0.041
		–	0.981 (73.1)	0.99	0.045
All vehicles combined	86	0.01 (3.5)	0.964 (122.4)	0.99	0.022
		–	0.984 (167.8)	0.99	0.024

Source: Analysis of Brazil-UNDP-World Bank highway research project data.

Figure 10.7: Plots of fuel consumption predicted using micro transitional model versus fuel consumption predicted using aggregate model

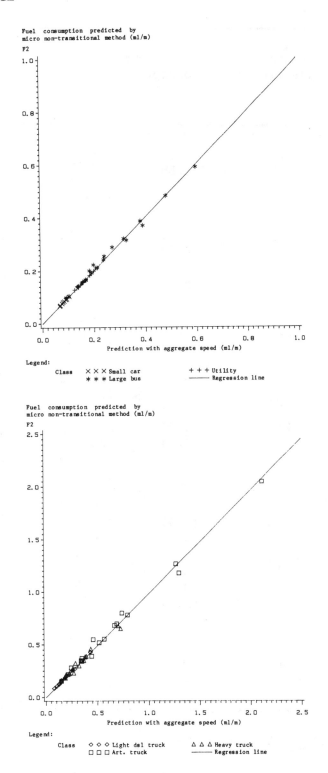

Source: Analysis of Brazil-UNDP-World Bank highway research project
          data.

Table 10.10: **Regression results: observed fuel consumption versus fuel consumption predicted using aggregate model**

Vehicle	Number of observations	Intercept	Slope	R^2	Standard error of residuals
Small car	8	−0.04 (−0.88)	1.475 (2.8)	0.57	0.017
		−	1.023 (14.1)	0.52	0.017
Utility	12	0.05 (2.8)	0.669 (5.4)	0.75	0.009
		−	1.012 (48.3)	0.55	0.011
Large bus	19	−0.01 (−0.6)	1.040 (29.9)	0.98	0.019
		−	1.022 (67.9)	0.98	0.019
Light diesel truck	15	0.02 (2.1)	0.930 (22.5)	0.97	0.013
		−	1.009 (52.6)	0.97	0.015
Heavy truck	15	0.05 (1.9)	0.845 (12.5)	0.92	0.042
		−	0.964 (31.8)	0.90	0.045
Articulated truck	17	0.06 (2.2)	0.910 (27.5)	0.98	0.066
		−	0.969 (44.3)	0.97	0.074
All vehicles combined	86	0.02 (3.2)	0.945 (70.4)	0.98	0.038
		−	0.976 (98.6)	0.98	0.040

Source: Analysis of Brazil–UNDP–World Bank highway research project data.

**Figure 10.8: Plots of observed fuel consumption versus consumption
predicted using aggregate model**

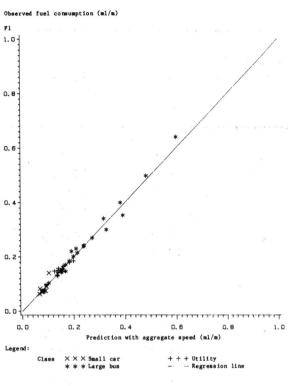

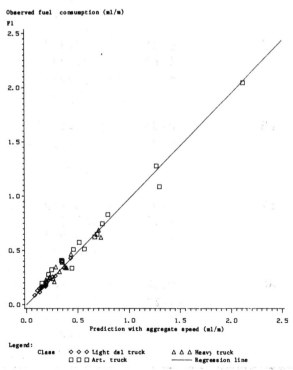

Source: Analysis of Brazil-UNDP-World Bank highway research project
data.

10.8.1   Sources of Discrepancy in Actual Fuel Consumption

The conditions under which the test vehicles were operated can be highlighted by the following features:

1.   The drivers were well-trained and well-controlled.

2.   The vehicles were relatively new and maintained in excellent mechanical condition, particularly the engine.

3.   The experiments were conducted generally when the road surface was dry.

4.   The experiments were conducted only after the engine had reached a steady-state operating temperature.

5.   The experiments were conducted with virtually no interference from other vehicular traffic.

According to the international data compiled by the Organization for Economic Cooperation and Development (OECD, 1982) deviations from the above ideals tend to cause significant increases in average fuel consumption. Table 10.11 gives approximate magnitudes of possible increases due to various sources. Though not exhaustive, they should explain most of the discrepancies between the experimental and survey data.

10.8.2   Data

For comparison purposes, only the survey vehicles that matched one of the test vehicles in terms of major characteristics such as the engine power, tare weight, rated load carrying capacity and fuel efficiency were included.   The resulting correspondence of test and survey vehicles is shown in Table 10.12.[4]

For each class of survey vehicles in Table 10.12, except for the total weight, the values of vehicle characteristics and model parameters (e.g., the aerodynamic drag coefficient, projected frontal area, tare weight and calibrated engine speed) obtained for the corresponding test vehicles were adopted. While these characteristics and parameters may be slightly different from those of the survey vehicles, the resulting fuel prediction errors should be relatively small. The total vehicle weight, which consists of the tare weight and payload, has a strong influence on predicted fuel consumption. However, as no reliable information was available for individual survey vehicles, estimates of their average values were made for each vehicle class.

For each survey vehicle, the characteristics of the routes on which the vehicle was operated were readily available in aggregate form, i.e., average road roughness (in QI), average rise plus fall (in

---

[4]   No matches were found for the following experimental vehicles: the Chevrolet Opala, the Dodge Dart and the Ford-400.

Table 10.11: Sources of fuel consumption discrepancy

Source	Possible variation in fuel consumption[1]
Driver behavior	20 percent difference between economical and hard driving for gasoline-engined passenger cars.
Mechanical condition	20 percent difference or more between well and badly tuned gasoline engines. 2-4 percent difference between correct and incorrect wheel alignment of passenger cars.
Road wetness	2 percent difference between dry and wet surfaces (paved only) for gasoline engined passenger cars.
Vehicle preparation	23 percent difference between a 1400 cc gasoline engine of a passenger car properly warm ed up and at ambiant temperature of 25 degree celsius. Over 4-km distance; 19 percent difference for a 2070 cc diesel engine. For trips longer than 10 km, the percent difference generally reduces to less than 2-3 percent.

[1] The percentage differences are very rough estimates.
Source: Adapted from OECD, 1982.

meters/km), horizontal curvature (in degrees/km), and percentage paved. Summary statistics of the survey routes by vehicle class are compiled in Table 10.13. It can be seen that these routes are generally of modest information was available on the superelevation of the survey routes, the average superelevation was computed as a function of the average horizontal curvature using the relationship given in Chapter 3 (Equation 3.25).

The above vehicle and road characteristics were used to predict the average fuel consumption for each survey vehicle. Only the aggregate model was used. This was because, as alluded to earlier, no detailed information on road geometry was readily available. For routes having mixed paved and unpaved portions, predictions were computed separately by surface type and then their average values were obtained using the paved/unpaved percentages as the weights.

Table 10.12: Correspondence between experimental and survey vehicles and estimates of tare weights and payloads

Vehicle class	Test vehicle	SURVEY VEHICLE		Tare weight (kg)	Average round trip payload(kg)
		Model	Number		
Car	Volkswagen 1300	1300	37	960	0
		1600	6		
		Total	43		
Utility	Volkswagen Kombi	Enclosed	2	1320	300
		Passenger	3		
		Total	5		
Bus	Mercedes Benz 0 362	0 362	32		
		LPO 321/45/48	12		
		LPO 1113/45	113		
		LP 113/48/51	145		
		OF 1113/61	8	8100	2300
		OH 1313/51	20		
		0 321	10		
		0 326	1		
		0 352	33		
		1111	2		
		Total	376		
Light diesel truck	Ford 4000	Ford 4000	8		
		Mercedes L-608	26	3270	2000
		Total	34		
Medium/ heavy truck	Mercedes Benz	L/LK/LS 1113	54		
		L/LK/LS 1313	29	3400/6600	4500/6000
		L/LK 1513	20		
		Total	103		
Articulated truck	Scania L 110	L 110	20		
		LS 1519	18		
		L 75	4		
		L 76	3	14700	13000
		LS 36	6		
		L 111	28		
		LT 111	7		
		LK 140	6		
		Total	92		

Source: Brazil-UNDP-World Bank highway research project data.

10.8.3   Results and Discussion

The observed and predicted fuel consumption are compared in the form of summary statistics in Table 10.14.   Generally, the range predicted is smaller than the range observed.

The high variability in the observed fuel consumption relative to the predicted may to be attributed mainly to the variability in the unmeasured factors discussed in Section 10.8.1, and, in particular, the variability in the total weights of the survey vehicles.

Regression of observed fuel consumption against predicted values by means of ordinary least squares[5], with and without intercept, yielded results as summarized in Table 10.15.   Figure 10.9 shows a plot of observed against predicted fuel consumption distinguished by vehicle class.   The regressions with-intercept for utilities and buses yielded intercepts substantially different from zero and slopes substantially different from one.   For the other vehicle classes, the regressions with and without the intercept yielded similar results.   The slopes of the regressions without-intercept are virtually identical to the simple ratios of mean observed to mean predicted fuel consumption in Table 10.14.

For the purposes of adjusting experimentally-based fuel consumption predictions to account for real-world conditions, the intercept is assumed to be zero for each vehicle class and the value of the slope from the regression without the intercept is taken as the required adjustment factor, α_2.   This procedure is justified by the following reasons:

1.   Besides convenience, a single multiplicative adjustment factor provides a desirable asymptotic property of fuel prediction, i.e., when actual fuel consumption approaches zero (for example, when a vehicle is traversing a downhill section under retarding power of the engine) the prediction should do the same.

2.   For vehicle classes with a large range of predicted fuel consumption (see the minimum and the maximum in Table 10.14), the results of regression with and without the intercept are very similar.

Except for the class of medium/heavy trucks the slopes of the without-intercept regression equations in Table 10.15 fall in a narrow range (1.11 - 1.20).   Since there is no fundamental reason why the adjust-

---

[5]   The regression should, strictly speaking, employ an error component technique since the observation errors are not independent but consist of components specific to both companies and vehicles (Harrison and Chesher, 1984).   The use of ordinary least squares would result in biased t-statistics although the coefficient estimates are still unbiased.   In this analysis t-statistics are used only to indicate relative significance.

Table 10.13: Summary statistics of observed and predicted fuel consumption

Vehicle class	Number of vehicles	Variables	Fuel consumption (liters/1000 km)				
			Mean	Std. dev.	Coef. of variation (%)	Minimum	Maximum
Car	43	Observed	100.8	12.4	12.0	80.0	129.0
		Predicted	87.8	3.6	4.1	84.3	94.3
		Ratio O/P	1.15				
Utility	5	Observed	177.2	20.9	11.8	142.0	195.0
		Predicted	149.8	2.6	1.7	146.1	151.6
		Ratio O/P	1.18				
Bus	376	Observed	305.8	36.5	11.9	211.0	486.0
		Predicted	253.5	12.0	4.7	236.4	294.1
		Ratio O/P	1.21				
Light diesel truck	34	Observed	193.3	31.9	16.5	157.0	304.0
		Predicted	174.3	12.2	7.0	164.8	216.3
		Ratio O/P	1.11				
Medium/heavy truck	103	Observed	319.8	45.2	14.1	251.0	424.0
		Predicted	311.1	40.5	13.0	272.1	392.8
		Ratio O/P	1.03				
Articulated truck	92	Observed	618.9	158.4	6 25.	373.0	1020.0
		Predicted	539.3	68.5	7 12.	472.9	759.4
		Ratio O/P	1.15				

Source: Brazil-UNDP-World Bank highway research project data and analysis.

Table 10.14: Summary of road characteristics

Vehicle class	Statistic	Rise plus fall (m/km)	Horizontal curvature (°/km)	Road roughness (QI)	Percent paved (%)
Car	Mean	26.8	45.4	76.4	63.1
	Std. dev.	7.9	50.1	39.9	35.5
	Maximum	39.2	202.3	140.0	100.0
	Minimum	12.0	12.0	26.9	10.0
Utility	Mean	21.5	27.4	94.0	38.0
	Std. dev.	7.1	7.8	31.0	27.4
	Maximum	32.3	33.0	115.0	68.0
	Minimum	16.6	18.6	46.0	18.0
Bus	Mean	24.4	34.7	86.7	48.9
	Std. dev.	6.8	39.1	46.4	42.3
	Maximum	39.1	188.8	172.6	100.0
	Minimum	9.8	6.2	23.0	0.0
Light diesel truck	Mean	25.5	43.9	66.3	68.4
	Std. dev.	5.6	43.0	40.8	38.5
	Maximum	38.7	214.9	166.5	100.0
	Minimum	15.9	6.1	28.0	0.0
Medium/heavy truck	Mean	32.5	43.2	42.8	88.9
	Std. dev.	3.9	30.9	11.7	10.9
	Maximum	41.4	108.8	85.0	100.0
	Minimum	27.4	5.7	24.0	43.0
Articulated truck	Mean	27.8	40.6	55.2	75.6
	Std. dev.	10.9	50.9	28.9	40.8
	Maximum	48.6	293.7	127.1	100.0
	Minimum	10.0	5.7	26.0	1.0

Source: Brazil-UNDP-World Bank highway research project data.

Table 10.15: Regression results observed versus predicted fuel consumption by vehicle class

Vehicle class	Number of vehicles	Intercept	Slope	R-square	Standard error of residuals
Car	43	−13.8 (−0.3)	1.31 (2.6)	0.14	11.60
			1.15 (57.7)	0.14	11.47
Utility	5	−897.8 (−3.0)	7.17 (3.6)	0.81	10.57
			1.18 (21.9)	0.24	18.14
Bus	376	272.8 (6.8)	0.13 (0.8)	0.00	36.57
			1.20 (153.0)	0.00	38.72
Light diesel truck	34	−8.5 (−0.1)	1.16 (2.8)	0.20	29.11
			1.11 (39.4)	0.19	28.67
Medium/heavy truck	103	89.8 (3.4)	0.74 (8.9)	0.44	34.03
			1.02 (91.0)	0.37	35.79
Articulated truck	92	41.4 (0.4)	1.07 (5.0)	0.21	141.14
			1.15 (42.6)	0.21	140.46
All vehicle classes	653	15.3 (2.3)	1.10 (51.7)	0.80	64.83
			1.15 (140.1)	0.80	65.04

Notes: Fuel consumption is expressed in liters/1000 km.
        Values in the parentheses are t-statistics.

Source: Analysis of Brazil-UNDP-World Bank highway research project data.

ment factors should be distinctly different, except for fuel type, the vehicles were lumped into light (gasoline) and heavy (diesel) groups, as follows:

Light (gasoline)	Heavy (diesel)
Car	Bus
Utility	All trucks

and regressions were run for these groups yielding results as summarized in Table 10.16. Figure 10.10 shows a plot of predicted vs. observed fuel consumption distinguishable by vehicle group; the plot is superimposed with the regression lines of slopes equal to 1.16 and 1.15 for the light and heavy vehicle groups, respectively.

As seen in the validation results in Section 10.7, the discrepancies between fuel predictions by the aggregate and micro models are on the order of less than 2 percent, which is considerably smaller than the 15-16 percent discrepancies between experimentally based fuel predictions and fuel consumption observed under actual operating conditions. Therefore, it seems appropriate to recommend the following values of adjustment factor, α_2, for use with all three prediction models, aggregate and micro:

Cars and utilities: 1.16
Buses and trucks : 1.15

Table 10.16: Regression results of observed versus predicted fuel consumption for heavy and light vehicle groups

Vehicle group	Number of vehicles	Intercept	Slope	R-square	Standard error of residuals
Heavy	605	20.5 (2.6)	1.09 (43.7)	0.76	67.18
			1.15 (134.6)	0.76	67.49
Light	48	-8.4 (-1.0)	1.24 (13.6)	0.80	12.17
			1.16 (63.5)	0.80	12.16

Note: Fuel consumption is expressed in liters/1,000 km.
Values in the parentheses are t-statistics.

Source: Analysis of Brazil-UNDP-World Bank highway research project data.

**Figure 10.9:   The plot of observed versus predicted fuel consumption
for all vehicle classes**

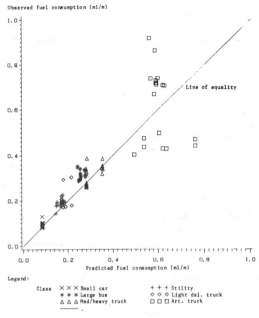

Note: Only randomly selected data points are shown

Note: Only randomly selected data points are shown.
Source: Brazil-UNDP-World Bank highway research project data and
          analysis.

**Figure 10.10:   The plot of observed versus predicted fuel consumption for
light and heavy vehicle groups and regression lines**

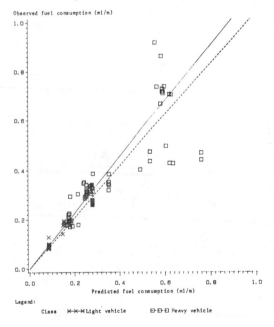

Source: Brazil-UNDP-World Bank highway research project data and
          analysis.

Aggregate Tire Wear Prediction Model

A major component of road user costs, especially for heavy goods vehicles, tire wear accounts for some 23 percent of the average running cost of a typical heavy truck operating on paved roads in rolling terrain in Brazil (GEIPOT, 1982, Volume 5). Current knowledge of tire mechanics indicates a strong dependence of tread wear on road alignment through forces acting on the tire which result from cornering, hill climbing, acceleration and braking. Also, a previous analysis of Brazil tire data (Chesher and Harrison, 1980) found that carcass failures are caused by increased severity of road alignment and surface conditions. This suggests that road improvements can have a disproportionate impact on tire costs relative to the other components. Therefore, to optimize highway investments, it is important to quantify properly the effects of geometric and surface characteristics on tire cost.

This chapter describes the formulation and estimation of a mathematical model which predicts tire wear as a function of vehicle and road characteristics (Section 11.1). Based largely on theories of tire mechanics, the model is an aggregate form of an algebraic function similar to the aggregate speed and fuel models (Chapters 7 and 10) and was statistically estimated using data obtained from the Brazil road user cost survey, for cross-ply tires only (GEIPOT, 1982 Volume 5). The data and estimation results, available for buses and trucks only, are presented in Sections 11.2 and 11.3, respectively. Section 11.4 presents the recommended tire wear prediction model based on the above results (for buses and trucks) and compares it with results from other studies. Also presented in Section 11.4 is a relatively simple tire wear prediction model obtained from highly aggregate data which is recommended for cars and utilities.

During the period of the study, the tires prevalent in Brazil were almost exclusively cross-ply type of tires and only this type of tires was included in the sample. Thus, the relationships presented here are applicable to cross-ply only.

11.1 MODEL FORMULATION

11.1.1 Tire Wear Cost Model

Two principal modes of tire wear contribute to tire cost:

1. Carcass wear; and
2. Tread wear.

Carcass wear

Carcass wear is defined in terms of the number of retreads to which a tire can be subjected before scrappage. Since the number of retreads, r, is an integer, its modelling should be done on a probabilistic basis, by defining:

PNR(r) = the probability that the tire will last through r retreads, r = 0, 1, 2, ..., N_r where N_r is the maximum practical number of retreads (equal to 6 in the Brazil data).

Tread wear

Treat wear is defined (for a given tire size and model) as the fraction of tread worn per 1,000 tire-km.[1] Since the wear rates of new treads and retreads may differ, the symbols TWN and TWR are used to denote the former and the latter, respectively.

Tire wear cost per unit travel distance

Let CN and CRT denote the cost of a new tire and one retreading, respectively. Then, the cost of tire wear per 1,000 tire-km, CTW, is given by:

$$CTW = \frac{CN + CRT\ NR}{DISTOT} \qquad (11.1)$$

where   NR = the average number of retreads, given by

$$NR = \sum_{r=1}^{N_r} r\ PNR(r) \qquad (11.2)$$

and DISTOT = the total distance of travel (in 1,000 km) provided by the tire carcass through its new tread and retreads, given by:

$$DISTOT = \frac{1}{TWN} + \frac{NR}{TWR} \qquad (11.3)$$

Two assumptions are implicit in Equations 11.1–11.3. First, all the treads completely wear out before any failure (e.g., irreparable damage to the carcass when the tread is only half worn). This assumption is considered to be acceptable since, as demonstrated in Section 11.2, the average distances afforded by terminal treads are greater than 85 percent those of the treads that were returned for retreading.

The second assumption is that the wear rate of retreads is constant regardless of the number of retreadings to which the carcass has been subjected. This assumption is substantiated to a large extent in the Brazil data, as shown in Section 11.3.

---

[1] There are other definitions of tread wear, viz., mils of tire tread thickness worn/km travelled, cubic inches/mile travelled, etc. These other definitions will be used on special occasions where appropriate.

Equivalent new tire life.

By rearranging Equation 11.1, the expression for the distance life of a cost-equivalent or simply equivalent new tire, TLNEW, is obtained:

$$TLNEW = \frac{DISTOT}{1 + NR\ CRT/CN} \tag{11.4}$$

We can interpret TLNEW as the distance life of CN dollars worth of tires (in 1000 km). The equivalent new tire life is useful for comparing the results from the mechanistic tire wear analysis herein with those from previous analyses and from other studies (Harrison and Chesher, 1984; CRRI, 1982; Hide, 1982; and Hide et al., 1975).

The above manner of tire wear model formulation offers several advantages. First, instead of lumping them together, the carcass and tread wear models are considered separately. This gives rise to a more meaningful interpretation of the causal mechanisms affecting the tire wear phenomenon. Second, the definition of tire cost per km of Equation 11.1 is provided as a function of the relative costs of retreads and new tires which appear to vary substantially across countries. While, as noted above, the ratio of the cost of a retreading to the cost of a new tire is about 15 percent in Brazil, it equals 50-60 percent in India (CRRI, 1982) and 40-50 percent in Costa Rica (Harral et al., 1984). Hence, Equation 11.1 provides greater flexibility in model transference to a new country than Equation 11.4 in which the ratio CR/CN is fixed to the originating country. Third, both the carcass life and tread wear models can be easily interpreted in physical terms and the estimates of the model parameters can be compared with data from other sources on a more systematic basis. This provides a greater scope for the model parameters to be adapted to local conditions, for example, with respect to the general recapping policy of vehicle operators, quality of recapping and rubber compound, abrasiveness of surfacing materials, etc.

11.1.2 Carcass Life Model

The effect of the carcass life on tire cost may be demonstrated by the following example. From the Brazil data the cost of a retreading is, as noted above, about 15 percent that of a new tire, whereas the average life of a retread is about 75 percent that of a new tread. So, CR = 0.15 CN and TWN = 0.75 TWR. Substituting these in Equations 11.1 and 11.3, we have the tire wear cost per 1,000 km given by:

$$CTW = \frac{CN(1 + 0.15\ NR)\ TWR}{1.33 + NR} \tag{11.5}$$

From Equation 11.5, the ratio of tire wear cost per km for an arbitrary number of retreadings to that for zero retreading is:

$$\frac{CTW(NR)}{CTW(NR=0)} = \frac{1 + 0.15\ NR}{1 + 0.75\ NR} \tag{11.6}$$

This ratio varies from 1 for NR = 0 to 0.45 for NR = 3. Thus, vehicle operators can achieve substantial savings by having the carcass retreaded as many times as practical subject to safety constraints.

Although, as shown in the above example, the carcass life is a major variable influencing tire operating cost, there seems to be little work done to date in relating quantitatively the number of retreads to road severity measures.[2] The only exception we are aware of is the analysis of Brazil data by Chesher and Harrison (1980) to obtain by multiple regression analysis relationships between the number of retreads to road characteristics, mainly road roughness, for bus and truck tires. On a priori grounds we would expect road roughness to reduce the carcass life in at least two ways: first, through fatigue, and second, through causing irreparable damage to the carcass structure. The former failure mechanism is gradual whereas the latter is sudden.

11.1.3 Micro Tread Wear Model

Our literature search revealed a wealth of theoretic-empiric knowledge on tire mechanics which is sufficient to permit a reasonable mathematical formulation of a tread wear model. However, as will be seen below, additional empirical information is still needed, especially with respect to actual driving tests over public roads.

Consider a homogeneous road section of uniform characteristics (i.e., constant gradient, curvature, roughness, surface texture) being traversed by a vehicle. At the tire-road contact area, there exists a force in the direction tangential to the road surface. The magnitude and direction of this tangential force depends on the circumferential force used to propel or retard the vehicle and the lateral force used to keep the vehicle from sliding when it is negotiating a bend. According to Schallamach (1981), the tangential force is transmitted through the elastic deformation of the part of the tire next to the road surface (called grip or adhesion). Upon return to its original shape, the tire surface at the contact area slips against the road surface. The abrasive slip action results in some loss of tire material. The amount of wear increases with the amount of tire slip and the magnitude of the accompanying shear force.

The physical mechanism of tread wear sketched above is described in detail in mathematical form by Schallamach (1981). Schallamach's comprehensive tread wear model is a synthesis of a series of theoretical and experimental findings dating back to the mid-nineteen fifties. Based on mechanical principles of pneumatic tires designed to handle large deflections and sliding distances, the full mathematical formulas are very complicated. However, for small tire slips these formulas reduce to a simple form. Since normal vehicle operations are associated with small slips, we are mainly concerned with the simplified formulas, the derivation of which is given in Appendix 11A.

---

[2] According to F. C. Brenner and T.E. Gillespie (private communication) and literature search.

For purposes of statistical analysis, the micro tread wear, TWT, model so derived can be stated as:

$$TWT = TWT_0 + TWT_c + TWT_\ell \tag{11.7}$$

or

$$TWT = TWT_0 + CT_c \frac{CFT^2}{NFT} + CT_\ell \frac{LFT^2}{NFT} \tag{11.8}$$

where TWT_c, TWT_ℓ = tire wear resulting from the circumferential and lateral forces, respectively (Equations 11A.8a and 11A.8b);

CFT, LFT = the circumferential and lateral forces acting on the tire, in newtons, respectively (as defined earlier);

NFT = the load on the tire in the direction normal to the tire-road contact area, in newtons;

TWT_0 = a constant term;

CT_c = K_0 b/k_c;

CT_ℓ = K_0 b/k_ℓ;

b = a parameter which depends on the tire dimensions and technical properties;

k_c, k_ℓ = parameters denoting circumferential and lateral lateral stiffness of the tire, respectively;

K_0 = a parameter which depends on the physical properties of the tire and the road surface (as elaborated in Appendix 11A);

and the parameters TWT_0, CT_c and CT_ℓ are to be estimated. According to Bergman and Crum (1973) who employed a similar model form in actual road tests, the constant term TWT_0 reflects unmeasured forces including the forces due to incorrect wheel alignment, tire construction properties, and road camber.

As shown in Appendix 11C, the above tread wear model has built into it a dependency of fourth or higher power on the vehicle speed on curves. This is supported by empirical findings given in Appendix 11B.

Seeing that circumferential and lateral forces are significant parameters affecting the tire wear, so are the tire properties in regard to circumferential and lateral stiffness. This issue is discussed in Appendix 11B, which draws on earlier empirical tire wear research. Theoretical analysis and practical testing on the basis of slip energy theory indicate that the tire wear rate is relatively independent of the direction of the total tangential force, and that circumferential and lateral tire stiffness can be assumed to be equal; this leads to a considerably simplified tire wear equation (Equation 11B.5).

The research results referred to in Appendix 11B also show a significant difference in tire wear:

1. Between radial and bias tires, radials having considerably smaller slip coefficients -- consistent with the general observation that radials provide better grip -- and hence also wearing slower than bias tires;

2. Between truck and car tires, the former having wear coefficients as large as 10 times or more those of car tires -- this results from both greater slip and slip energy coefficients for truck tires, which may be attributable to truck tires being operating typically under much higher loads and inflation pressures than passenger car tires;

3. Between dense and open-graded asphalt concrete -- the slip energy coefficient for the former being almost three times that of the latter; but

4. While there is conceptual difference in slip between paved and unpaved surfaces, the data available do not demonstrate a difference in tire wear on the basis of road surface type alone.

11.1.4 Aggregate Tread Wear Model

As physical phenomena, tire tread wear and fuel consumption share two common features: first, they occur continuously as the vehicle is traversing a road stretch; and, second, they are explained by well-established theories. Therefore, tread wear should ideally be modelled in a similar way to fuel consumption, as briefly outlined in the following manner. Detailed experiments using specially-instrumented test vehicles would be conducted to obtain data to relate tread wear as a function of the normal, circumferential and lateral forces acting on the tires, for different types of rubber compounds, tire construction, and road surfacing aggregates under different loads, inflation pressures, etc. These forces, in turn, would be related to the vehicle speed and characteristics of the vehicle and the road. Once a micro tread wear model is satisfactorily validated, it would be used as the building block for developing an aggregate tread wear model, in a manner similar to the aggregate fuel consumption model described in Chapter 10. Finally, experimentally based tread wear predictions can be adjusted to real-world operating conditions using actual operators records.

However, such detailed experimental data on tread wear were not collected in the Brazil study as the original intent was to acquire only survey-based data for modelling tire wear on the basis of empirical trends. The resulting empirical relationships are reported elsewhere (GEIPOT, 1982, Volume 5; Chesher and Harrison, 1985). In order to use this data base, the micro tread wear model formulated in Section 11.1.3 must be converted to aggregate form. Appendix 11C presents a detailed description of the aggregation procedure, along with the results of a numerical test to show that the accuracy of the aggregate model is close to that of the micro model.

11.2 DATA FOR ESTIMATION

Detailed data of 2886 tires were compiled for the final analysis; the data were obtained from the road user cost survey, as described in GEIPOT (1982, Volume 5) and Chesher and Harrison (1985). All tires included were of bias construction and were used by buses and medium, heavy and articulated trucks. The nominal dimensions of the tires (rim width/rim diameter, in inches) were 9.00/20 and 10.00/20 for buses and medium and heavy trucks and 9.00/20, 10.00/20 and 11.00/22 for articulated trucks.

Each tire had a complete historical record associated with various stages of its life cycle, from the first time it was mounted, through various recaps, and finally to the time it was removed for scrappage. The record of each tire contained not only the distance travelled during each stage, but also the aggregate characteristics of the routes.

To get an idea of what typical tires went through during their service lives, we examine the average survival rates and distances travelled by the tires during the various stages of their lives, as given in Table 11.1. It can be seen that of all the tires in the sample, none managed to survive to undergo the seventh recapping. In fact, the survival rate, expressed as a percentage of the total number of new tires, decreases quite rapidly with the recap stage. Only slightly more than 50 percent of the new tires could be recapped and less than 5 percent lasted long enough for the fourth recapping. The distances travelled by new tires were on average greater than those travelled by recaps by more than 20 percent. This may indicate differences in the workmanship and/or the quality of the rubber itself between new tires and recaps. It is interesting to note that: first, the average distance travelled by recapped tires were more or less constant regardless of the recapping stage; and, second, at each stage, new tire or recap, the average distance travelled by non-survivors were smaller than that by survivors but not by more than 16 percent margin. These observations support the assumptions made earlier in the tire wear cost model (Section 11.1.1).

The characteristics of the routes on which those tires were operated are summarized on Table 11.2. It can be seen that the tire data set covers a wide range of road roughness, from smooth paved to very rough unpaved. A large percentage of routes apparently have mixed paved/unpaved portions. The range of the vertical alignment is moderately high, with a maximum average gradient approaching 5 percent (rise plus fall = 50 m/km). However, the horizontal curvature suffers from a relatively narrow range of 7 to 294 degrees/km with a standard deviation of only 80 degrees/km.

Table 11.1: Survival rates and distances travelled at various stages of tire life cycle

Stage of tire life cycle	Number of survivors	Survival rate		Distance travelled by		
		Previous stage (%)	New stage (%)	Survivors (km)	Non-survivors (km)	Non-survivors vs. survivors (%)
New	2,886	100.0	100.0	26,939	22,612	84
1st recapping	1,549	53.7	53.7	18,628	18,051	97
2nd recapping	780	50.3	27.0	18,707	16,165	86
3rd recapping	360	46.1	12.5	18,495	16,178	87
4th recapping	138	38.3	4.8	18,581	16,211	87
5th recapping	43	31.2	1.5	19,165	16,451	86
6th recapping	11	25.6	0.4	–	13,818	–
7th recapping	0	0	0	–	–	–

Source: Brazil–UNDP–World Bank highway research project data.

As mentioned before, since the road user survey was not originally designed for the mechanistic approach, the data not only are in highly aggregate form but also lack the following information:

1. Superelevation: As curve superelevation was not measured in the survey of route characteristics, it was not possible to obtain a meaningful estimate of the coefficient for the lateral force component (LFT). Section 11.3 provides a further discussion of this effect.

2. Vehicle characteristics: No detailed information was surveyed except for the make/model and payloads of the vehicles on which the tires were mounted. For simplicity, except for the number of wheels per vehicle, average characteristics including the payload were used for each class of vehicles, as shown in Table 11.3.

   To predict aggregate vehicle speeds, the closest test vehicle was matched against each of the vehicle classes in Table 11.3, and the steady-state speed model parameters adapted for these test vehicles (as described in Chapter 10) were used.

3. Tire rubber volume: No data were obtained on the make/model and tread type of each tire which were necessary for accurate determination of the tire's wearable rubber volume. A procedure had to be devised to obtain an estimate of the average rubber volume per tire, as detailed in Appendix 11D.

Table 11.2: Summary statistics of tire survey routes

	Route Characteristics			
	Rise plus fall (m/km)	Curvature (degrees/km)	Roughness (QI)	Proportion paved (%)
Summary statistic:				
Mean	30.78	61.78	87.07	57.27
Minimum	9.80	7.50	23.00	0.00
Maximum	48.60	293.70	239.00	100.00
Standard deviation	8.50	80.82	40.30	32.75
Correlation coefficient with:				
Rise plus fall	1.000	0.800	−0.006	0.405
Curvature		1.000	0.217	0.089
Roughness			1.000	−0.874
Proportion paved				1.000

Source: Brazil–UNDP–World Bank highway research project data.

Table 11.3: Vehicle characteristics used in aggregate speed prediction

Characteristics	Vehicle Class			
	Large bus	Medium truck	Heavy truck	Articulated truck
Aerodynamic drag coefficient	0.65	0.85	0.85	0.63
Projected fromtal area (m^2)	6.30	5.20	5.20	5.75
Tare weight (kg)	81,00	54,00	66,00	14,700
Payload (kg)	23,00	4500	60,00	13,000
Number of highway tires	6	4	6	14
Number of mud and snow tires	0	2	4	4

Source: Brazil–UNDP–World Bank highway research project data.

11.3 ESTIMATION RESULTS

Using the tire data set described above, the carcass life and aggregate tread wear models were estimated on the basis of ordinary least-squares regression, but with an individual intercept estimated for each vehicle operator or company. Company-specific intercepts were intended to capture the differences in tire wear attributable to variations among companies in tire usage, maintenance and recapping policies. The rationale for this procedure is discussed in Harrison and Chesher (1984).

11.3.1 Carcass Life Model

The relationship selected relates the average number of recaps (NR) to the road roughness (QI) and horizontal curvature (C):

$$NR = NR_0 \exp[-0.00248 \; QI - 0.00118 \; \min(300,C)]-1$$
$$ (-3.32) (-2.20)$$

where: $\ell n \; NR_0$ = the natural logarithm of the average of the company-specific intercepts by tire size:

0.66 for 9.00/20 tires
(64.8)

1.22 for 10.00/20 tires
(52.5)

1.52 for 11.00/22 tires;
(58.7)

The number of data points is 2,886;
The t-statistics are shown in parentheses;
The standard error of regression = 0.40; and

R^2 = 0.478 (based on the average intercepts above).

In Equation 11.9 above the parameter NR_0 may be interpreted as equal to the average number of recaps for very smooth tangent roads. The effect of the horizontal curvature (C) is limited to the maximum value of 300 degrees per km which represents the upper end of the data range. It may be noted that the predicted NR can be negative for very rough and curvy roads (but not smaller than an asymptotic minimum of -1), indicating carcass failure before the tire is ready for the first recap. This means the total number of treads (new tread plus retreads) is smaller than one (but never smaller than zero). Graphs of predicted NR plotted against QI and C are shown in Figures 11.1(a) and (b), respectively, for each tire size. NR is depicted to decrease with increasing road severity. An increase in roughness by 150 QI (e.g., from a smooth paved to a rough unpaved surface) causes a 30 percent drop in the number of recaps. The same affect can be achieved by a 300 deg/km rise in the horizontal curvature (e.g., from a tangent to a moderately curved road).

Figure 11.1: Number of retreads, NR, for different tire sizes as a function of (a) roughness and (b) curvature

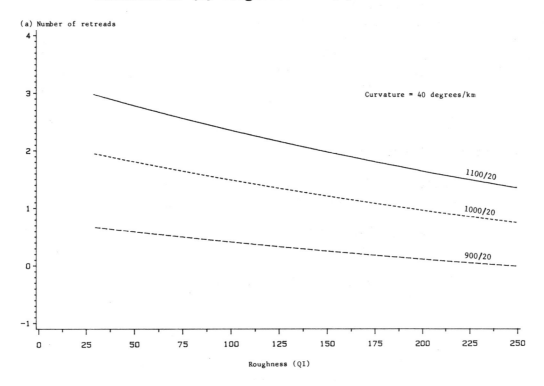

(a) Number of retreads

Curvature = 40 degrees/km

1100/20

1000/20

900/20

Roughness (QI)

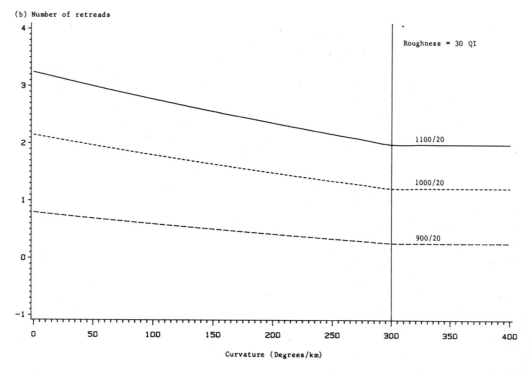

(b) Number of retreads

Roughness = 30 QI

1100/20

1000/20

900/20

Curvature (Degrees/km)

Source: Analysis of Brazil-UNDP-World Bank highway research project
          data.

11.3.2 Tread Wear Model

An earlier analysis (Rezende-Lima, 1984) yielded separate relationships for new treads and retreads, showing that the latter wear out faster than the former. However, due to the approximate nature of the coefficient estimates, it was decided for simplicity to pool the new tires and recaps, survivors and non-survivors, into one regression. This resulted in the following relationship which predicts tire tread wear, TWT, in dm^3/1000 tire-km:

$$TWT = 0.164 + 0.01278 \frac{CFT^2}{NFT} \tag{11.10}$$

$$(22.7) \quad (5.12)$$

where the constant term is the average of the company-specific intercepts; the number of data points is 2,886; the t-statistics are shown in parentheses; the standard error of regression = 3.63; and (v) R^2 = 0.181 (based on the average intercept above).

Conspicuously absent from the above relationship is the term for the lateral force, LFT^2/NFT (shown in Equation 11C.4). This does not mean the coefficient CT_ℓ for LFT^2/NFT is believed to be zero. In fact as discussed this coefficient should be of more or less the same magnitude as the CT_c coefficient of CFT^2/NFT. However, it was not possible to estimate the CT_ℓ coefficient with any degree of confidence. This is because the magnitude of the lateral force is highly dependent on the curve superelevation which, as noted earlier, was not recorded in the road user cost survey. An attempt was made to estimate the lateral force using relationships between superelevation (SP) and horizontal curvature (C) constructed from a sample of Brazilian roads[3]. Based on these lateral force estimates, the CT_ℓ coefficient was found to be insignificant. Two related factors were thought to be possible causes. First, the range of horizontal curvature in the data was too small (0 < C < 300). Second, within this range, superelevation was so well-designed that the actual lateral forces of the surveyed vehicles were indeed small. However, the lateral force is not believed to remain small for values of C greater than 400 degrees/km even with properly designed superelevation. In the high range of C, the curve speed constraint begins to dominate the vehicle speed, thereby raising the lateral force to a significant level. Therefore, the above tire wear formula is expected to produce conservative predictions for C greater than 400 and for roads without well-designed superelevation.

For straight driving, in which the lateral force, LFT, is zero, the estimate of 0.01278 for the circumferential force coefficient (CT_c) is directly comparable to the empirically obtained wear coefficients for bias truck tires presented in Table 11B.1. These empirical wear coefficients fall in the range 0.00225 to 0.00570, and the largest value is smaller than one-half of 0.01278. While there are numerous

---

[3] These superelevation-horizontal curvature relationships, obtained separately for paved and unpaved roads, are given in Chapter 3 (Equation 3.25).

possibilites for the discrepancy, the following are more plausible:

1. The non-survivors, which amounted to 46.3 percent of the data points used in the model estimation tended to make the estimated tread wear rate higher than should be.

2. The tires surveyed (new and recapped) were likely to be of lesser quality than those used in the controlled experiments (all new), thereby making them more susceptible to wear.

For straight driving, graphs of predicted tread wear, expressed in the number of treads per 1000 tire-km, plotted against road roughness (QI) and rise plus fall (RF) for a heavy truck, with and without the payload, are shown in Figures 11.2(a) and (b). The effect of 6,000 kg payload, compared to the 6,600 kg tare weight of the heavy truck, is shown to cause a significant extra tread wear which increases with road severity (roughness or steepness). As expected from the model formulation, tread wear is relatively insensitive to roughness which has only a small effect on the circumferential force through the rolling resistance. In contrast, tread wear is heavily influenced by road steepness. In particular, when rise plus fall exceeds 40 m/km the gravitational component of the circumferential force becomes dominant and causes the tires to wear at an increasing rate.

11.4 RECOMMENDED TIRE WEAR PREDICTION MODEL AND COMPARISON WITH OTHER STUDIES

Separate relationships for tire wear prediction are provided for buses and trucks as one group, and cars and utilities as another group. While the former is based on the mechanistic formulation and estimation results in the preceding section, the latter is based on a relatively simple formulation and highly aggregate data. Like the speed and fuel prediction models, the tire relationships are adapted specifically for each test vehicle.

11.4.1 Buses and Trucks

By adapting Equation 11.1, the formula for computing tire cost per 1,000 vehicle-km is given by:

$$CTV = \frac{NT \ (CN + CRT \ NR)}{DISTOT} \tag{11.11}$$

where NR is the predicted number of retreads, as given in Eq.11.14; NT is the number of tires on the vehicle; and the other variables are as defined before. Specific values of NR_0 are assigned to the bus and trucks in the test vehicle fleet, as shown in Table 11.4. Since no tires in the light truck classes (nominal dimensions of 7.50/16) were analyzed, $NR_0 = 1.93$ which correspond to the 9.00/20 dimensions, were adopted for these truck classes. Recalling that the total travel distance per tire carcass, DISTOT, is given by:

Figure 11.2: The plots of predicted number of equivalent new tires worn versus (a) roughness and (b) road rise plus fall for a heavy truck on a paved road.

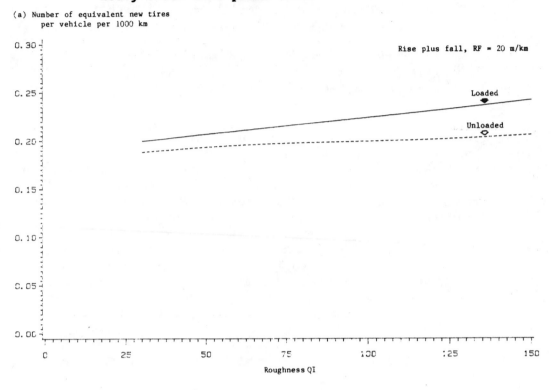

(a) Number of equivalent new tires
per vehicle per 1000 km

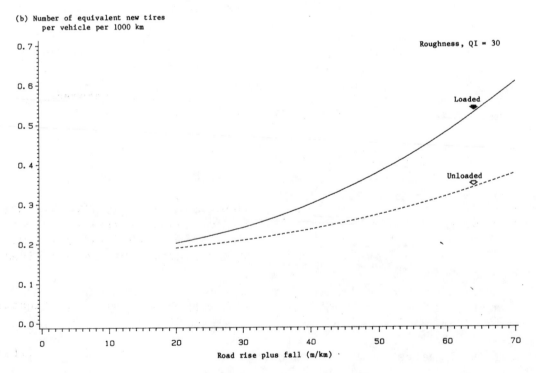

(b) Number of equivalent new tires
per vehicle per 1000 km

Source: Analysis of Brazil–UNDP–World Bank highway research project data.

Table 11.4: Basic parameters for tire wear prediction model for buses and trucks

Vehicle type Test vehicle	Nominal tire dimensions	NUMBER OF TIRES			Number of recaps at zero horizontal curvature NR_0	Average wearable rubber volume per per tire VOL (dm^3)
		Highway	Mud/snow	Total		
Large bus Mercedes Benz O-362	10.00/20	6	0	6	3.39	6.85
Light diesel truck Ford 4000	7.50/16	6	0	6	1.93	2.52
Light gasoline truck Ford 400	7.50/16	6	0	6	1.93	2.52
Medium truck MB 1113 with 2 axles	10.00/20	2	4	6	3.39	7.60
Heavy truck MB 1113 with 3 axles	10.00/20	6	4	10	3.39	7.30
Articulated truck Scania 110/39	11.00/22	14	4	18	4.57	8.39

Source: Adapted from Brazil-UNDP-World Bank highway research project data.

$$DISTOT = \frac{1}{TWN} + \frac{NR}{TWR} \qquad (11.12)$$

and assuming that TWN and TWR, the numbers of treads consumed per 1000 tire-km for new tires and recaps, respectively, are equal, then:

$$TWN = TWR = \frac{TWT}{VOL}$$

where TWT is the predicted volume of rubber loss, in dm^3/1,000 tire-km, as given in Equation 11.10; and VOL denotes the average volume of rubber per tire, in dm^3. Specific values of VOL for the test vehicles were computed on the basis of the vehicles' axle-wheel configurations and are given in Table 11.4.

To express tire costs in terms of equivalent new tires, Equation 11.11 may be rewritten as:

$$CTV = CN \ EQNTV \qquad (11.13)$$

where   EQNTV = the predicted number of "cost equivalent" or, simply, "equivalent" new tires consumed per 1,000 vehicle-km, given by:

$$EQNTV = \frac{(1 + RREC\ NR)}{DISTOT} \qquad (11.14)$$

where   RREC = the ratio of the cost of one retreading to the cost of
          one new tire (CRT/CN), or the "recap cost ratio."

Eliminating DISTOT, TWR and TWN in Equations 11.3, 11.12 and 11.4 results in:

$$EQNTV = \frac{NT\ (1 + RREC\ NR)}{1 + NR} \frac{TWT}{VOL} \qquad (11.15)$$

Substituting Equations 11.9 and 11.10 for NR and TWT in the above equation, and applying bias correction for model nonlinearity, we have:

$$EQNTV = NT \left\{ \frac{(1 + RREC\ NR)\ (0.164 + 0.01278\ (CFT^2/NFT))}{(1 + NR)\ VOL} + 0.0075 \right\}$$

$$\qquad (11.16)$$

where $NR = NR_0 \exp(-0.00248\ QI - 0.00118\ C) - 1.0$

0.0075 is value of the correction term for prediction bias.[4]

11.4.2 Cars and Utilities

As the tire data for cars and utilities obtained in the road user test survey are very aggregated, a relatively crude model was constructed for predicting the number of equivalent new tires per 1000 vehicle-km. The aggregate tire data for utilities (GEIPOT, 1982, Volume 5) come in two groups, paved and unpaved. The paved group has an average road roughness of 40 QI and average equivalent new tire life of 59,100 km. The corresponding averages for the unpaved group are 140 QI and 32,600 km. Assuming that EQNTV is a linear function of QI, the above aggregate data points yield the following relationship:

$$EQNTV = NT\ (0.0114 + 0.000137\ QI) \qquad (11.17)$$

---

[4] Since the above equation is a non-linear transformation of the original linear prediction relationships (Equations 11.9 and 11.11), a prediction bias is produced. This is similar to the prediction bias caused by the exponential transformation of the originally estimated speed model in logarithmic form. However, the non-linear transformation in Equation 11.16 is more complicated mathematically. Due to the approximate nature of Equation 11.16, a relatively simple additive bias correction term was applied. To quantify this bias correction term, EQNT was predicted for the survey vehicles in the tire data using Equation 11.16 and also computed based on the observed number of re treadings and total travel distance per carcass. The difference between the averages of the observed and predicted values of EQNT was found to equal 0.0075 and was taken as the bias correction term.

for predicting tire wear for cars and utilities with NT = 4; a road roughness ceiling of 200 QI is recommended.

11.4.3 Comparison of Tire Wear Prediction Model with Other Studies

Figures 11.3-11.6 compare the number of equivalent new tires predicted by Equations 11.16 and 11.17 with predictions using models obtained from other studies, namely those of TRRL-Kenya (Hide et al., 1975), TRRL-Caribbean (Hide, 1982), India (CRRI, 1982),[5] and Brazil in an earlier "aggregate-correlative" analysis (GEIPOT, 1982, Volume 5)[6]. As the "aggregate-correlative" Brazil models predict the equivalent new tire life (in the form of Equation 11.4) they had to be converted by inversion into the number of equivalent new tires. This non-linear transformation caused these Brazil models to predict generally lower tire consumption, measured in terms of the number of equivalent new tires, than the mechanistic models, even though they were derived from the same data base.

For medium/heavy trucks and buses, tire wear predictions by different models are plotted against roughness, curvature and rise plus fall in Figures 11.3-11.5[7]. For the mechanistic models, different curves are shown separately for paved and unpaved roads. Relative to the others, the Kenya and Caribbean models predict more than twice the influence of roughness (the steeper slopes of the prediction curves in Figure 11.3); however, these models assume no impact of road-geometry on tire wear (the flat slopes of the curves in Figures 11.4 and 11.5). One possible cause of these discrepancies is that the underlying data bases for the Kenya and Caribbean models were considerably smaller than for the India and Brazil models, thereby making the coefficient estimates somewhat less reliable. Among the models derived from the India and Brazil data bases, the predicted influence of roughness is very similar over the entire range, as indicated by almost equal slopes of the curves in Figure 11.3. As to the influence of road geometry, the mechanistic models predict increases in tire consumption over the extreme range of rise plus fall (0-70 m/km) and horizontal curvature (0-1,000 degrees/km) which are 3-4 times as large as the earlier low predictions made by the "aggregate-correlative" Brazil models. The predicted geometric effects by the India models are even lower.

---

[5] The TRRL Towed Fifth Wheel Bump Integrator Scale for road roughness (BI) was used in the TRRL-Kenya, TRRL-Caribbean, and India studies. As recommended by Paterson (1984), the conversion factor of 55 mm/km on the BI scale to one QI count was employed for comparison purposes. The models from these studies are summarized in Chesher and Harrison (forthcoming) and Watanatada, et al. (1987).

[6] The model coefficients originally reported in the 1982 GEIPOT report were slightly revised subsequently to make them conform with the revised definition of road roughness. The new coefficients, as reported in Chesher and Harrison (forthcoming), are used in the comparison.

[7] Because of variations in design and size among the study areas the prediction models are not strictly comparable. However, efforts were made to match the vehicle classes as closely as possible.

Figure 11.3 Tire wear versus roughness for (a) medium/heavy trucks and (b) buses as predicted by the mechanistic model and models from other studies

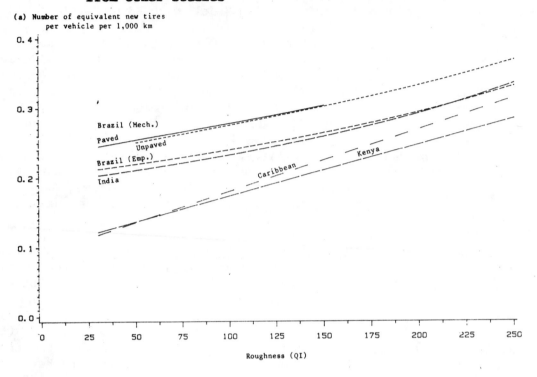

(a) Number of equivalent new tires
      per vehicle per 1,000 km

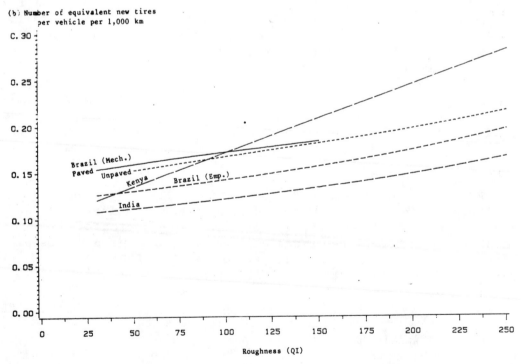

(b) Number of equivalent new tires
      per vehicle per 1,000 km

Source: See the first paragraph of Section 11.4.3.

Figure 11.4: Tire wear versus rise plus fall for (a) medium/heavy trucks and (b) buses as predicted by the mechanistic model and models from other studies

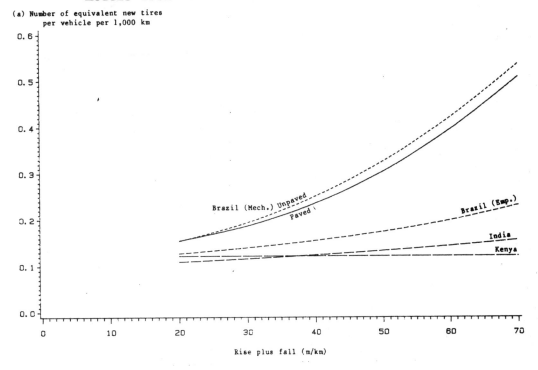

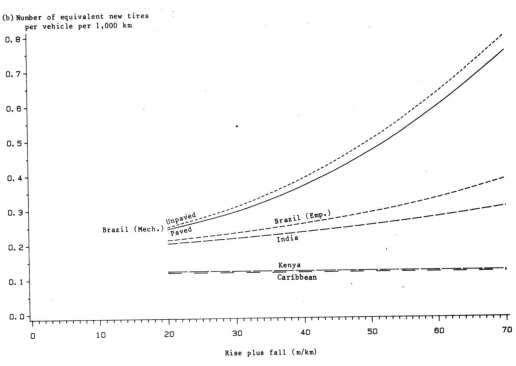

Source: See the first paragraph of Section 11.4.3.

Figure 11.5: Tire wear versus curvature for (a) medium/heavy trucks and (b) buses as predicted by the mechanistic model and models from other studies

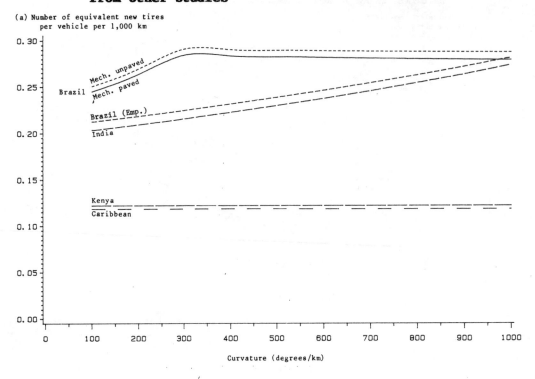

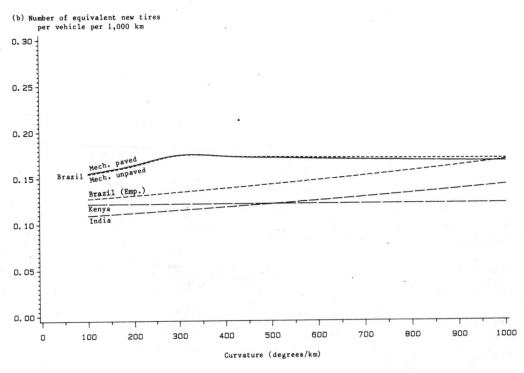

Source: See the first paragraph of Section 11.4.3.

**Figure 11.6: Tire wear versus roughness for cars and utilities as
               predicted by Equation 11.7 and models from other studies**

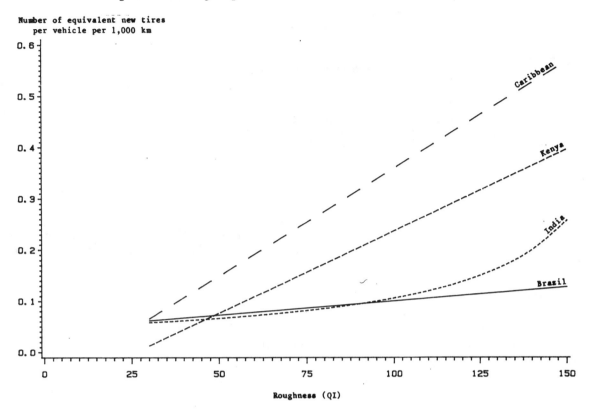

Source: See the first paragraph of Section 11.4.3.

For cars and utilities, tire wear predictions by the simple
model of Equation 11.17 and the Kenya, Caribbean and India models are
plotted against roughness in Figure 11.6. As before, the Kenya and
Caribbean models predict a very strong effect of roughness on tire wear
compared to the India and Brazil models which produce very similar
predictions up to about 120 QI[8].

---

[8] Like the aggregate-empiric Brazil models, the India models predict the
equivalent new tire life which can become zero. For cars and
utilities, the India model predicts zero tire life when roughness is
about 186 QI, at which point the number of equivalent new tires becomes
infinite. Therefore, an artificial ceiling must be imposed on the
India model for general application.

APPENDIX 11A

DERIVATION OF MICRO TREAD WEAR MODEL

This appendix provides a description of the micro tire tread wear model derived by Schallamach (1981). The physical mechanism of tire tread wear may be divided into two parts:

1.   the slip mechanism which deals with the relationship of the tire slip to the tangential and vertical forces on the tire; and

2.   the wear mechanism which deals with the relationship of the rate of tread wear to the tangential force and the tire slip.

Slip mechanism

Tire slip velocity T (in m/s) is defined as the vectorial difference between the travel and circumferential velocity of the wheel, Schallamach (1981):

$$T = R - W \qquad\qquad (11A.1)$$

where R = the velocity of the road relative to the wheel axle, in m/s; and
         W = the velocity of the wheel circumference relative to its 1211e, in m/s.

An illustration of the slip velocity definition is given in Figure 11A.1. Tire slip, λ, is defined on a relative basis:

$$\lambda = \frac{T}{\left|R\right|} \qquad\qquad (11A.2)$$

where $\left|R\right|$ = the magnitude of the wheel travel velocity (identically equal to the vehicle speed). Denote the magnitudes of the components of the tire slip in the tire's lateral and circumferential directions by λ_ℓ and λ_c, respectively. When the wheel rolls freely in a direction that makes "slip angle" η (in rad) to the travel direction (see Figure 11A.1), we have zero circumferential slip ($\eta = 0$) and the lateral slip is given by:

$$\lambda_\ell = \sin \eta \qquad\qquad (11A.3)$$

For small slips, $\lambda_\ell = \eta$, and we may use the slip angle, η, in the place of the lateral slip, λ_ℓ. When the wheel rolls in straight driving, the

Figure 11A.1: Illustration of slip velocity (tire-road contact area viewed from below)

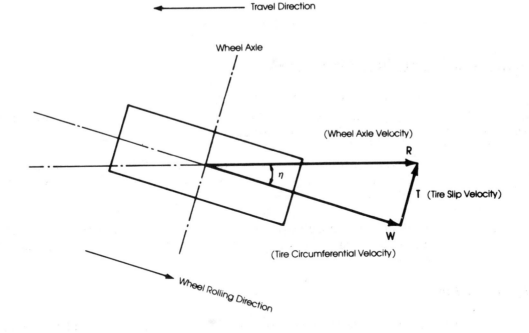

slip angle and lateral slip are zero, and the circumferential slip is given by:

$$_c\lambda = 1 - \frac{|W|}{|R|} \tag{11A.4}$$

where $|W|$ and $|R|$ denote the magnitudes of the wheel circumferential and travel velocities, respectively. The circumferential slip, λ_c, may be interpreted as the meters of slip per meter wheel travel. An illustation tire deformation and slip when rolling freely, side slipping, braking and propelling is given in Figure 11A.2.

The slip mechanism is mathematically described by means of an elastic toothed wheel (Schallamach and Turner, 1960). The teeth are assumed to deform independently of each other and to obey Hooke's law of linear stress-strain relationships, up to the limit of the available friction coefficient between the tire and the road surface. When a part of the contact area has its shear stress exceeding the available friction it begins to slide against the road surface and no further grip can be developed. For small slips (λ_ℓ below 0.07 radians or 4 degrees and λ_c below 5 percent) the elastic toothed wheel model yields the following simplified relationships:

$$_c\lambda = \frac{b}{k_c} \frac{CFT}{NFT} \tag{11A.5a}$$

Figure 11A.2: Illustration of tire deformation and slip in contact area model experiment of wheel on transparent track (viewed from below)

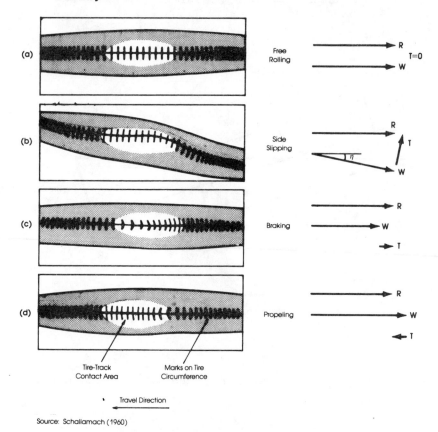

Source: Schallamach (1960)

Source: Adapted from Schallamach, 1960.

and
$$\ell^\lambda = \frac{b}{k_\ell} \frac{LFT}{NFT}$$
                                                                    (11.A5b)

where   b = a function of the tire's dimensions and mechanical
                 properties;

             k_c, k_ℓ = the circumferential and lateral stiffness of the
                 tire, respectively;

             CFT, LFT = the circumferential and lateral forces acting on
                 the tire, newtons, respectively; and

             NFT = the load on the tire in the direction normal to the
                 tire-road contact area, in newtons;

        Using a bias tire under different loads, Nordeen and Cortese
(1964) validated Schallamach and Turner's slip model in full form up to
the limit of the available friction coefficient when sliding occurred over
the whole contact area.

Wear mechanism

Based on an earlier experimental finding that the abrasion depth was an increasing function of the normal pressure on the contact area, Schallamach (1981) derived the following wear relationships (for small slips):

$$TWT_c = K_0 \, \lambda_c \, \frac{CFT^n}{NFT^{(n+1)/2}} \tag{11A.6a}$$

$$TWT_\ell = K_0 \, \lambda_\ell \, \frac{LFT^n}{NFT^{(n+1)/2}} \tag{11A.6b}$$

where TWT_c, TWT_ℓ = tire wear resulting from the circumferential and lateral forces, respectively;

K_0 = a function of the tire's geometry and mechanical properties as well as mechanical properties which depend on both the tire and the road surface (including available friction coefficient, road surface abrasiveness, and tire abrasion resistance); and

n = a constant, equal to 1 or more.

By substituting for λ_c and λ_ℓ from Equations 11A.5 in Equations 11A.6, the tire wear relationships may be expressed in terms of the forces as:

$$TWT_c = \frac{K_0 \, b}{k_c} \, \frac{CFT^{n+1}}{NFT^{(n+1)/2}} \tag{11A.7a}$$

and $$TWT_\ell = \frac{K_0 \, b}{k_\ell} \, \frac{LFT^{n+1}}{NFT^{(n+1)/2}} \tag{11A.7b}$$

The magnitude of the exponent n has been a subject of controversy. Veith (1974) provided a review of previous work on the exponent n. According to the theory that abrasive wear is proportional to the friction energy dissipated, the value of n should equal 1, and this is borne out in laboratory tests using relatively abrasive surfaces. However, tests using blunt surfaces and very high normal pressures resulted in n values as high as 2 or more. The departure from n=1 has been ascribed to fatigue failure accompanied by heightened temperatures in the contact area (Schallamach, 1981).

The experimental results which support the fatigue theory appear to have been based on testing severities considerably beyond those found under normal vehicle operating conditions. For example, from a trailer-cornering test of natural and synthetic rubber tires (Grosch and Schallamach, 1961) the average values of n are 1.4 and 1.5, respectively, for 1-4 degrees range of the slip angle (η). However, for the range 1-2 degrees slip angle, the values equal unity. Except for sharp steering on urban-street corners and sudden braking and other maneuvers to avoid accidents vehicle operators on rural roads are generally expected to use tire slips of no more than 2 degrees (or 0.035 radius) on sharp bends and under one percent on average. Results from tread wear tests using actual vehicles on public roads, carried out by Della-Moretta (1974), Bergman and Crum (1973) and Hodges and Koch (1979) give no indications that n should be greater than 1 for tires under normal usage. Therefore, n=1 was the value adopted for data analysis, and the wear relationships Equations 11A.7 reduce to

$$TWT_c = \frac{K_0\,b}{k_c}\,\frac{CFT^2}{NFT} \qquad\qquad (11A.8a)$$

and
$$TWT_\ell = \frac{K_0\,b}{k_\ell}\,\frac{LFT^2}{NFT} \qquad\qquad (11A.8b)$$

APPENDIX 11B

REVIEW OF PREVIOUS EMPIRICAL TREAD WEAR RESEARCH

Speed dependence of wear

The tread wear model developed in Appendix 11A has built-in fourth power or higher dependency on the vehicle speed on curves. This is illustrated in Figure 11B.1 using results obtained from race tracks in which measured tread wear is plotted against vehicle speed. In the Schallamach and Turner test (1960), tire wear increased by more than 5 times when the vehicle speed went from 50 to 80 km/h. In the Chiesa and Ghilandi test (1975), an increase in vehicle speed from 45 to 68 km/h resulted in a tire wear increase of more than 12 times.

Lateral versus circumferential stiffness

An issue of importance in road investment decision is concerned with the relative effects of the horizontal and vertical alignments on tread wear, which, in turn, depend on the relative magnitudes of the lateral and circumferential stiffness of the tire (k_ℓ and k_c, respectively). The results of road tests using actual vehicles conducted by Della-Moretta (1974), Bergman and Crum (1973) and Hodges and Koch (1979) provide useful information on this question, as discussed below.

Using a four-wheel drive vehicle and bias tires, Della-Moretta (1974) (also Della-Moretta and Sullivan, 1976) obtained a relationship between tread wear per unit "slip" energy[9]. The slip energy model is a simplified form of the more general tread wear relationship of Equations 11A.8a and 11A.8b in which the lateral and circumferential stiffness of the tire are assumed to be equal, i.e., $k_\ell = k_c = k$, and the constant term TWT_0 (in Equation 11.8) is set to zero. So, the tread wear equation reduces to:

$$TWT = \frac{K_0\ b}{k}\ \frac{TFT^2}{NFT} \tag{11B.1}$$

where   TFT = the total tangential force which is the vectorial sum of the (mutually perpendicular) lateral and circumferential components:

$$TFT = \sqrt{CFT^2 + LFT^2} \tag{11B.2}$$

Defining the slip energy, denoted by SE, as the product of tire slip $|\lambda|$ and the total tangential force:

---

[9] Although Henry C. Hodges did not produce any publications on slip energy he is acknowledged by Sullivan (1979) as another originator of the slip energy concept. A related report by Hodges and Koch (1979) is referenced later in this appendix.

Figure 11B.1:   Effect of vehicle curve speed on tread wear

(a)

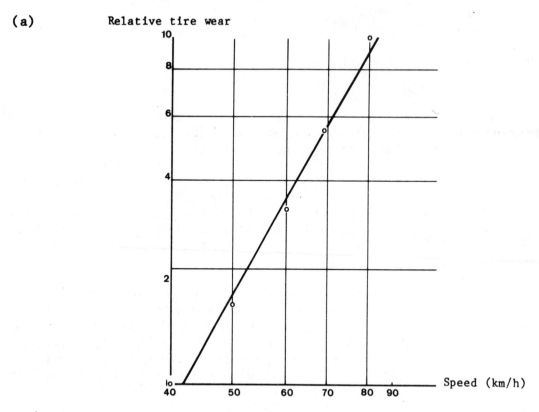

Source: Adapted from Schallamach and Turner, 1960.

(b)

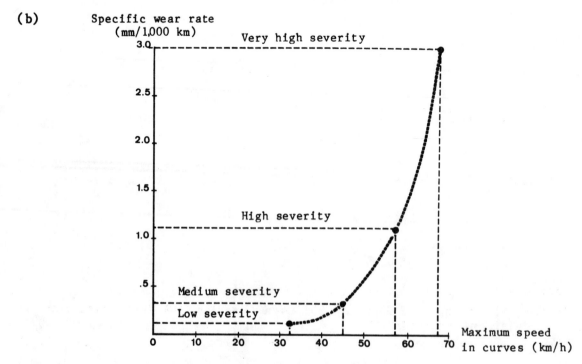

Source: Adapted from Chiesa and Ghilardi, 1978.

Defining the slip energy, denoted by SE, as the product of tire slip $|\lambda|$ and the total tangential force:

$$SE = |\lambda| \; TFT \tag{11B.3}$$

in joules per meter of travel,

where
$$|\lambda| = \frac{b}{k} \; \frac{TFT}{NFT} \tag{11B.4}$$

The dimensionless term b/k may be called the "slip coefficient." Thus, Equation 11B.1 above converts to the slip energy form:

$$TWT = K_0 \; S \; E \tag{11B.5}$$

where K_0 can be interpreted as the amount of tire wear per unit slip energy and may be called the "slip energy coefficient." The product K_0 b/k may be called the "wear coefficient" for the tangential force, and denoted by CT_t.

To test the lateral/circumferential tire stiffness assumption, Della-Moretta (1974) conducted experiments with the circumferential force alone (LFT = 0), the lateral force alone (CFT = 0), and both forces combined. The plot of results in Figure 11B.2 shows fairly close agreement among the three test modes. The Della-Moretta experiment was performed in an accelerated manner under conditions which ranged from light to highly

Figure 11B.2: Tread wear versus slip energy

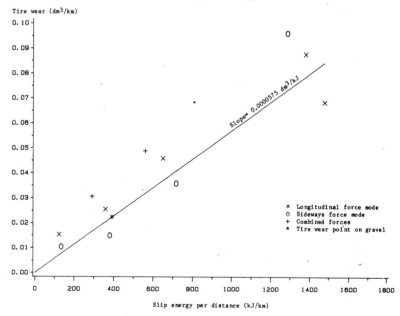

Source: Adapted from Della-Moretta and Sullivan, 1976.
Note: The ablative wear results have been omitted from the graph for
        illustration purposes.

severe involving values of the friction ratio TFT/NFT and the slip $|\lambda|$ as high as 0.5 and 0.15, respectively. This may explain why there is no detectable intercept term TWT_0 which is associated with the relatively small unmeasured forces.

The test conducted by Bergman and Crum (1973) was a close simulation of actual vehicle operations. A 5,100-lb passenger car with bias belted tires was driven over several routes of different surface textures at various average speeds. The lateral and longitudinal forces on the vehicle were measured along the route continuously. Each data point represents route-average tire wear and forces averaged over several runs, with tire rotation among the wheels after each run. The most and least severe test conditions had route-average friction ratios, TFT/NFT, of 0.050 and 0.007, respectively; their respective measured tread wear rates were 12.4 and 1.46 mils/100 miles. From the observed data, Bergman and Crum obtained regression results with $R^2 = 0.984$ and the intercept TWT_0 equal to 46 and 17 percent of the average and maximum wear rates, respectively. Most important, the lateral force coefficient was found to be greater than the circumferential one by 14 percent.

The foregoing results seem to indicate the relative independence of the tire wear rate on the direction of the total tangential force. In a later, larger scale experimental study, Hodges and Koch (1979) used the slip energy theory directly for tire wear prediction without explicitly testing the lateral/circumferential tire stiffness assumption. The study employed two four-wheel drive instrumented vehicles and six 4,100-lb passenger cars to test the wear behavior of bias, bias belted and radial tires. The instrumented vehicles were used to quantify the wear-slip energy relationships for the three types of tire construction and various surface textures. The passenger cars were used to provide independent wear observations for comparison with the wear prediction using these wear-slip energy relationships. Good agreement was obtained although the published results provided no information for evaluating the later/circumferential tire stiffness assumption.

Empirical slip, slip energy and wear coefficients

In constructing a tire wear prediction model, Zaniewski et al., (1982) compiled a set of slip and slip energy coefficients (b/k and K_0, respectively) obtained from several experimental studies. These coefficients are reproduced in Table 11B.1 (with adapted physical units), along with the corresponding wear coefficients (b K_0). The results are for both radial and bias tires tested over bituminous surfaces.

In the Hodges and Koch (1979) experiment in which passenger cars were used, the radial tires tended to have considerably smaller slip coefficients than the bias tires. This is consistent with the general tendency of radial tires to provide more grip for the same amount of slip. There is no consistent pattern between the slip energy coefficients of bias and radial tires. Overall, the passenger radial tires tended to wear slower than the bias tires, as indicated by the smaller wear coefficients.

Table 11B.1(a): Summary of available slip energy coefficients

Vehicle tested & source	Surface type, aggregate & location	Tire type	Slip coefficient		Wear coefficient
			$\dfrac{b}{k}$ [1]	Energy[2] K_0	$CT = \dfrac{b}{k} K_0$
Passenger cars 4,100 lb. (Hodges & Koch, 1979)	Nevada: Bituminous concrete of crushed & sifted aggregate from natural bank deposits with abrasion 20–25%[4]	Radial 1 [3]	0.031	0.0275	0.00086
		Radial 2	0.038	0.0219	0.00084
		Bias 1	0.067	0.0240	0.00160
		Bias 2	0.055	0.0230	0.00128
		Bias 3	0.045	0.0285	0.00129
		Bias 4	0.059	0.0275	0.00161
	Connecticut: Bituminous concrete of gravel from natural bank deposits with abrasion 35–37%	Radial 1	0.024	0.0163	0.00028
		Radial 2	0.026	0.0105	0.00027
		Bias 1	0.050	0.0076	0.00038
		Bias 2	0.059	0.0078	0.00046
		Bias 3	0.040	0.0103	0.00041
		Bias 4	0.042	0.0105	0.00044
	Texas: Bituminous concrete of crushed lime-stone aggregate from deposits with abrasion 26–29%	Radial 1	0.029	0.0131	0.00038
		Radial 2	0.023	0.0174	0.00040
		Bias 1	0.062	0.0115	0.00072
		Bias 2	0.050	0.0111	0.00055
		Bias 3	0.050	0.0106	0.00053
		Bias 4	0.042	0.0141	0.00059
Dump truck 5-ton (Della-Moretta Sullivan, 1977)	Nevada: Bituminous concrete of crushed basalt, 1"	10.00-20 12-ply, bias nylon-Goodyear Super High Miler	0.10	0.0570	0.00570

(See notes on following page)

Table 11B.1(b): Summary of available slip energy coefficients (continued)

Vehicle tested & source	Surface type, aggregate & location	Tire type	Slip coefficient		Wear coefficient
			$\dfrac{b}{k}$ [1]	Energy[2] K_0	$CT_t = \dfrac{b}{k} K_0$
Light truck, 5,000 lb (Barriere, et al., 1974)	Nevada: Bituminous concrete of crushed basalt, 1"	7.50–16 10 ply, Bias Goodyear Super High Miler	0.091	0.0616	0.00562
1970 Jeep Wagoneer (Barriere[6] et al. 1974)	Nevada: Bituminous concrete of crushed basalt, 1"	G78–14: B polyester/ fiberglass bias belted	0.045	0.0496	0.00225
1977 Jeep Wagoneer modified 4 wheel drive (Jones Della- Moretta, 1979)	California: Open graded asphalt concrete overlay	10R15LT Recap logging truck tires radial	0.077	0.0735	0.00566
	California: Dense graded asphalt concrete road-mixed		0.091	0.0257	0.00252

Footnotes for Table 11B.1(a) and 11B.1(b):

[1] Slip coefficient expressed in meters of wheel slip per meter of wheel travel.

[2] Slip energy coefficient expressed in $dm^3/1,000$ km of wheel travel per joule per meter of slip energy.

[3] Tire types – all mounted on 6.0 x 15.0 rims – passenger car tires:

    Radial 1 Goodyear steel belted radial – 76.5 in.[3] (total volume of available tread rubber)

    Radial 2 Firestone steel radial 500 – 78.3 in.[3]

    Bias 1   Uniroyal Tiger Paw – polyester bias – 82.0 in.[3]

    Bias 2   Goodyear Power Cushion – polyester/fiberglass bias belted 79.8 in.[3]

    Bias 3   B.F. Goodrich Long Miler – polyester/fiberglass belted 101.5 in.[3]

    Bias 4   Cooper Lifeliner Premium 78 – polyester/fiberglass belted 101.5 in.[3]

[4] ASTM Standard Abrasion Test C535

Source: Adapted from Zaniewski et al., 1982.

The data for truck tires show wear coefficients as large as 10 or more times those for passenger car tires. This results from both greater slip and slip energy coefficients for truck tires, which, in turn, may be attributable to the fact that truck tires are typically operated under much higher loads and inflation pressures than passenger car tires.

Jones and Della-Moretta (1979) conducted an experiment to compare tire tread wear over dense and open graded asphalt concrete. As shown in Table 11B.1, they found that while the slip coefficients were similar, the slip energy coefficient for the open graded surface were almost three times as large as that for the dense graded surface.

The wear coefficients in Table 11B.1 are compared with the estimation results in sub-section 11.3.2.

Paved versus unpaved surface

Della-Moretta (1974) explained the differences in tire slip behavior between paved and unpaved surfaces. For paved surfaces, slip occurs only between the tire and the road. For unpavedsurfaces, slip may be divided into two parts: the first between the tire and the road surface material immediately adjacent to the tire (termed the "bound slip") and the second between the road surface material adjacent to the tire and the material below it (termed the "loose slip"). Both slips give rise to the total slip observed on the tire but only the first causes tread wear. Since the bound slip on unpaved roads was not immediately observable, Della-Moretta assumed it to equal the slip observed on paved roads of similar aggregates.

One test run was made over a gravel road and the bound slip was estimated using the slip-friction ratio relationship obtained from an equivalent paved road with the friction ratio TFT/NFT measured for the run. The observed wear is plotted against the estimated slip energy as shown in Figure 11B.2. The good agreement with the paved road data points may be attributed to similarity in the abrasiveness of the surface aggregate as well as similarity in the bound slip values. In fact, according to the Schallamach-Turner slip model, small interfacial slips should depend only on the mechanical properties of the tire irrespective of the road surface, provided that the latter affords sufficient traction. The simplified slip relationships do not apply to slippery surfaces since their available coefficients of friction are small.

Della-Moretta's unpaved road bound slip assumption was used in the Brazil data analysis.

APPENDIX 11C

AGGREGATE TREAD WEAR MODEL: FORMULATION AND NUMERICAL TESTING

11C.1   FORMULATION OF AGGREGATE TREAD WEAR MODEL

Following the same aggregate prediction procedure for speed in Chapter 7, the route is represented by two homogenous segments, one positive and one negative grade of the same length, roughness, horizontal curvature (and superelevation), and absolute gradient. The length of each idealized segment equals that of the actual route.   The roughness, horizontal curvature, superelevation and absolute gradient are averages of the values measured over short homogeneous subsections of the actual roadway. The aggregate tire wear model computes tire consumption per unit distance travelled on each of these idealized segments and then averages out these predictions to obtain the tire wear prediction for the round trip.   For each idealized segment the following road characteristics are the same:

QI = the road roughness, in QI;
C = the horizontal curvature, in degrees per km road length;
and   SP = the superelevation, in fraction.

For the quantities that differ between the two segments, subscripts u and d are used to denote the uphill and downhill segments, respectively. Let RF be the average rise plus fall of the actual roadway, in m/km. The gradients for the uphill and downhill segments, expressed as fractions, are thus obtained as:

$$GR_u = \frac{RF}{1000} \qquad\qquad (11C.1a)$$

$$GR_d = - \frac{RF}{1000} \qquad\qquad (11C.1b)$$

For a given vehicle let TWT_u and TWT_d denote the volume of rubber worn per 1000 tire-km on the uphill and downhill segments, respectively. From the micro tread wear model of Equation 11.8, TWT_u and TWT_d are given by:

$$TWT_u = TWT_{0u} + CT_{cu} \frac{CFT_u^2}{NFT} + CT_{\ell u} \frac{LFT_u^2}{NFT} \qquad (11C.2a)$$

LF_u, LF_d = the vehicle lateral force on the uphill and
downhill segments, respectively; and

and $\qquad \text{TWT}_d = \text{TWT}_{0d} + \text{CT}_{cd} \dfrac{\text{CFT}_d^2}{\text{NFT}} + \text{CT}_{\ell d} \dfrac{\text{LFT}_d^2}{\text{NFT}}$ $\qquad\qquad$ (11C.2b)

where the terms are as defined earlier but with subscript u and d representing the uphill and downhill segments, respectively. The tire wear predicted for the whole route is computed as the average of the predictions for each road segment:

$$\text{TWT} = 0.5 \ (\text{TWT}_u + \text{TWT}_d) \qquad\qquad\qquad (11C.3)$$

or $\qquad \text{TWT} = \text{TWT}_0 + \text{CT}_c \dfrac{\text{CFT}^2}{\text{NFT}} + \text{CT}_\ell \dfrac{\text{LFT}^2}{\text{NFT}}$ $\qquad\qquad$ (11C.4)

where $\qquad \text{TWT}_0 = 0.5 \ (\text{TWT}_{0u} + \text{TWT}_{0d});$

$\qquad\qquad \text{CT}_c = 0.5 \ (\text{CT}_{cu} + \text{CT}_{cd});$

$\qquad\qquad \text{CT}_\ell = 0.5 \ (\text{CT}_{\ell u} + \text{CT}_{\ell d});$

$\qquad\qquad \text{CFT}^2 = 0.5 \ (\text{CFT}_u^2 + \text{CFT}_d^2);$

and $\qquad \text{LFT}^2 = 0.5 \ (\text{LFT}_u^2 + \text{LFT}_d^2).$

The parameters TWT_0, CT_c and CT_ℓ are to be estimated. The circumferential and lateral forces per tire are computed as:

$$\text{CFT}_u = \frac{\text{DF}_u}{\text{NT}} \qquad\qquad\qquad\qquad\qquad (11C.5a)$$

$$\text{CFT}_d = \frac{\text{DF}_d}{\text{NT}} \qquad\qquad\qquad\qquad\qquad (11C.5b)$$

$$\text{LFT}_u = \frac{\text{LF}_u}{\text{NT}} \qquad\qquad\qquad\qquad\qquad (11C.5c)$$

$$\text{LFT}_d = \frac{\text{LF}_d}{\text{NT}} \qquad\qquad\qquad\qquad\qquad (11C.5d)$$

where $\qquad \text{DF}_u$, DF_d = the vehicle drive force on the uphill and downhill segments, respectively;

$\qquad\qquad \text{LF}_u$, LF_d = the vehicle lateral force on the uphill and downhill segments, respectively;

and   NT = the total number of tires.

Similarly, the normal force per tire is given by:

$$NFT = \frac{m\ g}{NT} \qquad\qquad (11C.6)$$

where m is the vehicle mass and g the gravitational constant as defined in Chapter 2. The vehicle drive forces are computed as in Chapter 2, i.e.,

$$DF_u = m\ g\ GR_u + m\ g\ CR + 0.5\ RHO\ CD\ AR\ VSS_u \qquad (11C.7a)$$

$$DF_d = m\ g\ GR_d + m\ g\ CR + 0.5\ RHO\ CD\ AR\ VSS_d \qquad (11C.7b)$$

where VSS_u and VSS_d are the steady-state speeds on the idealized segments, computed according to the procedure in Chapter 7; and all other variables are defined before. The coefficient of rolling resistance, CR, is a function of road roughness, QI, as given in Chapter 2. The vehicle lateral forces are computed as in Chapter 3, i.e.,

$$LF_u = \frac{m\ VSS_u^2}{RC} - m\ g\ SP \qquad\qquad (11C.8a)$$

$$LF_d = \frac{m\ VSS_d^2}{RC} - m\ g\ SP \qquad\qquad (11C.8b)$$

where RC = the radius of curvature of each road segment, in meters, computed as inverse function of the horizontal curvature, C (as defined in Chapter 3):

$$RC = \frac{18,0000}{\pi\ C} \quad \text{for } C > 0 \qquad\qquad (11C.9)$$

and SP is the average superelevation, expressed as a fraction.

11C.2 NUMERICAL TESTING

The aggregate tread wear prediction model described above was tested for numerical accuracy using the micro transitional and non-transition tread wear prediction models as the benchmarks. The testing procedure employed the tread wear model coefficient estimates in Section 11.4 which were assumed for testing purposes to be the "correct" coefficients. This assumption was considered appropriate because we were mainly interested in relative, not absolute, errors. The micro tread wear model of Equation 11.8 was first quantified into the following:

$$TWT = 0.164 + 0.01278 \left[\frac{CFT^2}{NFT} + \frac{LFT^2}{NFT} \right] \qquad (11C.10)$$

where TWT is expressed in $dm^3/1,000$ tire-km. The above relationship served as the basis for both the aggregate and micro models. The micro prediction procedures are summarized as follows:

Micro transitional model

The prediction formula is:

$$TWT = \frac{\sum_j \Delta TIRE_j}{L} -$$
(11C.11)

where the summation is over all simulation intervals; and $\Delta TIRE_j$ is the predicted amount of rubber lost over simulation interval j, in dm^3, given by:

$$\Delta TIRE_j = \Delta L_j \left\{ 0.164 + 0.01278 \left[\frac{CFT_j^2}{NFT} + \frac{LFT_j^2}{NFT} \right] \right\}$$
(11C.12)

where CFT_j and LFT_j denote the average circumferential and lateral forces on the tire, in newtons; and NFT is the normal force on the tire as given in Eq.10.27. CFT_j and LFT_j are given by:

$$CFT_j = \frac{1}{NT} \left\{ m' a_j + m g (GR_j + CR_j) + A V_j^2 \right\}$$
(11C.13)

$$LFT_j = \frac{1}{NT} \left[\frac{m V_j^2}{RC_j} - m g SP_j \right]$$
(11C.14)

where a_j is the vehicle acceleration as defined in Equation 10.5 and the other variables are as defined previously, but with subscript j denoting those that are specific to simulation interval j.

Micro non-transitional model

The prediction formula is:

$$TWT = \frac{\sum_s TIRE_s}{L}$$
(11C.15)

where the summation is over all homogenous subsections; and $TIRE_s$ is the predicted amount of rubber lost over subsection s, in dm^3, given by:

$$TIRE_s = L_s \left\{ 0.164 + 0.01278 \left[\frac{CFT_s^2}{NFT} + \frac{LFT_s^2}{NFT} \right] \right\}$$
(11C.16)

where CFT_s and LFT_s denote the circumferential and lateral forces on the tire over homogeneous subsection s, respectively; and the other variables are as defined before. CFT_s and LFT_s are given by:

$$CFT_s = \frac{1}{NT} \left[m \ g \ (GR_s + CR_s) + A \ VSS_s^2 \right] \tag{11C.17}$$

$$LFT_s = \frac{1}{NT} \left[\frac{m \ VSS_s^2}{RC_s} - m \ g \ SP_s \right] \tag{11C.18}$$

where all variables are as defined previously, with subscript s denoting those that are specific to subsection s.

Results

The test vehicle characteristics and the steady-state model parameters adapted for the test vehicles (as described in Chapter 10) were used with the above prediction procedures. The detailed road characteristics employed were obtained from five 10-km road sections used in the fuel validation experiment (with summary statistics given in Table 8.2). The numerical results are summarized in Figures 11C.1 and 11C.2, and Tables 11C.1 and 11C.2. Figure 11C.1 plots aggregate tread wear predictions against predictions made by the micro non-transitional models for all test vehicles; each data point represents a 10-km journey of a test vehicle in one direction. The points are superimposed by the fitted ordinary least squares regression line passing through the origin. Figure 11C.2 does the same as Figure 11C.1, but for the micro transitional model. Tables 11C.1 and 11C.2 give a summary of regression results by test vehicle for aggregate vs micro non-transitional and aggregate vs micro transitional predictions, respectively.

It can be seen from the regression statistics (Table 11C.1) and data plot (Figure 11C.1) that the aggregate and macro transitional models produce almost identical predictions, implying negligible errors due to numerical approximation in the aggregation procedure. As seen in Table 11C.2 and Figure 11C.2, predictions by the aggregate model correlate very well with those obtained from speed profile simulation, with R^2 values for the without-intercept regressions falling within a 0.91–0.99 range. The slopes of all without-intercept regressions are smaller than one. The regression with all vehicles combined has a slope equal to 0.965, indicating a relatively small (3.5 percent) average upward bias on the part of the aggregate model. This seems sensible since the driver behavior assumptions underlying the simulated profiles are expected to cause less tire tread wear than that predicted on the basis of steady-state speed profiles.

Figure 11C.1   The plot of steady-state tire wear prediction vs. tire wear predicted using aggregate method

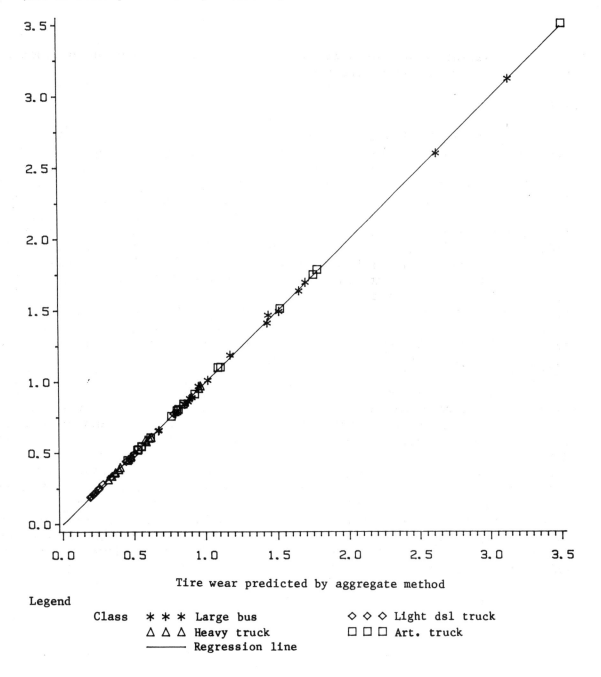

Tire wear predicted by micro non-transitional method
(No. of tires per vehicle per 1000 km)

Tire wear predicted by aggregate method

Legend

Class   ＊ ＊ ＊ Large bus   ◇ ◇ ◇ Light dsl truck
        △ △ △ Heavy truck   □ □ □ Art. truck
        —————— Regression line

Source: Road characteristics data from the Brazil-UNDP-World Bank
          highway research project, and relationships as given in the text.

Figure 11C.2: The plot of simulated tire wear prediction vs. tire wear predicted using aggregate method

Tire wear predicted by micro non-transitional method
(No. of tires per vehicle per 1000 km)

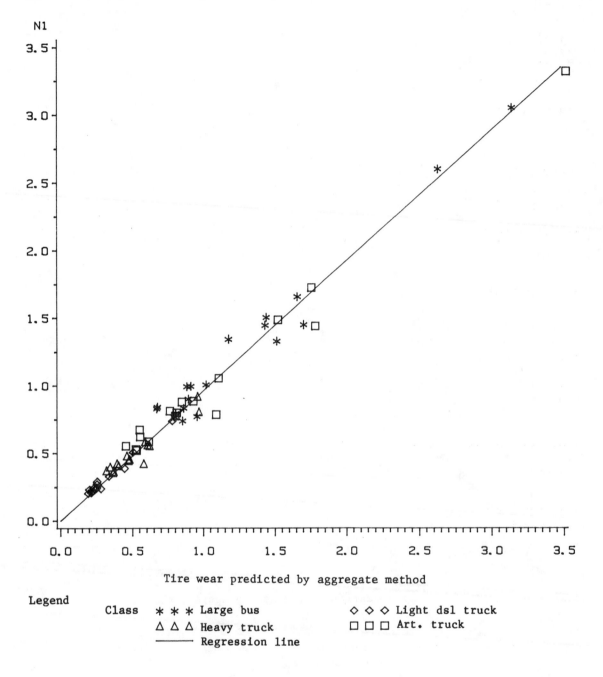

Tire wear predicted by aggregate method

Legend

Class   * * * Large bus   ◇ ◇ ◇ Light dsl truck
        △ △ △ Heavy truck   □ □ □ Art. truck
        ——— Regression line

Source: Road characteristics data from the Brazil-UNDP-World Bank
          highway research project, and relationships as given in the text.

Table 11C.1: **Regression results: micro non-transitional versus aggregate tread wear predictions**

Vehicle	Number of observations	Intercept	Slope	R^2	Standard error of residuals
Large bus	19	0.00 (-0.7)	0.999 (198.0)	1.00	0.014
		–	0.996 (441.8)	1.00	0.014
Light truck	15	-0.00 (-1.3)	0.999 (289.5)	1.00	0.002
		–	0.995 (634.8)	1.00	0.002
Heavy truck	15	-0.01 (-1.8)	1.010 (151.7)	1.00	0.005
		–	0.999 (400.8)	1.00	0.005
Articulated truck	17	-0.00 (-1.2)	1.001 (616.6)	1.00	0.049
		–	1.00 (1072.0)	1.00	0.050
All vehicles combined	66	-0.00 (-1.2)	0.999 (625.9)	1.00	0.008
		–	0.997 (1008.8)	1.00	0.008

Source: Analysis of Brazil-UNDP-World Bank highway research project data.

Table 11C.2: **Regression results: micro transitional versus aggregate tread wear predictions**

Vehicle	Number of observations	Intercept	Slope	R^2	Standard error of residuals
Large bus	19	0.07 (1.3)	0.938 (22.7)	0.97	0.115
		–	0.984 (51.7)	0.97	0.117
Light truck	15	0.03 (1.9)	0.908 (23.3)	0.98	0.023
		–	0.974 (51.5)	0.98	0.025
Heavy truck	15	0.09 (2.7)	0.777 (12.4)	0.92	0.047
		–	0.935 (35.8)	0.91	0.057
Articulated truck	17	0.07 (1.5)	0.900 (25.5)	0.98	0.107
		–	0.943 (45.5)	0.97	0.110

Source: Analysis of Brazil-UNDP-World Bank highway research project data.

APPENDIX 11D

AVERAGE RUBBER VOLUME PER TIRE

For a given tire size and type, the volume of rubber in the tire tread was calculated on the basis of dimensions furnished by Brazilian tire manufacturers. The dimensions considered for this calculation were the tire diameter, tread depth and upper and lower tread widths.

The formula for calculating the volume (1n dm^3) is:

$$Volume = \frac{\pi \times Diam \times Area}{1,000,000} \qquad (11D.1)$$

where   "Area" = the area of the tread cross section in mm^2, and
"Diam" = the tire diameter in mm.

The tread cross-section is a trapezoid with the upper and lower bases representing the upper and lower parts of the tread (the lower part being the tread surface in contact with the ground). In general, the two bases differ by 10 mm. The height of the trapezoid (which corresponds to the tread that will eventually be worn away) is equal to the tread depth minus the 1.6 mm remaining tread required by law. The empty parts of the trapezoid (which correspond to the grooves) are approximtely 30 percent ofthe total area of the trapezoid. Therefore, the cross-sectional area of the tread to be worn away is calculated (in mm^2) as follows:

$$Area = \frac{LL + LU}{2} \times (DE - 1.6) \times 0.70 \qquad (11D.2)$$

where   LL = the length of the lower trapezoid base, in mm;
LU = the length of the upper trapezoid base, in mm;
DE = the depth of the grooves, in mm;
Considering that LU = LL + 10, we have:
Area = (LL + 5) x (DE - 1.6) x 0.70

The estimated tread rubber volumes for different tire sizes and types are shown in Table 11D.1.

The tires listed in the data base are of two types: highway (h) and mud and snow (m/s). For a given size, the mud/snow tire has a greater volume of rubber in the tread area than the highway tire and is used only on the driving wheels of trucks. Unfortunately, no information was recorded in the road user survey to indicate the type of each tire. Therefore, it was necessary to estimate the average wearable rubber volume per tire on the basis of the axle-wheel configuration of the vehicles on which the tire were mounted. The axle-wheel configurations of the various vehicle classes are presented in Table 11D.1, along with the corresponding numbers of highway and mud/snow tires.

The average wearable rubber volume per tire, VOL, is computed as:

$$VOL = \frac{N_h VOL_h + N_{m/s} VOL_{m/s}}{N_h + N_{m/s}} \qquad (11D.3)$$

where VOL_h and $VOL_{m/s}$ denote the volumes of one highway and mud/snow tire, respectively; and N_h and $N_{m/s}$ denote the numbers of highway and mud/snow tires, respectively, for a given vehicle of known axle configuration.

Table 11D.1: Wearable tire rubber volumes by tire size, vehicle class, and axle configuration

Vehicle class	Axle configuration[1]	Number of tires	Tire size 9.00/20	10.00/20	11.00/22
Volume (dm^3) for highway tires:			5.76	6.85	8.00
Buses	1.2	6			
Medium trucks	1.2	2			
Heavy trucks	1.22	6			
Articulated trucks	1.2 - 222	14			
Volume (dm^3) for mud and snow tires:			7.24	7.98	9.77
Buses	1.2	0			
Medium trucks	1.2	4			
Heavy trucks	1.22	4			
Articulated trucks	1.2 - 222	4			
Average volume (dm^3) used in analysis:					
Buses	1.2	6	5.76	6.85	8.00
Medium trucks	1.2	6	6.75	7.60	9.18
Heavy trucks	1.22	10	6.35	7.30	8.71
Articulated trucks	1.2 - 222	18	6.09	7.10	8.39

[1] This code is the same as that used in the GEIPOT, 1982.

Source: Adapted from information provided by Brazilian tire manufacturers.

CHAPTER 12

Vehicle Maintenance, Depreciation, Interest and Utilization

Vehicle maintenance, depreciation and interest are important, interrelated components of the costs of vehicle ownership and operation. Maintenance parts and labor typically constitute 15-35 percent, and depreciation and interest 15-25 percent, of total costs excluding overhead; together they account for about the same proportion as fuel and tire consumption combined.

However, maintenance, and particularly the capital charges of depreciation and interest, are rather different in nature from such direct "running" costs as fuel and tire wear. First, depreciation and interest are less related to actual vehicle kilometers driven than they are to the passage of time, a point to which we return below. Second, vehicle owners normally interrelate expected future maintenance costs and capital costs of a new vehicle in decisions concerning maintenance and replacement, and the owner normally has some greater discretion over when or whether to incur these expenditures and in what form. Some owners may prefer to spend more on maintenance to prolong the life of the vehicle, while others may spend less on maintenance and replace the vehicle more frequently; either course may be optimal, depending on the individual owner's specific circumstances. A formal theoretical model of this type of integrated behavior is provided in Chapter 8 of Chesher and Harrison (1987).

We have not attempted to statistically estimate such "integrated" models, however, since our focus is not on vehicle maintenance and replacement decisions per se, but rather on the effect of road characteristics on the total costs of vehicle ownership and operation. Our particular objective permits some simplification of the task through separating the estimation of maintenance costs from the estimation of vehicle depreciation and interest.

Nonetheless, the task is still a difficult one. Because of limitations in both the underlying theory and the empirical data base, the estimation of the relationships of vehicle maintenance, depreciation and interest costs to road characteristics is somewhat cruder, and relies on more restrictive assumptions, than that for fuel consumption, tire wear and travel time. We deal first with vehicle maintenance and then with depreciation and interest costs.

12.1 VEHICLE MAINTENANCE PARTS AND LABOR

Vehicle usage-related stresses that cause wear or failure of vehicle parts are mainly of two types: those associated with road roughness and those associated with road geometry. The former type of stresses cause, through their repeated applications, wear on the steering and suspension systems as well as failure of certain components such as springs and brackets (Gillespie, 1981). The stresses associated with road geometry come in the form of forces imposed on the engine, the vehicle drive train (gear box, clutch, rear axle, etc.), and the brakes in order to propel or resist the vehicle against forces acting on the vehicle. Repeated applications of these forces cause wear and failures of the vehicle components that bear against those forces. In addition, abrasive dust frequently occurring in dry climates can enter the engine and thereby cause extra wear.

An attempt was made in Brazil to estimate a mechanistic model for vehicle maintenance parts similar to those given above for fuel and tire wear. A linear model form was postulated to relate parts consumption per 1,000 vehicle-km to vehicle suspension and propulsive energies, per distance unit. However, because of limitations in both the existing body of theory and the available data in Brazil, the exercise was not successful.

As a consequence, for vehicle maintenance costs, resort was made to simpler models correlating spare parts and mechanics' labor, respectively, with road characteristics, as reported by Chesher and Harrison (1985). Since these relationships have been adopted for the HDM-III model, we repeat their results here, with only minor changes for differences in units, for the reader's convenience.

12.1.1 Maintenance Parts Model

Spare parts consumption was found to depend on the roughness of the routes on which the vehicle ply and the average age of the fleet of vehicles of the same class. The proxy for vehicle age is the average cumulative distance driven by vehicles in the region. The age effect and the roughness effect combine multiplicatively. Holding the age constant, the relationship between parts consumption and roughness is generally non-linear with an exponential model providing the best fit, although for trucks a linear model was found to be more suitable. However, since the exponential relationship overpredicts parts consumption for high values of roughness, a linear form is assumed beyond a certain transitional roughness value.

The parts consumption cost model may be written as:

$$APART = CP_0 \exp(CP_q \, QI) \, CKM^{K_p} \qquad \text{for } QI \leq QIP_0 \qquad (12.1)$$

where $APART$ = parts cost per 1,000 vehicle-km for the given vehicle class expressed as a fraction of the cost of a new vehicle;

CP_0 = constant coefficient in the exponential relationship between spare parts consumption and roughness;

CP_q = roughness coefficient in the exponential relationships between spare parts consumption and roughness (per QI);

CKM = average age of the vehicle group in km, defined as the average number of kilometers the vehicles belonging to theparticular vehicle class in the region have been diven since they were built;

K_p = age exponent;

and QIP_0 = transitional value of roughness in QI beyond which the relationship between spare parts consumption and roughness is linear.

The tangential extension of the above relationship for values of roughness higher than QIP_0 may be derived analytically as:

$$APART = (P_0 + P_1 QI) CKM^{K_p} \quad \text{for } QI > QIP_0 \tag{12.2}$$

where $P_0 = CP_0 \exp(CP_q QIP_0)(1 - CP_q QIP_0)$

$P_1 = CP_0 \exp(CP_q QIP_0) CP_q$

Figure 12.1 depicts the above relationship for a large bus for two values of CKM. The broken lines show the part of the curves replaced by the tangential extension.

It should be noted that if the value of QIP_0 is very low (notionally zero), the relationship between parts consumption and roughness for a given value of age becomes linear. For the sake of uniformity of presentation the completely linear form is treated as a special case of the piece-wise exponential-linear form, with QIP_0 value being zero. In this case, the coefficients of the equation of the tangential extension become

$P_0 = CP_0$
$P_1 = CP_0 CP_q$

Using these relationships we can express a linear relationship in the "standard" form, as follows. If the linear prediction equation is:

$$APART = (P_0 + P_1 QI) CKM^{K_p}$$

then $CP_0 = P_0$
$CP_q = P_1/P_0$

and $QIP_0 = 0$

The values of the parameters using Brazil data are given in Table 14.4 of Chapter 14.

It may be noted that, generally, the age of the vehicle is an intermediate construct determined from the optimal scrapping date decision. However, it has been assumed in this volume that average age and vehicle lifetime are exogenous variables to be specified by the user. This amounts to the assumption that the age distribution of the vehicles

Figure 12.1:   Maintenance parts model for a large bus

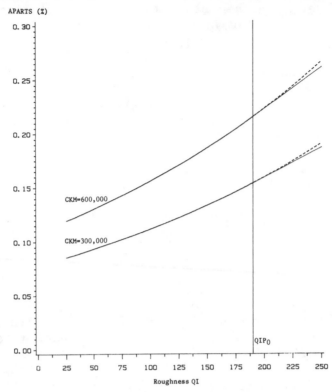

Source: Analysis of Brazil–UNDP–World Bank highway research project data.

in the region is stationary, and in any case does not affect the estimated maintenance costs significantly.

12.1.2 Maintenance Labor Hours Model

Maintenance labor resources required for operating a vehicle were found to be related to the maintenance parts consumption and, in the case of large buses in Brazil, roughness of the route on which the vehicle plies. The roughness effect, when significant, combines multiplicatively with the parts effect. The model, in its full generality, may be written,

$$\text{ALABOR} = CL_0 \; \text{APART}^{CL_p} \; \exp(CL_q \; QI) \tag{12.3}$$

where   ALABOR = predicted number of maintenance labor hours per 1,000 vehicle-km;

CL_0 = constant coefficient in the relationship between labor hours and parts consumption;

CL_p = exponent of parts cost in the relationship between labor hours and parts consumption;

CL_q = roughness coefficient in the exponential relationships between labor hours and roughness (per QI).

A value of zero for CL_q would imply that the roughness effect is not significant.

The constant coefficient CL_0 captures the result of labor-capital trade-off in the specific economic regime, and, as such, it is of importance to calibrate this parameter for a given application. On the other hand, the parts exponent CL_p reflects the economies of vehicle size and is found to be reasonably constant for a similar vehicle class between Brazil and India. Thus, it is not anticipated that the latter parameter needs to be locally calibrated, especially given the richness of vehicle classification in the Brazil study.

In the Brazil study, only buses had a significant roughness effect. However, in the Indian study the absence of roughness effect was not decisive in the case of a number of vehicle classes. Guidance for local calibration of the maintenance parts and labor models is provided in Chapter 13.

12.2 DEPRECIATION AND INTEREST CHARGES

A vehicle constitutes a medium-term capital asset; its purchase cost represents an investment which yields services over a period of several years. The market value of the asset declines with both the passage of time (typically rather quickly at first and then more slowly) and, generally to a much smaller degree, with the amount and type of usage. It is this loss of market value (as distinct from some physical or accounting concept) which is here taken to represent "depreciation", measured on an annual basis. Since depreciation occurs gradually, at any given point in time there is a residual (undepreciated) amount of capital tied up in the vehicle, which normally could be invested elsewhere, so that an annual interest charge, in addition to the annual depreciation, is incurred. The interest charge is purely a function of time and the undepreciated value of the vehicle.

In order to relate these predominantly time-related costs to other predominantly usage-related costs, it is convenient (and customary) to divide annual depreciation and interest charges by an annual utilization factor, such as average vehicle kilometerage. It should be noted, however, that where annual utilization is much above average, one would expect vehicle depreciation to increase and the vehicle life (in years) to be foreshortened, although probably less than proportionately.

Thus, in order to estimate the effects of varying road characteristics on vehicle depreciation and interest costs, one needs to establish the effects of road characteristics on (i) vehicle life and (ii) vehicle utilization. Unfortunately, neither of these relationships has ever been properly quantified empirically; traditionally they have simply been assumed in benefit-cost studies of road investments. In his classic treatise, de Weille (1966) assumed that annual utilization was fully proportional to any change in vehicle speeds due to changes in road characteristics, but the effect on depreciation and interest charges per vehicle kilometer was attenuated by the concomitant assumption that the vehicle life in years was reduced somewhat, so that the annual depreciation charge was increased.

Studies in Kenya (Hide et al., 1975) India (CRRI, 1982; Chesher, 1983), and Brazil (GEIPOT, 1982, Volume 5) have quantified the relationship of annual vehicle depreciation to the age of the vehicle in years (but not the effect of road characteristics thereon), and the studies in India and Brazil went on to investigate the effect of road characteristics on vehicle utilization.

In the Brazil models, as reported below, road characteristics affect depreciation and interest costs per kilometer through utilization; vehicle life in years (and hence annual depreciation) is left to be exogenously specified by the model user as estimated from local evidence. Utilization is modelled through a general set of accounting identities which interrelate route length, total annual operating time and non-driving time (which are estimated as parametric constants), with vehicle speed and driving times (as a function of road characteristics). A change in road characteristics which leads to a change in vehicle speeds results in a less than proportionate change in annual vehicle utilization, and the vehicle fleet size necessary to meet a given level of transport demand changes proportionately.

This model is not considered to provide an entirely adequate representation of the actual changes which will occur, particularly over the longer run, in vehicle utilization as a result of changes in the road network, since it is likely that the parameters of the utilization model (as well as the average life of vehicles) will be adjusted in response to any large scale improvements in the road network. Nonetheless, the model does rely less on such restrictive assumptions than do the traditional methods (which, indeed, rely entirely on a priori assumptions) for calculating depreciation and interest in quantifying the benefits of road improvements. When locally calibrated, as discussed below, the model should provide somewhat improved estimates of the impact of road changes on these important cost elements.

The remainder of this chapter presents:

1. The mathematical formulation of the Brazil models relating vehicle depreciation and interest to utilization, and utilization to speed (Section 12.3);

2. The results of statistical estimation of the model using the Brazil road user cost survey data (Section 12.3 and Appendix 12A); and

3. A recommended model for predicting vehicle utilization which utilizes local information (Section 12.4 and Appendix 12B).

12.3   MODEL FORMULATION

12.3.1   Relationship of Vehicle Depreciation and Interest Costs to Vehicle Utilization

The cost of vehicle depreciation per 1,000 km travelled, DEP, expressed as a fraction of the price of a new vehicle of the same class:

$$DEP = \frac{1,000}{LIFE \quad AKM} \qquad (12.4)$$

where   LIFE = the average vehicle service life in years;
and   AKM = the average annual vehicle utilization, in km of travel
                    per year.

Similarly, the interest cost per 1,000 km travelled, INT, expressed as a fraction of the price of a new vehicle of the same class:

$$INT = \frac{1,000 \; AINV}{200 \; AKM} \qquad (12.5)$$

where AINV is the interest rate in percent, and the annual interest charge is taken as the average of the residual vehicle value, decreasing in a linear fashion from full purchase price at the end of year 0 to zero at the end of year LIFE.

The average service life for a given vehicle class may be assumed to be equal to a constant value $LIFE_0$ (in years) for the region. That is,

$$LIFE = LIFE_0 \qquad (12.6a)$$

where $LIFE_0$ = the baseline average vehicle life, in years.

Alternatively, following de Weille (1966), the average vehicle service life may be assumed to be related to the predicted vehicle operating speed, as follows:

$$LIFE = \frac{1}{3} \left(\frac{S_0}{S} + 2 \right) LIFE_0 \qquad (12.6b)$$

where S_0 = the baseline average vehicle speed, in km/h,

given by: S_0 = AKM_0 / HRD_0
             AKM_0 = the baseline average annual kilometerage,
                       in km/year;
             HRD_0 = the baseline number of hours driven per
                       vehicle per year; and
             S = the predicted round-trip speed, in km/h.

12.3.2 Vehicle Utilization – Simple Model

Because of its importance in establishing the impact of changes in road characteristics, vehicle utilization became a major collection item of the road user cost surveys in Brazil and India. From the data obtained, GEIPOT (1982) and CRRI (1982) estimated vehicle utilization relationships as a function of vehicle and road characteristics as well as operating parameters including route length. In the Brazil road user cost survey, speed data were available only for some cars and buses, so in the statistical estimation vehicle utilization was not related to road characteristics through speed. This may partially explain why no clear geometric effects on vehicle utilization were found. In the India survey speed data were obtained from timetables and operating schedules. Although the speeds derived in this manner may be quite different from the actual speeds, vehicle utilization was found to be strongly influenced by speed.

Subsequently, using a constant elasticity model on India data, Chesher (1983) obtained alternative relationships between vehicle utilization and speed. For bus operations, the elasticity of bus utilization with respect to speed was found to equal approximately 0.7. As will be seen, a subsequent theoretical analysis suggests that the elasticity should lie between zero and one. However, possibly due to unsatisfactory speed data, elasticities of utilization for the other vehicle classes could not be meaningfully quantified.

The model formulated below is an adaptation of the "adjusted utilization" method in the earlier HDM-II model (Watanatada, et al., 1981). It assumes that each vehicle operates on a fixed route throughout a given year. The total time spent on making a complete round trip, TT, is given by:

$$TT = TN + TD \qquad (12.7)$$

where   TN = the amount of time spent on non-driving activities as part of the round trip tour, including loading, unloading, refueling, layovers, etc., in hours per trip; and

TD = the amount of time spent on driving over the route, in hours per trip.

For a given class of vehicles of similar operating characteristics (nature and size of cargo carried, etc.), the amount of non-driving time per trip, TN, is assumed on average to be constant. Let RL denote the round trip driving distance or route length in km, and S the average round trip speed in km/h. Thus, the driving time, TD, can be written as:

$$TD = \frac{RL}{S} \qquad (12.8)$$

Let HAV denote the vehicle availability, defined as the total amount of time the vehicle is available for vehicle operation, in hours per year. In general, HAV is equal to the total number of hours per year (8,760 h/y) less the time allowed for crew rest, infeasibility of vehicle operation (e.g., during holidays or hours labor does not normally work), vehicle repairs, etc. Within a given vehicle class, HAV is assumed to be constant and independent of vehicle speed; however, we would expect HAV to be dependent on labor work rules (e.g., scheduling of drivers and other crew members), vehicle age and condition, etc. Vehicle operators are assumed to maximize vehicle productivity by making as many trips possible within the vehicle availability constraint. Under this assumption, the number of trips per year, denoted by NTRIPS is given by:

$$\text{NTRIPS} = \frac{\text{HAV}}{\text{TT}} \tag{12.9}$$

The annual kilometerage, AKM, may be written as:

$$\text{AKM} = \text{NTRIPS RL} \tag{12.10}$$

The above assumption is considered appropriate when there is no "excess capacity" in the vehicle fleet within the region in question. During a period of economic downturn, it is possible that the total vehicle availability is not fully utilized, i.e., we have:

$$\text{NTRIPS} \leq \frac{\text{HAV}}{\text{TT}}$$

so that the number of trips and the annual utilization are constants independent of vehicle speed. Thus, in the "excess capacity" case, the assumption of constant annual utilization is more appropriate. Private passenger cars and commuting vehicles would also fall into this case, since vehicle utilization is expected to be somewhat independent of speed unless there is significant residential and workplace relocation. As will be seen subsequently, the "constant annual utilization" method is in fact a special case of the more general model described herein.

Where there is "no excess capacity," Equations 12.9 and 12.10 yield a speed-sensitive annual vehicle utilization, AKM, as given by:

$$\text{AKM} = \frac{\text{HAV RL}}{\text{TT}} \tag{12.11}$$

Substituting Equations 12.7 and 12.8 in Equation 12.11, we have annual vehicle utilization expressed as a function of the number of hours available, the operating speed, the non-driving time per trip, and the route length:

$$\text{AKM} = \frac{\text{HAV}}{\dfrac{\text{TN}}{\text{RL}} + \dfrac{1}{\text{S}}} \tag{12.12}$$

where HAV and TN are model parameters to be estimated within a given class of vehicles.

By differentiation it can be shown that the elasticity of vehicle utilization with respect to speed, denoted by EVU, is equal to the ratio of the driving time to the total trip time:

$$\text{EVU} = \frac{\partial \text{ AKM}}{\partial \text{ S}} \frac{\text{S}}{\text{AKM}} = \frac{\text{TD}}{\text{TT}} \tag{12.13}$$

Since by definition the driving time, TD, is never greater than the total trip time, TT, the elasticity is always smaller than one. Denoting the number of hours driven per year by HRD, we have:

$$HRD = TD \ NTRIPS \qquad\qquad (12.14)$$

Substituting NTRIPS from Equation 12.9 in Equation 12.14 yields:

$$\frac{HRD}{HAV} = \frac{TD}{TT} \qquad\qquad (12.15)$$

Thus, the elasticity of vehicle utilization with respect to speed can be alternatively expressed as equal to the ratio of the annual number of hours driven to the annual number of hours available:

$$EVU = \frac{HRD}{HAV} \qquad\qquad (12.16)$$

The estimation of model parameters HAV and TN is described in Appendix 12A. Using these estimated parameters and average route length in the estimation data, predicted vehicle utilization is graphed against vehicle speed for each vehicle class (except for the "bus without tachograph" and "medium/heavy truck non-tipper" classes) as shown in Figure 12.2. As expected, vehicle utilization for each vehicle class increases with vehicle speed but at a decreasing rate.

For cars, utilities, and medium and articulated trucks, Figure 12.3 compares vehicle utilization predicted by the model estimates above with that predicted by the constant annual hourly utilization method. The latter method, which is represented by lines bearing plus symbols in Figure 12.3, employed the following formula:

$$AKM = \frac{S}{S_{(avg)}} \ AKM_{(avg)} \qquad\qquad (12.17)$$

where $S_{(avg)}$ and $AKM_{(avg)}$ are the mean predicted vehicle speed and observed annual utilization for the survey vehicles, as computed in Table 12A.3. We can see that while predictions produced by these two methods are generally similar for average speeds, they are different for the low and high ends of the speed range. At the low end, the former method predicts a higher utilization than the latter. At the high end, the reverse occurs.

As discussed earlier, the elasticity of vehicle utilization with respect to operating speed (EVU) is a useful parameter, and it is desirable to estimate its representative values for the vehicle classes. Two alternative methods were used as described below.

Method 1

First, differentiate AKM in Equation 12.12 with respect to S to obtain the elasticity EVU expressed in the following form:

Figure 12.2: **Predicted vehicle utilization versus speed**

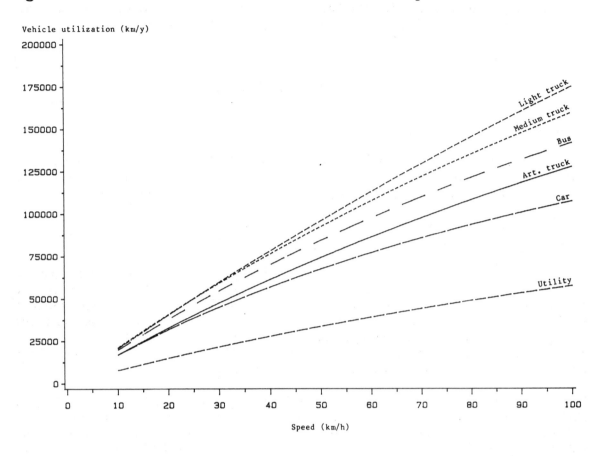

Note: These plots use the adjusted utilization method.

Note: These plots compare the adjusted and the constant hourly
        utilization method indicated by continuous and broken lines
        respectively.

Source: Analysis of Brazil-UNDP-World Bank highway research project data.

Figure 12.3:   Predicted vehicle utilization versus speed

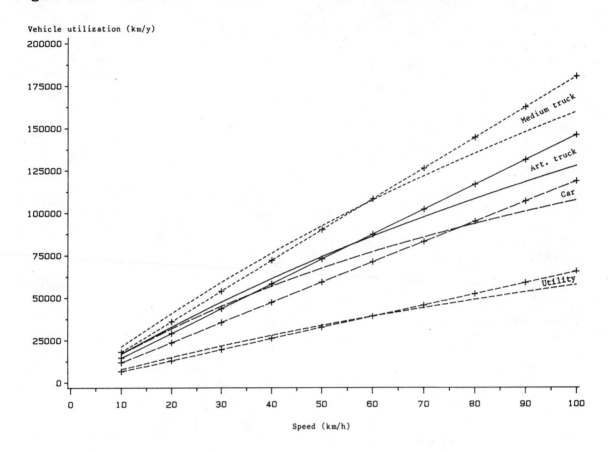

Note: These plots use the adjusted utilization method.

Source: Analysis of Brazil–UNDP–World Bank highway research project data.

$$EVU = \frac{\partial \; AKM}{\partial \; S} \; \frac{S}{AKM} = \frac{1}{\frac{S \; TN}{RL} + 1} \qquad (12.18)$$

Then, for each vehicle class, use the estimated value of TN in Table 12.5 and average values of RL and S to compute an estimate of EVU.

Method 2

This method uses the formula in Equation 12.16 (i.e., EVU = HRD/HAV) directly. For each vehicle class, the estimated value of HAV in Table 12A.5 is used. An average value of HRD is computed by averaging over the predicted values of HRD for the survey vehicles. The latter were computed by dividing the annual utilization of each survey vehicle by the corresponding predicted speed.

These two methods employ the same source of information in highly aggregate manner but in somewhat different ways. However, if the survey vehicles in the different vehicle classes are not too heterogeneous with respect to their operating behavior, then the resulting elasticities should not be very different. The results of the calculations for all vehicle classes except the "bus without tachograph" and "medium/heavy truck - non-tipper" classes are summarized in Table 12.1. Except for the "articulated truck" class, the elasticities of vehicle utilization based on the two methods are quite similar. The relatively high values for the truck classes indicate relatively low percentages of non-driving time compared to the other vehicle classes. This implies that truck utilization tends to be more responsive to increased operating speeds. In this respect, car utilization is the least responsive, as indicated by the smallest values of elasticities.

It should be noted that the average annual utilization value for cars (94,596 km/y) is significantly on the higher side even for commercial usage. It is probably due to the special nature of business in which the cars in the sample were employed, namely, courier work in and around Brasilia. While the Brazil values are treated as defaults, it is recommended that users determine representative values for the region of application. Figure 12.4 illustrates graphically how the relationship between vehicle utilization and speed varies with the elasticity (assuming 10,000 km/y utilization and 54 km/h average route speed at the designated elasticity values).

12.4 RECOMMENDED VEHICLE UTILIZATION PREDICTION MODEL

The estimated coefficients (in Table 12A.5) are specific to the Brazilian vehicle operators in the survey. As mentioned previously, the HAV and TN parameters depend on the trip distance, type of the cargo or passengers carried, the pick-up and delivery system, work rules, and other operating characteristics. Since these latter variables can vary from one locale to another, it is anticipated that the coefficients would be

Table 12.1: Estimation of average elasticities of vehicle utilization

| Vehicle class | Average | | | | | | Estimated Average | |
| | Annual utilization AKM (km/y) | Route length RL (km) | Predicted Speed S (km/h) | Predicted h/year driven RD | Hours available per year HAV | Non-drive h/trip TN | Elasticity of vehicle utilization, EVU | |
							Method 1	Method 2
Car	94,596	327	79.8	1,162	1,972	2.26	0.64	0.59
Utility	39,283	46	60.2	652	839	0.19	0.80	0.78
Bus with tachograph	102,404	328	64.0	1,601	2,302	1.57	0.77	0.70
Truck:								
Light	120,484	836	63.8	1,863	2,200	1.74	0.88	0.85
Medium/heavy truck-tipper	98,369	188	54.6	1,825	2,227	0.72	0.83	0.82
Articulated	95,517	1,230	65.6	1,400	2,414	4.86	0.79	0.58

Source: Analysis of Brazil-UNDP-World Bank highway research project data.

different in a new country or region. Therefore, it is advisable to develop a more generally applicable method for predicting vehicle utilization. The method should satisfy the following criteria:

1. Reliance on local data; and
2. Simplicity of input data requirements.

With the above criteria in mind, we propose a general model which requires three input parameters representing regional or national averages:

HRD_0 = an average annual number of hours driven;
AKM_0 = an average annual utilization, in km per year; and
EVU_0 = an average elasticity of vehicle utilization.

A relatively simple procedure for obtaining values of HRD_0, AKM_0 and EVU_0 is described in Chapter 14. Once these parameters are available for a given vehicle class, they can be used to "calibrate" the vehicle utilization model of Equation 12.2, using a simple algebraic procedure described in Appendix 12B. The resulting form of the vehicle utilization prediction model is given by:

$$AKM = \left[\frac{(1 - EVU_0)}{AKM_0} - + \frac{EVU_0}{HRD_0} \frac{}{S} \right]^{-1} \qquad (12.19)$$

The behavior of predicted vehicle utilization with respect to the elasticity EVU_0 is of interest. On one extreme, when EVU_0 equals zero, Equation 12.19 reduces to:

Figure 12.4: Predicted vehicle utilization versus speed for various EVU

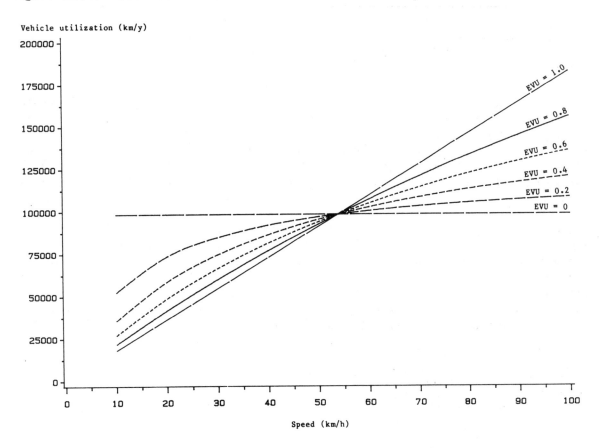

Note: These plots use the adjusted utilization method.

Note: These plots use the adjusted utilization method.

Source: Analysis of Brazil-UNDP-World Bank highway research project data.

$$AKM = AKM_0 \qquad\qquad\qquad\qquad (12.20)$$

which is recognized as the "constant annual utilization method" mentioned earlier.   On the opposite extreme, when EVU_0 equals one, Equation 12.19 becomes:

$$AKM = HRD_0 \; S \qquad\qquad\qquad\qquad (12.21)$$

which is recognized as the "constant annual hourly utilization method" used in many studies.   The two extremes of $EVU_0 = 0$ and $EVU_0 = 1$ are also shown in Figure 12.3 above (as a horizontal line and a positively sloped straight line through the origin, respectively).

APPENDIX 12A

ESTIMATION OF MODEL PARAMETERS

12A.1 DATA FOR ESTIMATION

The data used in model estimation were obtained from the road user cost survey as described in detail in GEIPOT (1982, Volume 5) and Chesher and Harrison (1985). For analysis purposes the survey vehicles were divided into the following classes: cars, utilities, buses with and without tachographs, and light, medium/heavy and articulated trucks, covering various models and makes as shown in Table 12A.1. Summary statistics of the route lengths and annual utilization of these vehicle classes are given in Table 12A.2. Table 12A.3 provides summary statistics by vehicle class of the routes' length, rise plus fall, horizontal curvature, roughness, and percentage paved.

Since speed data were not generally collected in the survey, the average operating speeds of the survey vehicles were predicted as a function of the above aggregate route characteristics using the aggregate speed prediction model described in Chapter 7. The closest test vehicle was matched against each of the vehicle classes as shown in Table 12A.1, and the steady-state speed model parameters adapted for those test vehicles (as described in Chapter 10) were used with the vehicle characteristics shown in Table 12A.4. The means and standard deviation of the predicted speeds by vehicle class are presented in Table 12A.2.

12A.2 MODEL ESTIMATION RESULTS AND ELASTICITIES OF UTILIZATION

The vehicle utilization model of Equation 12.12 is non-linear in the parameters TN and HAV, so a non-linear estimation procedure provided in the Statistical Analysis System (SAS) was employed (SAS Institute, 1982). Ideally HAV and TN should be estimated as a function of operating characteristics such as the type and size of commodities carried, route length, company operating policy, labor work rules, etc. However, because the necessary information was not available in the survey in suitable disaggregate form, it was possible only to obtain representative values of the HAV and TN parameters for broad vehicle classes.

Regression runs were carried out separately for the vehicle classes yielding results and coefficient estimates as summarized in Table 12A.5. Except for the "bus without tachograph" and "medium/heavy truck - non-tipper" classes, all coefficients are of the expected sign and reasonable magnitudes. For the vehicle classes with relatively short haul and presumably simple operations, namely, "utility" and "medium/heavy truck-tipper" with average route lengths of 46 and 188 km, respectively, the estimated non-driving time per trip of 0.19 and 0.72 hour, respectively, are smaller than the estimated values for the vehicle classes with relatively long haul operations, notably the "articulated

Table 12A.1 Classification of vehicle makes and models for vehicle utilization analysis

Vehicle class (test vehicle)	Make/model[1]	Number of vehicles	
Car (VW-1300)	VW-Brasilia	12	
	VW-1300	87	
	VW-1500	5	
	VW-1600	36	
	VW-1600 (double carburator)	6	
	Fiat-147L	51	
	Total	197	
Utility (VW-Kombi)	Ford F-75 Pick-up	11	
	VW-Kombi	6	
	Total	17	
		With tachograph	**Without tachograph**
Bus (MB-0362)	MB-LPO 321/45/48	0	13
	MB-LPO 1113/45	36	54
	MB-LP 113/48/51	19	121
	MB-OF 1113/51	7	1
	MB-OH 1313/51	3	7
	MB-O 321	7	2
	MB-O 326	1	0
	MB-O 352	22	8
	MB-O 362	0	33
	MB-O 355	23	1
	MB-1111 (truck chassis)	0	2
	Total	118	242
Light truck (Ford 4000)	Ford F 400	12	
	Ford F 4000	6	
	MB-L 608	14	
	Total	32	
		Tipper	**Non-tipper**
Medium/heavy truck (MB-1113)	MB-L/LPK/LPS 312	0	1
	MB-L/LK/LS 1113	40	41
	MB-L/LK/LS 1313	23	3
	MB-L/LK 1513	8	12
	MB-L 2013	0	8
	MB-L 2213	1	0
	MB-LK/LB 2213	6	0
	MB-L/LK 1519	16	0
	Total	94	65
Articulated truck (Scania 110/39)	MB-LS 1519	35	
	Scania-L 75	4	
	Scania-L 76	3	
	Scania-L 110	24	
	Scania-LS 36	2	
	Scania-L 111	45	
	Scania-LT 111	7	
	Scania-LK 140	7	
	Total	127	

[1] VW = Volkswagen; MB = Mercedes Benz
Source: Authors' judgement based on Brazil-UNDP-World Bank highway research project data.

Table 12A.2: Summary of route length and utilization

Vehicle class (Number of vehicles)	Types of statistics	Round trip route length (km)	Annual utilization (km)	Number of round trips per year	Average round trip speed(km/h)
Car	Mean	327	94596	374	79.8
(197)	Std. dev.	167	43314	256	7.1
Utility	Mean	46	39283	975	60.2
(17)	Std. dev.	35	10791	281	6.6
Bus:					
Tachograph	Mean	328	102404	411	64.0
(118)	Std. dev.	203	34994	214	7.0
W/o tachograph	Mean	319	82556	667	56.5
(242)	Std. dev.	187	28181	1227	8.8
Truck:					
Light	Mean	836	120484	209	63.8
(32)	Std. dev.	364	33731	242	7.1
Medium/heavy	Mean	188	98369	661	54.6
tipper (94)	Std. dev.	113	15556	319	9.5
Medium/heavy	Mean	836	93039	138	54.7
non-tipper (65)	Std. dev.	256	29000	97	4.2
Articulated	Mean	1230	95547	595	65.6
(127)	Std. dev.	1835	56811	820	13.2

Source: Brazil-UNDP-World Bank highway research project data.

truck" class with average route length of 1230 km and estimated TN equal to 4.86 hours. (Of course, the number of trips is inversely related to trip distance, so that the total non-driving time per year is much higher for the vehicles with short trip distances.)

The estimated non-driving time per round trip, TN, for the "bus without tachograph" and "medium/heavy truck - non-tipper" classes are virtually zero which is clearly unrealistic. An examination of the statistics in Table 12A.2 reveals that the standard deviation of predicted speed for the "medium/heavy truck - non-tipper" class is rather small, only 7.7 percent of the mean, which is seemingly a result of a relatively small range of road geometry and roughness variation. The poor TN estimate for the "bus without tachograph" class does not seem to be caused by the small variation in predicted speed, the standard deviation of which (8.8 km/h) is comparable to those of the other vehicle classes. A plausible explanation is that the speeds were predicted for free-flowing conditions whereas a substantial portion of these bus routes may have been built-up areas in which the actual operating speeds were considerably lower.

Table 12A.3: Summary of route characteristics

Vehicle class	Types of statistics	Rise plus fall (m/km)	Horizontal curvature (degrees/km)	Road roughness	Percentage paved
Car	Mean	30.0	64.5	61.5	80.8
	Std. dev.	6.8	48.1	31.1	29.2
Utility	Mean	13.4	17.6	121.3	21.4
	Std. dev.	2.1	9.8	32.7	23.9
Bus:					
Tachograph	Mean	22.7	16.3	64.3	65.4
	Std. dev.	4.8	10.2	39.5	42.3
W/o tachograph	Mean	26.1	42.8	96.0	44.3
	Std. dev.	7.8	42.9	48.1	42.2
Truck:					
Light	Mean	27.5	35.4	42.1	88.0
	Std. dev.	6.4	49.6	31.2	29.0
Medium/heavy tipper	Mean	35.7	86.1	63.8	76.3
	Std. dev.	6.5	92.1	39.2	26.4
Medium/heavy non-tipper	Mean	30.0	28.8	61.1	76.8
	Std. dev.	3.2	8.9	24.3	14.6
Articulated	Mean	27.6	40.8	57.1	73.9
	Std. dev.	10.8	48.1	28.9	40.3

Source: Brazil-UNDP-World Bank highway research project data.

Table 12A.4: Vehicle characteristics used in operating speed prediction

Vehicle class	Tare weight (kg)	Load (kg)	Aerodynamic drag coefficient	Frontal area (m^2)
Car	960	0	0.45	1.80
Utility	1,320	300	0.46	2.72
Bus (with/without tachograph)	8,100	2,300	0.65	6.30
Truck:				
Light	3,270	2,000	0.70	3.25
Medium	5,400	4,500		
Heavy	6,600	6,000		
Articulated	14,700	13,000	0.63	5.75

Source: Authors' adaptation based on Brazil-UNDP-World Bank highway
         research project data.

**Table 12A.5: Summary of regression results and estimates of model
parameters**

Vehicle class	Number of vehicles	Parameter estimates		R-square	Standard error of residuals
		HAV (h/y)	TN (h/trip)		
Car	197	1,972 (9.7)	2.26 (3.4)	0.43	32,760
Utility	17	839 (5.1)	0.19 (1.1)	0.31	9,120
Bus:					
Tachograph	118	2,302 (17.1)	1.57 (4.9)	0.35	28,320
W/o tachograph	242	1,460 (42.0)	0.01 (0.4)	0.12	26,520
Truck:					
Light	32	2,200 (10.8)	1.74 (1.4)	0.53	23,520
Medium/heavy tipper	94	2,227 (26.1)	0.72 (5.2)	0.51	10,900
Medium/heavy non-tipper	65	1,734 (13.5)	.0.0 (0.0)	0.24	25,495
Articulated	127	2,414 (24.0)	4.86 (6.6)	0.71	30,600

Note: Values shown in parentheses are asymptotic t-statistics.

Source: Analysis of Brazil-UNDP-World Bank highway research project data.

APPENDIX 12B

CALIBRATION OF RECOMMENDED VEHICLE UTILIZATION PREDICTION MODEL

The procedure for calibrating the general vehicle utilization prediction model with parameters HRD_0, AKM_0 and EVU_0 defined in Section 12.4 is described as follows. First, from Equation 12.16, we express HAV as the ratio of HRD_0 to EVU_0

$$HAV = \frac{HRD_0}{EVU_0} \qquad (12B.1)$$

Then, express the ratio of the non-driving time per trip to the route length as:

$$\frac{TN}{RL} = \frac{HAV - HRD_0}{AKM_0} \qquad (12B.2)$$

Substituting Equation 12B.1 for HAV in Equation 12B.2 gives:

$$\frac{TN}{RL} = \frac{\dfrac{HRD_0}{EVU_0} - HRD_0}{AKM_0} \qquad (12B.3)$$

Finally, substituting Equations 12B.1 and 12B.3 for HAV and TN/RL, respectivelyin Equation 12.12 yields the desired calibrated model:

$$AKM = \left[\frac{[1 - EVU_0]}{AKM_0} + \frac{EVU_0}{S\ HRD_0} \right]^{-1} \qquad (12B.4)$$

APPENDIX 12C

LUBRICANTS CONSUMPTION

Lubricants consumption was not part of the Brazil study. For completeness, the following relationships where lubricants consumption is a function of roughness are reported. These relationships are as modified by Chesher and Harrison (forthcoming) from those obtained from the India study (CRRI, 1982):

Passenger cars and utilities: AOIL = 1.55 + 0.011605 QI

Light trucks: AOIL = 2.20 + 0.011605 QI

Buses and medium and heavy trucks: AOIL = 3.07 + 0.011605 QI

Articulated trucks: AOIL = 5.15 + 0.011605 QI

where   AOIL = the lubricants consumption, in liters/1000 vehicle-km.

PART III

PART III

CHAPTER 13
Guidelines for Local Adaptations

As mentioned in Chapter 1, components of transport costs are generally assessed in the HDMS study as the product of a predicted physical quantity and an exogenously determined price or unit cost. This approach is clearly superior to that of directly predicting costs, since physical, as opposed to economic, models are more easily transfered geographically. Even so, transference problems still remain, and the objective of this chapter is to provide the user with some guidelines on how the vehicle operating cost models presented herein may be adapted to a new locality. Essentially the same issues arise as to the effect of large changes over time in the technological and economic circumstances of the countries where the models were originally estimated, and similar procedures may be pursued to update the models.

This chapter begins with a general discussion on the use of these guidelines (Section 13.1). The remaining sections provide specific guidelines dealing with models for predicting vehicle rolling resistance (13.2), speed (13.3), fuel consumption (13.4), tire wear (13.5), vehicle utilization (13.6) and maintenance parts and labor (13.7).

13.1 USE OF GUIDELINES

For economic profitability (or even survival), transport operators are expected to adapt their operations in response to the economic, social, technological and institutional setting of a given region. On the revenue side, the obvious tendency is to provide services where demand has not been satisfied or is growing. On the expenditure side, which is pertinent to this chapter, the operators may adapt by making appropriate choices not only on the vehicle technology (e.g., vehicle type, size, engine power, and suspension system) but also on the operating policy (e.g., vehicle operating hours, speeds, overloading, tire recapping and replacement). For example, in a high-wage economy, the tendency would be to purchase large, expensive trucks which carry large volumes of cargo, require minimum maintenance and provide comfort for high-speed travel over extended periods of time; on the other hand, since shift operations may be costly, the number of hours operated per year may be relatively short. In a low-wage economy, the opposite tendency would be expected. In another example, trucks operating in mountainous regions, e.g., in Nepal or Bolivia, need to employ large engines relative to their size, in order to provide the necessary propulsive power for hill-climbing; in contrast, operators in generally flat countries like Argentina or Australia can afford to use relatively small engines for even very heavy loads.

As discussed in Chapter 1, the ideal modelling framework would be to incorporate explicitly operators' adaptive behavior in the specifications of the prediction models. However, since this theoretical ideal was impractical to implement, an alternative, but workable framework of physical-component modelling was adopted. Within the latter framework, the calibrated values of the model parameters generally reflect the adaptations made by operators within a specific region and, strictly speaking, it would be desirable to re-calibrate them when applied in a new locality. However, attempts were made in two ways to maximize model transferability and thereby facilitate the task of local adaptation.

First, the mathematical forms of the models were made as general as possible. The mechanistic-behavioral theories made this possible to a large extent for the speed and fuel models, and to a lesser extent for the tire wear and vehicle utilization models. The "aggregate-correlative" models of maintenance parts and labor reported in Chesher and Harrison (forthcoming) and summarized in Chapter 12, on the other hand, had less theoretical support. However, empirical testing of the model forms across countries, i.e., Brazil and India, has yielded satisfactory results in certain respects. In particular, the exponents of the cumulative kilometerage age in the parts model and the parts variable in the labor model, were found to be reasonably stable.

Second, to the extent possible, the models were specified as explicit functions of as many relevant vehicle characteristics as possible (e.g., total weight and engine power), which are routine input requirements. Since these _variables_ are expected to explain much of the variation across countries, the calibrated _parameters_ in the functions so formulated tend to be less dependent on the peculiarities of a particular region. This was possible to a substantial extent with the speed and fuel models, and, because of data limitations, considerably less so with the tire wear model. The parameters of the vehicle utilization model, owing to their nature, as discussed in Chapter 12, are highly region-specific. As for the maintenance models, Chesher and Harrison, _op. cit._, found from empirical testing that, except for the exponent parameters mentioned above, the parameters of these models are sensitive to local conditions.

From the above discussion, we draw the following conclusions concerning local adaptation of the vehicle operating cost prediction models:

1. The mathematical forms of the models are generally adequate and need not be changed except for special reasons (e.g., to incorporate a new policy variable).

2. The vehicle attributes which appear as explanatory variables in the models should generally be determined for a new region. Table 13.1 compiles the list of the vehicle attributes and indicates possible sources of data needed.

3. Some of the parameters are obviously sensitive to local conditions while others appear less so, as discussed below.

Table 13.1: Summary of vehicle attributes used in aggregate vehicle operating cost prediction models

Prediction model	Vehicle attribute				
	Description	Symbol	Units	Chapter defined	Possible sources of data
Rolling resistance roughness equation	Contains no vehicle attributes	–	–	2	Field experiment required
Speed and fuel consumption	Gross vehicle mass Payload	m LOAD	kg kg	2 10	User survey/ field experiment
	Projected frontal area Aerodynamic drag coefficient	AR CD	m dimensionless	2 2	Vehicle manufacturers
Tire wear	Above attributes plus below: Number of tires per vehicle Wearable rubber volume	NT VOL	dimensionless dm	11 11	User survey/ tire manufacturers
Maintenance parts and labor	Cumulative kilometerage	CKM	km	12	User survey
Depreciation and interest	Life Utilization	LIFE AKM	years km/year	12 12	User survey Endogenously modelled (see Table 13.2)
Lubricants consumption	Contains no vehicle attributes	–	–	13	(Insignificant item, which does not warrant adjustment)

However, location-sensitivity should not be used as the only criterion for deciding whether a given parameter should be re-calibrated. Two other criteria are also important. The first has to do with how much influence the parameter has on the policy issues being addressed. The second is concerned with the amount of effort needed to carry out the re-calibration, involving data collection as well as analysis. Based on these three criteria we offer in Table 13.2 general guidelines for the recalibration of the model parameters. Since circumstances are expected to vary a good deal from one application to another, these recommendations need not be followed too strictly. Depending on the degree of prediction accuracy desired in an application, the user should exercise independent judgment against the three criteria above. To help the user in this respect Table 13.2 also provides broad subjective ratings, "low," "medium," or "high," for each parameter in the three categories, namely "sensitivity to local conditions," "influence on policy-making," and "re-calibration effort."

The ratings with respect to "influence on policy-making" were based on subjective assessment of the sensitivity of predictions of changes in total vehicle operating cost (in response to changes in road attributes) to a percentage change in the value of the model parameter. As to the "re-calibration effort," a "high" rating, (e.g., for the maintenance parts, roughness coefficient or for the parameters in the rolling resistance model) means that either a major user survey or a major

Table 13.2: Local adaptation of parameters used in aggregate vehicle operating cost prediction models

1 Prediction model	2 Description	3 Symbol	4 Units	5 Chapter defined	6 Sensitivity to local conditions	7 Influence on policy-making	8 Re-calibration effort	9 Re-calibration generally recommended	10 Possible source(s) of data
Rolling resistance-roughness equation	Constant term	CR^o	dimensionless	2	low	med	high	no	Field experiment
	Roughness coefficient	CR^o_q	QI^{-1}	2	low–med	high	high	no	Field experiment
Speed	Used driving power	HPDRIVE	metric hp	3	high	med–high	low	yes	Vehicle manufacturers/survey
	Used braking power	HPBRAKE	metric hp	3	med–high	low	low	yes	Vehicle manufacturers/survey
	Desired speed (road width > 5.5 m)	VDESIR	m/s	3	high	low–med	med	yes	Field experiment
	Perceived friction ratio	FRATIO	dimensionless	3	low	low–med	med	no	Field experiment
	Average rectified velocity	ARVMAX	mm/s	4	low	low–med	med	no	Field experiment
	Width effect parameter	BW	dimensionless	3	high	med–high	med	no	Field experiment
	Weibull shape parameter	β	dimensionless	3	low–med	med–high	high	no	Field experiment
Fuel consumption	Unit fuel consumption parameters	a_i	various	9	low–med	med–high	low	yes	Field experiment
	Calibrated engine speed	CRPM	rpm	10	med	low	low	no	Vehicle manufacturers
	Experimental-to-actual fuel conversion factor	α_2	dimensionless	10	med	low	high	no	Field experiment/survey
Tire wear	Ratio of retread to new tire cost	RREC	dimensionless	11	high	high	low	yes	Survey
	Base number of recaps	NR_o	dimensionless	11	high	med–high	med	yes	Survey
	Other carcass life model parameters	various	various	11	med–high	med–high	high	no	Survey
	Constant term in tread wear model	TWT_o	$dm^3/1000$ tire-km	11	med–high	med–high	med	yes	Survey
	Wear coefficient for circumferential force	CT_c	$dm^3/$joule-m/1000 tire-km	11	med–high	med–high	med	yes	Survey
Vehicle utilization	Base number of hours driven	HRD_o	hours/vehicle/year	12	high	high	med	yes	Survey
	Base utilization	AKM_o	km/year	12	high	high	med	yes	Survey
	Base elasticity of utilization	EVU_o	km/year	12	med–high	high	med	yes	Survey
Maintenance parts	Constant term	CP_o	complicated units	13	high	high	med	yes	Survey
	Roughness coefficient (exponential or linear form)	CP_q	QI^{-1}	13	med	high	high	no	Survey
	Exponent of kilometerage age	K_p	dimensionless	13	low	med	high	no	Survey
Maintenance labor	Constant term	CL_o	complicated units	13	high	high	med	yes	Survey
	Exponent of maintenance parts	CL_p	dimensionless	13	low	high	med	no	Survey
	Roughness coefficient (bus only)	CL_q	QI^{-1}	13	high	med	high	no	Survey
Lubricants consumption	Constant term	CO^o	liters/1000 veh-km	13	med	low	med	no	Survey
	Roughness coefficient	CO^o_q	(liters/1000 veh-km)		med	low	high	no	

field experiment would be called for; therefore, the parameters with a "high" rating in this category are not recommended for re-calibration, except under exceptional circumstances. Those users who intend to do so should first determine the scope of work involved based on the size of observations sample needed for a given degree of accuracy. Some further discussions on sampling are given in the remaining sections. A "medium" rating, e.g., for the maximum perceived friction ratio (FRATIO) or the the base number of recaps (NR_0), indicates that a minor user survey or field experiment would be required. Finally, a "low" re-calibration effort (e.g., for the maximum used driving power (HPDRIVE) or for the ratio of retread cost to new tire cost (RREC)) indicates that the information is either readily available or could be obtained easily from vehicle manufacturers or operators. For those parameters rated "low" or "medium" in re-calibration effort, simple guidelines are provided in the remaining sections (with the exception of the parameters in the lubricants consumption model which is clearly trivial).

13.2 COEFFICIENT OF ROLLING RESISTANCE

As discussed in Chapter 2, the rolling resistance coefficient CR, is primarily dependent on the tires and the suspension system. The tires affect the overall magnitude as well as the sensitivity of the coefficient to road roughness; the suspension system affects only the latter. From the current knowledge of vehicle mechanics, it is not possible to provide simple guidelines for adjusting the model for different tire and suspension types. An obvious way to obtain a new CR-roughness relationship is from an experiment similar to the coast-down runs described in Appendix 2A. This would amount to a major effort, however, and is therefore not generally recommended. It would be feasible only where a competent, well-equipped research unit exists.

13.3 SPEED PREDICTION MODELS

Of the parameters employed in the speed prediction models, both micro and aggregate, the most influential ones are the speed constraint parameters in the steady-state speed function, VDESIR, HPDRIVE, HPBRAKE, FRATIO and ARVMAX, and the β parameter.[1] As seen in the India case study (Section 4.4), it is not essential to re-calibrate all the speed constraing parameters, for example, FRATIO and ARVMAX. Further, the power parameters HPDRIVE and HPBRAKE can be calculated from rated power and weight, respectively. If warranted, any particular speed constraint parameter can be obtained from a small-scale experiment of spot speed observations at selected road sites. Where different road widths exist for observation, the experiment could also yield data for computing a new value of BW, the width effect parameter.

---

[1] No guidelines are provided herein for adaptation of the desired deceleration rate (DDESIR) used in the micro transitional model (Chapter 6). Although the DDESIR parameter could differ significantly across countries, the effect of the differential is expected to be of a much smaller magnitude than those for the VDESIR, HPDRIVE, HPBRAKE, FRATIO and ARVMAX parameters.

In order to re-calibrate the β parameter, a somewhat larger-scale experiment could be needed. However, it is expected that the Brazil estimates would, in general, be appropriate except for very specific traffic environments. The estimation bias correction factor, $E°$, need not be changed unless a full-fledged re-estimation of other parameters is attempted.

The estimation of each parameter requires a different type of road configuration depending on the type of the associated speed constraint. The general rule is to find sites that are dominated only by the speed constraint to which the parameter belongs. For example, for the VDESIR parameter, the sites selected should be over 6 meters wide, level, straight smooth, and with a slight decline (2-3 percent) so that only the "desired speed" constraint dominates. A slightly negatively sloped section is preferable to a level one since the maximum possible driving speed (VDRIVE) on the latter may become unacceptably low for heavily loaded trucks. Intuitively, the reason for this selection rule is that by allowing only the relevant speed constraint to prevail, we may get a better resolution of the parameter of interest. This point will become more apparent below.

For any speed constraint, care should be taken to make sure that the sections are long enough to allow steady-state conditions to be reached. At each section selected, 100 or more speed observations should be taken for each vehicle class. Assuming that individual speed observations have a standard error equal to 18 percent of the average speed at the site[2], the average observed speed over 100 observations would reduce the standard error to 1.8 percent ($18 ÷ \sqrt{100} = 1.8$). This degree of accuracy should be satisfactory for most purposes.

13.3.1 Desired Speed

The objective is to determine the original desired speed parameter (VDESIR) unadjusted for the road width effect for a given surface type (paved/unpaved). As noted earlier, only smooth, tangent roads with a decline of 2-3 percent and wider than 6 meters should be selected[3]. For each section-direction s, we compute an estimate of this parameter, denoted by $VDESIR_s$, as

$$VDESIR_s = \left[E°^{\frac{1}{\beta}} \ VSS_{so}^{-\frac{1}{\beta}} - VDRIVE_s^{-\frac{1}{\beta}} - VROUGH_s^{-\frac{1}{\beta}} \right]^{-\beta} \quad (13.1)$$

where VSS_{so} is the average observed speed at section-direction s; and the other symbols are as defined in Chapter 3 with subscript s denoting

---

[2] From the estimation results of the steady-state speed model in Table 4.3, the range of estimated standard errors due to random sampling of individual speed observations at a given site, σ_w, is 15.0 to 20.1 percent of the mean predicted speed.

[3] Although some sections may have a slightly negative effective gradient (i.e., $CR_s + GR_s < 0$), the braking speed constraint may be ignored for computational purposes.

the quantities which are specific to section-direction s. Equation 13.1 above was derived by algebraically solving the steady-state speed relationship of Equation 3.38 for VDESIR. Note that the curve speed constraint is irrelevant for tangent sections. As non-dominating constraining speeds, we would expect the terms $VDRIVE_s^{-1/\beta}$ and $VROUGH_s^{-1/\beta}$ to be much smaller than $VSS_{so}^{-1/\beta}$. Therefore, it should make little difference whether we use newly calibrated or originally estimated values of the HPDRIVE and ARVMAX parameters for computing $VDRIVE_s$ and $VROUGH_s$, respectively. This is the reason for choosing only sites that are dominated by the desired speed constraint and nothing else. However, if ideally suitable sections cannot be found and the locally calibrated parameter (say, $VDESIR_s$ in Equation 13.1) becomes sensitive to the other parameters (i.e., $VDRIVE_s$ and $VROUGH_s$), then it can be further refined by iteration.

The required parameter estimate is taken as the average of $VDESIR_s$ over all the section-directions sampled:

$$VDESIR = \frac{1}{N_s} \sum_{s=1}^{N_s} VDESIR_s \qquad (13.2)$$

where N_s is the total number of section-directions in the VDESIR experiment. The user should choose the value of N_s (i.e., the sample size) such that the standard error of the VDESIR estimate, given by:

$$\sigma_{VDESIR} = \left[\frac{1}{N_s-1} \sum_{s=1}^{N_s} \left[VDESIR_s - VDESIR \right]^2 \right]^{0.5} \qquad (13.3)$$

(where VDESIR is as given in Equation 13.2), is smaller than a predetermined level, e.g., 10 percent of VDESIR.

13.3.2 Used Driving Power

Two methods are available for determining the used driving power parameter (HPDRIVE), one based on a direct experiment and the other on a relationship of HPDRIVE to the maximum rated power (HPRATED). Because of its simplicity, the latter method is generally recommended.

Method 1: Direct experiment

This method follows the same approach as that taken for determining the desired speed parameter. The road sites selected for this experiment should be steep, smooth, relatively straight and wider than 6 meters, but can be either paved or unpaved. For very steep uphill grades (say, over 8 percent) where the driving power-limited speed constraint strongly dominates, the presence of moderate curvature (say, over 300 meters radius) and roughness (say, under 100 QI) would be acceptable. For section-direction s, the formula for computing HPDRIVE is:

$$HPDRIVE_s = \frac{1}{736} (m\ g\ (CR_s + GR_s)\ VDRIVE_s + 0.5\ RHO\ CD\ AR\ VDRIVE_s^3) \quad (13.4)$$

where $VDRIVE_s$ is the driving power-limited speed constraint computed for section-direction s; and the other variables are as defined in Chapter 2, subscript s denoting the quantities which are specific to section-direction s. $VDRIVE_s$ is obtained by solving Equation 3.38 yielding:

$$VDRIVE_s = (\ E^{\circ\frac{1}{\beta}}\ VSS_{so}^{-\frac{1}{\beta}} - VCURVE_s^{-\frac{1}{\beta}} - VROUGH_s^{-\frac{1}{\beta}} - VDESIR^{-\frac{1}{\beta}}\ )^{-\beta} \quad (13.5)$$

where VSS_{so} is as defined in Section 13.3.1 and the other variables are as defined in Chapter 3. For best results, the average vehicle weight should be obtained at each site. The required parameter estimate is taken as the average of $HPDRIVE_s$ over all section-directions sampled:

$$HPDRIVE = \frac{1}{N_s} \sum_{s=1}^{N_s} HPDRIVE_s \quad (13.6)$$

where N_s is the total number of section-directions in the HPDRIVE experiment. The value of N_s should be chosen so that the standard error of the HPDRIVE estimate,

$$\sigma_{HPDRIVE} = [\ \frac{1}{N-1} \sum_{s=1}^{N_s} [HPDRIVE_s - HPDRIVE]^2\ ]^{0.5} \quad (13.7)$$

(where HPDRIVE is as given in Equation 13.6), is smaller than a specified accuracy limit.

Method 2: Maximum rated power

The maximum rated power of a vehicle, denoted by HPRATED, is readily available in general from the vehicle manufacturer, and HPDRIVE can be derived from HPRATED. As described in Section 4.3, based on the test vehicles data, separate relationships were developed for gasoline and diesel vehicles:

For gasoline vehicles: $HPDRIVE = 2.0\ HPRATED^{0.7}$ (13.8a)

For diesel vehicles: $HPDRIVE = 0.7\ HPRATED$ (13.8b)

where HPRATED is the SAE maximum rated power of the average vehicle in the given class, in metric hp. These relationships are recommended for computing a crude estimate of the HPDRIVE parameter. Since the maximum rated power is usually quoted under standard atmospheric conditions, the value of HPRATED should be adjusted where the operating atmospheric conditions show a substantial departure from the standard conditions (e.g., in high-altitude driving or driving in severely cold weather). The standard conditions adopted by Brazilian vehicle manufacturers (with subscript 0 denoting standard conditions) are:

Temperature: TM_0 = 293 K (20°C or 68°F)

Barometric pressure: BP_0 = 101.3 kPa (76 cm of Mercury)

where TM_0 is the ambient temperature and BP_0 is measured at the carburetor air inlet. Based on Wong (1978) the following formulas are recommended as an approximation:

For gasoline vehicles: $HPRATED = HPRATED_0 \ (BP/BP_0) \ \sqrt{(TM_0/TM)}$ (13.9a)

For diesel vehicles: $HPRATED = HPRATED_0 \ (BP/BP_0) \ (TM_0/TM)$ (13.9b)

where $HPRATED_0$ and HPRATED denote the maximum rated power under standard and new conditions, respectively. It can be seen from the above formulas that, by lowering the atmospheric pressure (BP), high altitude has an attenuating effect on the vehicle power. Similarly, a hot climate (high TM) causes the vehicle power to drop. However, it should be noted that the loss of power at high elevations can be alleviated by turbocharging. Hence, the proportion of turbocharged vehicles in the vehicle population of the region should be ascertained while adapting the HPDRIVE parameter.

13.3.3 Used Braking Power

Similar to the used driving power, two methods are available for determining the used braking power (HPBRAKE), one based on a direct experiment and the other on a relationship of HPBRAKE to the rated gross vehicle weight. Relative to HPDRIVE, HPBRAKE has a relatively small influence on the predicted speed. Therefore, the method based on the rated gross vehicle weight, which is much less costly than the direct experiment method, is generally recommended.

Method 1: Direct experiment

The road sites selected for this experiment should be steep, opposite directions). It is important to ensure that steady-state conditions can be reached at each site in both travel directions. This may not be possible as the uphill direction usually requires a considerably shorter travel distance to reach the steady-state speed than the downhill direction. One way to remedy this is to use a moderately curved section which is led and followed by moderately curved sections. This winding configuration tends not only to reduce the transient distance needed to attain the steady-state speed but also to suppress the occurrence of downhill momentum situations.

For given section-direction s, the formula for computing HPBRAKE is obtained from Equation 3.6:

$$HPBRAKE_s = -\frac{m\,g\,(GR_s + CR_s)\,VBRAKE_s}{736} \tag{13.10}$$

where $VBRAKE_s$ is the braking power-limited speed constraint computed for section-direction s; and the other variables are defined in Chapter 2 subscript s denoting the quantities which are specific to section-direction s. $VBRAKE_s$ is obtained by solving Equation 3.38 producing:

$$VBRAKE_s = \left[\, E^{\circ\frac{1}{\beta}}\, VSS_{so}^{-\frac{1}{\beta}} - VDRIVE_s^{-\frac{1}{\beta}} - VCURVE_s^{-\frac{1}{\beta}} - VROUGH_s^{-\frac{1}{\beta}} - VDESIR_s^{-\frac{1}{\beta}} \,\right]^{-\beta} \tag{13.11}$$

where the variables above are as defined previously. Following the same remaining procedure as for HPDRIVE, we compute the HPDRIVE estimate and the standard error of the estimate as:

$$HPBRAKE = \frac{1}{N_s} \sum_{s=1}^{N_s} HPBRAKE_s \tag{13.12}$$

$$\sigma_{HPBRAKE} = \left\{ \frac{1}{N_s - 1} \sum_{s=1}^{N_s} (HPBRAKE_s - HPBRAKE)^2 \right\}^{0.5} \tag{13.13}$$

Method 2: Rated gross vehicle weight

As presented in Section 4.3, the used braking power may be computed from the following simple formula as an approximation:

$$HPBRAKE = 14\ GVW \text{ or } 15\ GVW \tag{13.14}$$

where GVW is the manufacturer's rated gross weight, in tons, of the average vehicle in the given class. This formula is based on the assumption that vehicle designers generally strive to match the vehicle's braking capability with its design weight. As shown in Section 4.3, this assumption is supported by data from the test vehicles.

13.3.4 Perceived Friction Ratio

As indicated in Section 13.1, because of its expected insensitivity to local conditions, the perceived friction ratio need not be re-calibrated in general. However, where circumstances warrant, the following guideline may be followed.

For each surface type (paved/unpaved), a set of road sites are needed to determine the FRATIO parameter. For paved roads, FRATIO should be determined separately for loaded and unloaded trucks. The road sites selected should have a sharp horizontal curvature (under 50 meter radius), and be smooth, level or with a slight decline (2-3 percent) and wider than 6 meters. By following essentially the same procedure as for the preceding model parameters, the FRATIO estimate and its standard error are given by:

$$\text{FRATIO} = \frac{1}{N_s} \sum_{s=1}^{N_s} \text{FRATIO}_s \qquad (13.15)$$

and

$$\sigma_{\text{FRATIO}} = \left[\frac{1}{N_s-1} \sum_{s=1}^{N_s} \left[\text{FRATIO}_s - \text{FRATIO}\right]^2 \right]^{0.5} \qquad (13.16)$$

where N_s is the total number of section-directions selected for determining FRATIO; and FRATIO_s is the value computed for section-direction s, given by

$$\text{FRATIO}_s = \frac{\text{VCURVE}_s^2}{g\,\text{RC}_s} - \text{SP}_s \qquad (13.17)$$

where VCURVE_s is the curvature-limited speed constraint computed for section-direction s; and the other variables are as defined in Chapter 3, with subscript s denoting the quantities specific to section-direction s. VCURVE_s is obtained from Equation 3.38:

$$\text{VCURVE}_s = \left(\text{E}^{\circ\frac{1}{\beta}}\, \text{VSS}_{so}^{-\frac{1}{\beta}} - \text{VDRIVE}_s^{-\frac{1}{\beta}} - \text{VROUGH}_s^{-\frac{1}{\beta}} - \text{VDESIR}^{-\frac{1}{\beta}} \right)^{-\beta} \qquad (13.18)$$

13.3.5 Average Rectified Velocity

As indicated in Section 13.1, the expected insensitivity of the maximum average rectified velocity (ARVMAX) to local conditions makes re-calibration unnecessary in general. Where circumstances warrant, however (e.g., where vehicle suspension systems are very different from those in Brazil), the ARVMAX parameter may be re-calibrated using the guideline below. For each vehicle class, only one value of the ARVMAX parameter needs to be determined. The road sites selected should be straight, level or with a slight decline (2-3 percent), over 6 meters wide and have roughness of at least 125 QI for paved and 200 QI for unpaved roads. Similarly to the preceding parameters, the ARVMAX estimate and its standard error are given by:

$$ARVMAX = \frac{1}{N_s} \sum_{s=1}^{N_s} ARVMAX_s \tag{13.19}$$

$$\sigma_{ARVMAX} = \left[\frac{1}{N_s-1} \sum_{s=1}^{N_s} [ARVMAX_s - ARVMAX]^2 \right]^{0.5} \tag{13.20}$$

where N_s is the total number of section-directions selected for determining ARVMAX. $ARVMAX_s$ is the value computed for section-direction s:

$$ARVMAX_s = k_0 \, QI_s \, VROUGH_s \tag{13.21}$$

where k_0 is a constant (as defined in Chapter 3), QI_s the roughness of section-direction s, and $VROUGH_s$ the roughness-limited speed constraint computed for section-direction s. $VROUGH_s$ may be computed using:

$$VROUGH_s = \left[E^{\circ \frac{1}{\beta}} VSS_{so}^{-\frac{1}{\beta}} - VDRIVE_s^{-\frac{1}{\beta}} - VDESIR_s^{-\frac{1}{\beta}} \right]^{-\beta} \tag{13.22}$$

As before, the above formula is obtained by solving Equation 3.38 (with $VCURVE_s$ eliminated since no curved sections are included).

13.3.6 Width Effect Parameter

Unlike the parameters dealt with above, the width effect parameters, BW, were not originally estimated with the Brazil data; rather, they were added to the steady-state speed model using results from the India case study (Section 4.4). If recalibration is desired, a relatively simple procedure would be to use the method described in Section 13.3.1 to obtain desired speeds for two groups of smooth and level-tangent sections, one with two lanes (carriageway width greater than 5.5 m), and the other with single lane (carriageway width less than 4 m). Let VDESIR and VDESIR' denote the mean desired speeds for the wider and the narrower groups of sections, respectively. Then the estimate of the BW parameter VDESIR'/VDESIR.

13.3.7 Weibull Shape Parameter

As indicated in Section 4.4 and earlier, while predicted speeds are sensitive to the value of β, in order to obtain reliable estimates of β a larger scale field study would be required. As seen above, a given speed constraint parameter can be calibrated by collecting speed data on a group of sections of a particular characteristic. On the other hand, speed data would be needed on a larger range of section characteristics to calibrate the β parameter, thus necessitating a nearly full-fledged experiment. However, it is expected that the estimates of β derived in the Brazil study would be applicable in most cases. The only exceptions are likely to be countries such as India, where the traffic environment is characterized by severe congestion and diversity of traffic composition. For applications in such areas, values of β closer to those obtained in the case study of India (Section 4.4) may be used.

13.4 FUEL CONSUMPTION PREDICTION MODEL

Granted accurate speed prediction, the accuracy in the prediction of fuel consumption depends largely on how well the unit fuel consumption (UFC) function estimated for each test vehicle (Chapter 9) represents the vehicle fleet in question. As discussed in Chapter 9, while the estimated UFC functions are considered to be adequate in most cases, some are based on a relatively dated engine design and may not well represent the fuel efficiency of the vehicle classes in question. In this case, a recalibration may be desirable.

The simplest way for the user would be to choose a suitable value of the "relative energy-efficiency factor", α_1, suggested in Chapter 9 (Table 9.6) — to bring the fuel predicton made for Brazil engines of the early seventies closer to modern-day engines. For example, the energy efficiency factor of 0.8 recommended for adjusting the fuel prediction for the Scania means unit fuel consumption computed by the original relationship would be multiplied by 0.8; this is equivalent to re-calibrating each UFC model parameter by applying the 0.80 factor. The fuel efficiency factor, α_1, is, of course, applied over and above the "fuel adjustment factor," α_2, which has to do with non-engine related efficiencies. Another way to re-calibrate the UFC function would be through a major field experiment similar to that described in Chapter 9. This is obviously a major effort and not generally recommended.

The fuel consumption predictions also depend on the value of average nominal engine speed or calibrated rpm (CRPM). It is not expected to be location-sensitive. If warranted, the CRPM parameter may easily be re-calibrated if the maximum rated engine speed (MRPM) of the typical vehicles in the region is known. As described in Section 10.6, the value of CRPM parameter for most of the vehicles in the Brazil test fleet was found to be about 0.75 MRPM, and this formula may be used to re-calibrate the CRPM parameter.

As regards the fuel adjustment factors, α_2, they can be re-calibrated only with a major effort, because both field experiment and survey of vehicle operators would be needed in order to obtain sound estimates. Further, these factors are not likely to be highly sensitive to regional factors under free-flow conditions. Thus, it is recommended that the values of α_2 derived in the Brazil study be used.

Major differences in atmospheric conditions can cause some differences in fuel consumption. However, according to Taylor (1960), such differences are small relative to the discrepancies of some 10-25 percent between experimentally-based and surveyed fuel consumption.

13.5 TIRE WEAR PREDICTION MODEL

As indicated in Table 13.2, the following parameters in the tire wear prediction model should be locally determined if possible:

1. The ratio of retreading cost to new tire price, RREC (Equation 11.14);

2. The base number of recaps, NR_0 (Equation 11.9);

3. The constant term of the tread wear model, TWT_0 (Equation 11.10); and

4. The wear coefficient of the tread wear model, CT_c (Equation 11.10).

Because of the nature of the underlying survey data, these parameters are highly aggregated in nature and implicitly lump together the effects of numerous factors which it has not been possible to separate. The RREC parameter basically reflects relative prices of retreadings, manufacturing or importing new tires. The NR_0 parameter largely represents the average effect of the recapping policies of the vehicle operators in the region. For these parameters, it is appropriate to use company-level data for re-calibration.

For the RREC parameter, a relatively simple survey of a few representative vehicle operators, and recapping and new tire companies should produce fairly reliable information. As for the NR_0 parameter, it should be possible to obtain from a sample of companies the total numbers of new tires installed and retreadings consumed by tire size for each company over a period of, say, 2 or more years. The ratio of these variables is the average number of recaps per tire carcass under the company's operating conditions (NR). The base number of recaps for each company (NR_0) can be determined by virtue of the original carcass life model of Equation 11.9, given NR, C and QI values. The road attributes C and QI may be roughly assessed for each company on a subjective basis. The desired base number of recaps can then be computed as a simple average of the averages for the companies surveyed.

As mechanistically oriented parameters, the constant term (TWT_0) and wear coefficient (CT_c) of the tread wear model should ideally be re-calibrated on the basis of tire material and construction properties. Since the latter information seems relatively easy to obtain, the task of local adaptation would be substantially facilitated. However, further research would be needed before mechanistic re-calibration could be done. For the time being, a relatively simple method based on a small-scale user survey is suggested, as outlined below.

The survey suggested for re-calibrating the RREC and NR_0 parameters above could be slightly expanded -- mainly to obtain the total number of vehicle kilometers each vehicle class in a company covered over the same historical period as the total numbers of new tires and retreadings consumed. For this information the average number of tire treads worn per 1,000 vehicle-km for each vehicle class is given by

$$\frac{\text{Total number of new tires} + \text{total number of retreadings}}{\text{Total number of vehicle kilometers}}$$

The "actual" rubber volume consumed per 1,000 tire-km (denoted by TWT') is estimated from the above and the average number of tires per vehicle (NT) and the average rubber volume per tire (VOL), as:

$$\text{TWT'} = \frac{\text{Number of tire treads per 1,000 vehicle-km}}{\text{NT VOL}}$$

The re-calibrated TWT_0 and CT_c coefficients (denoted by $TWT_0"$ and $CT_c"$, respectively) are computed based on the ratio of the "actual" and "predicted" rubber volume consumption per 1,000 tire-km (assuming that changes in the mechanical properties of the vehicles, the tires and the road surface affect the two parameters by the same percentage):

$$TWT_0' = 0.164 \frac{\text{TWT'}}{\text{TWT}}$$

and

$$CT_c' = 0.1278 \frac{\text{TWT'}}{\text{TWT}}$$

where, 0.164 = the default constant term (TWT_0);
0.1278 = the default wear coefficient (CT_c); and
TWT = the predicted rubber volume worn per 1,000 tire-km, as given in Equation 11.10.

Because they are expected to vary significantly across countries or regions, the coefficients of road horizontal curvature (C) and roughness (QI) in the carcass life model should a priori be re-calibrated. However, re-calibration is not generally recommended mainly because it would require a road user cost survey as well as a field experiment to be carried out on a rather major scale. A simpler method exists, however, as a possibility, based on a small-scale sample design suggested by Chesher (1982a & b).

Chesher's sample design is expected to produce considerably more efficient estimates for "slope" coefficients (such as those for the C and QI variable). While the Brazil survey design primarily emphasized disposition of companies over the design factorial and homogeneity of vehicle operating routes, the small-scale sample design concentrates on within-company variation in the road attribute of interest, e.g., horizontal curvature (C) or roughness (QI). This emphasis results in not only a relatively small sample size needed but also removal of possible calibration biases due to company policies. The design might be adapted for use with the carcass life model, by separately calibrating the two coefficients (before calibrating the constant term), as follows:

Consider first the C-coefficient. The sample design calls for companies that operate on both tangent and "curvy" routes which have approximately the same roughness level. The curvy routes should be as extreme as possible so as to maximize the resolution of the calibrated parameter. The sample design for the QI-coefficient follows the same pattern, i.e., calling for companies that operate on as extreme, smooth and rough routes as possible, but which have similar horizontal curvatures.

Using actual parts consumption data for cars, buses and trucks as an example, Chesher, op. cit., found that satisfactory results with coefficient estimates differing by less than 15 percent from estimates based on the full data set could be obtained from as few as 2-7 companies having 13-23 vehicles per company on average. These results are obviously encouraging and suggest the potential of this sample design in small-scale local adaptation, which is the object of this chapter. However, successful implementation, as Chesher pointed out, depends crucially on our ability to find companies that operate under opposite extreme road conditions. In the actual Brazil user cost sample, out of a total of 72 non owner-driver companies, only 12 exhibited the necessary operating characteristics. This fact seems to suggest that the average user may not be able to find a sufficient number of such companies. However, the potential of this sample design should not be ruled out. Experience from future empirical testing should reveal the feasibility of the design for small-scale local adaptation.

13.6 VEHICLE UTILIZATION PREDICTION MODEL

As noted in Chapter 12, to adapt the proposed vehicle utilization model, three parameters are needed for each vehicle class:

1. The base number of hours driven per vehicle per year, HRD_0;

2. The base kilometerage driven per vehicle per year, AKM_0; and

3. The base elasticity of vehicle utilization (or hourly utilization ratio), EVU_0.

For each of the companies sampled, the first two items (HRD_0 and AKM_0) should be readily available as company-level averages. The last item (EVU_0) may be obtained by first selecting a representative sample of routes operated by the company. For each route, determine the driving time (TD) and total trip time (TT). In addition to the driving time the latter includes the time spent on loading/unloading, picking up and dropping off passengers, stopping for meals and fuel, and layovers (waiting for the next scheduled departure). The elasticity for each route (EVU) is the ratio TD/TT. By averaging over these representative routes we obtain the average elasticity for the company. By averaging over the companies in the sample we obtain desired values of HRD_0, AKM_0 and EVU_0 for the vehicle class.

13.7 MAINTENANCE PARTS AND LABOR PREDICTION MODELS

13.7.1 Maintenance Parts Model

As discussed in Chapter 12, Section 12.1.1, parts consumption (PC) is affected by roughness (QI) and cumulative kilometerage (CKM) as given by the general model form below:

$$PC = \begin{cases} CP_0 \exp(CP_q \, QI) \, CKM^{K_p} & \text{for } QI < QIP_0 \\ (P_0 + P_1 \, QI) \, CKM^{K_p} & \text{for } QI \geq QIP_0 \end{cases} \qquad (13.25)$$

$$P_0 = CP_0 \exp(CP_q \, QIP_0)(1 - CP_q QIP_0) \qquad (13.26)$$

$$P_1 = CP_0 \exp(CP_q \, QIP_0) \, CP_q \qquad (13.27)$$

where CP_0, CP_q and K_p are model parameters and QIP_0 is the threshold roughness level. The above formula applies differently to trucks and non-trucks in the following way. For non-trucks, the threshold roughness, QIP_0, corresponds to a relatively rough road (roughness exceeding 100 QI). Thus the second part of the above formula represents a straight line extrapolation beyond a high roughness level where the extrapolated line is tangent to the exponential curve represented by the first part of the formula. For trucks, the threshold roughness QIP_0 is zero by definition as the formula is linear over the entire range of roughness. Thus the above formula reduces to the following form for trucks:

$$PC = CP_0(1 + CP_q \, QI) \, CKM^{K_p} \qquad (13.28)$$

It can be seen from both Equations. 13.25 and 13.28 above that for all vehicle classes the constant term CP_0 is a multiplicative factor in the parts consumption formula. This means that changing the value of CP_0 affects both the general level and the sensitivity of parts consumption to roughness. The CP_0 parameter should be re-calibrated in general because it reflects relative prices of vehicle parts and new vehicles which vary significantly across economies.

The required data for each vehicle class may be obtained from a few representative companies each operating on a set of routes having similar roughness. For each company average values of the following characteristics should be obtained over all vehicles and over a period of one year or more: parts consumption per 1,000 vehicle-km (PC), expressed as a percentage of new vehicle price; cumulative kilometerage (CKM); and road roughness (QI). Substituting these values and the original estimates for the CP_q and K_p in Equations 13.25 or 13.28, whichever is applicable, will yield the value of CP_0 for each company. The desired value of CP_0 is computed as the simple average over the individual companies' CP_0 values.

As noted in Section 13.1, the exponent of cumulative

kilometerage, K_p, is expected to be relatively insensitive to local conditions and therefore need not be re-calibrated. The roughness coefficient, CP_q, on the other hand, is believed to reflect durability of the vehicles as well as average maintenance practices in the region or country, and therefore could be sensitive to local conditions, although not as much as the multiplicative parameter, CP_0. Again, as discussed in Section 13.1, re-calibration of the roughness coefficient represents a major effort and consequently not recommended in general. However, should the user desire to do so the possibility of employing the small-scale sample design suggested by Chesher (Section 13.3) should be considered if companies that operate on both smooth and rough roads (QI $\leq$ 40 and QI $\geq$ 120) can be found in sufficient numbers.

13.7.2 Maintenance Labor Hours Model

From Chapter 12, Section 12.1.2, the amount of maintenance labor-hours required (LH) is dependent on the amount of maintenance parts consumption (PC) and, in the case of buses only, roughness (QI) as given by the following general formula:

$$LH = CL_0 \ PC^{CL_p} \ \exp(CL_q \ QI) \qquad\qquad (13.29)$$

where CL_0 CL_p and CL_q are model parameters. The exponent of parts consumption (CL_p), which has been found from the Brazil and India studies to lie in the range $0.34 - 0.48$ (Chesher and Harrison, 1987), relfects the diminishing amount of labor input per unit parts consumption as parts consumption increases. As noted in Section 14.1 this parameter has been found to be stable across conditions as disparate as Brazil and India and therefore re-calibration is not recommended. The roughness coefficient (CL_q) is, of course, zero except for buses. Since re-calibration of this coefficient calls for a relatively major data collection effort, it is not recommended generally.

The constant term (CL_0) basically represents the amount of labor input resulting from a tradeoff between labor and capital given their relative prices; therefore, the CL_0 parameter should be re-calibrated. For a given vehicle class, the procedure would be similar to that for calibrating the constant term in the parts model (CP_0). This involves first selecting representative companies, which should be the same as those selected for calibrating the parts model constant term (CP_0). Then, for each company obtain average values of the following variables over all vehicles and a period of one year or more: labor-hours required per 1,000 vehicle-km (LH); parts consumption (PC), expressed as a percentage of new vehicle price; and, in the case of buses, roughness (QI). Substituting these values and the original CL_p and CL_q parameter estimates in Equation 13.29 above will produce the value of CL_0 for each company. The desired value of CL_0 is established as the simple average over the individual companies' CL_0 values.

percentage of new vehicle price; and, in the case of buses, roughness (QI). Substituting these values and the original CL_p and CL_q parameter estimates in Equation 13.29 above will produce the value of CL_0 for each company. The desired value of CL_0 is established as the simple average over the individual companies' CL_0 values.

CHAPTER 14

User's Guide to Aggregate Prediction

This chapter is a step-by-step user's guide to predict speed and various components of vehicle operating costs at the aggregate level using information on the roadway (geometry, roughness, surface type and width class) and information on the vehicle (including, at a minimum, class and, for trucks, load). Its main purpose is to bring together in one place material that is covered in different parts of the text and to complement it with prediction equations for the remaining cost components from other sources. The aggregate prediction models are presented in such a way that they can easily be programmed on a personal computer. For convenience, the steps are cross-referenced with equations from earlier chapters from which they are derived.

For various model parameters needed in the predictions, the values arrived at in the Brazil study are included as defaults. The user is urged to go over the discussion on local adaptation of model parameters given in Chapter 13 carefully and determine values appropriate for the region of application.

14.1 OUTLINE OF METHODOLOGY

Completing the sequence of steps once would yield the following predictions for one combination of roadway and vehicle class:

1. a. Space-mean speed of travel over the roadway in km/h;

   b. Average passenger time, crew labor and cargo holding in hours/1,000 vehicle-km;

2. Average fuel consumption over the roadway in liters/1,000 vehicle-km;

3. Average tire wear over the roadway in number of equivalent new tires per 1,000 vehicle-km;

4. a. Average yearly utilization of the vehicle in making trips over the roadway in vehicle-km/year;

   b. Average depreciation and interest as percentages of new vehicle price per 1,000 vehicle-km;

5. a. Average consumption of maintenance parts over the roadway as percentage of new vehicle price per 1,000 vehicle-km;

     b. Average maintenance labor needed for trips over the roadway in hours/1,000 vehicle-km;

     c. Average consumption of lubricants over the roadway in liters/1,000 vehicle-km.

     Given a stretch of road between points, say A and B, three distinct types of journey on the road may be identified for a vehicle. These are:

     1. One-way journey from A to B;

     2. One-way journey from B to A; and

     3. Round-trip journey either from A to B and back to A, or from B to A and back to B.

     Of the three, the first two are basic in the sense that predictions for the round-trip journey may be obtained from the predictions for the two one-way journeys by means of appropriate averages. In order to obtain desired predictions for each journey type, three aggregate attributes of vertical geometry of the roadway are required. However, as pointed out in Section 7.3, the aggregate information on vertical geometry obtained for either journey type (1) or (2) is also sufficient for the other type and also for the round trip journey. For most applications, predictions for a round trip are adequate. The only significant exception is in the case of a truck with very different load levels in the two opposite directions. In this case, it is recommended that predictions be obtained separately for (1) and (2). Further, it may be noted that, while in the cases of speed, fuel consumption and tire wear all the three modes of travel are natural modes for prediction purposes, in the case of vehicle utilization round-trip travel is the natural mode because non-driven time on a trip is not well-defined for a one-way travel. At the aggregate level, the choice among the three modes of travel is governed exclusively by the way the average attributes of vertical geometry are computed for the roadway (Section 7.3).

     The roadway for which predictions are desired may be of arbitrary length and geometry. However, for one set of predictions, the surface type and width class of the roadway must be the same. If the roadway is made up of both paved and unpaved, or narrow and wide segments, it should be treated as different roadways and the sequence of steps performed separately for each.

     Two sets of inputs are required from the user for arriving at predicted aggregate speed: information on the roadway and information on the vehicle. In addition, for each operating cost component for which predictions are desired some specific inputs would be needed. Classified lists of information items, as well as instructions for entering the information, are provided.

The sequence of steps to arrive at the aggregate speed and fuel consumption predictions is organized as follows:

These steps are illustrated through a numerical example in Appendix 14A.

14.2 INSTRUCTIONS FOR PROVIDING INFORMATION ON THE ROADWAY

The information required on the roadway is as follows:

Information item	Symbol	Units	Recommended Value range	
1. Surface type	–	Categorical	Paved/unpaved	. .
2. Average roughness	QI	QI counts	15 – 300	. .
3. Average positive gradient	PG	Fraction	0.0 – 0.12	. .
4. Average negative gradient	NG	Fraction	0.0 – 0.12	. .
5. Proportion of uphill travel	LP	Fraction	0.0 – 1.0	. .
6. Average horizontal curvature	C	deg/km	0 – 1000	. .
7. Average superelevation	SP	Fraction	0.0 – 0.2	. .
8. Altitude of the terrain above Mean Sea Level	ALT	m	0.0 – 5000	. .
9. Effective number of lanes	–	Categorical	Single-lane/ More than one lane	. .

In completing the above table, care should be taken that the values are within the recommended range given above, subject to the following qualifications:

1. For prediction of maintenance parts and labor, the data used in model estimation covered the following range of roughness:

   Cars and utilities   25–120 QI
   Buses   25–190 QI
   Trucks   25–120 QI

Even though extrapolation is difficult to avoid, the user should be aware of it when roughness values fall outside of the range indicated above.

2.   For tire wear prediction, the maximum recommended horizontal curvature is 300 degrees/km, which corresponds to the minimum average radius of curvature of 190 m. Overprediction of tire wear is expected when extrapolated beyond this limit (see Chapter 11 for discussion).

The detailed procedure for data input is as follows:

1.   Enter surface type (paved or unpaved).

2.   Enter average roughness in QI units if, available. If roughness is given as m/km IRI (International Roughness Index), convert into QI units using the formula:

$$QI = 13 \ IRI$$

If roughness is given in BI units (as measured with the TRRL Towed Fifth Wheel Bump Integrator), convert into QI units using the formula:

$$QI = BI/55$$

If roughness is measured using any other methodology, transform into QI units using an appropriate calibration method.

If a roughness value is not available in any of the above units, the user may translate his subjective assessment of the roughness of the roadway into QI units by using a five-point scale as shown below (since these guidelines can only provide very broad approximations, the user is urged to work with actual roughness measures, if possible):

Qualitative evaluation	QI	
	Paved roadway	Unpaved roadway
Smooth	25	50
Reasonably smooth	50	100
Medium rough	75	150
Rough	100	200
Very rough	125	250

3, 4, 5, 6.   Enter geometric attributes (defined in Chapter 7). If starting with detailed vertical and horizontal geometric profiles of the roadway, follow the steps in Appendix 7A to determine average geometric attributes. This procedure provides the required aggregate information for both one-way journey directions as well as the round trip. Note the sign convention for gradients: both "average positive gradient" and "average negative gradient," as entered in the table, are non-negative quantities.

If starting with the HDM-II or HDM-III input data, the following formulas can be used, but for round trip predictions only:

3. Average positive gradient,   PG = RF/1000
4. Average positive gradient,   NG = RF/1000
5. Proportion of uphill travel, LP = 0.5

where RF = average rise plus fall, in m/km.

The information in the HDM input data is not sufficient to compute predictions for one-way journeys. As pointed out in Section 7.3, because of symmetry, the average negative gradient for a round trip journey is identical to average positive gradient, and proportion of level and uphill travel is, by definition, 0.5.

7. Enter superelevation. If the superelevation is known on a detailed basis as part of the horizontal profile, the steps in Appendix 7A will yield the average superelevation.

If the superelevation is known on an average basis for the roadway, enter it as a fraction.

If the superelevation is not known, either on a detailed basis or on an average basis, the following formula obtained from a sample of roads in Brazil may be used to determine superelevation:

For a paved roadway: SP = 0.00012 C   (3.25)
For an unpaved roadway: SP = 0.00017 C

8. Enter the altitude of the terrain above the Mean Sea Level, if known. (This value is not crucial.)

9. Enter the effective number of lanes in the roadway. The only important distinction in the current model is between single-lane roads and other roads. If the carriageway width is less than 4 m the roadway may be classified as single-lane. If the roadway is wider than 5.5 m, it may be classified as having more than one lane.

Roadways with width between 4 and 5.5 m, will have to be classified judgementally, based on other factors such as, shoulder width and condition, average daily traffic, and traffic composition. It might be of help to note that, in India, cars seemed to experience the effect of narrow widths more than buses and trucks.

14.3 INSTRUCTIONS FOR PROVIDING INFORMATION ON THE VEHICLE

The information required on the vehicle for speed prediction is as follows:

Information item	Symbol	Units	Value
1 Vehicle class	–	Categorical	. .
2 (a) Tare weight	TARE	kg	. .
(b) Load carried	LOAD	kg	. .
3 Used driving power	HPDRIVE	metric hp	. .
4 Used braking power	HPBRAKE	metric hp	. .
5 Surface type-specific desired speed	VDESIR	m/s	. .
6 Aerodynamic drag coefficient coefficient	CD	Dimensionless number	. .
7 Projected frontal area	AR	m^2	. .

It may be observed that the only required inputs are the vehicle class and, in the case of a truck, the load carried. As for other input items the user has the option of using the "standard" values associated with the particular vehicle class as default values. These values are given in Table 14.1. (Please note that for user convenience, all tables in this chapter are given at the end). Alternatively, the user may retain some of the default values and substitute more suitable values for others, if necessary. Using a value of zero for the load carried by a truck signifies that predictions are desired for an empty (unloaded) truck.

In completing the above table, care should be taken that the values of vehicle attributes are within the recommended range given in Table 14.5. The detailed procedure for data input is as follows:

1. The user may choose one of the following vehicle classes (representative makes and models for the respective classes as employed in the Brazil-UNDP Study are given in parentheses):

Small car	(Volkswagen 1300)
Medium car	(Chevrolet – Opala)
Large car	(Chrysler – Dodge Dart)
Utility or pick-up	(Volkswagen Kombi)
Bus	(Mercedes Benz 0-362)
Light gasoline truck	(Ford F-400)
Light diesel truck	(Ford F-4000)
Medium truck	(Mercedes Benz 1113 with 2 axles)
Heavy truck	(Mercedes Benz 1113 with 3 axles)
Articulated truck	(Scania 110/39)

2.   a. Look up the tare weight value for the particular vehicle class from Table 14.1 or enter own value.

b. If the vehicle is a car, a bus or a utility, look up the default value provided in Table 14.1 or enter own value. Here the load carried represents the weight of the passengers and some light load.

If the vehicle is a truck, the user is urged to enter the value of load carried after carefully considering factors such as the nature of the material transported in the region, the loading practice, and the maximum rated tonnage for the vehicle. The following chart is intended to be illustrative of the order of the magnitude involved:

	Load carried (LOAD) in kg by truck			
Loading condition	Light	Medium	Heavy	Articulated
Unloaded	0	0	0	0
Partially loaded	1800	4500	6000	13000
Fully loaded	3600	9000	12000	26000

3, 4, 5.   Determine the values of used driving power (HPDRIVE), used braking power (HPBRAKE), and desired speed (VDESIR) values for the particular vehicle class using the procedure given in Section 14.1, or look up the default values given in Table 14.1. Note that the value of VDESIR is different for paved and unpaved surfaces.

6, 7.   Look up the standard values of CD and AR for the particular vehicle class from Table 14.1 and enter. If the values are not representative of the vehicles in the region of the roadway, enter appropriate values.

In completing the above table in respect of cost components for which predictions are desired, the following procedure should be used for data input:

1a.   Look up the calibrated RPM (CRPM) value for the particular vehicle class from Table 14.1. The table also gives the value of maximum rated RPM (MRPM) for the vehicle class. If the maximum rated RPM value for the typical vehicle in user's region is markedly different from the one given, enter 0.75 times the maximum rated RPM as the value of calibrated RPM. That is, the recommended formula in order to override the default value of CRPM is:

14.4 INSTRUCTIONS FOR PROVIDING INFORMATION NEEDED FOR PREDICTING VARIOUS COMPONENTS OF VEHICLE OPERATING COST

The information required for predicting various cost components follows:

Prediction desired	Information item	Symbol	Units	Value
1. **Fuel consumption** (Chapters 9 and 10)	(a) Calibrated rpm	CRPM	rpm	..
	(b) Relative energy-efficiency factor	α_1	dimensionless	..
	(c) Fuel adjustment factor	α_2	dimensionless	..
2. **Tire wear** (buses and trucks) (Chapter 11)	(a) Number of tires per vehicle	NT	integer	..
	(b) Average wearable volume of rubber per tire	VOL	dm^3	..
	(c) Ratio of cost of retreading to cost of new tire	RREC	fraction	..
	(d) Maximum number of recaps	NR_0	dimensionless	..
	(e) Constant term of tire consumption model	TWT_0	dm^3/m	..
	(f) Tire wear coefficient	CT_c	$dm^3/J\text{-}m$	..
3. **Vehicle utilization depreciation and interest** (Chapter 12)	(a) Average annual utilization in a baseline case	AKM_0	km	..
	(b) Average annual number of hours driven in a baseline case	HRD_0	h	..
	(c) Hourly utilization ratio (or elasticity of vehicle utilization) in a baseline case	EVU_0	fraction	..
	(d) Average vehicle service life	$LIFE_0$	year	..
4. **Maintenance parts and labor** (Chapter 12)	(a) Constant term of parts consumption model	CP_0	dimensionless	..
	(b) Roughness coefficient of parts consumption model	CP_q	dimensionless	..
	(c) Threshold roughness value	QIP_0	QI	..
	(d) Constant term of maintenance labor model	CL_0	dimensionless	..
	(e) Parts exponent of maintenance labor model	CL_p	dimensionless	..
	(f) Roughness coefficient of maintenance labor model	CL_q	dimensionless	..
	(g) Average kilometerage of vehicles belonging to this class	CKM	km	..

CRPM = 0.75 MRPM

1b. Enter the value of relative energy-efficiency factor, α_1.
     If the typical vehicle in user's region is similar to the
     make and model of the representative vehicle in the
     Brazilian study, the value of 1.00 may be used. If the
     typical vehicle in the region mber is more modern, enter a
     suitable value based on the discussion in Section 9.4.

1c. Enter the value of fuel adjustment factor, α_2, which
     eonverts fuel predictions based on controlled experiments
     to those based on real life operating conditions. If
     suitable, the following values derived in the Brazil study
     may be used:

Vehicle class	α_2
Car or utility	1.16
Bus or truck	1.15

     For a detailed discussion, the user is referred to Section
     10.8.

2a. Enter the number of tires on a typical vehicle of the
     vehicle class. Table 14.1 gives the values for the
     representative makes and models.

2b. Enter the average volume of wearable rubber on a new tire
     of a size suitable for the vehicle class. It should be
     possible to obtain this information from tire manufacturers
     in the country. Table 14.1 gives the average volume for
     tires commonly used in Brazil (in cubic decimeters).

2c. Determine the ratio of the cost of one retreading (or
     recapping) to the cost of a new tire. Note that the
     default value of 0.15, based on the Brazil case, is quite
     low in comparison with many countries.

2d. Enter the hypothetical maximum number of recaps for a
     typical carcass used on vehicles of this class in the
     region given that the vehicle would always traverse on
     extremely smooth and straight road sections. Conceptually,
     this value can be fractional. For guidelines for
     calibrating NR_0 see Section 13.5.

2e,f. Look up the TWT_0 and CT_C values for the particular
     vehicle class from Table 14.4 or enter own values. See
     Section 13.5 for discussion on how to determine
     appropriate values for the region.

3a,b.   For a baseline case of a roadway in the region, for a representative vehicle belonging to the vehicle class of interest, and for a typical year of operation, determine:

    1.   The number of kilometers covered by the vehicle in the year (AKM_0); and

    2.   The number of hours the vehicle was driven to cover that distance (HRD_0).

In the case of improvement of an existing link, the baseline case could be the present roadway itself. In the case of a new link, the baseline case may be taken to be any similar, or an average, roadway in the region. In either case, these values are relatively easily obtained from vehicle operators.

3c.   For the baseline case, determine the average proportion of time the vehicle was in motion relative to the time it was in use: in other words, the hourly utilization ratio, also called the elasticity of vehicle utilization (EVU_0). The method for determining the hourly utilization ratio is given in Section 13.6.

Since the operating parameters on which the hourly utilization ratio depends vary considerably from country to country or even from one region in a country to another, the user is urged to provide estimates specific to the country or region. However, if the information is not available the following values based on Brazil data are suggested (provided that operating conditions in the region in question are similar to those in Brazil):

$$EVU_0 = \begin{cases} 0.60 \text{ for a car} \\ 0.80 \text{ for a utility} \\ 0.75 \text{ for a bus} \\ 0.85 \text{ for a truck} \end{cases}$$

3d.   Enter the average service life of the vehicles belonging to the particular vehicle class in the region, in years.

4a.   Enter the value of CP_0, the constant term of the parts consumption model, which relates to the relative price of spare parts items typical for vehicles of this class vis-a-vis the average price of a new vehicle of this class. The user is urged to calibrate this parameter following the guidelines in Section 13.7. However, if conditions are similar, the Brazilian values given in Table 14.4 may be used.

4b,c.   Enter the values of CP_q and QIP_0 for the particular vehicle class from Table 14.4. See Section 4.d for discussion on how to determine appropriate values.

4d.   Enter the value of CL_0, the constant term of the maintenance labor hours model, which relates to the labor-capital trade-off in the region of interest. The user is urged to calibrate this parameter following the guidelines given in Section 13.7. For countries or regions similar to Brazil, the default values given in Table 14.4 may be used.

4e,f.   Enter the values of CL_p and CL_q for the particular vehicle class from Table 14.4. For reasons explained in Chapter 13, these values are generally recommended for use without re-calibration. However, should the user desire to re-calibrate them, Section 13.7 provides a disucssion on how to determine appropriate values.

4g.   Enter the average cumulative kilometerage, that is, the average number of kilometers driven over the lifetime of a vehicle of the particular vehicle class. This value may be arrived at using information from steps 3a and 3d above, subject to the ceiling CKM' given in Table 14.4:

$$CKM = min(0.5 \ LIFE_0 \ AKM_0, \ CKM')$$

14.5 STEPS FOR COMPUTING PREDICTED SPEED

14.5.1 Compute the Rolling Resistance Coefficient (CR):

If the vehicle is a car or a utility:

$$CR = 0.0218 + 0.0000467 \ QI \qquad \text{(2.18a)}$$

If the vehicle is a bus or a truck:

$$CR = 0.0139 + 0.0000198 \ QI \qquad \text{(2.18b)}$$

14.5.2 Compute RHO, the Mass Density of Air in the Terrain of the Roadway, in kg/m^3:

If the altitude (ALT) above the Mean Sea Level is known, compute the air density from the following formula:

$$RHO = 1.225 \left[1 - 2.26 \frac{ALT}{100,000}\right]^{4.255} \qquad \text{(2.15)}$$

Otherwise use the default value:

RHO = 1.225

14.5.3 Compute the "Mass" of the Vehicle, m, in kg:

m = TARE + LOAD

14.5.4 Compute the Driving Power-constrained Speed for Uphill Travel, $VDRIVE_u$, in m/s (the formulas are from Section 3.3.1 and Appendix 3B):

First compute the following intermediate quantities:

A = 0.5 RHO CD AR

$$b = \frac{HPDRIVE\ 736}{2\ A}$$

$$c_1 = \frac{m\ g\ (CR + PG)}{3\ A} \qquad \text{where } g = 9.81 \text{ m/s}^2$$

$$D_1 = b^2 + c_1^3$$

$$d_1 = \sqrt{D_1}$$

Then,

$$VDRIVE_u = \sqrt[3]{d_1 + b} - \sqrt[3]{d_1 - b}$$

Note: HPDRIVE is the used driving power value obtained in Section 14.3.

14.5.5 Compute the Driving Power-constrained Speed for Downhill Travel, $VDRIVE_d$, in m/s (formulas are from Appendix 3B):

First compute the following intermediate quantities:

$$c_2 = \frac{m\ g\ (CR - NG)}{3\ A}$$

$$D_2 = b^2 + c^3$$

where A and b are as computed in 14.5.4 above. Next, examine the sign of the quantity D_2.

Case 1: $D_2 > 0$.

If D_2 is positive, then,

$d_2 = \sqrt{D_2}$ and

$VDRIVE_d = \sqrt[3]{d_2 + b} - \sqrt[3]{d_2 - b}$

Case 2: $D_2 \leq 0$.

If D_2 is non-positive, proceed as follows:

$r = 2 \sqrt{-c_2}$

$z = \dfrac{1}{3} \text{ arc cos } \left\{ -\dfrac{2 \, b}{c_2 r} \right\}$

where z is in radians.

Then compute the following three roots of the cubic equation:

$v_1 = r \cos (z)$

$v_2 = r \cos \left(z + \dfrac{2}{3}\pi\right)$

$v_3 = r \cos \left(z + \dfrac{4}{3}\pi\right)$

Note that exactly one of the three roots is positive.   Set $VDRIVE_d$ to the positive root.   That is:

$VDRIVE_d = \max \left\{v_1, \, v_2, \, v_3\right\}$

14.5.6   Compute the Braking Power–constrained Speed, VBRAKE, in m/s:

First examine the sign of the quantity (CR − NG).

Case 1: CR − NG $\geq$ 0.

If (CR − NG) is non-negative, set VBRAKE to infinity.   This is an acceptable value because VBRAKE will appear only as a denominator.   That is,

$\dfrac{1}{VBRAKE} = 0$

and this factor will then drop out of the denominator of the speed prediction formula.

Case 2: CR − NG < 0.

If (CR− NG) is negative:

$$VBRAKE = -\frac{HPBRAKE\ 736}{m\ g\ (CR - NG)} \tag{3.6}$$

Note: HPBRAKE is the used braking power value obtained in Section 14.3.

14.5.7   Compute the Maximum Allowable Curve Speed, VCURVE, in m/s:

Look up the values of $FRATIO_0$ and $FRATIO_1$ for the particular vehicle class and surface type from Table 14.2. Then,

$$VCURVE = \sqrt{((FRATIO_0 - FRATIO_1\ LOAD) + SP)\ g\ RC} \tag{3.14, 4.7}$$

where $RC = 180,000/\pi C$

If the curvature C is zero or very small, VCURVE may be taken to be infinity, i.e.:

$1/VCURVE = 0$.

14.5.8   Compute the Roughness-constrained Speed, VROUGH, in m/s:

Look up the value of ARVMAX in Table 14.2 for the particular vehicle class. Then,

$$VROUGH = \frac{ARVMAX}{0.0882\ QI} \tag{3.24}$$

14.5.9   Determine the Desired Speed Adjusted for Width Effect, VDESIR', in m/s:

Look up the value of VDESIR for the particular vehicle class and surface type as obtained in Section 14.3. If the roadway is classified as single-lane, look up the value of "width effect parameter," BW, for the particular vehicle class and width class from Table 14.2. If the roadway is classified as having more than one lane, there is no width effect, and the value of BW is 1.00 for all vehicle classes. Then,

VDESIR' = BW VDESIR

14.5.10   Look up the Values of β and $E°$ for the Particular Vehicle Class from Table 14.2.

14.5.11   Compute the Aggregate Uphill Steady-state Speed, VSS_u, in m/s:

$$VSS_u = E° \left\{ \left(\frac{1}{VDRIVE_u}\right)^{\frac{1}{\beta}} + \left(\frac{1}{VCURVE}\right)^{\frac{1}{\beta}} + \left(\frac{1}{VROUGH}\right)^{\frac{1}{\beta}} + \left(\frac{1}{VDESIR'}\right)^{\frac{1}{\beta}} \right\}^{-\beta} \quad (3.38)$$

14.5.12   Compute the Aggregate Downhill Steady-state Speed, VSS_d, in m/s:

$$VSS_d = E° \left\{ \left(\frac{1}{VDRIVE_d}\right)^{\frac{1}{\beta}} + \left(\frac{1}{VBRAKE}\right)^{\frac{1}{\beta}} + \left(\frac{1}{VROUGH}\right)^{\frac{1}{\beta}} + \left(\frac{1}{VCURVE}\right)^{\frac{1}{\beta}} + \left(\frac{1}{VDESIR'}\right)^{\frac{1}{\beta}} \right\}^{-\beta}$$

14.5.13   Final Step for Speed Prediction: Compute the Predicted Average Speed, ASPEED for the Journey (converted from m/s to km/h):

$$ASPEED = \frac{3.6}{\dfrac{LP}{VSS_u} + \dfrac{1 - LP}{VSS_d}} \quad km/h.$$

Note: Some resources which may be straight-forwardly computed using predicted speed are as follows:

1.   The number of passenger-hours spent per 1,000 vehicle-km of travel, PHX:

$$PHX = 1,000 \ \frac{PAX}{ASPEED}$$

where PAX is the average number of passengers per vehicle.

2.   The number of crew hours required per 1,000 vehicle-km, CRH:

$$CRH = \frac{1,000}{ASPEED}$$

3.   The cargo holding cost per 1,000 vehicle-km, CHC:

$$CHC = \frac{10 \ MVC \ AINV}{8760 \ ASPEED}$$

where: MVC is the monetary value of the cargo;
AINV is the annual interest rate in percentage; and
8760 is the number of hours per year.

14.6 STEPS FOR COMPUTING PREDICTED FUEL CONSUMPTION, TIRE WEAR AND VEHICLE UTILIZATION

Steps for computing predicted fuel consumption:

14.6.1   Compute the Gravitational Resistances in N:

$$\text{Uphill} \quad : GF_u = m \ g \ PG \qquad\qquad\qquad (2.13)$$
$$\text{Downhill} : GF_d = m \ g \ NG$$

14.6.2   Compute the Rolling Resistance in N:

$$\text{Uphill and downhill: } RR = m \ g \ CR \qquad\qquad (2.17)$$

14.6.3   Compute the Air Resistances in N:

$$\text{Uphill} \quad : AF_u = 0.5 \ RHO \ CD \ AR \ (VSS_u)^2 = A \ (VSS_u)^2 \qquad (2.9)$$
$$\text{Downhill} : AF_d = 0.5 \ RHO \ CD \ AR \ (VSS_d)^2 = A \ (VSS_d)^2$$

14.6.4   Compute the Drive Forces in N:

$$\text{Uphill} \quad : DF_u = (GF_u + RR + AF_u) \qquad\qquad (2.6)$$
$$\text{Downhill} : DF_d = (-GF_d + RR + AF_d)$$

14.6.5   Compute the Vehicle Power in Metric hp:

$$\text{Uphill} \quad : HP_u = \frac{DF_u \ VSS_u}{736} \qquad\qquad\qquad (2.11)$$

$$\text{Downhill} : HP_d = \frac{DF_d \ VSS_d}{736}$$

14.6.6   Compute the Aggregate Uphill Unit Fuel Consumption, UFC_u, in Liters/1000 Vehicle-km:

Look up the fuel consumption coefficients a_0, a_1, a_3, a_4 and a_5 for the particular vehicle from Table 14.3. Then,

$$UFC_u = (a_0 + a_1 \ CRPM + a_2 \ CRPM^2 + a_3 HP_u + a_4 HP_u \ CRPM$$
$$+ a_5 \ HP_u^2) \times 10^{-2} \qquad\qquad (9.4)$$

(CRPM is the calibrated RPM value obtained in Section 14.4.)

14.6.7   Compute the Aggregate Downhill Unit Fuel Consumption, UFC_d, in Liters/1,000 Vehicle-km:

First check whether $HP_d \geq 0$; if so look up fuel consumption coefficients a_0, a_1, a_2, a_3, a_4, a_5 from Table 14.3. Then compute:

$$UFC_d = (a_0 + a_1 \, CRPM + a_2 \, CRPM^2 + a_3 \, HP_d + a_4 \, HP_d \, CRPM$$

$$+ \; a_5 \, HP_d{}^2) \times 10^{-2} \tag{9.4}$$

On the other hand, if $HP_d < 0$, look up the threshold negative power value, NH_0, and the coefficients a_0, a_1, a_2, a_6, a_7 for the particular vehicle from Table 14.3. Compare HP_d and NH_0.

If $NH_0 \leq HP_d < 0$, then,

$$UFC_d = (a_0 + a_1 \, CRPM + a_2 \, CRPM^2 + a_6 \, HP_d + a_7 \, HP_d{}^2) \times 10^{-2}$$

Finally, if $HP_d < NH_0$, then,

$$UFC_d = (a_0 + a_1 \, CRPM + a_2 \, CRPM^2 + a_6 \, NH_0 + a_7 \, NH_0{}^2) \times 10^{-2}$$

14.6.8 **Compute the Predicted Aggregate Experimental Fuel Consumption per Distance Unit, FUELA, in Liters/1,000 Vehicle-km:**

$$FUELA = \alpha_1 \left(UFC_u \; \frac{LP}{VSS_u} + UFC_d \; \frac{1 - LP}{VSS_d} \right)$$

where α_1 is the "relative energy-efficiency factor" obtained in Section 14.4.

14.6.9 **Finally, Adjust the Predicted Experimental Fuel Consumption to Account for Real World Operating Conditions Yielding the Predicted Aggregate Operating Fuel Consumption, AFUEL, in Liters/1,000 Vehicle-km.:**

$$AFUEL = \alpha_2 \, FUELA$$

where α_2 is the "fuel adjustment factor" obtained in Section 14.4.

Steps for computing predicted tire wear:

14.6.10 **If the Vehicle is a Car or a Utility Go Directly to Step 14.6.17.**

Otherwise, continue with step 14.6.11.

14.6.11 **Compute the Square of Circumferential Force, CFT^2, in N^2:**

$$CFT^2 = LP \, (DF_u^2) + (1 - LP) \, (DF_d^2)$$

14.6.12   Compute the Circumferential Energy per Tire, CE, in J:

$$CE = \frac{CFT^2}{m\ g\ NT}$$

where NT is the number of tires in the vehicle (default value is given in Table 14.1).

14.6.13   Compute the Predicted Volume of Rubber Worn, TWT, in $dm^3/1,000$ km:

$$TWT = TWT_0 + CT_c\ CE \qquad\qquad (11.8,\ 11.10)$$

where TWT_0 and CT_c are given in Table 14.4.

14.6.14   Compute the Predicted Number of Retreadings, NR:

$$NR = (NR_0 + 1)\ \exp\left[-\ 0.00248\ QI - 0.00118\ \min\ (C.300)\right] -1 \qquad (11.9)$$

where NR_0 is the maximum number of recaps (default value is given in Table 14.4).

14.6.15   Compute the Total Travel Distance Afforded by One Tire Carcass, DISTOT, in 1,000 km:

$$DISTOT = \frac{(1 + NR)\ VOL}{TWT} \qquad\qquad (11.3,\ 11.2)$$

where VOL is the volume of wearable rubber per tire (default value is given in Table 14.1).

14.6.16   Compute the Predicted Number of Equivalent New Tires Consumed per 1,000 km for Each Tire on the Vehicle (EQNT):

Trucks and buses:

$$EQNT = \frac{1 + RREC\ NR}{DISTOT} + 0.0075 \qquad\qquad (11.16)$$

where RREC is the percentage ratio of the cost of one retreading to the cost of a new tire (default value from Brazil is 15%).

14.6.17   Compute the Predicted Number of Equivalent New Tires Consumed per 1,000 km of Vehicle Travel (EQNTV):

1. If the vehicle is a truck or a bus:
    EQNTV = NT EQNT $\qquad$ (11.16)

2. If the vehicle is a car or a utility:
    EQNTV = NT min [0.0388, 0.0114 + 0.000137 QI] $\qquad$ (11.17)

Steps for computing predicted utilization, depreciation and interest:

14.6.18 Compute the Predicted Annual Vehicle Utilization, AKM, in km:

$$AKM = [\frac{1 - EVU_0}{AKM_0} + \frac{EVU_0}{ASPEED\ HRD_0}]^{-1} \qquad (12.9)$$

14.6.19 Determine the Average Service Life of the Vehicle, LIFE, in Years, Using one of the Following Formulas:

If the vehicle service life is expected to be constant, then:

$$LIFE = LIFE_0 \qquad (12.6a)$$

If sensitivity of service life to speed is desired, then

$$LIFE = (\frac{AKM_0}{HRD_0\ ASPEED} + 2)\frac{LIFE_0}{3} \qquad (12.6b)$$

14.6.20 Compute the Vehicle Depreciation per 1,000 Vehicle-km, DEP, in Fraction of the Price of a New Vehicle of the Same Class:

$$DEP = 1,000/(LIFE\ AKM)$$

14.6.21 Compute the Amount of Interest Charge per 1,000 Vehicle-km, INT, in Fraction of the Price of a New Vehicle of the Same Class:

$$INT = 5\ AINV/AKM \qquad (12.5)$$

14.7 STEPS FOR COMPUTING PREDICTED MAINTENANCE RESOURCES AND LUBRICANT CONSUMPTION

14.7.1 Compute Standardized Parts Cost per 1000 vehicle-km as Fraction of the Average Price of a New vehicle of the Same Class, APART:

Look up K_p from Table 14.4 for the particular vehicle class. Look up the values of QIP_0, CP_0 and CP_q as obtained in Table 14.4. Compare QIP_0 and the value of QI for the road section.

If $QI < QIP_0$, then,

$$APART = CP_0\ \exp(CP_q\ QI_0)\ CKM^k p \qquad (12.1)$$

If $QI > QIP_0$, then,

$$APART = CP_0 \ exp(CP_q \ QIP_0) \ CKM^{Kp}((1 - CP_q \ QIP_0) + CP_q \ QI)$$

14.7.2 Compute the Predicted Maintenance Labor, ALABOR in Labor-hours per 1,000 vehicle-km:

Look up the values of CL_0, CL_p and CL_q as obtained in Table 14.4. Then,

$$ALABOR = CL_0 \ APART^{CL_p} \ exp(CL_q \ QI) \tag{12.3}$$

14.7.3 Compute the Predicted Lubricants Consumption, AOIL, in Liters per 1,000 vehicle-km:

Look up the value CO_0 in Table 14.4. Then,

$$AOIL = CO_0 + 0.011605 \ QI \tag{Appendix 12C}$$

Table 14.1: Vehicle classes and their standard characteristics

Vehicle class Characteristics	Cars			Utility	Bus	Light truck		Medium/ Heavy truck	Heavy truck	Articulated truck
	Small	Med.	Large			Gas	Diesel			
1. **Representative vehicle make model**	Volks wagen 1300	Chev- rolet Opel	Chrys ler Dodge Dart	Volks wagen Kombi	Merc. Benz O-362	Ford F-400	Ford F-4000	Merc. Benz 1113 (two axles)	Merc. Benz 1113 (three axles)	Scania 110/39
2. **Weight (kg):**										
Tare weight (TARE)	960	1200	1650	1320	8100	3120	3270	5400	6600	14730
Load carried (LOAD)	400	400	400	900	4000					
3. **Driving power (SAE):**										
Maximum used (HPDRIVE)	30.0	70.0	85.0	40.0	100.0	80.0	60.0	100.0	100.0	210.0
Maximum rated (HPRATED)	48.0	146.0	198.0	60.0	147.0	169.0	102.0	147.0	147.0	285.0
4. **Maximum used braking:**										
power (HPBRAKE)	17.0	21.0	27.0	30.0	160.0	100.0	100.0	250.0	250.0	500.0
5. **Desired speed (m/s) (VDESIR):**										
Paved sections	27.3	27.3	27.3	26.4	25.9	22.7	22.7	24.7	24.7	23.4
Unpaved sections	22.8	22.8	22.8	21.8	19.3	20.0	20.0	20.0	20.0	13.8
6. **RPM:**										
Calibrated (CRPM)	3500	3000	3300	3300	2300	3300	2600	1800	1800	1700
Maximum rated (MRPM)	4600	4000	4400	4600	2800	4400	3000	2800	2800	2200
7. **Aerodynamic drag:**										
coefficient (CD)	0.45	0.50	0.45	0.46	0.65	0.70	0.70	0.85	0.85	0.63
8. **Projected frontal area:**										
(m^2) (AR)	1.80	2.08	2.20	2.72	6.30	3.25	3.25	5.20	5.20	5.75
9. **Tires:**										
Number (NT)	4	4	4	4	6	6	6	6	10	18
Nominal diameter (mm)					1000	900	900	1000	1000	1100
Wear rubber volume (dm^3) (VOL)					6.85	4.30	4.30	7.60	7.30	8.39

To be specified by the user.

Source: Adapted from Brazil-UNDP-World Bank highway research project data and analysis.

Table 14.2: Parameter values for computing speed predictions

Vehicle class Parameter		Car[1]	Utility	Bus	Truck		
					Light	Medium/ Heavy[3]	Articulated
$FRATIO_0$	Paved roads	0.268	0.221	0.233	0.253	0.292	0.179
	Unpaved roads	0.124	0.117	0.095	0.099	0.087	0.040
$FRATIO_1$	Paved roads	0	0	0	0.128×10^{-4}	0.094×10^{-4}	0.023×10^{-4}
	Unpaved roads	0	0	0	0	0	0
ARVMAX		259.7	239.7	212.8	194.0	177.7	130.9
BW		0.74	0.74	0.78	0.73	0.73	0.73
β		0.274	0.306	0.273	0.304	0.310	0.244
E°		1.003	1.004	1.012	1.008	1.013	1.018

[1] The parameter values are the same for small, medium and large cars
[2] The parameter values are the same for both kinds of light trucks, gasoline and diesel.
[3] The parameter values are the same for medium and heavy trucks.

Source: Adapted from Brazil–UNDP–World Bank highway research project data and analysis.

Table 14.3: Parameter values for computing fuel consumption predictions

Vehicle class	Car			Utility	Bus	Light truck		Medium/ Heavy	Articu- lated
Parameter	Small	Medium	Large			Gas	Diesel	truck	truck
a_0	−8201	23453	−23705	6014	−7276	−48381	−41803	−22955	−30559
a_1	33.4	40.6	100.8	37.6	63.5	127.1	71.6	95.0	156.1
a_2	0	0.01214	0	0	0	0	0	0	0
a_3	5630	7775	2784	3846	4323	5867	5129	3758	4002
a_4	0	0	0.938	1.398	0	0	0	0	0
a_5	0	0	13.91	0	8.64	43.70	0	19.12	4.41
a_6	4460	6552	4590	3604	2479	3843	2653	2394	4435
a_7	0	0	0	0	11.50	0	0	13.76	26.08
NH_0	−10	−12	−15	−12	−50	−50	−30	−85	−85

Source: Adapted from Brazil-UNDP-World Bank highway research project data and analysis.

Table 14.4: Parameters for computing tire wear, maintenance parts, maintenance labor and lubricant consumption

Prediction model	Vehicle class Parameter Values	Car or Utility[1]	Bus	Truck			
				Light[2]	Medium	Heavy	Articulated
Tire wear	NR_0	–	2.39	0.93	2.39	2.39	3.57
	TWT_0	–	0.164	0.164	0.164	0.164	0.164
	CT_c	–	12.78×10^{-3}	12.78×10^{-3}	12.78×10^{-3}	12.78×10^{-3}	12.78×10^{-3}
Maintenance parts consumption	K_p	0.308	0.483	0.371	0.371	0.371	0.371
	CP_0	32.49×10^{-6}	1.77×10^{-6}	1.49×10^{-6}	1.49×10^{-6}	8.61×10^{-6}	13.94×10^{-6}
	CP_q	13.70×10^{-3}	3.56×10^{-3}	251.79×10^{-3}	251.79×10^{-3}	35.31×10^{-3}	15.65×10^{-3}
	QIP_0	120	190	0	0	0	0
	CKM'	300,000	1,000,000	600,000	600,000	600,000	600,000
Maintenance labor	CL_0	77.14	293.44	242.03	242.03	301.46	652.51
	CL_p	0.547	0.517	0.519	0.519	0.519	0.519
	CL_q	0	0.0055	0	0	0	0
Lubricants consumption	OO_0	1.55	3.07	2.20	3.07	3.07	5.15

[1] The parameter values are the same for cars of all three sizes as well as for utilities.

[2] The parameter values are the same for gasoline as well as diesel trucks.

Source: Adapted from Brazil-UNDP-World Bank highway research project data and analysis.

Table 14.5: Recommended range of vehicle attributes

Vehicle attribute	Units	Recommended range
Gross vehicle weight, m	kg	
Cars		800- 2,000
Utilities		1,100- 2,500
Buses		7,500-12,000
Light trucks		3,000- 6,500
Medium trucks		5,000-16,000
Heavy trucks		6,000-22,000
Articulated trucks		13,000-45,000
Payload, LOAD	kg	
Cars		0- 400
Utilities		0- 1,400
Buses		0- 4,500
Light trucks		0- 3,500
Medium trucks		0-11,000
Heavy trucks		0-16,000
Articulated trucks		0-32,000
Projected frontal area, AR	m^2	
Cars		1.5 - 2.4
Utilities		2.3 - 3.2
Buses		6.0 - 7.0
Light trucks		3.0 - 5.0
Medium trucks		5.0 - 8.0
Heavy trucks		5.0 - 8.0
Articulated trucks		5.5 - 10.0
Aerodynamic drag coefficient, CD	dimensionless	0.3 - 1.0
Wearable rubber volume per tire, VOL	cm^3	
Buses		5.6 - 8.0
Light trucks		2.0 - 3.5
Medium trucks		6.5 - 9.3
Heavy trucks		6.3 - 8.8
Articulated trucks		6.0 - 8.5
Cumulative kilometerage CKM	km	
Cars and utilities		0- 300,000
Buses		0-1,000,000
Trucks		0- 600,000

Source: Authors' recommendation.

APPENDIX 14A

ILLUSTRATIVE EXAMPLE

In this appendix, the procedure to predict aggregate speeds and various components of vehicle operating costs is illustrated through a numerical example. For this purpose, use is made of the roadway for which the aggregate geometrical attributes were computed in Appendix 7B. It is further assumed that the roadway is paved, quite smooth (QI = 40) and wide (width = 7m); it is 700 meters above the mean sea level. Predictions are desired for a one-way trip, starting from point A and ending at point B (Figure 7B.1). Using the aggregate geometric attributes computed in Appendix 7B, all the information required on the roadway may be furnished and is given in Table 14A.1.

The vehicle for which predictions are desired is a heavy truck. It carries a load of 9,900 kg. In this illustrative example the default values provided in Table 14.1 are judged to be adequate, and therefore used to furnish the information required on the vehicle, as shown in Table 14A.2.

We desire predictions for fuel consumption, tire wear, vehicle utilization, maintenance resources and oil consumption. We judge that the Brazil default values for the fuel parameters, the tire parameters, and the maintenance resource parameters are appropriate, and we expect a heavy truck in the region to be driven about 80,000 km in a year over about 2,000 hours on an average roadway. Further, we estimate that, in order for a heavy truck to be driven for 2,000 hours, it needs non-driven time of about 350 hours yielding an hourly utilization ratio of approximately 0.85. Finally, an avereage heavy truck in the region lasts for about 8 years. Thus, we estimate the average cumulative kilometerage to be 320,000 km. Now we are ready to furnish the information required to predict the desired cost components (Table 14A.3).

The steps for predicting speed and other quantities are shown below. For each step, the final result is given. Note that the number of significant digits shown is more than necessary--they are included to facilitate the user's checking of calculations.

Speed Prediction

14.5.1 The coefficient of rolling resistance is CR = 0.01469 using the equation for the truck.

Table 14A.1: Roadway information

Information item	Symbol	Units	Value
1. Surface type	–	categorical	Paved
2. Average roughness	QI	QI counts	40
3. Average positive gradient	PG	fraction	0.040
4. Average negative gradient	NG	fraction	0.049
5. Proportion of uphill travel	LP	fraction	0.307
6. Average horizontal curvature	C	deg/km	127.835
7. Average superelevation	SP	fraction	0.018
8. Altitude of the terrain above Mean Sea Level	ALT	m	700
9. Effective number of lanes	–	categorical	More than one

Table 14A.2: Vehicle information for heavy truck

Information item	Symbol	Units	Value
1. Vehicle class		categorical	Heavy truck
2.(a) Tare weight	TARE	kg	6,600
(b) Load carried	LOAD	kg	9,900
3. Maximum used driving power	HPDRIVE	metric hp	100.0
4. Maximum used braking power	HPBRAKE	metric hp	250.0
5. Desired speed on:		m^2	
(a) Paved sections	VDESIR(P)	m/s	23.8
(b) Unpaved sections	VDESIR(U)	m/s	19.8
6. Calibrated RPM	CRPM	rpm	2,000
7. Drag coefficient	CD	dimensionless number	0.85
8. Projected frontal area	AR	m^2	5.20

Table 14A.3: Input information for prediction of fuel consumption tire wear, vehicle utilization, depreciation and interest, and maintenance resources

	Symbol	Value
1.(a)	CRPM	2,000
(b)	α_1	1.00
(c)	α_2	1.15
2.(a)	NT	10
(b)	VOL	7.3
(c)	RREC	0.15
(d)	NR_0	2.39
(e)	TWT_0	0.164
(f)	CT_c	0.01278
3.(a)	AKM_0	80,000
(b)	HRD_0	2,000
(c)	EVU_0	0.85
(d)	$LIFE_0$	8
4.(a)	CP_0	0.0000861
(c)	CP_q	0.03531
(d)	QIP_0	0
(e)	CL_0	0.519
(f)	CL_q	0
(g)	CKM	320,000

14.5.2 The mass density of air is computed using the formula since the altitude is known. RHO = 1.1446.

14.5.3 m = 16500

14.5.4 The value of HPDRIVE is 100. We start with,

A   = 2.529649
b   = 14,547.47
c_1 = 1,166.53
D_1 = 1,799,023,609, and
d_1 = 42,414.93

Thus, $VDRIVE_u$ = 8.15865

14.5.5   We start with,

$$c_2 = -731.7569, \text{ and}$$
$$D_2 = -180{,}203{,}600.$$

Now, since D_2 is non-positive we follow the steps outlined in Case 2:

$$r = 54.10201$$
$$z = 0.2484181$$

The three roots of the cubic equation are:

$$v_1 = 52.44123$$
$$v_2 = -37.74059$$
$$v_3 = -14.70064$$

We select the positive root, in this case v_1, as the value of $VDRIVE_d$.

Thus, $VDRIVE_d = 52.44123$

14.5.6   Since CR − NG is negative, we use the formula in Case 2 to get the value of VBRAKE.

VBRAKE = 33.13366 using   HPBRAKE = 250

14.5.7   VCURVE = 30.89198 using $FRATIO_0 = 0.2926$ $FRATIO_1 = 0.00000945$.

14.5.8   VROUGH = 50.37982 using ARVMAX value of 177.74.

14.5.9   Since the effective number of lanes is more than one,
BW = 1.00   and   VDESIR' = VDESIR = 24.67

14.5.10   For a heavy truck:
$\beta = 0.3095$ and $E° = 1.013$.

14.5.11 $VSS_u = 8.15447$

14.5.12 $VSS_d = 19.99359$

14.5.13   ASPEED = 49.78622 km/h.

Fuel Consumption Prediction

14.6.1 $GF_u = 6,474.600$
$GF_d = 7,931.386$

14.6.2 $RR = 2,378.121$

14.6.3 $AF_u = 168.210$
$AF_d = 1,011.050$

14.6.4 $DF_u = 9,020.92$
$DF_d = -4,542.054$

14.6.5 $HP_u = 99.94688$
$HP_d = -123.3859$

14.6.6 $UFC_u = 7,146.423$

14.6.7   Since HP_d is negative, we compare it with NH_0 for a heavy truck which is -10. Since it is smaller than NH_0 we use the last formula for UFC_d.

$UFC_d = 439.71$

14.6.8 $FUELA = 284.2899$

14.6.9 $AFUEL = 326.9333$

Tire Wear Prediction

14.6.10   We proceed with the next step since the vehicle is a truck.

14.6.11 $CFT^2 = 39280487$

14.6.12 $CE = 24.26687$

14.6.13 $TWT = 0.4741306$

14.6.14   NR = 1.63963

14.6.15   DISTOT = 40.64727

14.6.16   EQNT = 0.03815402

14.6.17   EQNTV = 0.3815402

Predicting Vehicle Utilization Depreciation and Interest

14.6.18   AKM = 96,047.64

14.6.19   Using the speed sensitive service life formula:
LIFE = 7.475828

14.6.20   DEP = 0.001392689

14.6.21   Using an investment rate, AINV, of 12%, we have:
INT = 0.00062469

Predicting Maintenance Resources and Oil Consumption

14.7.1   Since QI is more than the value of QIP_O, which is 0 for a heavy truck, we use the linear equation: APART = 0.002290146 and,

14.7.2   ALABOR = 12.85282

Finally,

14.7.3   AOIL = 3.5342.

Model Predictions and Policy Sensitivity

As noted before, a desirable feature of the vehicle operating cost prediction models is their power to distinguish subtle differences among investment alternatives. For example, one would expect the time-related savings of paving a gravel road with poor alignment to be somewhat lower than that of paving a level-tangent gravel road. This is because even after paving, the poor alignment still prevents speed from increasing above that dictated by geometry.

This type of discriminatory power plays an important role in the optimization of highway investments under budget constraints. As evident from practical experience, the more severe the funding constraints the more difficult it becomes to choose from a number of competing alternatives, all appearing to be equally attractive. The discriminatory power afforded by the prediction models helps the policy-maker decide, on the basis of total transport cost minimization, where best to allocate scarce highway funds.

Although ideally it is essential to consider other costs also in the context of total transport cost minimization, the scope of this chapter is confined to vehicle operating costs. Specifically, the chapter has two main purposes:

1. To explore, with graphs and tables of model predictions, the effects of road roughness and geometry on vehicle operating costs (Sections 15.1-15.3); and

2. To provide a set of comprehensive and detailed tables of predicted physical resource consumption to serve as an initial reference in project or policy analyses to indicate the sensitivity of costs to alternative standards -- provided that the country or region in question is not too different from Brazil (Section 15.4).

Most of the graphs are presented in terms of physical quantities so that use or interpretations can be made in a broader context of other countries. However, to get a better perspective of policy implications, it is necessary to examine model predictions in cost terms based on typical unit costs.

15.1 VEHICLE RUNNING COSTS VERSUS ROAD ATTRIBUTES

All predictions presented in this chapter are based on the aggregate models as well as the default vehicle characteristics and model parameters compiled in Chapter 13. The basis for predicting vehicle

Table 15.1: Basis for calculation of depreciation and interest

	Vehicle class			
	Car	Utility	Bus	All trucks
Base number of hours driven HRD_0 (h/vehicle/y)	1,200	1,200	1,600	1,600
Base number of km driven AKM_0 (km/vehicle/y)	95,000[1]	95,000	110,000	100,000
Elasticity of vehicle utilization (EVU_0	0.6	0.8	0.75	0.85

For all vehicles[1]:	Vehicle depreciation:	"vehicle life" method
	Vehicle utilization :	adjusted utilization method
	Vehicle service life:	6 years

Note: The information in this table should be regarded as indicative
       only.

[1] Note that the average km driven for the car, reflecting commercial
usage in the Brazilian case, is much higher than would normally be the
case for a passenger car in private usage. Consequently, the
depreciation and interest costs per kilometer are much lower.

**Table 15.2: Economic unit costs for calculation of vehicle operating
costs in pesos**

Vehicle class	Representative test vehicle	New vehicle price (pesos/vehicle)	New tire price (pesos/tire)	Crew wages (pesos/crew-h)
Small car	VW-1300	3,300	19	1.93
Utility	VW-Kombi	5,900	27	1.93
Bus	MB-D362	40,000	168	4.40
Light truck	F-4000	11,700	66	1.93
Medium truck	MB-1113/2-axle	18,300	168	2.20
Heavy truck	MB-1113/3-axle	22,700	168	2.20
Artic.truck	Scania 110/39	56,300	258	4.13

Unit costs applicable to all vehicles:

Maintenance labor wages (pesos/labor-h)	2.75
Interest rate (percent/year)	11
Gasoline (pesos/liter)	0.266
Diesel (pesos/liter)	0.282
Lubricants (pesos/liter) gasoline	1.16
diesel	1.07

Note: Adjustments for taxes have been made to approximate economic (as
       distinct from financial) costs, but the information in this table
       should be regarded as indicative only.

depreciation, interest and passenger value-of-time costs is shown in Table 15.1. Table 15.2 presents unit costs for different vehicle classes expressed in economic terms in arbitrary monetary units, which are called "pesos." While the data in these tables are considered to be fairly typical, they are not intended to be construed as being specific to any particular country.

Appendix 15A contains graphs of predictions of the heavy truck's total running cost, speed and individual cost components (per 1000 vehicle-km) plotted against rise plus fall (RF), horizontal curvature (C), and roughness (QI) for paved roads under both loaded and unloaded conditions. The total running cost includes the following components: fuel and lubricants consumption, tire wear, maintenance parts and labor, depreciation and interest, and crew labor. The range of the RF, C and QI variables are:

RF	0 - 80 m/km	level - steep
C	0 - 1,000 degrees/km	tangent - curvy
QI	25 - 125	smooth - rough

The plots in Figures 15A.1-15A.9 are intended to illustrate by means of one vehicle class how the total running cost and its components vary with road and vehicle attributes. Although only plots for paved roads are presented, the patterns are very similar between paved and unpaved roads. While the graphs are largely self-explanatory, the following observations are particularly noteworthy:

Speed, depreciation and interest, and crew hours (Figures 15A.1-15A.3)

1. Vehicle load has an adverse effect on speed (and consequently depreciation and interest and crew hours). The effect becomes increasingly pronounced with increasing rise plus fall but attenuates slightly with increasing roughness or curvature or both. This behavior is consistent with the derivation of the constraining speeds in Chapter 3.

2. For all geometric combinations, an increase in roughness causes a reduction in speed, with the greatest reduction occurring when the geometry is the most severe (steep and curvy) and the smallest when the geometry is the least severe (level and tangent), given the same load level.

3. When the road is steep (RF = 80 m/km) the speed of the loaded truck is hardly affected by large changes in roughness and horizontal curvature. This is because to the maximum possible driving and allowable braking speeds are dominant.

4. Horizontal curvature always has an adverse effect on speed. At the same load level, the magnitude of the effect is the largest when the road is smooth and level and the

smallest when the road is rough and steep.

Fuel consumption (Figure 15A.4)

5. At a given speed, vehicle load affects fuel consumption through vehicle power, which in turn is directly dependent on rolling resistance and gravitational forces. Both of these forces are directly proportional to vehicle load. This explains why the truck consumes more fuel when loaded than when unloaded for any given road geometry.

6. Vehicle load and rise plus fall are the key determinants of fuel consumption and almost completely dominate roughness and horizontal curvature. In Figure 15A.4(b), the effect of rise plus fall on fuel consumption is much stronger when the truck is loaded than when it is unloaded.

7. For both loaded and unloaded conditions, fuel consumption goes up slowly with rise plus fall up to about 20-30 m/km, and then climbs rapidly. This non-linear behavior is explained by the non-linear (upwards concave) shape of the unit fuel consumption function quantified in Chapter 9. The policy implication of this is that improvement in vertical alignment of a road by more than a certain threshold level (say 2-3 percent average gradient) may not be worthwhile from the standpoint of fuel savings.

8. Figure 15A.4(a) shows that when the road is level-tangent the increase in rolling resistance due to increasing roughness over the range of 50-125 QI is more than countervailed by the reduction in air resistance caused by reduced speed on a rougher surface. (However, beyond 125 QI, which is generally applicable to unpaved roads, the rolling resistance effect becomes dominant.)

Tire wear (Figure 15A.5)

9. Because vehicle load is a major contributor to vehicle drive force which causes tread wear, tire consumption is larger when the truck is loaded than when it is unloaded, given the same road geometry. The vehicle load effect becomes more prominent with road severity (except when implicit ceilings are imposed on tire consumption as shown in Figure 15A.5(c)).

10. As shown in Figure 15A.5(a), given the same load level, roughness has a small effect on tire wear when the road is level and a large effect when it is steep.

11. The effect of rise plus fall on tire wear is particularly strong. Figure 15A.5(b) shows that tire wear increases with rise plus fall at an increasing rate. At the same load level, the increase is the largest when the road is

curvy and rough and the smallest when it is tangent and smooth.

12. Similarly for roughness, as depicted in Figure 15A.5(c), at the same roughness and load level the effect of horizontal curvature on tire wear is relatively small when the road is level and relatively large when it is steep.

Maintenance parts and labor and lubricants consumption (Figure 15A.6)

13. Our data show that these three contributors to the total running cost are dependent only on roughness (not on geometry and vehicle load), as predicted by the "aggregate-correlative" models reported in Chesher and Harrison (1985). The graphs show the relationships.

Total running cost (Figure 15A.7)

14. For each geometric combination, the total running cost is significantly larger when the truck is loaded than when it is unloaded.

15. For all geometric combinations, roughness has a strong effect on the total running cost. It is shown in Appendix 15B (for heavy truck) that vehicle maintenance (parts and labor) can represent as much as 50 percent of the total running cost. This explains why the trend of the total running cost curves are similar to that of the maintenance parts curve. The effect of roughness on the total running cost is the greatest when the road is level and tangent and the smallest when the road is curvey and steep; however, the differential is small.

16. The total running cost is more sensitive to rise plus fall when the vehicle is loaded than when it is unloaded, other things being equal. At the same roughness and load level, the sensitivity is greater when the road is curvy than when it is tangent. This trend is similar to that of tire wear.

17. Horizontal curvature has a significant effect on the total running cost. At a given roughness and load level, the effect is greater when the road is steep than when it is level (up to the limit imposed by an implicit ceiling).

Sensitivity of model predictions to superelevation coefficient (Figures 15A.8 and 15A.9)

18. In these graphs the predicted speed, fuel consumption, tire curvature using the following relationship which relates superelevation (SP) to horizontal curvature (C) for paved roads (from Chapter 13):

SP = 0.00012 C x (sensitivity factor)

where the "sensitivity factor" were given values of 0.5, 1.0 and 1.5. The value of 1.0 means that the recommended formula was used whereas the values of 0.5 and 1.5 mean that the computed superelevation was +50 and −50 percent of the recommended value, respectively. It can be seen from the graphs that speed predictions are slightly sensitive to the superelevation coefficient, but fuel consumption, tire wear and the total running cost are hardly affected. Speed predictions based on the recommended formula (sensitivity factor = 1) are larger than predictions based on ±50 percent perturbations from the recommended value. This is an indication that the superelevations employed in deriving the SP-C relationship were reasonably well chosen, given the model's sensitivity to superelevation.

15.2 BREAKDOWN INTO COMPONENTS OF VEHICLE RUNNING COSTS

Appendix 15B contains in tabular form percentage breakdowns of the running costs of three selected vehicle classes (utility, bus and heavy truck - all loaded) for various combinations of the rise plus fall, horizontal curvature and roughness variables for paved and unpaved surfaces, as laid out below:

	RF	C	QI	Vertical alignment	Horizontal alignment	Roughness
1	0	0	25/50	level	tangent	smooth
2	80	0	25/50	steep	tangent	smooth
3	0	1,000	25/50	level	curvy	smooth
4	80	1,000	25/50	steep	curvy	smooth
5	0	0	125/250	level	tangent	rough
6	80	0	125/250	steep	curvy	rough
7	0	1,000	125/250	level	tangent	rough
8	80	1,000	125/250	steep	curvy	rough

The purpose of this appendix is to illustrate the relative contributions of the various vehicle operating cost components for different vehicle class under different operating conditions. The following observations are noted:

1. The tables show clearly that fuel cost is the largest single cost component. This is brought out most forcefully in the case of utility vehicles, where, for the "smooth" roads, fuel consumption represents some 40 percent of total running costs on paved roads, and slightly lower on unpaved roads. While the absolute total costs (as well as the fuel cost component) go up with increasing roughness, the fuel cost relative to the total is reduced sharply, down to some 32 percent on very rough paved roads, and to some 25 percent on unpaved roads. The same finding holds true for curvature and rise and fall: the more severe the road

condition, the smaller the percentage share of fuel costs, i.e., the increase in total running costs are on the account of other cost components. The above findings also apply generally for the cases of buses and heavy trucks, although here the proportions of fuel costs are lower, and thus more in line with what is normally expected.

2.   The data show that tire costs are fairly insignificant for utility vehicles, but very large for both buses and heavy trucks and in fact generally assume an ever increasing percentage of an ever increasing total cost, from around 10 percent under the most favorable conditions to around 25 percent under the most unfavorable. Since at the same time total running costs increase by a factor of 2.2-3 this means a six to seven 7 fold increase in absolute tire costs (for paved and unpaved roads, respectively) between the most favorable and the most unfavorable conditions here considered.

3.   The crew cost component, which is linearly proportionate to the inverse of speed, varies as expected with road attributes. The component is very large in the case of utility vehicles and buses, but considerably less for heavy trucks.

4.   The maintenance cost component increases sharply with increase in roughness; for a utility vehicle increasing some three-fold on unpaved roads going from QI 50 to QI 250, and slightly less on paved roads, going from QI 25 to QI 125. This effect is equally clear for buses and heavy trucks, but with a factor of 1.5 to 2 between the extreme conditions. In this sense again, the maintenance takes on an increasing proportion of an increasing total running cost; in the case of a utility van on a gravel road, the absolute costs typically increasing by a factor of about 6 due to roughness increase alone.

5.   Finally, depreciation and interest account for a substantial proportion of the total running costs for all vehicles on both road types, again with somewhat lower values for the heavy trucks.

15.3   TOTAL RUNNING COST VERSUS VEHICLE WEIGHT

In Appendix 15C, Figure 15C.1(a) plots the predicted total running cost per 1,000 vehicle-km against the total vehicle weight for all vehicle classes and a number of load levels. The data points represent two extreme road conditions: the best (level-tangent and smooth paved with RF=0, C=0 and QI=25) and the worst (steep-curvy and rough unpaved with RF=80 m/km, C=1,000 degrees/km and QI=250). Each set of data points, which exhibit a straight-line trend, is accompanied by the line of best fit using ordinary least-squares regression. Both regression lines have a positive slope and positive intercept, and the line corresponding to the worst road condition is steeper and has a larger intercept.

        This observation suggests an economy of scale with respect to vehicle size under a wide range of operating conditions. As also illustrated in Figure 15C.1(b), the predicted total running cost per 1,000 ton-km of vehicle weight tends to decline as the vehicle weight increases, assuming constant load factors. Even more striking is Figure 15C.1(c) in which the predicted total running cost per 1,000 ton-km of payload is plotted against the vehicle weight (for trucks only), exhibiting an even sharper declining trend.

15.4 DETAILED PREDICTION TABLES

        Appendix 15D contains 30 tables (15 for paved and 15 for unpaved roads), each comprising predicted physical quantities consumed per 1,000 vehicle-km of operation on a given surface type (paved or unpaved) under different sets of road conditions for a given vehicle class and load level. The road conditions are represented by all possible combinations of:

RF		0 — 40	80	m/km
C		0 — 500	1000	degrees/km
and	QI	25 — 75	125	paved
or	QI	50 — 150	250	unpaved

The tables are identified for the following vehicle classes and load levels:

Vehicle class — load level

---

1. Small car
2. Medium car
3. Large car
4. Utility
5. Bus (with passengers)
6. Light gasoline truck — unloaded
7. Light gasoline truck — loaded
8. Light diesel truck — unloaded

9. Light diesel truck — loaded
10. Medium truck — unloaded
11. Medium truck — loaded
12. Heavy truck — unloaded
13. Heavy truck — loaded
14. Articulated truck — unloaded
15. Articulated truck — loaded.

        In order to save space the components of crew labor, passenger delay and cargo holding share the same column labelled "time per distance" and expressed in vehicle-hours per 1,000 vehicle-km. This implies that one passenger per vehicle is assumed. However, the user can obtain the desired passenger-hours delayed by simply multiplying the value shown with the actual number of passengers per vehicle.

The predictions in each table are for the following vehicle operating cost components:

	Cost component	Units (per 1,000 vehicle-km)
1.	Fuel consumption	liters
2.	Lubricants consumption	liters
3.	Tire wear	equivalent new tires
4.	Maintenance parts	percent of new vehicle price
5.	Maintenance labor	labor-hours
6.	Depreciation	percent of new vehicle price
7.	Interest	percent of new vehicle price
8.	Crew labor	crew-hours
9.	Passenger delay	passenger-hours
10.	Cargo holding	vehicle-hours

APPENDIX 15A

SENSITIVITY OF VEHICLE OPERATING COSTS TO ROAD CHARACTERISTICS FOR HEAVY TRUCKS ON PAVED ROADS

Figure 15A.1: Speed versus characteristic road parameters for a heavy truck on paved roads: (a) roughness, (b) rise plus fall, and (c) curvature

Notes: 1. (U) stands for unloaded, and (L) stands for loaded.
        2. Roughness: Smooth means 25 QI, and rough means 125 QI.
        3. Rise plus fall: Level means 0 m/km, and steep means 80 m/km
        4. Curvature: Tangent means 0 deg/km, and curvy means 1,000 deg/km
        5. For other variables default values as given in Chapter 14 are used.
Source: Analysis of Brazil-UNDP-World Bank highway research project data

(a)

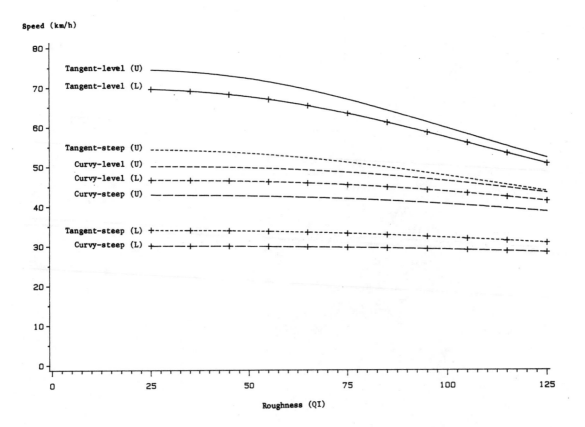

(b)

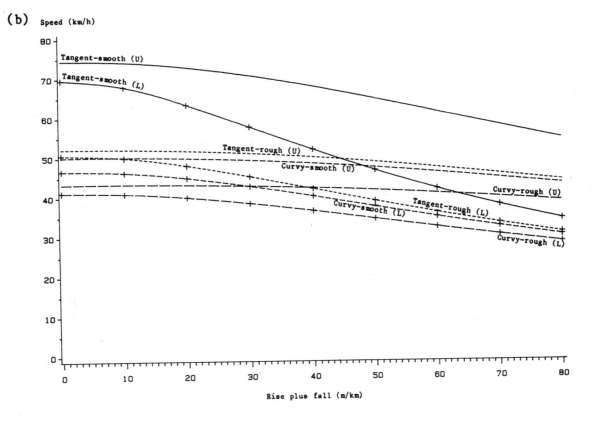

(c)

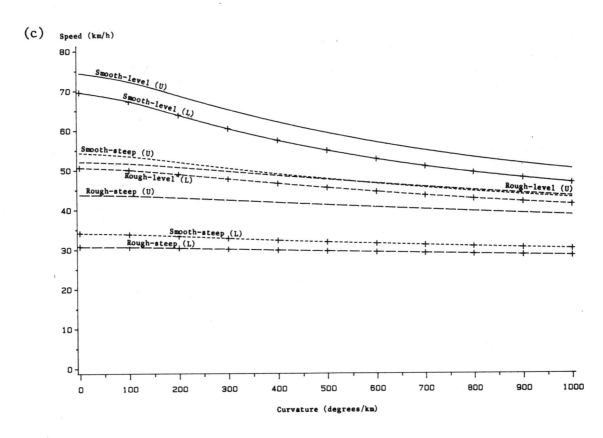

**Figures 15A.2: Depreciation and interest versus characteristic road
parameters for a heavy truck on paved roads:
(a) roughness, (b) rise plus fall, and (c) curvature**

Notes: 1. (U) stands for unloaded, and (L) stands for loaded.
2. Roughness: Smooth means 25 QI, and rough means 125 QI.
3. Rise plus fall: Level means 0 m/km, and steep means 80 m/km
4. Curvature: Tangent means 0 deg/km, and curvy means 1,000 deg/km
5. For other variables default values as given in Chapter 14 are
used.

Source: Analysis of Brazil–UNDP–World Bank highway research project data

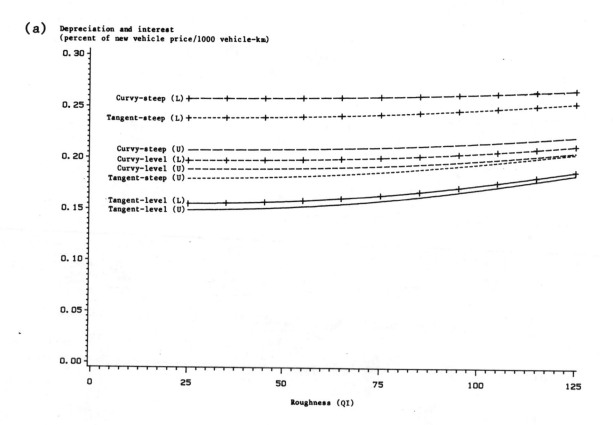

(b)

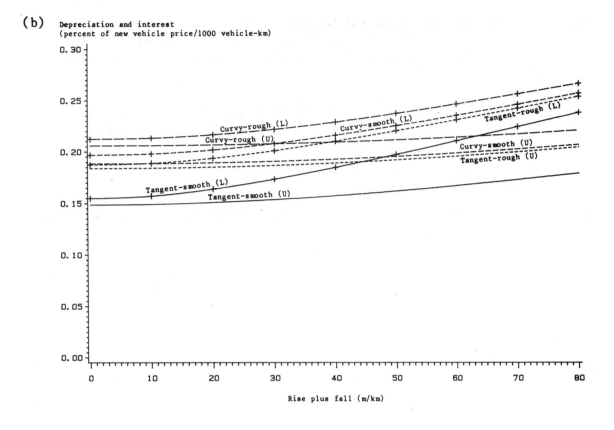

(c)

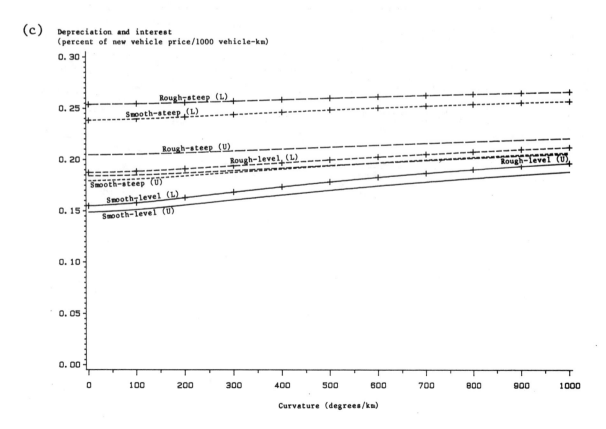

**Figure 15A.3: Crew hours versus characteristic road parameters for a
heavy truck on paved roads: (a) roughness, (b) rise plus
fall, and (c) curvature**

Notes: 1. (U) stands for unloaded, and (L) stands for loaded.
2. Roughness: Smooth means 25 QI, and rough means 125 QI.
3. Rise plus fall: Level means 0 m/km, and steep means 80 m/km
4. Curvature: Tangent means 0 deg/km, and curvy means 1,000 deg/km
5. For other variables default values as given in Chapter 14 are
used.

Source: Analysis of Brazil-UNDP-World Bank highway research project data

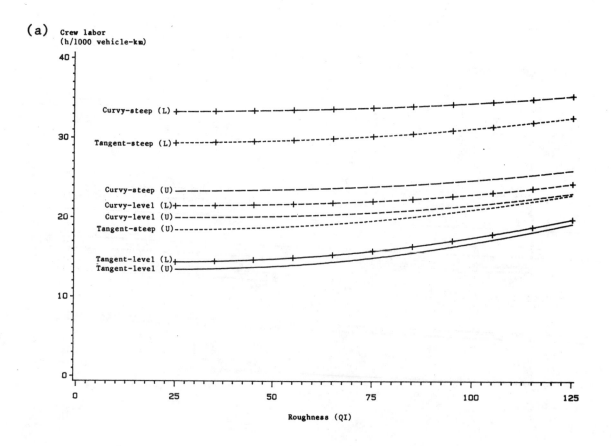

(b) **Crew labor**
     (h/1000 vehicle-km)

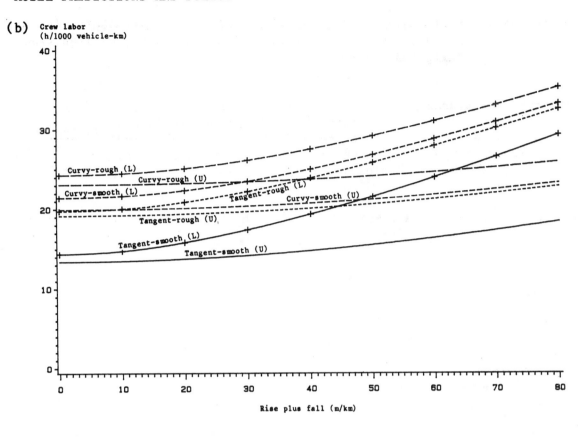

(c) **Crew labor**
     (h/1000 vehicle-km)

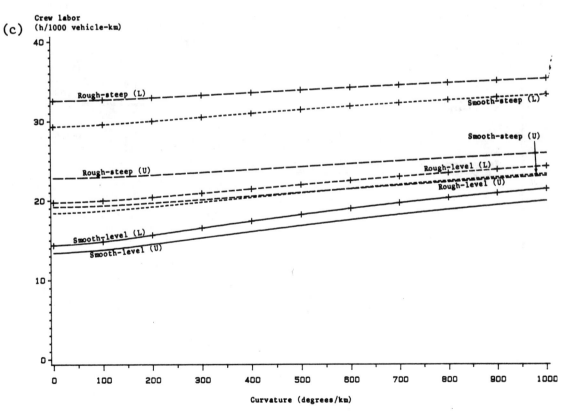

Figure 15A.4: **Fuel consumption versus characteristic road parameters for a heavy truck on paved roads: (a) roughness, (b) rise plus fall, and (c) curvature**

Notes: 1. (U) stands for unloaded, and (L) stands for loaded.
       2. Roughness: Smooth means 25 QI, and rough means 125 QI.
       3. Rise plus fall: Level means 0 m/km, and steep means 80 m/km
       4. Curvature: Tangent means 0 deg/km, and curvy means 1,000 deg/km
       5. For other variables default values as given in Chapter 14 are used.

Source: Analysis of Brazil-UNDP-World Bank highway research project data

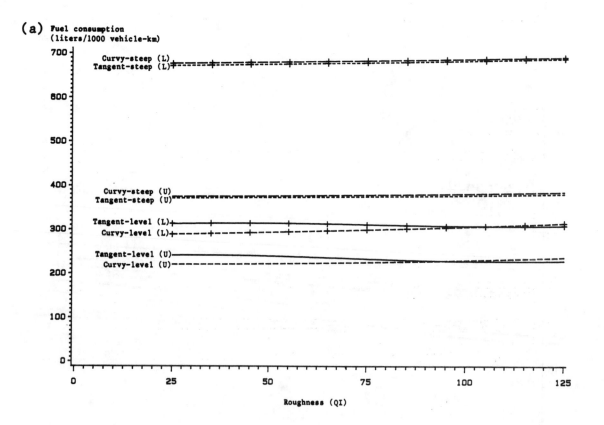

(b) Fuel consumption
(liters/1000 vehicle-km)

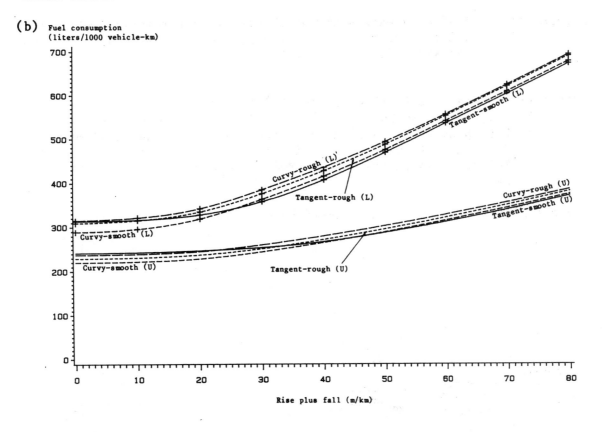

Rise plus fall (m/km)

(c) Fuel consumption
(liters/1000 vehicle-km)

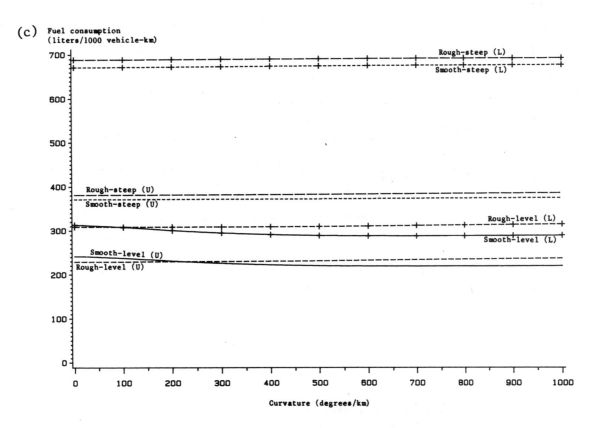

Curvature (degrees/km)

Figure 15A.5: **Tire wear versus characteristic road parameters for a heavy truck on paved roads: (a) roughness, (b) rise plus fall, and (c) curvature**

Notes: 1. (U) stands for unloaded, and (L) stands for loaded.
2. Roughness: Smooth means 25 QI, and rough means 125 QI.
3. Rise plus fall: Level means 0 m/km, and steep means 80 m/km
4. Curvature: Tangent means 0 deg/km, and curvy means 1,000 deg/km
5. For other variables default values as given in Chapter 14 are used.

Source: Analysis of Brazil-UNDP-World Bank highway research project data

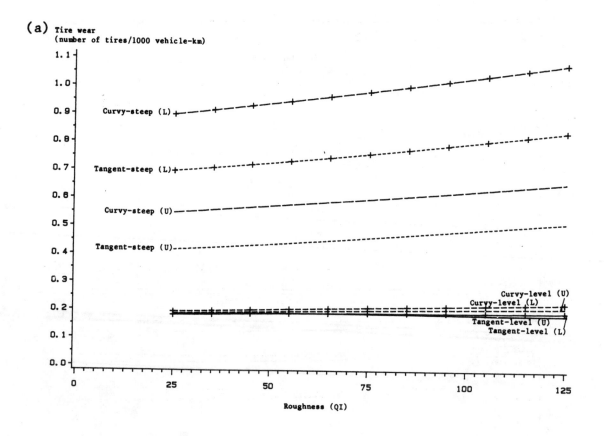

(b)

Tire wear
(number of tires/1000 vehicle-km)

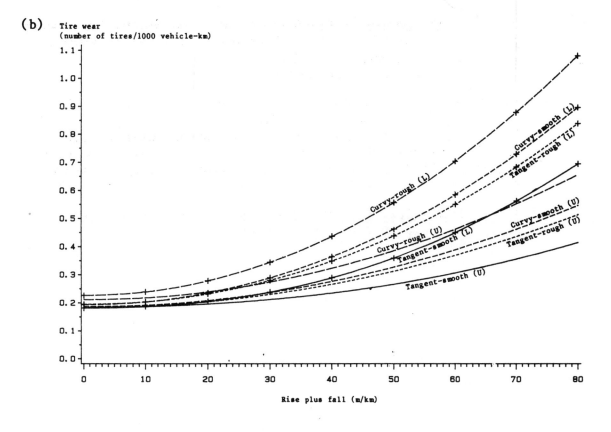

Rise plus fall (m/km)

(c)

Tire wear
(number of tires/1000 vehicle-km)

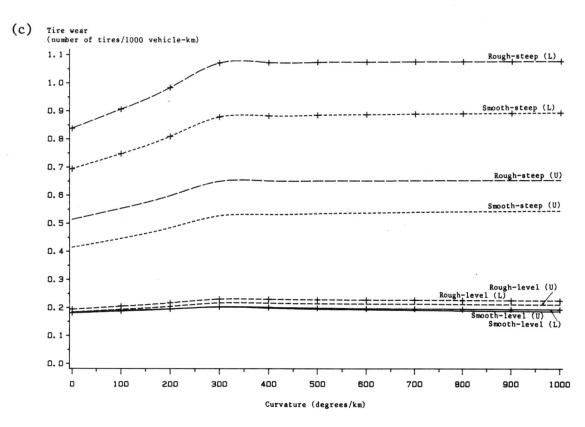

Curvature (degrees/km)

Figure 15A.6: Maintenance parts consumption and labor and lubricants consumption versus roughness for a heavy truck on paved roads: (a) maintenance parts consumption, (b) maintenance labor, and (c) lubricants consumption

Note: These resources depend only on roughness among the road characteristics.

Sources: Analysis of Brazil-UNDP-World Bank highway research project data for (a) and (b). (See Chesher and Harrison (1987) and GEIPOT (1982).)
Analysis of Indian Road User Costs Study data for (c). (See Chesher and Harrison (1987) and CRRI (1982).)

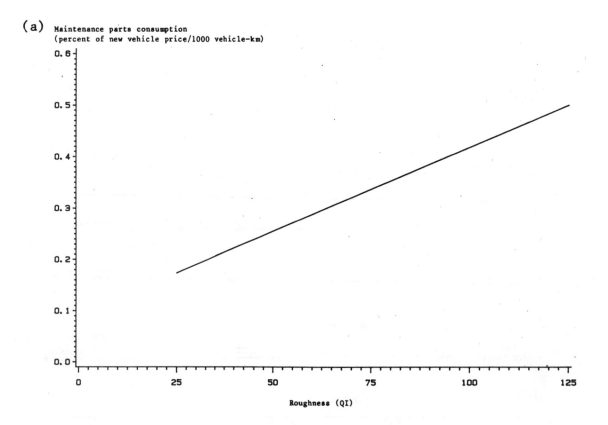

(a) Maintenance parts consumption
(percent of new vehicle price/1000 vehicle-km)

(b)

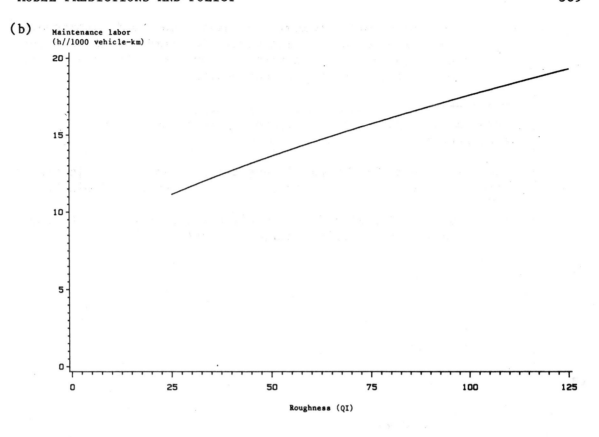

(c)

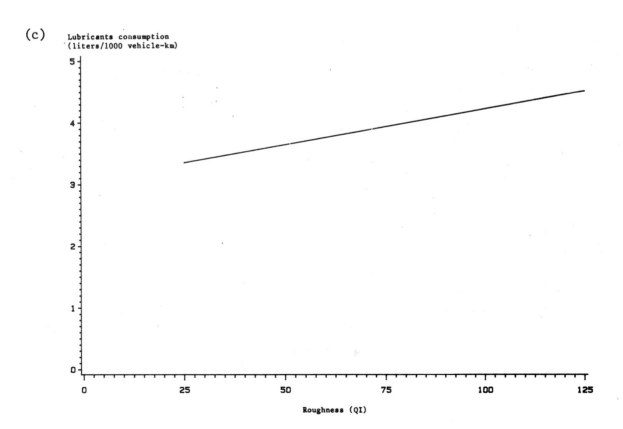

Figure 15A.7:   Total running cost versus characteristic road   parameters for a heavy truck on paved roads: (a) roughness, (b) rise plus fall, and (c) curvature

Notes: 1. (U) stands for unloaded, and (L) stands for loaded.
        2. Roughness: Smooth means 25 QI, and rough means 125 QI.
        3. Rise plus fall: Level means 0 m/km, and steep means 80 m/km
        4. Curvature: Tangent means 0 deg/km, and curvy means 1,000 deg/km
        5. For other variables default values as given in Chapter 14 are used.

Source: Analysis of Brazil–UNDP–World Bank highway research project data

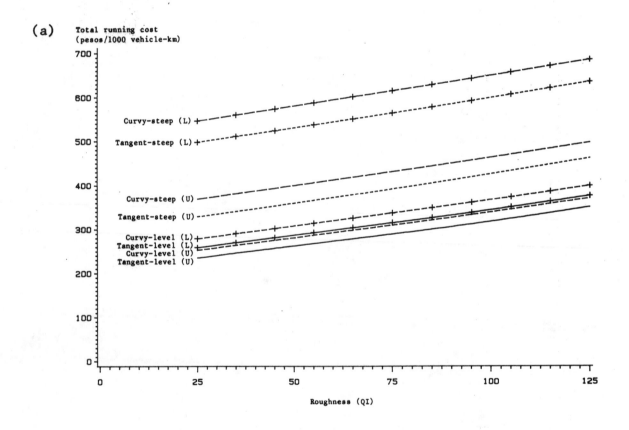

(b)

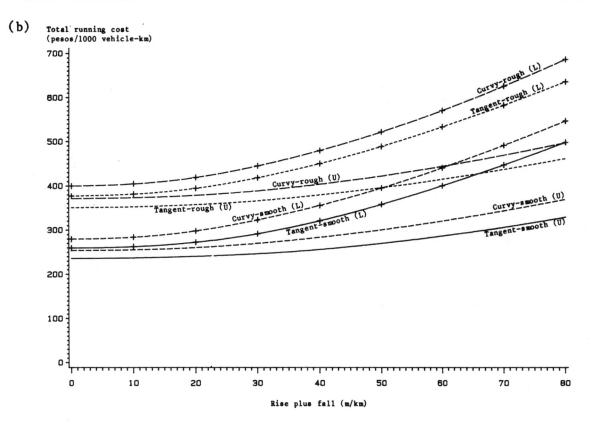

(c)

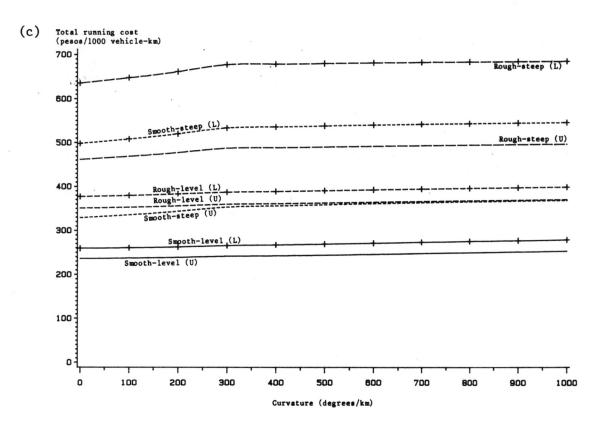

**Figure 15A.8:   Sensitivity of (a) fuel use and (b) tire wear to super-
elevation formula for a heavy truck on paved roads**

(a)

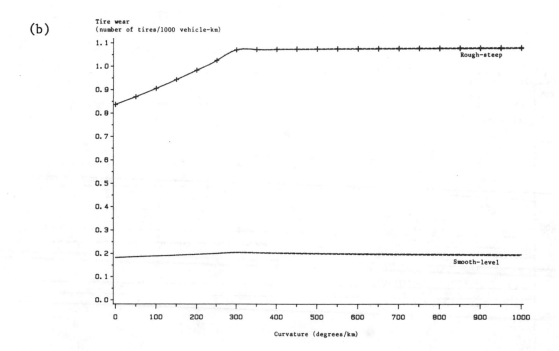

(b)

Legend: Sensitivity factors:

Notes: 1. Smooth means 25 QI, and rough means 125 QI.
       2. Level means 0 m/km, and steep means 80 m/km.
Source: Analysis of Brazil-UNDP-World Bank highway research project data

Figure 15A.9: Sensitivity of (a) speed and (b) total running cost to
superelevation formula for a heavy truck on paved roads

(a)

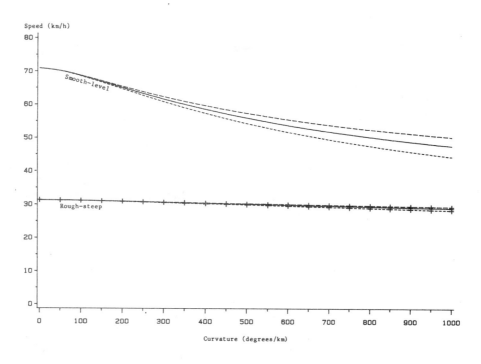

(b)

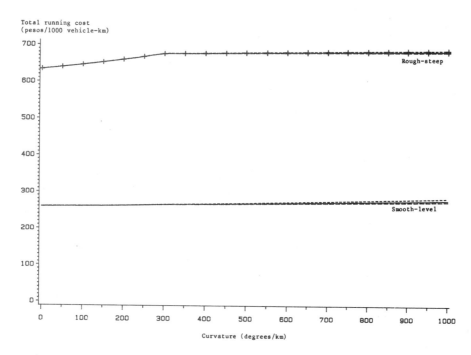

Legend: Sensitivity factors:

Notes: 1. Smooth means 25 QI, and rough means 125 QI.
       2. Level means 0 m/km, and steep means 80 m/km.
Source: Analysis of Brazil-UNDP-World Bank highway research project data

APPENDIX 15B

BREAKDOWN OF OPERATING COSTS

This appendix gives the vehicle cost breakdowns under various operating conditions both as "peso" costs per 1,000 vehicle-km and as percentage of the total cost. The quantities in the columns with labels prefixed by "%" are the percentage breakdowns. The "fuel" column comprises both fuel and lubricants and the "parts" column comprises both parts and labor.

Table 15B.1: Cost breakdown by percentage and total running cost for 1,000 vehicle km on paved roads

RF	C	QI	% fuel	% tire	% crew	% maint.	% depr. + int.	Total cost : (pesos/1000km)
0	0	25	41.3	1.4	21.3	13.4	22.6	112.80
		125	31.3	1.9	18.9	30.1	17.8	160.18
	1000	25	35.7	1.1	29.0	10.7	23.6	141.12
		125	30.2	1.7	23.4	26.2	18.6	184.18
80	0	25	41.4	1.2	23.7	11.5	22.1	130.65
		125	33.4	1.8	19.9	27.4	17.5	175.73
	1000	25	39.0	1.0	28.1	9.7	22.2	155.37
		125	32.7	1.6	23.3	24.5	17.9	196.60

RF	C	QI	% fuel	% tire	% crew	% maint.	% depr. + int.	Total cost : (pesos/1000km)
0	0	25	28.0	9.0	19.9	19.2	23.8	290.61
		125	23.0	7.8	20.7	26.8	21.7	355.26
	1000	25	22.8	7.9	27.1	16.7	25.5	334.41
		125	21.0	8.0	24.6	24.2	22.3	393.93
80	0	25	28.7	19.6	22.5	10.7	18.5	520.26
		125	26.0	20.4	20.8	16.1	16.7	592.38
	1000	25	26.5	22.9	23.0	9.8	17.9	569.85
		125	24.0	24.3	20.9	14.7	16.0	645.88

RF	C	QI	% fuel	% tire	% crew	% maint.	% depr. + int.	Total cost : (pesos/1000km)
0	0	25	35.5	11.7	12.2	27.1	13.6	259.15
		125	24.4	8.6	11.5	44.2	11.3	376.98
	1000	25	30.4	11.6	16.9	25.1	16.0	279.27
		125	23.4	9.5	13.4	41.7	12.1	399.50
80	0	25	38.7	23.4	12.9	14.1	10.8	498.13
		125	31.3	22.1	11.3	26.2	9.1	635.49
	1000	25	35.6	27.5	13.4	12.8	10.7	546.41
		125	29.2	26.4	11.3	24.3	8.8	685.88

Table 15B.2 Cost breakdown by percentage and running cost for 1,000 vehicle km on unpaved roads

RF	C	QI	% fuel	% tire	% crew	% maint.	% depr. + int.	Total cost : (pesos/1000km)
0	0	50	38.0	1.6	22.2	16.2	22.0	123.73
		250	24.0	1.5	18.9	41.8	13.8	272.03
	1000	50	34.5	1.3	28.9	12.9	22.5	155.52
		250	24.4	1.5	20.4	39.7	14.0	286.26
80	0	50	39.6	1.4	23.6	14.2	21.2	140.90
		250	25.9	1.5	18.8	40.2	13.5	282.52
	1000	50	37.5	1.2	28.1	11.9	21.3	168.43
		250	26.3	1.4	20.2	38.4	13.7	296.08

RF	C	QI	% fuel	% tire	% crew	% maint.	% depr. + int.	Total cost : (pesos/1000km)
0	0	50	25.1	8.1	22.3	20.5	24.1	311.15
		250	17.6	5.7	23.5	34.8	18.4	550.35
	1000	50	21.8	7.3	28.7	17.3	24.9	367.94
		250	17.4	6.6	24.4	33.2	18.3	577.29
80	0	50	27.9	19.8	22.4	11.8	18.2	540.31
		250	20.9	19.9	20.1	24.7	14.4	777.68
	1000	50	25.5	22.9	23.3	10.6	17.6	598.22
		250	19.5	24.2	19.7	22.9	13.7	837.77

RF	C	QI	% fuel	% tire	% crew	% maint.	% depr. + int.	Total cost : (pesos/1000km)
0	0	50	30.8	10.5	12.5	33.1	13.2	288.55
		250	20.1	6.7	13.6	49.1	10.6	567.50
	1000	50	27.7	10.3	17.1	29.7	15.2	321.51
		250	20.0	7.9	14.0	47.4	10.7	587.75
80	0	50	36.4	22.9	12.5	17.8	10.3	535.00
		250	25.2	21.7	11.4	33.6	8.2	828.83
	1000	50	33.3	26.9	13.3	16.2	10.3	588.81
		250	23.5	26.3	11.1	31.3	7.8	890.13

APPENDIX 15C

EFFECT OF VEHICLE WEIGHT ON OPERATING COSTS

Figure 15C.1: **Total running costs per (a) 1,000 vehicle-km, (b) 1,000 ton-km of vehicle weight and (c) 1,000 ton-km of payload, versus gross vehicle weight for two extreme road conditions**

(a)

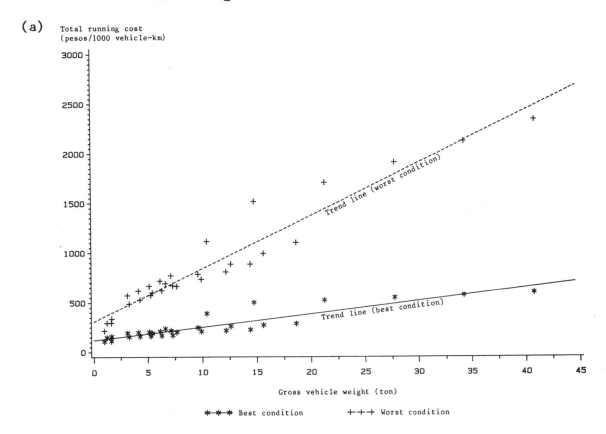

(b)

Total running cost
(pesos/1000 ton-km of vehicle weight)

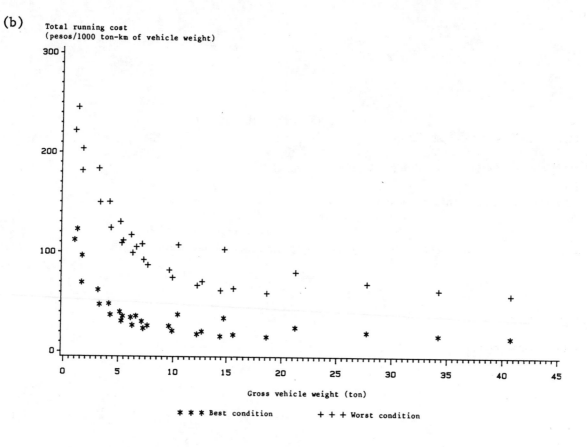

Gross vehicle weight (ton)

✱ ✱ ✱ Best condition   + + + Worst condition

(c)

Total running cost
(pesos/1000 ton-km of payload)

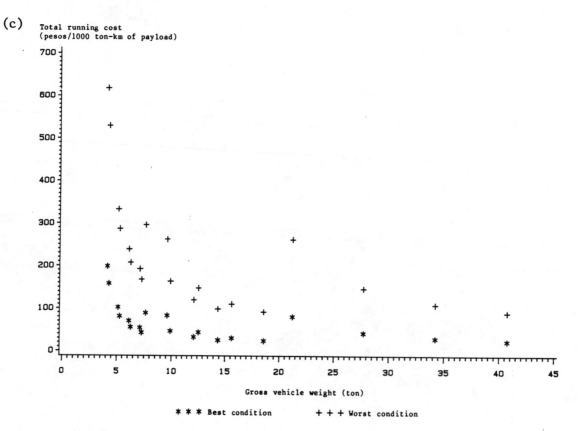

Gross vehicle weight (ton)

✱ ✱ ✱ Best condition   + + + Worst condition

APPENDIX 15D

DETAILED PREDICTION TABLES

The units for the quantities predicted in these tables are as follows:

Units	Quantities
Fuel consumption	liters/1,000 vehicle-km
Tire wear	number of equivalent new tires/1,000 vehicle-km
Depreciation and interest	percentage of new vehicle price/1,000 vehicle-km
Time per distance	vehicle hours/1,000 vehicle-km
Maintenance and parts	percentage of new vehicle price/1,000 vehicle-km
Maintenance and labor	labor hours/1,000 vehicle-km
Lubricant consumption	liters/1,000 vehicle-km

Table 15D.1: Physical quantities for a small car on a paved road surface

RF	C	QI	Fuel	Lubricants	Tire wear	Maint.-parts	Maint.-labor	Depre-ciation	Interest	Time per-distance
0	0	25	97.0	1.8	0.0593	0.1241	2.0	1.1111	0.3056	11.5
		75	99.2	2.4	0.0867	0.2461	2.9	1.1111	0.3056	12.1
		125	104.2	3.0	0.1141	0.4872	4.2	1.1111	0.3056	14.1
	500	25	104.8	1.8	0.0593	0.1241	2.0	1.1111	0.3056	16.0
		75	107.5	2.4	0.0867	0.2461	2.9	1.1111	0.3056	16.2
		125	112.8	3.0	0.1141	0.4872	4.2	1.1111	0.3056	17.3
	1000	25	116.8	1.8	0.0593	0.1241	2.0	1.1111	0.3056	19.6
		75	119.3	2.4	0.0867	0.2461	2.9	1.1111	0.3056	19.7
		125	123.7	3.0	0.1141	0.4872	4.2	1.1111	0.3056	20.4
40	0	25	97.7	1.8	0.0593	0.1241	2.0	1.1111	0.3056	11.9
		75	99.9	2.4	0.0867	0.2461	2.9	1.1111	0.3056	12.5
		125	105.0	3.0	0.1141	0.4872	4.2	1.1111	0.3056	14.4
	500	25	105.5	1.8	0.0593	0.1241	2.0	1.1111	0.3056	16.2
		75	108.1	2.4	0.0867	0.2461	2.9	1.1111	0.3056	16.4
		125	113.4	3.0	0.1141	0.4872	4.2	1.1111	0.3056	17.5
	1000	25	117.8	1.8	0.0593	0.1241	2.0	1.1111	0.3056	19.7
		75	120.1	2.4	0.0867	0.2461	2.9	1.1111	0.3056	19.8
		125	124.4	3.0	0.1141	0.4872	4.2	1.1111	0.3056	20.5
80	0	25	104.4	1.8	0.0593	0.1241	2.0	1.1111	0.3056	14.5
		75	106.7	2.4	0.0867	0.2461	2.9	1.1111	0.3056	14.7
		125	112.2	3.0	0.1141	0.4872	4.2	1.1111	0.3056	16.1
	500	25	113.5	1.8	0.0593	0.1241	2.0	1.1111	0.3056	17.5
		75	115.7	2.4	0.0867	0.2461	2.9	1.1111	0.3056	17.7
		125	120.4	3.0	0.1141	0.4872	4.2	1.1111	0.3056	18.5
	1000	25	124.5	1.8	0.0593	0.1241	2.0	1.1111	0.3056	20.6
		75	126.6	2.4	0.0867	0.2461	2.9	1.1111	0.3056	20.7
		125	130.6	3.0	0.1141	0.4872	4.2	1.1111	0.3056	21.2

Table 15D.2: Physical quantities for a medium car on a paved surface

RF	C	QI	Fuel	Lubricants	Tire wear	Maint.-parts	Maint.-labor	Depreciation	Interest	Time per-distance
0	0	25	199.5	1.8	0.0593	0.1282	2.0	1.0000	0.2750	10.8
		75	203.9	2.4	0.0867	0.2543	2.9	1.0000	0.2750	11.4
		125	217.3	3.0	0.1141	0.5033	4.3	1.0000	0.2750	13.7
	500	25	224.0	1.8	0.0593	0.1282	2.0	1.0000	0.2750	15.6
		75	229.1	2.4	0.0867	0.2543	2.9	1.0000	0.2750	15.9
		125	241.3	3.0	0.1141	0.5033	4.3	1.0000	0.2750	17.0
	1000	25	255.3	1.8	0.0593	0.1282	2.0	1.0000	0.2750	19.4
		75	259.9	2.4	0.0867	0.2543	2.9	1.0000	0.2750	19.5
		125	269.4	3.0	0.1141	0.5033	4.3	1.0000	0.2750	20.2
40	0	25	199.7	1.8	0.0593	0.1282	2.0	1.0000	0.2750	10.9
		75	204.2	2.4	0.0867	0.2543	2.9	1.0000	0.2750	11.5
		125	217.7	3.0	0.1141	0.5033	4.3	1.0000	0.2750	13.7
	500	25	224.3	1.8	0.0593	0.1282	2.0	1.0000	0.2750	15.7
		75	229.4	2.4	0.0867	0.2543	2.9	1.0000	0.2750	15.9
		125	241.6	3.0	0.1141	0.5033	4.3	1.0000	0.2750	17.0
	1000	25	256.2	1.8	0.0593	0.1282	2.0	1.0000	0.2750	19.4
		75	260.5	2.4	0.0867	0.2543	2.9	1.0000	0.2750	19.6
		125	269.8	3.0	0.1141	0.5033	4.3	1.0000	0.2750	20.2
80	0	25	210.2	1.8	0.0593	0.1282	2.0	1.0000	0.2750	12.8
		75	214.3	2.4	0.0867	0.2543	2.9	1.0000	0.2750	13.0
		125	227.6	3.0	0.1141	0.5033	4.3	1.0000	0.2750	14.7
	500	25	235.8	1.8	0.0593	0.1282	2.0	1.0000	0.2750	16.5
		75	239.8	2.4	0.0867	0.2543	2.9	1.0000	0.2750	16.7
		125	250.7	3.0	0.1141	0.5033	4.3	1.0000	0.2750	17.6
	1000	25	265.4	1.8	0.0593	0.1282	2.0	1.0000	0.2750	19.9
		75	269.2	2.4	0.0867	0.2543	2.9	1.0000	0.2750	20.0
		125	277.8	3.0	0.1141	0.5033	4.3	1.0000	0.2750	20.6

Table 15D.3: Physical quantities for a large car on a paved surface

RF	C	QI	Fuel	Lubricants	Tire wear	Maint.-parts	Maint.-labor	Depreciation	Interest	Time per-distance
0	0	25	214.9	1.8	0.0593	0.1320	2.1	0.9091	0.2500	10.7
		75	221.9	2.4	0.0867	0.2618	3.0	0.9091	0.2500	11.3
		125	243.3	3.0	0.1141	0.5182	4.3	0.9091	0.2500	13.6
	500	25	255.1	1.8	0.0593	0.1320	2.1	0.9091	0.2500	15.6
		75	261.3	2.4	0.0867	0.2618	3.0	0.9091	0.2500	15.8
		125	277.1	3.0	0.1141	0.5182	4.3	0.9091	0.2500	17.0
	1000	25	297.0	1.8	0.0593	0.1320	2.1	0.9091	0.2500	19.4
		75	302.2	2.4	0.0867	0.2618	3.0	0.9091	0.2500	19.5
		125	313.8	3.0	0.1141	0.5182	4.3	0.9091	0.2500	20.2
40	0	25	218.4	1.8	0.0593	0.1320	2.1	0.9091	0.2500	10.8
		75	225.3	2.4	0.0867	0.2618	3.0	0.9091	0.2500	11.4
		125	246.4	3.0	0.1141	0.5182	4.3	0.9091	0.2500	13.7
	500	25	258.7	1.8	0.0593	0.1320	2.1	0.9091	0.2500	15.7
		75	264.5	2.4	0.0867	0.2618	3.0	0.9091	0.2500	15.9
		125	279.9	3.0	0.1141	0.5182	4.3	0.9091	0.2500	17.0
	1000	25	300.6	1.8	0.0593	0.1320	2.1	0.9091	0.2500	19.4
		75	305.4	2.4	0.0867	0.2618	3.0	0.9091	0.2500	19.5
		125	316.6	3.0	0.1141	0.5182	4.3	0.9091	0.2500	20.2
80	0	25	254.6	1.8	0.0593	0.1320	2.1	0.9091	0.2500	13.1
		75	257.5	2.4	0.0867	0.2618	3.0	0.9091	0.2500	13.3
		125	272.0	3.0	0.1141	0.5182	4.3	0.9091	0.2500	14.9
	500	25	285.1	1.8	0.0593	0.1320	2.1	0.9091	0.2500	16.7
		75	288.1	2.4	0.0867	0.2618	3.0	0.9091	0.2500	16.8
		125	299.4	3.0	0.1141	0.5182	4.3	0.9091	0.2500	17.7
	1000	25	318.8	1.8	0.0593	0.1320	2.1	0.9091	0.2500	20.1
		75	322.8	2.4	0.0867	0.2618	3.0	0.9091	0.2500	20.1
		125	332.8	3.0	0.1141	0.5182	4.3	0.9091	0.2500	20.7

Table 15D.4: Physical quantities for a utility vehicle on a paved surface

RF	C	QI	Fuel	Lubricants	Tire wear	Maint.-parts	Maint.-labor	Depreciation	Interest	Time per-distance
0	0	25	167.1	1.8	0.0593	0.1523	2.2	0.3556	0.0770	12.4
		75	170.5	2.4	0.0867	0.3021	3.2	0.3653	0.0799	13.2
		125	175.7	3.0	0.1141	0.5979	4.7	0.3944	0.0888	15.6
	500	25	169.5	1.8	0.0593	0.1523	2.2	0.4157	0.0957	17.5
		75	175.4	2.4	0.0867	0.3021	3.2	0.4199	0.0971	17.9
		125	184.4	3.0	0.1141	0.5979	4.7	0.4348	0.1021	19.3
	1000	25	181.2	1.8	0.0593	0.1523	2.2	0.4545	0.1091	21.2
		75	187.0	2.4	0.0867	0.3021	3.2	0.4570	0.1100	21.4
		125	195.7	3.0	0.1141	0.5979	4.7	0.4666	0.1134	22.4
40	0	25	167.7	1.8	0.0593	0.1523	2.2	0.3633	0.0793	13.1
		75	171.3	2.4	0.0867	0.3021	3.2	0.3725	0.0820	13.8
		125	176.8	3.0	0.1141	0.5979	4.7	0.3998	0.0905	16.1
	500	25	173.2	1.8	0.0593	0.1523	2.2	0.4197	0.0970	17.9
		75	178.0	2.4	0.0867	0.3021	3.2	0.4238	0.0984	18.3
		125	186.7	3.0	0.1141	0.5979	4.7	0.4382	0.1033	19.6
	1000	25	187.3	1.8	0.0593	0.1523	2.2	0.4570	0.1100	21.4
		75	191.9	2.4	0.0867	0.3021	3.2	0.4596	0.1109	21.7
		125	199.6	3.0	0.1141	0.5979	4.7	0.4690	0.1143	22.6
80	0	25	195.5	1.8	0.0593	0.1523	2.2	0.3989	0.0902	16.0
		75	199.3	2.4	0.0867	0.3021	3.2	0.4039	0.0918	16.5
		125	207.7	3.0	0.1141	0.5979	4.7	0.4226	0.0980	18.2
	500	25	208.1	1.8	0.0593	0.1523	2.2	0.4385	0.1034	19.6
		75	211.6	2.4	0.0867	0.3021	3.2	0.4415	0.1045	19.9
		125	218.3	3.0	0.1141	0.5979	4.7	0.4532	0.1086	21.0
	1000	25	219.5	1.8	0.0593	0.1523	2.2	0.4694	0.1145	22.6
		75	222.9	2.4	0.0867	0.3021	3.2	0.4715	0.1153	22.9
		125	228.7	3.0	0.1141	0.5979	4.7	0.4797	0.1183	23.7

Table 15D.5: Physical quantities for a loaded bus on a paved surface

RF	C	QI	Fuel	Lubricants	Tire wear	Maint.- parts	Maint.- labor	Depre- ciation	Interest	Time per- distance
0	0	25	276.3	3.4	0.1559	0.0813	8.5	0.1359	0.0370	13.2
		75	277.5	3.9	0.1644	0.0971	12.3	0.1391	0.0383	13.9
		125	272.7	4.5	0.1659	0.1160	17.7	0.1497	0.0428	16.7
	500	25	255.6	3.4	0.1649	0.0813	8.5	0.1515	0.0436	17.2
		75	263.3	3.9	0.1795	0.0971	12.3	0.1529	0.0443	17.6
		125	271.5	4.5	0.1924	0.1160	17.7	0.1589	0.0471	19.3
	1000	25	257.6	3.4	0.1570	0.0813	8.5	0.1635	0.0493	20.6
		75	265.8	3.9	0.1714	0.0971	12.3	0.1643	0.0497	20.9
		125	276.2	4.5	0.1864	0.1160	17.7	0.1680	0.0516	22.0
40	0	25	319.5	3.4	0.2437	0.0813	8.5	0.1507	0.0433	17.0
		75	325.0	3.9	0.2658	0.0971	12.3	0.1532	0.0444	17.7
		125	333.2	4.5	0.2939	0.1160	17.7	0.1611	0.0482	19.9
	500	25	322.4	3.4	0.3067	0.0813	8.5	0.1618	0.0485	20.1
		75	328.8	3.9	0.3357	0.0971	12.3	0.1631	0.0492	20.5
		125	337.9	4.5	0.3700	0.1160	17.7	0.1678	0.0515	21.9
	1000	25	329.1	3.4	0.3089	0.0813	8.5	0.1707	0.0530	22.9
		75	335.6	3.9	0.3377	0.0971	12.3	0.1716	0.0535	23.2
		125	344.3	4.5	0.3709	0.1160	17.7	0.1747	0.0551	24.2
80	0	25	516.7	3.4	0.6058	0.0813	8.5	0.1818	0.0591	26.6
		75	522.0	3.9	0.6570	0.0971	12.3	0.1826	0.0596	26.9
		125	528.7	4.5	0.7205	0.1160	17.7	0.1859	0.0615	28.0
	500	25	519.3	3.4	0.7685	0.0813	8.5	0.1860	0.0616	28.1
		75	524.5	3.9	0.8411	0.0971	12.3	0.1867	0.0620	28.3
		125	530.8	4.5	0.9273	0.1160	17.7	0.1892	0.0635	29.2
	1000	25	522.3	3.4	0.7755	0.0813	8.5	0.1905	0.0643	29.7
		75	527.4	3.9	0.8484	0.0971	12.3	0.1911	0.0647	30.0
		125	533.4	4.5	0.9332	0.1160	17.7	0.1930	0.0659	30.7

Table 15D.6: Physical quantities for an unloaded, light gasoline truck on a paved surface

RF	C	QI	Fuel	Lubricants	Tire wear	Maint.-parts	Maint.-labor	Depre-ciation	Interest	Time per-distance
0	0	25	321.6	2.5	0.3994	0.0968	6.6	0.1616	0.0420	13.3
		75	329.6	3.1	0.4203	0.2639	11.1	0.1688	0.0444	14.4
		125	362.8	3.7	0.4243	0.4309	14.3	0.1898	0.0520	18.0
	500	25	348.6	2.5	0.4509	0.0968	6.6	0.1858	0.0505	17.3
		75	358.9	3.1	0.4956	0.2639	11.1	0.1896	0.0519	18.0
		125	390.2	3.7	0.5337	0.4309	14.3	0.2031	0.0571	20.4
	1000	25	386.3	2.5	0.4294	0.0968	6.6	0.2043	0.0576	20.6
		75	395.3	3.1	0.4749	0.2639	11.1	0.2067	0.0585	21.1
		125	421.6	3.7	0.5209	0.4309	14.3	0.2160	0.0623	22.9
40	0	25	347.3	2.5	0.5276	0.0968	6.6	0.1642	0.0429	13.7
		75	356.8	3.1	0.5700	0.2639	11.1	0.1711	0.0452	14.8
		125	390.3	3.7	0.6034	0.4309	14.3	0.1912	0.0525	18.3
	500	25	376.9	2.5	0.6449	0.0968	6.6	0.1873	0.0511	17.6
		75	386.7	3.1	0.7120	0.2639	11.1	0.1910	0.0525	18.2
		125	416.6	3.7	0.7784	0.4309	14.3	0.2041	0.0575	20.6
	1000	25	413.1	2.5	0.6288	0.0968	6.6	0.2052	0.0580	20.8
		75	421.5	3.1	0.6961	0.2639	11.1	0.2076	0.0589	21.3
		125	446.6	3.7	0.7678	0.4309	14.3	0.2168	0.0627	23.0
80	0	25	419.7	2.5	0.9244	0.0968	6.6	0.1740	0.0463	15.3
		75	429.2	3.1	1.0236	0.2639	11.1	0.1795	0.0482	16.2
		125	458.2	3.7	1.1376	0.4309	14.3	0.1968	0.0547	19.2
	500	25	445.4	2.5	1.2237	0.0968	6.6	0.1932	0.0533	18.6
		75	454.4	3.1	1.3574	0.2639	11.1	0.1965	0.0546	19.2
		125	480.2	3.7	1.5083	0.4309	14.3	0.2083	0.0592	21.4
	1000	25	475.5	2.5	1.2240	0.0968	6.6	0.2092	0.0596	21.6
		75	483.5	3.1	1.3566	0.2639	11.1	0.2115	0.0605	22.0
		125	505.8	3.7	1.5057	0.4309	14.3	0.2200	0.0640	23.6

Table 15D.7: Physical quantities for a loaded, light gasoline truck on a paved surface

RF	C	QI	Fuel	Lubricants	Tire wear	Maint.-parts	Maint.-labor	Depreciation	Interest	Time per-distance
0	0	25	360.6	2.5	0.3941	0.0968	6.6	0.1630	0.0425	13.5
		75	370.2	3.1	0.4222	0.2639	11.1	0.1700	0.0449	14.6
		125	402.7	3.7	0.4381	0.4309	14.3	0.1906	0.0523	18.1
	500	25	387.7	2.5	0.4570	0.0968	6.6	0.1890	0.0517	17.9
		75	400.2	3.1	0.5067	0.2639	11.1	0.1926	0.0531	18.5
		125	431.9	3.7	0.5540	0.4309	14.3	0.2053	0.0580	20.8
	1000	25	425.9	2.5	0.4404	0.0968	6.6	0.2077	0.0590	21.3
		75	437.0	3.1	0.4903	0.2639	11.1	0.2100	0.0599	21.7
		125	464.1	3.7	0.5430	0.4309	14.3	0.2187	0.0635	23.4
40	0	25	425.1	2.5	0.5999	0.0968	6.6	0.1714	0.0454	14.9
		75	437.1	3.1	0.6617	0.2639	11.1	0.1776	0.0475	15.9
		125	469.2	3.7	0.7270	0.4309	14.3	0.1956	0.0542	19.0
	500	25	455.3	2.5	0.7721	0.0968	6.6	0.1940	0.0536	18.7
		75	466.7	3.1	0.8580	0.2639	11.1	0.1973	0.0549	19.3
		125	494.9	3.7	0.9520	0.4309	14.3	0.2090	0.0595	21.5
	1000	25	488.7	2.5	0.7658	0.0968	6.6	0.2110	0.0603	21.9
		75	498.8	3.1	0.8511	0.2639	11.1	0.2133	0.0612	22.3
		125	523.1	3.7	0.9461	0.4309	14.3	0.2215	0.0646	24.0
80	0	25	596.9	2.5	1.2959	0.0968	6.6	0.1987	0.0554	19.6
		75	605.1	3.1	1.4339	0.2639	11.1	0.2022	0.0568	20.2
		125	622.7	3.7	1.6032	0.4309	14.3	0.2138	0.0614	22.4
	500	25	612.1	2.5	1.7278	0.0968	6.6	0.2125	0.0609	22.2
		75	619.4	3.1	1.9196	0.2639	11.1	0.2149	0.0619	22.6
		125	634.5	3.7	2.1444	0.4309	14.3	0.2234	0.0654	24.3
	1000	25	627.3	2.5	1.7394	0.0968	6.6	0.2247	0.0660	24.6
		75	634.1	3.1	1.9306	0.2639	11.1	0.2265	0.0668	25.0
		125	652.2	3.7	2.1508	0.4309	14.3	0.2330	0.0697	26.3

Table 15D.8: Physical quantities for an unloaded, light diesel truck on a paved surface

RF	C	QI	Fuel	Lubricants	Tire wear	Maint. parts	Maint. labor	Depreciation	Interest	Time per distance
0	0	25	164.7	2.5	0.3903	0.0968	6.6	0.1645	0.0430	13.8
		75	167.4	3.1	0.4142	0.2639	11.1	0.1713	0.0453	14.9
		125	177.1	3.7	0.4233	0.4309	14.3	0.1913	0.0526	18.3
	500	25	169.9	2.5	0.4491	0.0968	6.6	0.1873	0.0511	17.6
		75	174.4	3.1	0.4943	0.2639	11.1	0.1910	0.0525	18.2
		125	185.5	3.7	0.5340	0.4309	14.3	0.2041	0.0575	20.6
	1000	25	181.2	2.5	0.4295	0.0968	6.6	0.2052	0.0580	20.8
		75	185.6	3.1	0.4753	0.2639	11.1	0.2076	0.0589	21.3
		125	195.9	3.7	0.5219	0.4309	14.3	0.2168	0.0627	23.0
40	0	25	169.8	2.5	0.5131	0.0968	6.6	0.1699	0.0448	14.6
		75	174.1	3.1	0.5603	0.2639	11.1	0.1761	0.0470	15.7
		125	187.3	3.7	0.6050	0.4309	14.3	0.1946	0.0538	18.8
	500	25	180.7	2.5	0.6453	0.0968	6.6	0.1907	0.0523	18.2
		75	185.2	3.1	0.7141	0.2639	11.1	0.1942	0.0537	18.8
		125	197.1	3.7	0.7857	0.4309	14.3	0.2066	0.0585	21.1
	1000	25	194.0	2.5	0.6351	0.0968	6.6	0.2075	0.0589	21.2
		75	198.0	3.1	0.7036	0.2639	11.1	0.2099	0.0598	21.7
		125	208.3	3.7	0.7779	0.4309	14.3	0.2187	0.0635	23.4
80	0	25	212.8	2.5	0.9157	0.0968	6.6	0.1865	0.0508	17.4
		75	216.8	3.1	1.0195	0.2639	11.1	0.1912	0.0525	18.3
		125	226.8	3.7	1.1496	0.4309	14.3	0.2057	0.0582	20.9
	500	25	221.9	2.5	1.2344	0.0968	6.6	0.2024	0.0568	20.3
		75	225.2	3.1	1.3721	0.2639	11.1	0.2053	0.0580	20.8
		125	233.3	3.7	1.5351	0.4309	14.3	0.2156	0.0622	22.8
	1000	25	230.9	2.5	1.2470	0.0968	6.6	0.2161	0.0624	22.9
		75	233.7	3.1	1.3831	0.2639	11.1	0.2182	0.0633	23.3
		125	240.6	3.7	1.5402	0.4309	14.3	0.2259	0.0665	24.8

Table 15D.9: Physical quantities for a loaded, light diesel truck on a paved surface

RF	C	QI	Fuel	Lubricants	Tire wear	Maint.-parts	Maint.-labor	Depreciation	Interest	Time per-distance
0	0	25	187.2	2.5	0.3863	0.0968	6.6	0.1669	0.0438	14.1
		75	191.9	3.1	0.4167	0.2639	11.1	0.1734	0.0461	15.2
		125	203.6	3.7	0.4371	0.4309	14.3	0.1927	0.0531	18.5
	500	25	194.4	2.5	0.4558	0.0968	6.6	0.1909	0.0524	18.2
		75	200.6	3.1	0.5059	0.2639	11.1	0.1945	0.0538	18.8
		125	213.2	3.7	0.5545	0.4309	14.3	0.2067	0.0586	21.1
	1000	25	206.8	2.5	0.4408	0.0968	6.6	0.2090	0.0595	21.5
		75	212.8	3.1	0.4909	0.2639	11.1	0.2112	0.0604	21.9
		125	224.4	3.7	0.5442	0.4309	14.3	0.2198	0.0639	23.6
40	0	25	208.7	2.5	0.5858	0.0968	6.6	0.1822	0.0492	16.7
		75	214.6	3.1	0.6497	0.2639	11.1	0.1877	0.0512	17.6
		125	228.8	3.7	0.7238	0.4309	14.3	0.2034	0.0572	20.5
	500	25	220.9	2.5	0.7685	0.0968	6.6	0.2014	0.0564	20.1
		75	226.7	3.1	0.8554	0.2639	11.1	0.2045	0.0577	20.7
		125	239.3	3.7	0.9544	0.4309	14.3	0.2150	0.0619	22.7
	1000	25	234.4	2.5	0.7688	0.0968	6.6	0.2164	0.0625	22.9
		75	239.7	3.1	0.8550	0.2639	11.1	0.2186	0.0634	23.4
		125	250.6	3.7	0.9527	0.4309	14.3	0.2263	0.0667	24.9
80	0	25	315.0	2.5	1.3044	0.0968	6.6	0.2194	0.0637	23.5
		75	319.2	3.1	1.4440	0.2639	11.1	0.2224	0.0650	24.1
		125	327.9	3.7	1.6182	0.4309	14.3	0.2318	0.0691	26.1
	500	25	322.0	2.5	1.7437	0.0968	6.6	0.2302	0.0684	25.7
		75	325.9	3.1	1.9383	0.2639	11.1	0.2324	0.0694	26.2
		125	333.3	3.7	2.1695	0.4309	14.3	0.2394	0.0725	27.7
	1000	25	329.0	2.5	1.7605	0.0968	6.6	0.2399	0.0727	27.8
		75	332.6	3.1	1.9547	0.2639	11.1	0.2416	0.0735	28.1
		125	339.2	3.7	2.1806	0.4309	14.3	0.2471	0.0761	29.3

Table 15D.10: Physical quantities for an unloaded, medium truck on a paved surface

RF	C	QI	Fuel	Lubricants	Tire wear	Maint.-parts	Maint.-labor	Depreciation	Interest	Time per distance
0	0	25	227.9	3.4	0.1492	0.1140	7.2	0.1180	0.0373	13.3
		75	218.2	3.9	0.1483	0.3109	12.1	0.1252	0.0404	14.8
		125	213.8	4.5	0.1411	0.5077	15.6	0.1437	0.0491	19.1
	500	25	206.4	3.4	0.1518	0.1140	7.2	0.1339	0.0444	16.8
		75	209.4	3.9	0.1604	0.3109	12.1	0.1381	0.0464	17.7
		125	216.9	4.5	0.1640	0.5077	15.6	0.1510	0.0529	20.9
	1000	25	207.0	3.4	0.1417	0.1140	7.2	0.1468	0.0507	19.9
		75	212.2	3.9	0.1517	0.3109	12.1	0.1495	0.0521	20.5
		125	222.9	4.5	0.1597	0.5077	15.6	0.1588	0.0571	23.0
40	0	25	244.0	3.4	0.1888	0.1140	7.2	0.1221	0.0391	14.1
		75	241.4	3.9	0.1987	0.3109	12.1	0.1287	0.0420	15.6
		125	244.1	4.5	0.2063	0.5077	15.6	0.1458	0.0502	19.6
	500	25	235.8	3.4	0.2182	0.1140	7.2	0.1366	0.0457	17.4
		75	239.4	3.9	0.2352	0.3109	12.1	0.1405	0.0476	18.3
		125	247.6	4.5	0.2508	0.5077	15.6	0.1527	0.0538	21.4
	1000	25	238.8	3.4	0.2132	0.1140	7.2	0.1486	0.0516	20.3
		75	243.4	3.9	0.2305	0.3109	12.1	0.1512	0.0530	21.0
		125	253.2	4.5	0.2480	0.5077	15.6	0.1602	0.0578	23.4
80	0	25	317.2	3.4	0.3231	0.1140	7.2	0.1333	0.0441	16.6
		75	320.0	3.9	0.3579	0.3109	12.1	0.1388	0.0467	17.9
		125	325.6	4.5	0.4009	0.5077	15.6	0.1528	0.0538	21.4
	500	25	317.8	3.4	0.4188	0.1140	7.2	0.1450	0.0498	19.4
		75	321.4	3.9	0.4595	0.3109	12.1	0.1483	0.0515	20.2
		125	327.9	4.5	0.5088	0.5077	15.6	0.1586	0.0570	23.0
	1000	25	320.4	3.4	0.4258	0.1140	7.2	0.1549	0.0549	22.0
		75	324.3	3.9	0.4649	0.3109	12.1	0.1572	0.0562	22.6
		125	331.4	4.5	0.5106	0.5077	15.6	0.1651	0.0606	24.7

Table 15d.11: Physical quantities for a loaded, medium truck on a paved surface

RF	C	QI	Fuel	Lubricants	Tire wear	Maint.-parts	Maint.-labor	Depreciation	Interest	Time per-distance
0	0	25	280.6	3.4	0.1433	0.1140	7.2	0.1210	0.0386	13.9
		75	275.3	3.9	0.1478	0.3109	12.1	0.1277	0.0415	15.4
		125	271.6	4.5	0.1478	0.5077	15.6	0.1451	0.0498	19.5
	500	25	256.8	3.4	0.1527	0.1140	7.2	0.1380	0.0463	17.7
		75	263.8	3.9	0.1643	0.3109	12.1	0.1418	0.0482	18.6
		125	273.7	4.5	0.1733	0.5077	15.6	0.1536	0.0542	21.6
	1000	25	257.2	3.4	0.1459	0.1140	7.2	0.1509	0.0528	20.9
		75	266.0	3.9	0.1581	0.3109	12.1	0.1534	0.0541	21.6
		125	279.1	4.5	0.1698	0.5077	15.6	0.1618	0.0588	23.8
40	0	25	339.4	3.4	0.2203	0.1140	7.2	0.1351	0.0450	17.0
		75	344.8	3.9	0.2406	0.3109	12.1	0.1407	0.0476	18.4
		125	354.4	4.5	0.2643	0.5077	15.6	0.1544	0.0547	21.8
	500	25	340.4	3.4	0.2740	0.1140	7.2	0.1483	0.0515	20.2
		75	347.3	3.9	0.2998	0.3109	12.1	0.1515	0.0532	21.1
		125	358.0	4.5	0.3295	0.5077	15.6	0.1612	0.0584	23.7
	1000	25	344.7	3.4	0.2755	0.1140	7.2	0.1586	0.0569	22.9
		75	351.9	3.9	0.3007	0.3109	12.1	0.1608	0.0582	23.6
		125	362.6	4.5	0.3294	0.5077	15.6	0.1681	0.0623	25.6
80	0	25	533.6	3.4	0.5095	0.1140	7.2	0.1628	0.0593	24.1
		75	539.9	3.9	0.5612	0.3109	12.1	0.1663	0.0613	25.1
		125	548.0	4.5	0.6275	0.5077	15.6	0.1756	0.0669	27.8
	500	25	536.5	3.4	0.6609	0.1140	7.2	0.1711	0.0642	26.5
		75	542.3	3.9	0.7260	0.3109	12.1	0.1734	0.0656	27.2
		125	549.4	4.5	0.8064	0.5077	15.6	0.1801	0.0697	29.2
	1000	25	538.6	3.4	0.6713	0.1140	7.2	0.1780	0.0684	28.6
		75	544.1	3.9	0.7352	0.3109	12.1	0.1797	0.0695	29.1
		125	550.8	4.5	0.8113	0.5077	15.6	0.1849	0.0728	30.8

Table 15D.12: Physical quantities for an unloaded, heavy truck on a paved surface

RF	C	QI	Fuel	Lubricants	Tire wear	Maint.-parts	Maint.-labor	Depreciation	Interest	Time per distance
0	0	25	241.8	3.4	0.1842	0.1740	11.1	0.1129	0.0359	13.4
		75	233.1	3.9	0.1868	0.3371	15.7	0.1196	0.0388	14.9
		125	228.7	4.5	0.1837	0.5002	19.3	0.1369	0.0471	19.2
	500	25	219.8	3.4	0.1951	0.1740	11.1	0.1276	0.0425	16.9
		75	223.6	3.9	0.2072	0.3371	15.7	0.1316	0.0444	17.8
		125	231.4	4.5	0.2150	0.5002	19.3	0.1438	0.0506	21.0
	1000	25	219.7	3.4	0.1858	0.1740	11.1	0.1397	0.0485	19.9
		75	225.7	3.9	0.1990	0.3371	15.7	0.1423	0.0499	20.6
		125	236.9	4.5	0.2109	0.5002	19.3	0.1511	0.0546	23.1
40	0	25	267.0	3.4	0.2349	0.1740	11.1	0.1188	0.0385	14.8
		75	267.3	3.9	0.2505	0.3371	15.7	0.1248	0.0412	16.2
		125	271.8	4.5	0.2659	0.5002	19.3	0.1402	0.0488	20.1
	500	25	262.0	3.4	0.2787	0.1740	11.1	0.1317	0.0445	17.9
		75	266.4	3.9	0.3014	0.3371	15.7	0.1354	0.0463	18.8
		125	274.9	4.5	0.3246	0.5002	19.3	0.1465	0.0521	21.8
	1000	25	264.9	3.4	0.2760	0.1740	11.1	0.1426	0.0500	20.7
		75	270.1	3.9	0.2986	0.3371	15.7	0.1451	0.0513	21.4
		125	279.9	4.5	0.3226	0.5002	19.3	0.1533	0.0559	23.7
80	0	25	371.2	3.4	0.4145	0.1740	11.1	0.1338	0.0455	18.4
		75	375.2	3.9	0.4582	0.3371	15.7	0.1385	0.0479	19.6
		125	381.2	4.5	0.5135	0.5002	19.3	0.1503	0.0542	22.8
	500	25	372.7	3.4	0.5361	0.1740	11.1	0.1435	0.0505	20.9
		75	376.7	3.9	0.5879	0.3371	15.7	0.1464	0.0521	21.7
		125	383.0	4.5	0.6521	0.5002	19.3	0.1552	0.0570	24.3
	1000	25	374.7	3.4	0.5461	0.1740	11.1	0.1519	0.0551	23.3
		75	378.9	3.9	0.5960	0.3371	15.7	0.1540	0.0562	23.9
		125	385.7	4.5	0.6555	0.5002	19.3	0.1607	0.0602	25.9

411

Table 15D.13: Physical quantities for a loaded, heavy truck on a paved surface

RF	C	QI	Fuel	Lubricants	Tire wear	Maint.-parts	Maint.-labor	Depreciation	Interest	Time per-distance
0	0	25	313.2	3.4	0.1809	0.1740	11.1	0.1170	0.0377	14.4
		75	311.2	3.9	0.1893	0.3371	15.7	0.1232	0.0405	15.8
		125	308.7	4.5	0.1941	0.5002	19.3	0.1390	0.0482	19.7
	500	25	288.9	3.4	0.1988	0.1740	11.1	0.1331	0.0452	18.2
		75	298.4	3.9	0.2146	0.3371	15.7	0.1366	0.0469	19.1
		125	309.8	4.5	0.2290	0.5002	19.3	0.1473	0.0525	22.0
	1000	25	288.7	3.4	0.1928	0.1740	11.1	0.1452	0.0514	21.4
		75	299.8	3.9	0.2090	0.3371	15.7	0.1475	0.0526	22.0
		125	314.6	4.5	0.2256	0.5002	19.3	0.1552	0.0569	24.2
40	0	25	406.4	3.4	0.2888	0.1740	11.1	0.1374	0.0473	19.3
		75	414.4	3.9	0.3157	0.3371	15.7	0.1422	0.0498	20.6
		125	426.9	4.5	0.3483	0.5002	19.3	0.1538	0.0561	23.8
	500	25	410.0	3.4	0.3611	0.1740	11.1	0.1489	0.0534	22.4
		75	418.5	3.9	0.3950	0.3371	15.7	0.1517	0.0550	23.2
		125	430.7	4.5	0.4353	0.5002	19.3	0.1597	0.0596	25.6
	1000	25	414.7	3.4	0.3642	0.1740	11.1	0.1575	0.0583	24.9
		75	423.3	3.9	0.3975	0.3371	15.7	0.1595	0.0595	25.5
		125	435.1	4.5	0.4363	0.5002	19.3	0.1656	0.0631	27.4
80	0	25	671.3	3.4	0.6940	0.1740	11.1	0.1713	0.0668	29.3
		75	679.0	3.9	0.7574	0.3371	15.7	0.1739	0.0685	30.2
		125	688.6	4.5	0.8377	0.5002	19.3	0.1806	0.0731	32.5
	500	25	674.2	3.4	0.8661	0.1740	11.1	0.1774	0.0709	31.4
		75	681.5	3.9	0.9713	0.3371	15.7	0.1792	0.0721	32.0
		125	690.2	4.5	1.0742	0.5002	19.3	0.1843	0.0757	33.9
	1000	25	676.5	3.4	0.8955	0.1740	11.1	0.1826	0.0744	33.2
		75	683.6	3.9	0.9799	0.3371	15.7	0.1840	0.0755	33.8
		125	691.8	4.5	1.0794	0.5002	19.3	0.1880	0.0784	35.3

Table 15D.14: Physical quantities for an unloaded, articulated truck on a paved surface

RF	C	QI	Fuel	Lubricants	Tire wear	Maint.-parts	Maint.-labor	Depreciation	Interest	Time per-distance
0	0	25	342.0	5.4	0.2951	0.2306	27.9	0.0846	0.0306	12.3
		75	348.7	6.0	0.3005	0.3602	35.2	0.0958	0.0363	15.5
		125	402.9	6.6	0.3075	0.4899	41.3	0.1195	0.0505	23.4
	500	25	346.4	5.4	0.3184	0.2306	27.9	0.1029	0.0403	17.7
		75	363.7	6.0	0.3359	0.3602	35.2	0.1071	0.0427	19.1
		125	412.9	6.6	0.3527	0.4899	41.3	0.1229	0.0528	24.7
	1000	25	370.1	5.4	0.3142	0.2306	27.9	0.1145	0.0472	21.6
		75	385.5	6.0	0.3326	0.3602	35.2	0.1167	0.0487	22.4
		125	426.8	6.6	0.3517	0.4899	41.3	0.1273	0.0559	26.4
40	0	25	414.4	5.4	0.4013	0.2306	27.9	0.0909	0.0337	14.1
		75	423.3	6.0	0.4256	0.3602	35.2	0.0997	0.0384	16.7
		125	457.7	6.6	0.4488	0.4899	41.3	0.1206	0.0513	23.8
	500	25	420.4	5.4	0.4667	0.2306	27.9	0.1055	0.0418	18.5
		75	431.5	6.0	0.4982	0.3602	35.2	0.1093	0.0440	19.8
		125	464.7	6.6	0.5319	0.4899	41.3	0.1239	0.0535	25.1
	1000	25	433.6	5.4	0.4651	0.2306	27.9	0.1158	0.0481	22.1
		75	444.8	6.0	0.4966	0.3602	35.2	0.1180	0.0495	22.8
		125	475.0	6.6	0.5312	0.4899	41.3	0.1281	0.0565	26.7
80	0	25	668.8	5.4	0.7393	0.2306	27.9	0.1053	0.0416	18.5
		75	678.4	6.0	0.8017	0.3602	35.2	0.1113	0.0453	20.5
		125	694.3	6.6	0.8697	0.4899	41.3	0.1263	0.0552	26.0
	500	25	674.2	5.4	0.9081	0.2306	27.9	0.1150	0.0476	21.8
		75	682.2	6.0	0.9808	0.3602	35.2	0.1178	0.0494	22.8
		125	696.4	6.6	1.0666	0.4899	41.3	0.1288	0.0570	27.0
	1000	25	678.8	5.4	0.9138	0.2306	27.9	0.1224	0.0525	24.5
		75	686.3	6.0	0.9849	0.3602	35.2	0.1241	0.0537	25.2
		125	699.6	6.6	1.0673	0.4899	41.3	0.1322	0.0596	28.4

Table 15D.15: Physical quantities for a loaded, articulated truck on a paved surface

RF	C	QI	Fuel	Lubricants	Tire wear	Maint.-parts	Maint.-labor	Depreciation	Interest	Time per-distance
0	0	25	483.4	5.4	0.3049	0.2306	27.9	0.0869	0.0317	13.0
		75	497.2	6.0	0.3161	0.3602	35.2	0.0971	0.0370	15.9
		125	551.6	6.6	0.3283	0.4899	41.3	0.1198	0.0507	23.5
	500	25	484.8	5.4	0.3338	0.2306	27.9	0.1065	0.0423	18.9
		75	510.6	6.0	0.3559	0.3602	35.2	0.1100	0.0444	20.0
		125	563.0	6.6	0.3788	0.4899	41.3	0.1241	0.0537	25.2
	1000	25	507.1	5.4	0.3306	0.2306	27.9	0.1177	0.0493	22.7
		75	531.3	6.0	0.3532	0.3602	35.2	0.1195	0.0506	23.4
		125	577.5	6.6	0.3778	0.4899	41.3	0.1289	0.0571	27.1
40	0	25	721.3	5.4	0.5099	0.2306	27.9	0.1079	0.0432	19.3
		75	737.0	6.0	0.5487	0.3602	35.2	0.1141	0.0470	21.5
		125	758.4	6.6	0.5914	0.4899	41.3	0.1283	0.0567	26.9
	500	25	728.0	5.4	0.6103	0.2306	27.9	0.1190	0.0502	23.2
		75	741.6	6.0	0.6580	0.3602	35.2	0.1216	0.0519	24.2
		125	760.8	6.6	0.7136	0.4899	41.3	0.1313	0.0589	28.1
	1000	25	732.8	5.4	0.6121	0.2306	27.9	0.1261	0.0551	26.0
		75	746.0	6.0	0.6593	0.3602	35.2	0.1278	0.0563	26.6
		125	764.1	6.6	0.7137	0.4899	41.3	0.1349	0.0616	29.6
80	0	25	1230.3	5.4	1.1877	0.2306	27.9	0.1363	0.0627	30.2
		75	1244.9	6.0	1.2779	0.3602	35.2	0.1391	0.0650	31.5
		125	1264.6	6.6	1.3850	0.4899	41.3	0.1474	0.0721	35.4
	500	25	1235.0	5.4	1.4556	0.2306	27.9	0.1417	0.0671	32.7
		75	1248.6	6.0	1.5773	0.3602	35.2	0.1433	0.0685	33.4
		125	1266.2	6.6	1.7204	0.4899	41.3	0.1492	0.0737	36.3
	1000	25	1238.6	5.4	1.4609	0.2306	27.9	0.1458	0.0707	34.6
		75	1251.9	6.0	1.5818	0.3602	35.2	0.1469	0.0717	35.2
		125	1268.3	6.6	1.7220	0.4899	41.3	0.1514	0.0757	37.4

Table 15D.16: Physical quantities for a small car on an unpaved surface

RF	C	QI	Fuel	Lubricants	Tire wear	Maint.-parts	Maint.-labor	Depreciation	Interest	Time per distance
0	0	50	99.5	2.1	0.0730	0.1748	2.4	1.1111	0.3056	13.2
		150	111.4	3.3	0.1278	0.6433	4.9	1.1111	0.3056	16.5
		250	143.8	4.5	0.1552	1.2680	7.1	1.1111	0.3056	24.3
	500	50	117.4	2.1	0.0730	0.1748	2.4	1.1111	0.3056	19.5
		150	126.8	3.3	0.1278	0.6433	4.9	1.1111	0.3056	21.0
		250	152.1	4.5	0.1552	1.2680	7.1	1.1111	0.3056	26.3
	1000	50	128.8	2.1	0.0730	0.1748	2.4	1.1111	0.3056	22.5
		150	136.9	3.3	0.1278	0.6433	4.9	1.1111	0.3056	23.5
		250	158.5	4.5	0.1552	1.2680	7.1	1.1111	0.3056	27.8
40	0	50	100.2	2.1	0.0730	0.1748	2.4	1.1111	0.3056	13.5
		150	112.1	3.3	0.1278	0.6433	4.9	1.1111	0.3056	16.7
		250	144.1	4.5	0.1552	1.2680	7.1	1.1111	0.3056	24.4
	500	50	118.3	2.1	0.0730	0.1748	2.4	1.1111	0.3056	19.6
		150	127.4	3.3	0.1278	0.6433	4.9	1.1111	0.3056	21.1
		250	152.4	4.5	0.1552	1.2680	7.1	1.1111	0.3056	26.4
	1000	50	129.8	2.1	0.0730	0.1748	2.4	1.1111	0.3056	22.6
		150	137.5	3.3	0.1278	0.6433	4.9	1.1111	0.3056	23.6
		250	158.9	4.5	0.1552	1.2680	7.1	1.1111	0.3056	27.9
80	0	50	107.9	2.1	0.0730	0.1748	2.4	1.1111	0.3056	15.5
		150	119.0	3.3	0.1278	0.6433	4.9	1.1111	0.3056	17.9
		250	149.4	4.5	0.1552	1.2680	7.1	1.1111	0.3056	24.8
	500	50	125.0	2.1	0.0730	0.1748	2.4	1.1111	0.3056	20.5
		150	133.5	3.3	0.1278	0.6433	4.9	1.1111	0.3056	21.7
		250	157.5	4.5	0.1552	1.2680	7.1	1.1111	0.3056	26.7
	1000	50	135.7	2.1	0.0730	0.1748	2.4	1.1111	0.3056	23.2
		150	143.1	3.3	0.1278	0.6433	4.9	1.1111	0.3056	24.1
		250	163.7	4.5	0.1552	1.2680	7.1	1.1111	0.3056	28.2

Table 15D.17: Physical quantities for a medium car on an unpaved surface

RF	C	QI	Fuel	Lubricants	Tire wear	Maint.-parts	Maint.-labor	Depre-ciation	Interest	Time per-distance
0	0	50	206.9	2.1	0.0730	0.1805	2.4	1.0000	0.2750	12.6
		150	236.6	3.3	0.1278	0.6646	5.0	1.0000	0.2750	16.2
		250	315.1	4.5	0.1552	1.3098	7.2	1.0000	0.2750	24.1
	500	50	256.1	2.1	0.0730	0.1805	2.4	1.0000	0.2750	19.3
		150	276.4	3.3	0.1278	0.6646	5.0	1.0000	0.2750	20.8
		250	335.4	4.5	0.1552	1.3098	7.2	1.0000	0.2750	26.2
	1000	50	284.3	2.1	0.0730	0.1805	2.4	1.0000	0.2750	22.3
		150	301.2	3.3	0.1278	0.6646	5.0	1.0000	0.2750	23.4
		250	350.8	4.5	0.1552	1.3098	7.2	1.0000	0.2750	27.7
40	0	50	207.2	2.1	0.0730	0.1805	2.4	1.0000	0.2750	12.7
		150	236.9	3.3	0.1278	0.6646	5.0	1.0000	0.2750	16.2
		250	315.3	4.5	0.1552	1.3098	7.2	1.0000	0.2750	24.2
	500	50	256.8	2.1	0.0730	0.1805	2.4	1.0000	0.2750	19.3
		150	276.8	3.3	0.1278	0.6646	5.0	1.0000	0.2750	20.8
		250	335.5	4.5	0.1552	1.3098	7.2	1.0000	0.2750	26.2
	1000	50	285.3	2.1	0.0730	0.1805	2.4	1.0000	0.2750	22.4
		150	301.7	3.3	0.1278	0.6646	5.0	1.0000	0.2750	23.4
		250	351.0	4.5	0.1552	1.3098	7.2	1.0000	0.2750	27.7
80	0	50	218.7	2.1	0.0730	0.1805	2.4	1.0000	0.2750	14.0
		150	245.8	3.3	0.1278	0.6646	5.0	1.0000	0.2750	16.8
		250	321.4	4.5	0.1552	1.3098	7.2	1.0000	0.2750	24.3
	500	50	265.8	2.1	0.0730	0.1805	2.4	1.0000	0.2750	19.8
		150	284.3	3.3	0.1278	0.6646	5.0	1.0000	0.2750	21.1
		250	341.4	4.5	0.1552	1.3098	7.2	1.0000	0.2750	26.3
	1000	50	293.1	2.1	0.0730	0.1805	2.4	1.0000	0.2750	22.7
		150	308.6	3.3	0.1278	0.6646	5.0	1.0000	0.2750	23.7
		250	356.7	4.5	0.1552	1.3098	7.2	1.0000	0.2750	27.9

Table 15D.18: Physical quantities for a large car on an unpaved surface

RF	C	QI	Fuel	Lubricants	Tire wear	Maint.-parts	Maint.-labor	Depre-ciation	Interest	Time per distance
0	0	50	228.8	2.1	0.0730	0.1859	2.5	0.9091	0.2500	12.6
		150	270.3	3.3	0.1278	0.6844	5.0	0.9091	0.2500	16.2
		250	370.1	4.5	0.1552	1.3488	7.3	0.9091	0.2500	24.1
	500	50	297.6	2.1	0.0730	0.1859	2.5	0.9091	0.2500	19.3
		150	322.5	3.3	0.1278	0.6844	5.0	0.9091	0.2500	20.8
		250	395.3	4.5	0.1552	1.3488	7.3	0.9091	0.2500	26.2
	1000	50	333.7	2.1	0.0730	0.1859	2.5	0.9091	0.2500	22.3
		150	353.8	3.3	0.1278	0.6844	5.0	0.9091	0.2500	23.4
		250	414.4	4.5	0.1552	1.3488	7.3	0.9091	0.2500	27.7
40	0	50	232.2	2.1	0.0730	0.1859	2.5	0.9091	0.2500	12.7
		150	272.9	3.3	0.1278	0.6844	5.0	0.9091	0.2500	16.2
		250	372.0	4.5	0.1552	1.3488	7.3	0.9091	0.2500	24.1
	500	50	301.0	2.1	0.0730	0.1859	2.5	0.9091	0.2500	19.3
		150	325.2	3.3	0.1278	0.6844	5.0	0.9091	0.2500	20.8
		250	397.2	4.5	0.1552	1.3488	7.3	0.9091	0.2500	26.2
	1000	50	337.2	2.1	0.0730	0.1859	2.5	0.9091	0.2500	22.4
		150	356.5	3.3	0.1278	0.6844	5.0	0.9091	0.2500	23.4
		250	416.3	4.5	0.1552	1.3488	7.3	0.9091	0.2500	27.7
80	0	50	264.1	2.1	0.0730	0.1859	2.5	0.9091	0.2500	14.3
		150	293.1	3.3	0.1278	0.6844	5.0	0.9091	0.2500	17.0
		250	384.8	4.5	0.1552	1.3488	7.3	0.9091	0.2500	24.4
	500	50	319.0	2.1	0.0730	0.1859	2.5	0.9091	0.2500	19.9
		150	340.6	3.3	0.1278	0.6844	5.0	0.9091	0.2500	21.2
		250	409.2	4.5	0.1552	1.3488	7.3	0.9091	0.2500	26.4
	1000	50	352.4	2.1	0.0730	0.1859	2.5	0.9091	0.2500	22.8
		150	370.2	3.3	0.1278	0.6844	5.0	0.9091	0.2500	23.7
		250	427.8	4.5	0.1552	1.3488	7.3	0.9091	0.2500	27.9

Table 15D.19: Physical quantities for a utility vehicle on an unpaved surface

RF	C	QI	Fuel	Lubricants	Tire wear	Maint.-parts	Maint.-labor	Depre-ciation	Interest	Time per-distance
0	0	50	167.3	2.1	0.0730	0.2145	2.7	0.3780	0.0837	14.3
		150	183.8	3.3	0.1278	0.7896	5.5	0.4239	0.0984	18.3
		250	226.5	4.5	0.1552	1.5562	7.9	0.5069	0.1290	26.6
	500	50	181.2	2.1	0.0730	0.2145	2.7	0.4476	0.1066	20.5
		150	199.2	3.3	0.1278	0.7896	5.5	0.4692	0.1144	22.6
		250	236.8	4.5	0.1552	1.5562	7.9	0.5264	0.1370	28.8
	1000	50	192.2	2.1	0.0730	0.2145	2.7	0.4758	0.1169	23.3
		150	209.1	3.3	0.1278	0.7896	5.5	0.4916	0.1229	25.0
		250	243.6	4.5	0.1552	1.5562	7.9	0.5386	0.1423	30.2
40	0	50	168.1	2.1	0.0730	0.2145	2.7	0.3842	0.0856	14.8
		150	185.0	3.3	0.1278	0.7896	5.5	0.4279	0.0998	18.6
		250	228.1	4.5	0.1552	1.5562	7.9	0.5086	0.1297	26.8
	500	50	186.3	2.1	0.0730	0.2145	2.7	0.4504	0.1076	20.8
		150	202.5	3.3	0.1278	0.7896	5.5	0.4715	0.1153	22.9
		250	238.7	4.5	0.1552	1.5562	7.9	0.5278	0.1376	29.0
	1000	50	198.4	2.1	0.0730	0.2145	2.7	0.4778	0.1176	23.5
		150	213.1	3.3	0.1278	0.7896	5.5	0.4935	0.1237	25.2
		250	245.8	4.5	0.1552	1.5562	7.9	0.5398	0.1428	30.4
80	0	50	200.6	2.1	0.0730	0.2145	2.7	0.4120	0.0945	17.2
		150	216.5	3.3	0.1278	0.7896	5.5	0.4446	0.1055	20.2
		250	256.1	4.5	0.1552	1.5562	7.9	0.5156	0.1325	27.6
	500	50	218.5	2.1	0.0730	0.2145	2.7	0.4636	0.1124	22.1
		150	231.6	3.3	0.1278	0.7896	5.5	0.4819	0.1192	23.9
		250	266.3	4.5	0.1552	1.5562	7.9	0.5335	0.1401	29.6
	1000	50	228.2	2.1	0.0730	0.2145	2.7	0.4876	0.1214	24.5
		150	241.6	3.3	0.1278	0.7896	5.5	0.5017	0.1269	26.0
		250	273.1	4.5	0.1552	1.5562	7.9	0.5449	0.1450	31.0

Table 15D.20: Physical quantities for a loaded bus on an unpaved surface

RF	C	QI	Fuel	Lubricants	Tire wear	Maint.-parts	Maint.-labor	Depre-ciation	Interest	Time per-distance
0	0	50	262.8	3.7	0.1492	0.0888	10.2	0.1462	0.0413	15.8
		150	276.1	4.8	0.1646	0.1268	21.3	0.1611	0.0481	19.9
		250	321.6	6.0	0.1855	0.1775	43.9	0.1895	0.0637	29.3
	500	50	263.2	3.7	0.1628	0.0888	10.2	0.1662	0.0507	21.5
		150	284.8	4.8	0.1931	0.1268	21.3	0.1733	0.0544	23.7
		250	328.7	6.0	0.2292	0.1775	43.9	0.1937	0.0663	30.9
	1000	50	270.5	3.7	0.1595	0.0888	10.2	0.1742	0.0549	24.0
		150	291.9	4.8	0.1905	0.1268	21.3	0.1794	0.0577	25.7
		250	333.7	6.0	0.2283	0.1775	43.9	0.1964	0.0681	32.0
40	0	50	323.3	3.7	0.2590	0.0888	10.2	0.1582	0.0468	19.1
		150	342.2	4.8	0.3092	0.1268	21.3	0.1695	0.0524	22.5
		250	382.5	6.0	0.3703	0.1775	43.9	0.1930	0.0659	30.7
	500	50	334.1	3.7	0.3230	0.0888	10.2	0.1729	0.0542	23.6
		150	351.9	4.8	0.3892	0.1268	21.3	0.1790	0.0575	25.6
		250	388.5	6.0	0.4743	0.1775	43.9	0.1967	0.0683	32.1
	1000	50	340.9	3.7	0.3231	0.0888	10.2	0.1794	0.0577	25.7
		150	358.1	4.8	0.3889	0.1268	21.3	0.1840	0.0604	27.4
		250	392.7	6.0	0.4739	0.1775	43.9	0.1991	0.0699	33.1
80	0	50	520.7	3.7	0.6354	0.0888	10.2	0.1845	0.0607	27.5
		150	533.9	4.8	0.7593	0.1268	21.3	0.1902	0.0641	29.6
		250	554.2	6.0	0.9234	0.1775	43.9	0.2050	0.0740	35.6
	500	50	525.5	3.7	0.8120	0.0888	10.2	0.1918	0.0652	30.2
		150	537.6	4.8	0.9818	0.1268	21.3	0.1957	0.0676	31.7
		250	556.4	6.0	1.2070	0.1775	43.9	0.2076	0.0758	36.7
	1000	50	528.1	3.7	0.8158	0.0888	10.2	0.1956	0.0676	31.7
		150	539.9	4.8	0.9847	0.1268	21.3	0.1988	0.0697	33.0
		250	557.9	6.0	1.2078	0.1775	43.9	0.2093	0.0771	37.5

Table 15D.21: Physical quantities for an unloaded, light gasoline truck on an unpaved surface

RF	C	QI	Fuel	Lubricants	Tire wear	Maint.-parts	Maint.-labor	Depreciation	Interest	Time per-distance
0	0	50	330.5	2.8	0.3928	0.1803	9.1	0.1718	0.0455	14.9
		150	399.5	3.9	0.4285	0.5145	15.7	0.2064	0.0584	21.0
		250	559.0	5.1	0.4978	0.8486	20.4	0.2591	0.0820	32.1
	500	50	397.4	2.8	0.4490	0.1803	9.1	0.2083	0.0592	21.4
		150	449.7	3.9	0.5428	0.5145	15.7	0.2259	0.0665	24.8
		250	583.5	5.1	0.6573	0.8486	20.4	0.2661	0.0855	33.8
	1000	50	432.3	2.8	0.4397	0.1803	9.1	0.2219	0.0648	24.0
		150	477.1	3.9	0.5369	0.5145	15.7	0.2354	0.0707	26.8
		250	598.7	5.1	0.6557	0.8486	20.4	0.2703	0.0877	34.8
40	0	50	358.4	2.8	0.5385	0.1803	9.1	0.1739	0.0462	15.3
		150	425.3	3.9	0.6209	0.5145	15.7	0.2073	0.0588	21.2
		250	579.4	5.1	0.7379	0.8486	20.4	0.2594	0.0821	32.2
	500	50	423.6	2.8	0.6594	0.1803	9.1	0.2092	0.0595	21.5
		150	473.6	3.9	0.8042	0.5145	15.7	0.2265	0.0668	25.0
		250	603.4	5.1	0.9838	0.8486	20.4	0.2664	0.0856	33.8
	1000	50	457.1	2.8	0.6516	0.1803	9.1	0.2226	0.0651	24.2
		150	500.1	3.9	0.7989	0.5145	15.7	0.2359	0.0710	26.9
		250	618.3	5.1	0.9822	0.8486	20.4	0.2706	0.0878	34.9
80	0	50	430.3	2.8	0.9774	0.1803	9.1	0.1818	0.0491	16.6
		150	488.0	3.9	1.1953	0.5145	15.7	0.2113	0.0604	21.9
		250	627.3	5.1	1.4574	0.8486	20.4	0.2608	0.0828	32.5
	500	50	484.9	2.8	1.2878	0.1803	9.1	0.2129	0.0610	22.3
		150	529.8	3.9	1.5860	0.5145	15.7	0.2291	0.0679	25.5
		250	649.6	5.1	1.9623	0.8486	20.4	0.2676	0.0863	34.1
	1000	50	513.9	2.8	1.2854	0.1803	9.1	0.2253	0.0663	24.7
		150	553.4	3.9	1.5833	0.5145	15.7	0.2381	0.0719	27.4
		250	663.6	5.1	1.9611	0.8486	20.4	0.2717	0.0884	35.1

Table 15D.22: Physical quantities for a loaded, light gasoline truck on an unpaved surface

RF	C	QI	Fuel	Lubricants	Tire wear	Maint.-parts	Maint.-labor	Depreciation	Interest	Time per distance
0	0	50	369.1	2.8	0.3955	0.1803	9.1	0.1728	0.0459	15.1
		150	438.5	3.9	0.4474	0.5145	15.7	0.2069	0.0586	21.1
		250	598.7	5.1	0.5313	0.8486	20.4	0.2593	0.0821	32.1
	500	50	431.0	2.8	0.4646	0.1803	9.1	0.2087	0.0593	21.5
		150	486.8	3.9	0.5705	0.5145	15.7	0.2262	0.0667	24.9
		250	622.8	5.1	0.7030	0.8486	20.4	0.2663	0.0856	33.8
	1000	50	464.8	2.8	0.4566	0.1803	9.1	0.2222	0.0649	24.1
		150	513.5	3.9	0.5652	0.5145	15.7	0.2357	0.0709	26.9
		250	637.8	5.1	0.7015	0.8486	20.4	0.2705	0.0878	34.8
40	0	50	437.1	2.8	0.6288	0.1803	9.1	0.1799	0.0484	16.3
		150	500.9	3.9	0.7600	0.5145	15.7	0.2105	0.0601	21.8
		250	646.1	5.1	0.9246	0.8486	20.4	0.2606	0.0827	32.4
	500	50	493.3	2.8	0.8071	0.1803	9.1	0.2120	0.0607	22.1
		150	543.5	3.9	0.9973	0.5145	15.7	0.2286	0.0677	25.4
		250	668.6	5.1	1.2380	0.8486	20.4	0.2674	0.0862	34.1
	1000	50	523.1	2.8	0.8026	0.1803	9.1	0.2247	0.0660	24.6
		150	567.5	3.9	0.9938	0.5145	15.7	0.2377	0.0717	27.3
		250	682.7	5.1	1.2368	0.8486	20.4	0.2715	0.0883	35.1
80	0	50	604.3	2.8	1.3693	0.1803	9.1	0.2035	0.0573	20.5
		150	638.3	3.9	1.6965	0.5145	15.7	0.2246	0.0660	24.6
		250	754.8	5.1	2.1019	0.8486	20.4	0.2664	0.0856	33.8
	500	50	630.5	2.8	1.8318	0.1803	9.1	0.2255	0.0663	24.7
		150	668.8	3.9	2.2726	0.5145	15.7	0.2388	0.0723	27.5
		250	773.7	5.1	2.8399	0.8486	20.4	0.2725	0.0888	35.3
	1000	50	649.4	2.8	1.8365	0.1803	9.1	0.2354	0.0707	26.8
		150	687.6	3.9	2.2745	0.5145	15.7	0.2463	0.0757	29.2
		250	785.6	5.1	2.8396	0.8486	20.4	0.2762	0.0908	36.3

Table 15D.23: Physical quantities for an unloaded, light diesel truck on an unpaved surface

RF	C	QI	Fuel	Lubricants	Tire wear	Maint.-parts	Maint.-labor	Depre-ciation	Interest	Time per-distance
0	0	50	166.5	2.8	0.3882	0.1803	9.1	0.1740	0.0463	15.3
		150	189.3	3.9	0.4290	0.5145	15.7	0.2074	0.0588	21.2
		250	249.1	5.1	0.5001	0.8486	20.4	0.2594	0.0821	32.2
	500	50	185.6	2.8	0.4494	0.1803	9.1	0.2091	0.0595	21.5
		150	206.4	3.9	0.5444	0.5145	15.7	0.2265	0.0668	25.0
		250	258.2	5.1	0.6606	0.8486	20.4	0.2664	0.0856	33.8
	1000	50	197.4	2.8	0.4405	0.1803	9.1	0.2225	0.0651	24.2
		150	216.2	3.9	0.5387	0.5145	15.7	0.2359	0.0710	26.9
		250	263.9	5.1	0.6590	0.8486	20.4	0.2706	0.0878	34.9
40	0	50	174.3	2.8	0.5315	0.1803	9.1	0.1785	0.0479	16.1
		150	200.8	3.9	0.6273	0.5145	15.7	0.2097	0.0598	21.7
		250	261.2	5.1	0.7512	0.8486	20.4	0.2603	0.0825	32.4
	500	50	198.4	2.8	0.6668	0.1803	9.1	0.2113	0.0604	22.0
		150	218.9	3.9	0.8162	0.5145	15.7	0.2281	0.0675	25.3
		250	270.4	5.1	1.0021	0.8486	20.4	0.2671	0.0860	34.0
	1000	50	210.9	2.8	0.6608	0.1803	9.1	0.2241	0.0658	24.5
		150	229.0	3.9	0.8119	0.5145	15.7	0.2372	0.0715	27.2
		250	276.2	5.1	1.0007	0.8486	20.4	0.2713	0.0882	35.0
80	0	50	217.1	2.8	0.9759	0.1803	9.1	0.1930	0.0532	18.6
		150	235.8	3.9	1.2180	0.5145	15.7	0.2183	0.0633	23.3
		250	290.5	5.1	1.5023	0.8486	20.4	0.2637	0.0842	33.2
	500	50	233.9	2.8	1.3140	0.1803	9.1	0.2194	0.0637	23.5
		150	250.2	3.9	1.6268	0.5145	15.7	0.2342	0.0702	26.5
		250	299.3	5.1	2.0245	0.8486	20.4	0.2701	0.0876	34.7
	1000	50	242.3	2.8	1.3173	0.1803	9.1	0.2305	0.0685	25.8
		150	259.6	3.9	1.6273	0.5145	15.7	0.2423	0.0739	28.3
		250	304.9	5.1	2.0238	0.8486	20.4	0.2740	0.0896	35.7

Table 15D.24: Physical quantities for a loaded, light diesel truck on an unpaved surface

RF	C	QI	Fuel	Lubricants	Tire wear	Maint.-parts	Maint.-labor	Depreciation	Interest	Time per-distance
0	0	50	190.3	2.8	0.3915	0.1803	9.1	0.1759	0.0469	15.6
		150	216.6	3.9	0.4479	0.5145	15.7	0.2084	0.0592	21.4
		250	279.2	5.1	0.5336	0.8486	20.4	0.2598	0.0823	32.3
	500	50	209.6	2.8	0.4650	0.1803	9.1	0.2099	0.0598	21.7
		150	233.6	3.9	0.5721	0.5145	15.7	0.2272	0.0671	25.1
		250	288.3	5.1	0.7063	0.8486	20.4	0.2667	0.0858	33.9
	1000	50	221.4	2.8	0.4575	0.1803	9.1	0.2231	0.0653	24.3
		150	243.2	3.9	0.5671	0.5145	15.7	0.2365	0.0712	27.0
		250	294.0	5.1	0.7049	0.8486	20.4	0.2709	0.0880	34.9
40	0	50	214.0	2.8	0.6190	0.1803	9.1	0.1895	0.0519	17.9
		150	242.3	3.9	0.7623	0.5145	15.7	0.2166	0.0626	23.0
		250	302.6	5.1	0.9367	0.8486	20.4	0.2631	0.0840	33.0
	500	50	236.9	2.8	0.8105	0.1803	9.1	0.2174	0.0629	23.1
		150	259.3	3.9	1.0060	0.5145	15.7	0.2329	0.0696	26.3
		250	311.5	5.1	1.2551	0.8486	20.4	0.2696	0.0873	34.6
	1000	50	248.7	2.8	0.8090	0.1803	9.1	0.2289	0.0678	25.5
		150	268.8	3.9	1.0042	0.5145	15.7	0.2413	0.0734	28.1
		250	317.1	5.1	1.2541	0.8486	20.4	0.2736	0.0894	35.6
80	0	50	318.6	2.8	1.3792	0.1803	9.1	0.2233	0.0654	24.3
		150	335.3	3.9	1.7165	0.5145	15.7	0.2405	0.0730	27.9
		250	369.7	5.1	2.1418	0.8486	20.4	0.2754	0.0904	36.1
	500	50	330.7	2.8	1.8543	0.1803	9.1	0.2406	0.0731	27.9
		150	344.2	3.9	2.3066	0.5145	15.7	0.2519	0.0784	30.4
		250	374.9	5.1	2.8960	0.8486	20.4	0.2807	0.0933	37.4
	1000	50	336.9	2.8	1.8630	0.1803	9.1	0.2486	0.0768	29.7
		150	349.3	3.9	2.3116	0.5145	15.7	0.2580	0.0814	31.8
		250	378.3	5.1	2.8967	0.8486	20.4	0.2839	0.0951	38.3

Table 15D.25: Physical quantities for an unloaded, medium truck on an unpaved surface

RF	C	QI	Fuel	Lubricants	Tire wear	Maint.-parts	Maint.-labor	Depre-ciation	Interest	Time per-distance
0	0	50	212.2	3.7	0.1389	0.2125	9.9	0.1285	0.0419	15.5
		150	223.4	4.8	0.1392	0.6061	17.1	0.1573	0.0563	22.6
		250	286.4	6.0	0.1516	0.9998	22.2	0.1967	0.0810	34.8
	500	50	214.5	3.7	0.1427	0.2125	9.9	0.1556	0.0553	22.2
		150	237.6	4.8	0.1618	0.6061	17.1	0.1706	0.0639	26.3
		250	295.1	6.0	0.1849	0.9998	22.2	0.2012	0.0843	36.4
	1000	50	223.4	3.7	0.1394	0.2125	9.9	0.1648	0.0604	24.7
		150	245.7	4.8	0.1599	0.6061	17.1	0.1766	0.0675	28.1
		250	300.1	6.0	0.1845	0.9998	22.2	0.2036	0.0862	37.3
40	0	50	238.4	3.7	0.1900	0.2125	9.9	0.1316	0.0433	16.2
		150	253.5	4.8	0.2101	0.6061	17.1	0.1588	0.0570	23.0
		250	311.3	6.0	0.2391	0.9998	22.2	0.1972	0.0814	35.0
	500	50	245.9	3.7	0.2192	0.2125	9.9	0.1571	0.0561	22.5
		150	266.6	4.8	0.2557	0.6061	17.1	0.1716	0.0644	26.6
		250	319.5	6.0	0.3006	0.9998	22.2	0.2016	0.0847	36.6
	1000	50	254.0	3.7	0.2169	0.2125	9.9	0.1659	0.0611	25.0
		150	273.9	4.8	0.2542	0.6061	17.1	0.1774	0.0680	28.4
		250	324.2	6.0	0.3002	0.9998	22.2	0.2040	0.0865	37.5
80	0	50	318.8	3.7	0.3476	0.2125	9.9	0.1410	0.0478	18.4
		150	332.2	4.8	0.4212	0.6061	17.1	0.1639	0.0599	24.4
		250	375.0	6.0	0.5010	0.9998	22.2	0.1990	0.0827	35.6
	500	50	325.2	3.7	0.4467	0.2125	9.9	0.1622	0.0590	23.9
		150	340.5	4.8	0.5356	0.6061	17.1	0.1752	0.0666	27.7
		250	381.6	6.0	0.6471	0.9998	22.2	0.2032	0.0859	37.2
	1000	50	330.2	3.7	0.4478	0.2125	9.9	0.1699	0.0634	26.1
		150	345.5	4.8	0.5356	0.6061	17.1	0.1805	0.0699	29.3
		250	385.4	6.0	0.6468	0.9998	22.2	0.2055	0.0877	38.1

424

Table 15D.26: Physical quantities for a loaded, medium truck on an unpaved surface

RF	C	QI	Fuel	Lubricants	Tire wear	Maint.-parts	Maint.-labor	Depre-ciation	Interest	Time per-distance
0	0	50	266.9	3.7	0.1396	0.2125	9.9	0.1305	0.0428	16.0
		150	280.2	4.8	0.1485	0.6061	17.1	0.1583	0.0568	22.9
		250	344.4	6.0	0.1675	0.9998	22.2	0.1971	0.0813	34.9
	500	50	264.0	3.7	0.1501	0.2125	9.9	0.1565	0.0558	22.4
		150	292.1	4.8	0.1749	0.6061	17.1	0.1712	0.0642	26.5
		250	352.7	6.0	0.2061	0.9998	22.2	0.2015	0.0846	36.5
	1000	50	271.4	3.7	0.1474	0.2125	9.9	0.1654	0.0608	24.8
		150	299.2	4.8	0.1733	0.6061	17.1	0.1771	0.0678	28.3
		250	357.4	6.0	0.2056	0.9998	22.2	0.2039	0.0864	37.4
40	0	50	342.1	3.7	0.2322	0.2125	9.9	0.1427	0.0486	18.9
		150	363.5	4.8	0.2760	0.6061	17.1	0.1652	0.0607	24.8
		250	413.3	6.0	0.3272	0.9998	22.2	0.1997	0.0832	35.9
	500	50	350.4	3.7	0.2877	0.2125	9.9	0.1632	0.0596	24.2
		150	372.5	4.8	0.3449	0.6061	17.1	0.1762	0.0673	28.0
		250	419.8	6.0	0.4174	0.9998	22.2	0.2038	0.0864	37.4
	1000	50	355.9	3.7	0.2876	0.2125	9.9	0.1708	0.0639	26.4
		150	377.7	4.8	0.3445	0.6061	17.1	0.1813	0.0705	29.6
		250	423.6	6.0	0.4171	0.9998	22.2	0.2061	0.0881	38.3
80	0	50	537.8	3.7	0.5429	0.2125	9.9	0.1676	0.0620	25.5
		150	552.8	4.8	0.6629	0.6061	17.1	0.1830	0.0716	30.1
		250	577.9	6.0	0.8048	0.9998	22.2	0.2089	0.0903	39.3
	500	50	542.0	3.7	0.7047	0.2125	9.9	0.1812	0.0704	29.6
		150	555.1	4.8	0.8549	0.6061	17.1	0.1907	0.0768	32.7
		250	581.2	6.0	1.0495	0.9998	22.2	0.2122	0.0930	40.7
	1000	50	543.5	3.7	0.7089	0.2125	9.9	0.1865	0.0739	31.3
		150	556.7	4.8	0.8569	0.6061	17.1	0.1945	0.0794	34.0
		250	583.1	6.0	1.0498	0.9998	22.2	0.2140	0.0945	41.4

Table 15D.27: Physical quantities for an unloaded, heavy truck on an unpaved surface

RF	C	QI	Fuel	Lubricants	Tire wear	Maint.-parts	Maint.-labor	Depreciation	Interest	Time per-distance
0	0	50	226.4	3.7	0.1768	0.2555	13.6	0.1226	0.0402	15.6
		150	238.0	4.8	0.1835	0.5818	20.9	0.1497	0.0538	22.7
		250	301.4	6.0	0.2030	0.9081	26.3	0.1869	0.0775	34.8
	500	50	227.3	3.7	0.1885	0.2555	13.6	0.1481	0.0530	22.2
		150	251.7	4.8	0.2151	0.5818	20.9	0.1622	0.0611	26.4
		250	310.0	6.0	0.2481	0.9081	26.3	0.1911	0.0807	36.4
	1000	50	235.8	3.7	0.1852	0.2555	13.6	0.1567	0.0578	24.7
		150	259.5	4.8	0.2133	0.5818	20.9	0.1678	0.0646	28.2
		250	315.0	6.0	0.2476	0.9081	26.3	0.1934	0.0825	37.4
40	0	50	264.5	3.7	0.2411	0.2555	13.6	0.1274	0.0424	16.8
		150	280.8	4.8	0.2733	0.5818	20.9	0.1520	0.0551	23.3
		250	336.2	6.0	0.3143	0.9081	26.3	0.1877	0.0781	35.1
	500	50	271.7	3.7	0.2853	0.2555	13.6	0.1504	0.0542	22.8
		150	292.6	4.8	0.3342	0.5818	20.9	0.1638	0.0621	26.9
		250	344.0	6.0	0.3952	0.9081	26.3	0.1918	0.0812	36.7
	1000	50	279.0	3.7	0.2836	0.2555	13.6	0.1584	0.0588	25.2
		150	299.3	4.8	0.3330	0.5818	20.9	0.1692	0.0654	28.6
		250	348.5	6.0	0.3948	0.9081	26.3	0.1940	0.0830	37.6
80	0	50	373.8	3.7	0.4452	0.2555	13.6	0.1403	0.0488	20.1
		150	386.9	4.8	0.5409	0.5818	20.9	0.1597	0.0596	25.6
		250	424.1	6.0	0.6469	0.9081	26.3	0.1907	0.0804	36.3
	500	50	379.0	3.7	0.5737	0.2555	13.6	0.1581	0.0587	25.1
		150	393.4	4.8	0.6891	0.5818	20.9	0.1695	0.0656	28.7
		250	429.7	6.0	0.8354	0.9081	26.3	0.1945	0.0833	37.8
	1000	50	382.7	3.7	0.5763	0.2555	13.6	0.1648	0.0626	27.2
		150	397.3	4.8	0.6899	0.5818	20.9	0.1741	0.0686	30.2
		250	433.0	6.0	0.8353	0.9081	26.3	0.1966	0.0850	38.6

Table 15D.28: Physical quantities for a loaded, heavy truck on an unpaved surface

RF	C	QI	Fuel	Lubricants	Tire wear	Maint.-parts	Maint.-labor	Depreciation	Interest	Time per distance
0	0	50	301.4	3.7	0.1802	0.2555	13.6	0.1256	0.0416	16.4
		150	316.8	4.8	0.1970	0.5818	20.9	0.1512	0.0547	23.1
		250	381.5	6.0	0.2253	0.9081	26.3	0.1874	0.0779	35.0
	500	50	295.7	3.7	0.1994	0.2555	13.6	0.1493	0.0536	22.5
		150	327.0	4.8	0.2336	0.5818	20.9	0.1632	0.0617	26.7
		250	389.4	6.0	0.2776	0.9081	26.3	0.1916	0.0811	36.6
	1000	50	302.1	3.7	0.1968	0.2555	13.6	0.1576	0.0583	25.0
		150	333.5	4.8	0.2321	0.5818	20.9	0.1686	0.0651	28.4
		250	393.9	6.0	0.2771	0.9081	26.3	0.1938	0.0828	37.5
40	0	50	411.4	3.7	0.3051	0.2555	13.6	0.1438	0.0506	21.0
		150	436.6	4.8	0.3650	0.5818	20.9	0.1627	0.0614	26.5
		250	484.1	6.0	0.4363	0.9081	26.3	0.1924	0.0817	37.0
	500	50	420.4	3.7	0.3807	0.2555	13.6	0.1607	0.0601	25.9
		150	444.4	4.8	0.4577	0.5818	20.9	0.1719	0.0672	29.5
		250	489.6	6.0	0.5569	0.9081	26.3	0.1960	0.0845	38.4
	1000	50	425.2	3.7	0.3815	0.2555	13.6	0.1669	0.0640	27.9
		150	448.7	4.8	0.4578	0.5818	20.9	0.1762	0.0700	31.0
		250	492.8	6.0	0.5567	0.9081	26.3	0.1980	0.0861	39.2
80	0	50	676.1	3.7	0.7308	0.2555	13.6	0.1746	0.0690	30.4
		150	694.4	4.8	0.8819	0.5818	20.9	0.1863	0.0771	34.6
		250	716.6	6.0	1.0688	0.9081	26.3	0.2065	0.0933	42.9
	500	50	680.6	3.7	0.9382	0.2555	13.6	0.1846	0.0759	34.0
		150	696.9	4.8	1.1359	0.5818	20.9	0.1922	0.0815	36.9
		250	718.5	6.0	1.3939	0.9081	26.3	0.2091	0.0955	44.1
	1000	50	682.3	3.7	0.9425	0.2555	13.6	0.1886	0.0788	35.5
		150	698.0	4.8	1.1382	0.5818	20.9	0.1950	0.0838	38.0
		250	719.6	6.0	1.3943	0.9081	26.3	0.2105	0.0968	44.7

Table 15D.29: Physical quantities for an unloaded, articulated truck on an unpaved surface

RF	C	QI	Fuel	Lubricants	Tire wear	Maint.-parts	Maint.-labor	Depre-ciation	Interest	Time per-distance
0	0	50	365.2	5.7	0.2870	0.2954	31.7	0.1103	0.0446	20.1
		150	455.0	6.9	0.3135	0.5547	44.0	0.1340	0.0609	29.2
		250	629.9	8.1	0.3505	0.8141	53.7	0.1669	0.0917	46.3
	500	50	406.5	5.7	0.3209	0.2954	31.7	0.1255	0.0547	25.7
		150	475.5	6.9	0.3614	0.5547	44.0	0.1393	0.0652	31.6
		250	635.7	8.1	0.4143	0.8141	53.7	0.1679	0.0928	46.9
	1000	50	419.4	5.7	0.3202	0.2954	31.7	0.1294	0.0575	27.3
		150	483.2	6.9	0.3611	0.5547	44.0	0.1412	0.0667	32.4
		250	638.2	8.1	0.4142	0.8141	53.7	0.1683	0.0933	47.2
40	0	50	431.5	5.7	0.4124	0.2954	31.7	0.1121	0.0457	20.7
		150	497.2	6.9	0.4611	0.5547	44.0	0.1345	0.0613	29.4
		250	651.3	8.1	0.5251	0.8141	53.7	0.1670	0.0918	46.4
	500	50	458.8	5.7	0.4789	0.2954	31.7	0.1263	0.0552	26.0
		150	514.0	6.9	0.5494	0.5547	44.0	0.1397	0.0655	31.8
		250	656.8	8.1	0.6406	0.8141	53.7	0.1680	0.0929	47.0
	1000	50	468.4	5.7	0.4783	0.2954	31.7	0.1300	0.0579	27.5
		150	520.4	6.9	0.5492	0.5547	44.0	0.1416	0.0670	32.6
		250	659.1	8.1	0.6405	0.8141	53.7	0.1684	0.0934	47.3
80	0	50	680.1	5.7	0.7850	0.2954	31.7	0.1197	0.0507	23.5
		150	708.8	6.9	0.9025	0.5547	44.0	0.1376	0.0638	30.8
		250	784.6	8.1	1.0486	0.8141	53.7	0.1677	0.0926	46.8
	500	50	688.6	5.7	0.9504	0.2954	31.7	0.1306	0.0583	27.8
		150	714.9	6.9	1.1122	0.5547	44.0	0.1422	0.0675	32.9
		250	788.0	8.1	1.3192	0.8141	53.7	0.1686	0.0937	47.4
	1000	50	691.8	5.7	0.9508	0.2954	31.7	0.1336	0.0607	29.1
		150	717.3	6.9	1.1122	0.5547	44.0	0.1438	0.0689	33.7
		250	789.5	8.1	1.3192	0.8141	53.7	0.1690	0.0941	47.7

Table 15D.30: Physical quantities for a loaded, articulated truck on an unpaved surface

RF	C	QI	Fuel	Lubricants	Tire wear	Maint.-parts	Maint.-labor	Depreciation	Interest	Time per-distance
0	0	50	502.0	5.7	0.3021	0.2954	31.7	0.1108	0.0449	20.3
		150	604.3	6.9	0.3366	0.5547	44.0	0.1341	0.0611	29.3
		250	791.2	8.1	0.3847	0.8141	53.7	0.1670	0.0918	46.3
	500	50	538.7	5.7	0.3401	0.2954	31.7	0.1257	0.0548	25.8
		150	623.6	6.9	0.3908	0.5547	44.0	0.1394	0.0653	31.6
		250	796.9	8.1	0.4586	0.8141	53.7	0.1680	0.0929	47.0
	1000	50	550.7	5.7	0.3395	0.2954	31.7	0.1295	0.0576	27.3
		150	630.8	6.9	0.3906	0.5547	44.0	0.1413	0.0668	32.5
		250	799.3	8.1	0.4586	0.8141	53.7	0.1684	0.0933	47.2
40	0	50	735.8	5.7	0.5347	0.2954	31.7	0.1219	0.0521	24.3
		150	774.9	6.9	0.6131	0.5547	44.0	0.1390	0.0649	31.4
		250	887.4	8.1	0.7132	0.8141	53.7	0.1681	0.0930	47.1
	500	50	743.6	5.7	0.6353	0.2954	31.7	0.1320	0.0594	28.4
		150	781.9	6.9	0.7436	0.5547	44.0	0.1433	0.0685	33.4
		250	891.6	8.1	0.8844	0.8141	53.7	0.1690	0.0941	47.7
	1000	50	746.4	5.7	0.6354	0.2954	31.7	0.1349	0.0616	29.6
		150	784.8	6.9	0.7435	0.5547	44.0	0.1449	0.0698	34.2
		250	893.4	8.1	0.8844	0.8141	53.7	0.1694	0.0946	47.9
80	0	50	1242.6	5.7	1.2414	0.2954	31.7	0.1434	0.0686	33.5
		150	1277.0	6.9	1.4422	0.5547	44.0	0.1540	0.0782	38.8
		250	1327.0	8.1	1.6976	0.8141	53.7	0.1740	0.1001	51.0
	500	50	1248.0	5.7	1.5219	0.2954	31.7	0.1493	0.0738	36.4
		150	1279.7	6.9	1.8003	0.5547	44.0	0.1566	0.0808	40.3
		250	1328.3	8.1	2.1606	0.8141	53.7	0.1747	0.1010	51.5
	1000	50	1249.7	5.7	1.5231	0.2954	31.7	0.1511	0.0754	37.3
		150	1280.7	6.9	1.8007	0.5547	44.0	0.1576	0.0818	40.8
		250	1328.8	8.1	2.1606	0.8141	53.7	0.1750	0.1014	51.7

CHAPTER 16

Conclusions

The major conclusions from this study may be drawn from the perspectives of a planner as well as a researcher, as laid down in the following paragraphs.

16.1 PLANNING TOOLS

The study has yielded the following tools useful for a range of highway planning purposes:

1. A set of aggregate models for predicting speed, fuel consumption, tire wear and vehicle utilization of cars, utilities, buses, and light to articulated trucks under free-flowing conditions. These predictions constitute some 75 percent of the total operating cost of a typical Brazilian heavy truck through the component costs of fuel, tires, depreciation and interest and crew (the remaining 25 percent comprise lubricants and vehicle maintenance). Expressed generally as non-linear algebraic functions of vehicle characteristics and road geometry, surface type and roughness, these models were mostly formulated under reasonable assumptions on driver/operator behavior and well-established principles of vehicle mechanics.[1] With one exception[2], they have been either calibrated (vehicle utilization model) or validated with independent data (speed and fuel models). To a substantial extent, the models are sensitive to vehicle and road characteristics and their interactions, and therefore are capable of discriminating among similar investment alternatives involving total transport cost tradeoffs. They are suitable for a number of highway planning applications ranging from project to sector level, involving alternative surfacing and geometric standards, as well as policy issues on road user taxes and vehicle axle load limits. Local adaptation of these models is facilitated by the fact that most of the model parameters can be readily interpreted in

---

[1] Because of the lack of data the tire wear prediction model for cars and utilities was calibrated as a simple linear function of road roughness.

[2] As shown in Chapter 11, because of unsuitable data the wear coefficient of the aggregate tread wear model could not be calibrated for the lateral force component. This is expected to cause some underprediction for roads with average horizontal curvatures greater than 300 degrees/km.

physical terms. Now incorporated in the World Bank's HDM-III model for total transport cost prediction, these models can be used for predicting vehicle operating costs alone and can be implemented on hand-held or personal computers (e.g., through a spreadsheet package).

2. Micro prediction models for speed, fuel and tires. Although developed primarily as a basis for formulating and testing the aggregate models, when implemented in a production version[3] these micro models can be used to evaluate the economic benefits of specific road link improvements.

16.2 RECOMMENDATIONS FOR FUTURE RESEARCH

While the study has yielded planning tools that can be of immediate use, there is still a wide scope for possible future research to improve or extend the results, as discussed below:

1. The probabilistic limiting speed theory, which served as the basis for formulating the steady-state speed model reported herein, provides a generalized framework which can and should be used to incorporate additional policy variables such as, speed limit and curve sight distance. Also, the effect of road width could be further enhanced.[4]

The unit fuel consumption functions, quantified for normally aspirated gasoline and diesel engines, should be adequate for most applications after appropriate adjustment for the progress in engine efficiency since the early seventies. New functions could be calibrated for substantially different engine designs (e.g., supercharged engines with an intercooler or gasohol/alcohol powered engines). And further tests could be carried out to improve the adjustment factors.

3. The technique for transforming the micro speed, fuel consumption and tire wear prediction models into

---

[3] For research purposes these models were coded in SAS (Statistical Analysis System) which is generally available only on mainframe IBM computers. Work is currently underway at GEIPOT in Brazil to develop a production version of the micro transitional prediction models for predicting speed, fuel consumption and tire wear.

[4] The Brazil data did not include roads narrower than 5 meters. As presented in Chapter 4, based on data from India, the effect of narrow roads on speed has been added to the steady-state speed model in a rather simple way. If possible, a future field study should incorporate other factors related to road width in the data collection effort such as shoulder conditions.

convenient aggregate form has been found to produce acceptable accuracy over a moderately wide range of road geometry. However, it should be tested over a more extreme range to ascertain whether an adjustment factor is needed to accommodate more severe transitional driving effects.

4. While a reasonable relationship between vehicle rolling resistance and road roughness has been quantified, alddi- tional field data should be collected to strengthen the existing coefficients. Future research efforts should also investigate the effects of tire properties, suspen- sion characteristics and road roughness pattern on the magnitudes of the coefficients. This should yield a more generalized and easily adaptable relationship.

5. The micro prediction models can be used as a building block of a model for simulating traffic flow interaction and the resulting fuel consumption, and the wear of tires and possibly parts under impeded flow conditions.

6. Conjunctive use of detailed experimental and more aggre- gate survey data has been found to be more effective than either type of data alone. This is clearly evident in the contrast between the fuel consumption and tire wear models; for the former there was an abundance of both experimental and survey data whereas for the latter there were survey data alone. As a result, the estimated coefficients of fuel consumption models are much better determined and refined than those of the tire wear models. Future field studies should include a comprehen- sive program of controlled experiments on tire wear as well as a road user survey covering sufficiently detailed information for mechanistic tire wear modelling purposes. More comprehensive and detailed data should permit the tire wear prediction models to be not only better quanti- fied but also able to distinguish between tire construc- tion types (e.g., bias vs. radial), types of rubber com- pounds and road surface aggregates, etc. Special efforts should be devoted to quantification of the effect of hori- zontal geometry on tire tread wear. This would make the models more policy-responsive as well as enhance their local adaptability.

7. The treatment of vehicle depreciation and interest costs could be improved with incorporation of models for the economic life of the vehicle and with more detailed data on operating characteristics (e.g., actual operating speed, type and size of loads, time spent on driving, loading/unloading, etc.) for calibration of the vehicle utilization model. Emphasis should be given to examining possible effects of road characteristics on vehicle life, non-driving time and vehicle availability.

Units

Quantity	Unit	Symbol	Note
Length	Meter	m	Fundamental
	Kilometer	km	1,000 m
	Millimeter	mm	m/1,000
Mass	Kilogram	kg	Fundamental
	Ton	ton	1,000 kg (Also written "tonne")
Time	Second	s	Fundamental
	Hour	h	3,600 s
	Year	year or y	Auxiliary
Angle	Radian	rad	Supplementary-fundamental
	Degree	deg	$\pi/180$ rad
Thermodynamic temperature	Kelvin	K	Fundamental
Area	Square meter	m^2	–
Volume	Cubic meter	m^3	–
	Cubic decimeter	dm^3	$m^3/1,000$ (for tire rubber volume)
Liquid volume	Liter	liter	$m^3/1,000$
	Milliliter	ml	liter/1,000
Mass density	Kilogram per per cubic meter	kg/m^3	–

Quantity	Unit	Symbol	Note
Moment of inertia of mass	Kilogram-square meter	$kg-m^2$	–
Linear velocity	Meter per second Kilometer per hour Millimeter per second	m/s km/h mm/s	– 3.6 m/s (m/s)/1,000 (for average rectified velocity)
Time per distance	Second per meter	s/m	1/(m/s)
Linear acceleration	Meter per second square	m/s^2	–
Angular velocity	Revolution per minute	rpm	$\pi/30$ rad/s
Force	Newton Kilogram force	N kgf	$kg-m/s^2$ 9.81 N
Power	Watt Metric horsepower	W metric hp or hp	N-m/s 736 W or 75 kgf-m/s (equal to 0.986 British hp)
Energy	Joule Kilojoule	J kJ	N-m or W-s 1,000 J
Pressure	Pascal Kilopascal	Pa kPa	N/m^2 1,000 Pa

Glossary of Symbols

Notes:

1. An additional entry for a subscripted form of a symbol is included for significant instances only. A separate list of subscripts is given following the Greek symbols.

2. For each entry a brief explanation is given. The chapter and section offirst occurrence may be consulted for details.

3. In the column for units:

    1   means that the symbol stands for a dimensionless quantity.

    NVP   signifies that the quantity has units of the average price of a new vehicle of the same class, i.e., it is expressed as a fraction of new vehicle price.

    km   refers to vehicle-km unless specifically stated otherwise (e.g., tire-km).

    $ denotes any monetary unit.

    --   is used whenever units are inapplicable (e.g., expectation operator) or unhelpful (e.g., logarithm of speed) or various (e.g., a vector of disparate quantities).

Symbol	Meaning	Units	Section
A	Intermediate expression (= 0.5 RHO CD AR)	--	2B
a	Acceleration	m/s^2	2.2
$a_0 \ldots, a_7$	Coefficients of unit fuel consumption function	--	9.2
ADEP	Annual depreciation	NVP/1,000 km	12.3
AF	Air resistance	N	2.2
AFUEL	Predicted aggregate operating fuel consumption	liters/1,000 km	14.6
AINT	Annual interest	NVP/1,000 km	12.3
AKM	Vehicle utilization	km/year	12.3
ALABOR	Predicted maintenance labor	h/1,000 km	12.1
ALT	Road elevation above mean sea level	m	2.2
AMOMEN	Acceleration governed by braking capacity	m/s^2	6.2
AOIL	Lubricants consumption	liters/1,000 km	12.1
APART	Predicted maintenance parts	NVP/1,000 km	12.1
APOWER	Acceleration resulting from the use of HPRULE	m/s^2	6.3
AR	Vehicle projected frontal area	m^2	2.2
ARS	(= ARS(V)) Average rectified slope: rear axle suspension motion per distance	mm/m	3.3
ARS80	= ARS(80 km/h)	mm/m	3.3
ARV	(= ARV(V)) Average rectified velocity: rate of cumulative absolute displacement of rear-axle relative to vehicle body	mm/s	3.3
ASPEED	Predicted aggregate space-mean speed	km/h	14.5

Symbol	Meaning	Units	Section
B	Intermediate expression	--	
$b_0 \ldots, b_4$	$(= b_i(RPM))$ Parametric coefficients of intermediate form of UFC	--	9A
BI	Road roughness measured by Bump Integrator trailer at 32 km/h	mm/km	14.2
BP	Barometric pressure	kPa	13.3
BW	Free-flow width effect parameter	1	4.4
C	Horizontal curvature	degrees/km	2.1
c_s	Curvature of homogeneous sections	degrees/km	7A
$c_0, \ldots, c_4$	Coefficients of $b_i(RPM)$	--	9A
CD	Aerodynamic drag coefficient	1	2.2
CFT	Circumferential force on a tire	N	11.1
CHC	Cargo holding cost	$/1,000 km	14.5
CKM	Average road age of vehicle group	km	12.1
CL_p	Parts exponent in maintenance labor equation	1	12.1
CL_q	Roughness coefficient in maintenance labor equation	$(QI)^{-1}$	12.1
CL_0	Constant term in the maintenance labor equation	1	12.1
$c\ell_s$	$= c_s \ell_s$	1,000 degrees	7A
CN	Cost of a new tire	$	11.1
CO_0	Constant term in the lubricants equation	liters/1,000 km	14.7
CP_q	Roughness coefficient in parts-roughness relation	$(QI)^{-1}$	12.1
CP_0	Constant term in parts-roughness relation	1	12.1

Symbol	Meaning	Units	Section
CR	Rolling resistance coefficient	1	2.2
CRH	Crew hours	h/1,000 km	14.5
CRPM	"Average" (calibrated) nominal engine speed	rpm	10.6
CRT	Cost of a retread	$	11.1
CT_c	Tire tread wear coefficient – circumferential	dm^3/kJ	11.1
CT_ℓ	Tire tread wear coefficient – lateral	dm^3/kJ	11.1
CTV	Cost of tire wear (by vehicle)	$/1,000 km	11.4
CTW	Cost of tire wear (by tire)	$/1,000 tire-km	11.1
CV[.]	Coefficient of variation of . (= standard deviation/mean)	--	--
D	Discriminant of a cubic	--	3B
D	Kolmogorov–Smirnov statistic for test of normality	1	4B
D_1, D_2	Intermediate expressions	--	14.5
d	Differential sign	--	--
$d_0, \ldots, d_4$	Coefficients of b_1(RPM)	--	9A
d_1, d_2	Intermediate expressions	--	14.5
DBRAKE	Deceleration goverened by used braking power	m/s^2	6.2
DDESIR	Desired deceleration	m/s^2	6.2
DDRIVE	Decleration governed by used driving power	m/s^2	6.2
DE	Depth of tire tread grooves	mm	11D
DECEL	Predicted deceleration	m/s^2	6.2
DF	Drive force	N	2.2

Symbol	Meaning	Units	Section
DISTOT	Total distance of travel provided by a tire carcass	1,000 km	11.1
DRT	Differential speed ratio	1	9.1
E°	Estimation bias correction factor for section-specific steady-state speed prediction	1	3.4
$E[.]$	Expectation of .	--	--
$E^2[.]$	$=(E[.])^2$	--	--
e	Section-specific error in log-speed model	--	3.4
$e_0,\ldots e_4$	Coefficients of $b_1(RPM)$	--	9A
EQNT	Predicted number of equivalent new tires (by tire)	$(1,000\ \text{tire-km})^{-1}$	14.6
EQNTV	Predicted number of equivalent new tires (by vehicle)	$(1,000\text{-km})^{-1}$	11.4
EVU	Elasticity of vehicle utilization	1	12.2
F	Predicted amount of fuel consumed	ml	10.1
FC	Fuel consumption per distance	ml/m	10.1
FL	Road "fall"	1	2.1
FRATIO	Perceived friction ratio	1	3.3
FRATIO_0	Intercept term in the relation between FRATIO and payload	1	4.3
FRATIO_1	Slope term in the relation betweem FRATIO and payload	kg^{-1}	4.3
FUELA	Predicted aggregate experimental fuel consumption	liters/1,000 km	14.6
g	Acceleration due to gravity (≈ 9.81)	m/s^2	--
g_s	Vertical gradient of homogeneous section s	1	7A
GF	Gravitational force	N	2.2

Symbol	Meaning	Units	Section
GR	Road gradient	1	2.2
GRT	Gear speed ratio	1	9.1
GVW	Rated gross vehicle weight	kg	4.3
HAV	Vehicle availability	h/year	12.3
HP	Vehicle power delivered at the driving wheels	metric hp	2.2
HPBRAKE	Used braking power	metric hp	3.3
HPDRIVE	Used driving power	metrip hp	3.3
HPGRAD	Used driving power modified to take into account the effective gradient	metric hp	6.3
HPRATED	Vehicle maximum rated power	metric hp	4.3
HPRULE	Driving power used according to the rule derived from assumed transitional driver behavior	metric hp	6.3
HPSS	Power required to sustain steady-state speed	metric hp	6.3
HRD	Hours driven	h/year	12.2
I	Number of sections in steady-state speed model estimation	1	4A
I_e	Moment of inertia of mass of rotating parts of the vehicle	$kg\text{-}m^2$	2.2
I_w	Moment of inertia of mass of wheels	$kg\text{-}m^2$	2.2
IRI	International Roughness Index	m/km	2.1
J_i	Number of vehicles of a class observed at section i	1	4A
K	$= \sum_s c\ell_s$	1,000 degrees	7A
K_p	Age exponent in parts consumption equation	1	12.1

Symbol	Meaning	Units	Section
K_0	Tread wear per unit slip energy	dm^3/kJ	11.1
k	Tire stiffness	1	11.1
k_0	Conversion factor between the ARS80 and the QI measures of roughness (= 0.0882)	counts/m	3.3
L	Length	m	Various
ℓ_s	Length of homogeneous section s	m	7A
LF	Lateral force on vehicle	N	3.3
LFT	Lateral force on tire	N	11.1
LL	Length of lower trapezoid base of tire tread	mm	11D
LN	Proportional length of downhill travel	1	7.3
$LOAD$	Vehicle payload	kg	4.3
LP	Proportional length of uphill travel	1	7.3
LU	Length of upper trapezoid base of tire tread	mm	11D
M_w	Mass of wheels	kg	2.2
m	Vehicle mass	kg	2.2
m'	Effective vehicle mass	kg	2.2
m_e	Equivalent translatory mass of vehicle rotating parts	kg	2.2
m_w	Equivalent translatory mass of wheels	kg	2.2
$MRPM$	Maximum rated engine speed	rpm	13.4
MVC	Cargo monetary value	$	14.5
N	Iteration counter	1	6.2
N_h	Number of highway tires on a vehicle	1	11D

Symbol	Meaning	Units	Section
N_r	Maximum practical number of retreads for a tire	1	11.2.1
N_s	Number of section-directions	1	13.3
n	Sample size	1	4C
n	An exponent	1	11A
NF	Normal force on vehicle	N	3.4
NFT	Normal force on tire	N	11.1
NG	Weighted average of absolute values of negative grades	1	7.3
ng_s	$= -\text{Min}\,(0,\,g_s)$	1	7A
NH	Negative power	metric hp	9A
NH_0	Lower limit on negative power	metric hp	9.2
NHX	Bounded negative power	metric hp	9A
NL	$= \sum_s n\ell_s$	m	71
$n\ell_s$	$= ng_s\,\ell_s$	m	7A
NL	$= \sum_s n\ell_s$	m	7A
NR	Average number of retreads for a carcass	1	11.1
NR_0	Base number of recaps for a carcass	1	11.3
NTRIPS	Number of trips a year	1	12.3
P	$= \sum_s p_s$	m	7A
P[.]	Probability of .	1	--
P_0	Constant term in tangential extension of parts-roughness relation	1	12.1
P_1	Roughness coefficient in tangential extension of parts-roughness relation	$(QI)^{-1}$	12.1

Symbol	Meaning	Units	Section
p, p_0, p_1, etc.	Coefficients in an algebraic expression	--	Various
p_s	Length of a homogeneous section s with a non-negative grade, zero otherwise	m	7A
PAX	Average number of passengers per vehicle	1	14.5
PG	Weighted average of positive and level grades	1	7.3
pg_s	$= \text{Max}(0, g_s)$	1	7A
PH	Positive power	metric hp	9A
PHX	Number of passenger-hours	h/1,000 km	14.5
PL	$= \sum_s p\ell_s$	m	7A
$p\ell_s$	$= pg_s\, \ell_s$	m	7A
PNG	Average of PG and NG	1	7.3
PNR(r)	The probability that tire will last through r retreads	1	11.1
PP	Proportion of paved part of a roadway	1	7.3
q, q_0, q_1, etc	Coefficients in an algebraic expression	--	Various
QI	Road roughness measured by quarter-car index scale	counts/km	2.1
QIP_0	Exponential-linear transitional value of roughness in parts consumption equation	QI	12.1
R	Road velocity relative to wheel axle	m/s	11A
R^2	Explained variance/total variance	1	--
r	Intermediate expression	--	3B
r	Variable denoting number of retreads for a tire	1	11.1

Symbol	Meaning	Units	Section
r_0, r_1	Surface type-specific parameter in the speed-sensitive ARS formula	--	3.3
RC	Radius of curvature	m	2.1
RF	Roadway rise plus fall	m/km	7.3
RHO	Mass density of air	kg/m^3	2.2
RL	Route length	km	12.3
RMT	Average of the inner and outer radii of a tire	m	2A.2
RNT	Nominal radius of a tire	m	2A.2
RPM	Engine speed	rpm	9.1
RR	Rolling resistance	N	2.2
RREC	Ratio of costs of a retreading and a new tire	1	11.4
RRT	Tire rolling radius	m	2.2
RS	Road "rise"	1	2.1
RWG	Wheel radius of gyration	m	2.2
S	Round-trip speed on a given route	km/h	12.3
S	$\sum_s s\ell_s$	m	7A
s_s	Superelevation of homogeneous section s	1	7A
SE	Slip energy	J	11B
SFC	(=SFC(HP, RPM)) Specific fuel consumption	ml/metric hp.s	9.3
$s\ell_s$	$s_s \ell_s$	m	7A
SMS	Space-mean speed	m/s	5.1
SP	Superelevation	1	3.2

Symbol	Meaning	Units	Section
SR	Speed reduction ratio	1	2.2
SSQ(.)	Sum of squares to be minimized with respect to .	--	--
SSR	Sum of squared residuals	--	--
ST	Surface type	Qualitative	3.2
STDLOAD	Assumed average payload of observed population vehicles	kg	4.3
T	Tire slip velocity	m/s	11A
t	Student's test statistic	1	--
t	Elapsed time	s	2A.2
TARE	Vehicle tare weight	kg	14.3
TF	Nominal tire diameter	m	9.1
TD	Driving time	h/trip	12.3
TF	Tangential force on vehicle	N	3.3
TFT	Tangential force on tire	N	11.1
TIRE	Predicted amount of rubber lost	dm^3	11C
TLNEW	Distance life of a cost-equivalent new tire	1,000 km	11.1
TM	Temperature	K	13.3
TN	Non-driving time	h/trip	12.3
TT	Trip time	h	12.3
TWN	New tread wear rate	$(1,000 \text{ tire-km})^{-1}$	11.1
TWR	Retread wear rate	$(1,000 \text{ tire-km})^{-1}$	11.1
TWT	Tire tread wear - total	$dm^3/1,000$ tire-km	11.1
TWT_c	Tire tread wear - due to circumferential force	"	"
TWT_ℓ	Tire tread wear - due to lateral force	"	"

Symbol	Meaning	Units	Section
TWT_0	Tire tread wear - due to unmeasured influences	"	"
U, U_z, U, etc.^{z}	Logarithms of respective V quantities	--	3.4
u_i	Mean of log-speeds at section i	--	4A
UFC	(= UFC(HP, RPM)) Unit fuel consumption	ml/s	9.1
UFC_0	$= a_0 + a_1 RPM + a_2 RMP^2$	ml/s	9.2
V	Vehicle speed	m/s	2.2
V_{br}	Braking power-limited speed constraint as a random variable	m/s	3.4
V_c	Curvature-limited speed constraint as a random variable	m/s	3.4
V_d	Desired speed as a random variable	m/s	3.4
V_{dr}	Driving power-limited speed constraint as a random variable	m/s	3.4
V_r	Roughness-limited speed constraint as a random variable	m/s	3.4
V_z	General expression for speed constraint treated as a random variable	m/s	3.4
V'	Arithmetic minimum of mean speed constraints	m/s	3.4
V	(=$V(X,Y:\theta,\beta)$) Systematic part of observed speed variate V	m/s	3.4
V_z	Systematic part of speed constraint variate V_z	m/s	3.4
v	Realization of observed speed random variable V	m/s	3.4
v_z	Realization of speed constraint variate V_z	m/s	3.4
V_w	Wind speed	m/s	2.2
Var[.]	Variance of .	--	--

Symbol	Meaning	Units	Section
VAVG	Average of VENMAX and VEXMAX	m/s	6.2
VAVG2	Average of squares of VENMAX and VEXMAS	--	6.2
VBRAKE	Constraining speed related to braking power	m/s	3.2
VCTL	Control speed: maximum allowed "safe" speed	m/s	6.2
VCURVE	Constraining speed related to curvature	m/s	3.2
VDECEL	Maximum allowed "deceleration" speed	m/s	6.2
VDESIR	Desired speed: constraining speed related to subjective factors	m/s	3.2
VDESIR '	VDESIR modified to take into account effect of road width	m/s	4.4
VDRIVE	Constraining speed related to driving power	m/s	3.2
VEN	Predicted entry speed	m/s	6.3
VENTMAX	Maximum allowed entry speed	m/s	6.2
VEX	Predicted exit speed	m/s	6.3
VEXMAX	Maximum allowed exit speed	m/s	6.2
VMOMEN	Maximum allowed "momentum" speed	m/s	6.2
VOL	Tire rubber volume	dm^3	11.5
VPOWER	Exit speed resulting from acceleration APOWER	m/s	6.3
VROUGH	Constraining speed related to roughness	m/s	3.2
VSS	Steady-state speed	m/s	3.2
VSS_{s_0}	Average observed speed at section-direction s	m/s	13.3
W	Weibull random variable	--	3A.1
W	Roadway width	m	4.4

Symbol	Meaning	Units	Section
w	Error specific to speed observation in log-speed model	--	3.4
x	(= x(t)) Distance traversed	m	2A.2
x_1, x_2	Arbitrary distance points	m	2A.2
Y	Intermediate expression	--	2A.2
Y	Vector of vehicle characteristics	--	3.2
Z	Gumbel random variable	--	3A.2
z	Intermediate expression	--	3B
α	Scale parameter of a Weibull distribution	--	3A.1
α_1	Relative energy-efficiency factor	1	9.4
α_2	Fuel adjustment factor	1	10.8
β	Shape parameter of Weibull distribution	--	3.4
Γ	Gamma function	--	3A.1
μ	Location parameter of Gumbel distribution	--	3A.2
γ	Central angle subtended by a curve	Degree	2.1
γ	Euler's constant ($\simeq 0.577$)	1	3A.2
γ_i	Weights in the steady-state speed model estimation	--	4A
Δ	Increment sign	--	--
ΔAR_{12}	Energy loss due to air resistance between points 1 and 2	J	2A.2
ΔKE_{12}	Change in kinetic energy between points 1 and 2	J	2A.2
ΔPE_{12}	Change in potential energy between points 1 and 2	J	2A.2

Symbol	Meaning	Units	Section
ΔRE_{12}	Energy loss due to rolling resistance between points 1 and 2	J	2A.2
δ_{ij}	Weibull model error treated additively	--	4A
ε	$(=\varepsilon(X))$ Section-specific error in observed speed	--	3.4
ζ	$(=\zeta(X,Y))$ Vehicle-specific error in observed speed	--	3.4
η	Slip angle	rad	11A
θ	Vector of steady-state speed model parameters	--	3.2
λ	Scale parameter of Gumbel distribution	--	3A
λ	Wheel slip	1	11A
ν	$(=\nu(X,Y,))$ Joint contribution of speed constraint errors to observed speed variate	--	3.4
ν_z	$(=\nu_z(X,Y))$ Random part of speed constraint variate V_z	--	3.4
ξ	Random part of observed speed variate V	--	3.4
ξ_z	Random part of speed constraint variate V_z	--	3.4
π	Ratio of circumference to diameter $(\simeq 3.146)$	1	--
$\sum$	Summation sign	--	--
σ	Standard error of log-speed	--	3.4
σ_e	Standard error of section-specific error in log-speed model	--	3.4
σ_w	Standard error of error specific to speed observation in log-speed model	--	3.4

Symbol	Meaning	Units	Section
τ	Time per distance	s/m or h/1000 km	5.1
$\emptyset$	Road inclination	rad	2.1
χ	Likelihood ratio	1	4C
χ^2_f	Chi-square test statistic with f degrees of freedom	--	4C
ω	$(=\omega(X,Y))$ Error specific to a speed observation	--	3.4

References

Abaynayaka, S.W. and others. <u>A Study of Factors Affecting Traffic Speeds on Rural Roads in Kenya.</u> TRRL Supplementary Report 28 UC. Department of the Environment, Transport and Road Research Laboratory. Crowthorne, England, 1974.

Andersen, S.W. and S. Gravem. "Fuel Consumption Model and Preliminary Abstract." Private communication. October 1979.

Beck, R. <u>Parametric Analysis of the Off-Road Performance of a Special Tracked Test Vehicle.</u> Proceedings of the 6th International Conference, International Society of Terrain Vehicle Systems, vol. 3, August 22-25. Vienna, Austria, 1978.

Ben-Akiva, M. and S.R. Lerman. <u>Discrete Choice Analysis: Theory and Application to Predict Travel Demand.</u> MIT Press, Cambridge, Massachusetts, 1985.

Benjamin, J.R. and C.A. Cornel. <u>Probability, Statistics and Decision for Civil Engineers.</u> McGraw-Hill, New York, 1970.

Bergman, W. and W.B. Crum. "New Concepts of Tire Wear: Measurement and Analysis." <u>Society of Automotive Engineers</u>, SAE transactions 730615. Warrendale, Pennsylvania, 1973.

Bester, C.J. <u>Effect of Pavement Type and Condition of the Fuel Consumption of Vehicles.</u> Transportation Research Record (1,000), pp. 28-32, 1984.

——————— . "Fuel Consumption of Highway Traffic." Doctoral dissertation, University of Pretoria. Pretoria, South Africa, 1981.

Bhandari, A. and others. <u>An Investigation of Cost Effective Road Maintenance and Improvement Options.</u> Discussion Paper No. 5. Transportation Department, World Bank. Washington, DC (forthcoming).

Brademeyer, B. <u>The Road Investment Analysis Model: User Manual</u> Technology Adaptation Program, Massachusetts Institute of Technology, (TAP report 77-10). Cambridge, Massachusetts, 1977.

Brodin, A., G. Gynnerstedt and G. Levander. <u>A Program for Monte Carlo Simulation of Vehicle along Two-Lane Rural Roads. An Application of Structured Programming Technique and Simula-67 Language.</u> Meddelande Institute, No. 143, National Road and Traffic Research. Linkoping, Sweden, 1979.

Central Road Research Institute. Road User Cost Study in India.   Final report. New Delhi, India, 1982.

Chesher, A. "Vehicle Operating Cost Equations Developed from the Indian Road User Cost Survey Data." Unpublished report prepared for Transportation and Water Department, World Bank. Washington, D.C., May 1983.

——————. "Transferability of User Cost Equations: Methodology for Country Studies." GEIPOT/PICR project memorandum ICR/AC/002/82. March 5, 1982(a).

——————. "A Method for Estimating Limiting Velocity Vehicle Speed Models." Unpublished note prepared for Transportation Department, World Bank. Washington, DC, April 1982(b).

——————. "Transferability of User Cost Equations: An Example Using the Brazil Study Data." GEIPOT/PICR project memorandum ICR/AC/099/82. May 24, 1982(c).

Chesher, A. and R. Harrison. Vehicle Operating Costs: Evidence from Developing Countries.   Transportation Department, World Bank. Washington, DC (forthcoming).

Chesher, A. and R. Harrison. "Tire Wear and the Effect of Highway Characteristics: Preliminary Report." Unpublished internal technical memorandum of GEIPOT/PICR Research. GEIPOT, Brasilia, Brazil, 1980.

Chiesa, A. and G. Ghilardi. "Evaluation of Tire Abrasion in Terms of Driving Severity." Society of Automotive Engineers, SAE transactions 750459. Warrendale, Pennsylvania, 1975.

Della-Moretta, L. "Relating Operational Variables to Tire Wear." Paper presented at the International Society for Terrain Vehicle Systems, Regional Meeting. Carson City, Nevada, October 1974.

Della-Moretta, L. and E.C. Sullivan. "U.S. Forest Service Vehicle Operating Cost Model." Proceedings of the Workshop on Lessening Energy Waste in the Road-Tire-Vehicle-Driven System, sponsored by the U.S. Department of Agriculture, Forest Service and the University of California, Institute of Transportation Studies.   Claremont, California, 1976.

de Weille, J. Quantification of Road User Savings. World Bank Staff Occasional Paper no. 2, World Bank. Washington, DC, 1966.

Dickson, L.E. New First Course in the Theory of Equations. Wiley, New York, 1957.

Domencich, T.A. and D. McFadden. Urban Travel Demand: A Behavioral Analysis. North-Holland Publishing Co., Amsterdam, Netherlands, 1975.

Fisher, W.D. Clustering and Aggregation in Economics. Johns Hopkins University Press, Baltimore, Maryland, 1969.

GEIPOT. Research on the Interrelationships Between Costs of Highway Construction Maintenance and Utilization: Final Report on Brazil-UNDP Highway Research Project. (12 volumes). Brasilia, Brazil, 1982.

Galanis, N.H. Users Manual for Program RODES. National Institute for Transport and Road Research. Reports RX/1/80, RX/11/80, RX/12/80. Pretoria, South Africa, 1980.

Gillespie, T.D. "Technical Consideration in the Worldwide Standardizatio and Road Roughness Measurement." Highway Safety Research Institute. University of Michigan, Report No. UM-HSRI-81-28. Ann Arbor, Michigan: 1981.

Gillespie, T.D., M.W. Sayers and L. Segel. Calibration of Response-Type and Roughness Measuring Systems. NCHRP Report 228, National Cooperative Highway Research Program. Washington, DC, 1980.

Good, M.C. Road Curve Geometry and Driver Behavior. ARRB Special Report No. 15, Australian Road Research Board. Victoria, Australia, 1978.

Gourieroux, C. and others. Pseudo Maximum Likelihood Methods: Theory. Econometrica (52), pp. 681-700, 1984.

Gravem, S. "A Microscopic Discrete-Event Simulation Model for Two-Lane Highway Network." Unpublished report. Preliminary report. A Traffic Simulation Model for Two-Lane Roads, Institute of Transport. Economics, Norway, 1978.

Green, J.H.A. Aggregation in Economic Analysis: An Introductory Survey. Princeton University Press, Princeton, New Jersey, 1964.

Grosch, K.A. and A. Schallamach. "Tire Wear of Controlled Slip." Vol. 4 (356). 1961.

Guenther, Karl W. Predictive Models for Vehicle Operating Consequences. M.S. thesis, Civil Engineering Department, Massachusetts Institute of Technology. Cambridge, Massachusetts, 1969.

Gupta, K.L. Aggregation in Economics: A Theoretical and Empirical Study Rotterdam University Press, Rotterdam, Netherlands, 1969.

Gynnerstedt, G., A. Carlsson and B. Westerlund. A Model for the Monte Carlo Simulation of Traffic Flow along Two-Lane Single-Carriageway Rural Roads, National Road and Traffic Research Institute. Linkoping, Sweden, 1977.

Gynnerstedt, G. and R.J. Troutbeck. Computer Programs and Simulation Models with Associated Field Experiments for the Indian Road User Cost Study. Australian Road Research Board Internal Report AIR 838-2, Australian Road Research Board. July 1981.

Hide, O. Vehicle Operating Costs in the Caribbean: Results of a Survey of Vehicle Operators. TRRL Report 1031. Department of the Environment, Transport and Road Research Laboratory. Crowthorne, England, 1982.

————— . Vehicle Operating Costs in the Caribbean. Working Paper no. 81. TRRL Overseas Unit. Department of the Environment, Transport and Road Research Laboratory. Crowthorne, England, 1980.

Hide, H. and others. The Kenya Road Transport Cost Study: Research on Vehicle Operating Costs. TRRL Report LR 672. Department of the Environment, Transport and Road Research Laboratory. Crowthorne, England, 1975.

Hoban, C.J. "Methods of Evaluation used in ARRB Simulation Studies." Paper presented at the Workshop on Rural Traffic Simulation. Australian Road Research Board. Victoria, Australia, 1983.

Hodges, H.C. and K.D. Koch. Tire Treadwear Validation, vol 1: Technical Report. National Highway Traffic Safety Administration, U.S. Department of Transportation. Washington, DC, 1979.

Johnson, N.L. and S. Kotz. Continuous Univariate Distributions, vol. I. Houghton Mifflin, Boston, 1970.

Jones, D. and L. Della-Moretta. Truck Tire Wear Rates on Open vs. Dense-Graded Asphalt Pavement. Report No. 7977-1210. U.S. Department of Agriculture, Forest Service. Washington, DC, 1979.

Kadiyali, L.R. and others. Rolling Resistance and Air Resistance Factors for Simulation Study. Road User Costs Study Technical Paper No. 92, Seventeenth Quarterly Report, Central Road Research Institute. New Delhi, India, 1982.

Koppelman, F.S. Aggregation in Economic Analysis: An Introductory Survey, Princeton University Press, Princeton, New Jersey, 1964.

Korst, H.H. and R.A. White. "Aerodynamic and Rolling Resistances of Vehicles as Obtained from Coast-down Experiments." In the Proceedings of the Second International Conference on Vehicle Mechanics, edited by P. Rapin and H.K. Sachs. Swets and Zeitlinger, Amsterdam, Netherlands, 1973.

Lee, R.A. and F. Pradko. Analytical Analysis of Human Vibration. Society of Automotive Engineers No. 680091. Warrendale, Pennsylvania, 1968.

Limpert, R. "Tires and Rims." Vehicle System Components. Wiley, New York, 1982.

Lind, Robert C. and others. Discounting for Time and Risk in Energy Policy. Resources for the Future, Inc., Washington, DC, 1982.

Lu, X.P. "Effects of Road Roughness on Vehicular Rolling Resistance." Paper presented at the ASTM Symposium on Roughness Methodology. Bal Harbor, Florida, 1983.

Malinvaud, E. Statistical Methods of Econometrics. 3d ed. North-Holland Publishing Co.. Amsterdam, Netherlands, 1980.

McAdams, H.T. and others. Fuel Economy of Automotive Vehicles: A Compendium of Statistical Techniques. National Technical Information Service, U.S. Department of Commerce. Springfield, Virginia, 1977.

McFadden, D. "Qualitative Response Models." In Advances in Econometrics, edited by Werner Hildenbrand, Cambridge University Press. Cambridge, England: 1982.

McFadden, D. "Econometric Models for Probabilistic Choice." In Structural Analysis of Discrete Choice Data with Econometric Applications, edited by C.F. Manski and D. McFadden. MIT Press, Cambridge, Massachusetts, 1981.

McFadden, D. and F. Reid. "Aggregate Travel Demand Forecasting from Disaggregated Behavioral Models." Paper presented at the 54th Annual Meeting of the Transportation Research Board. Washington, DC, 1975.

McLean, J.R. Observed Speed Distribution and Rural Road Traffc Operations.Australian Road Research Board Proceedings, vol. 9 part 5. Vermont-South, Australia, 1978.

Moavenzadeh, F. and others. Highway Design Standards Study Phase I: The Model. Staff Working Paper No. 96, World Bank. Washington, DC. 1971.

Morosiuk, G. and S.W. Abaynayaka. Vehicle Operating Costs in the Caribbean: An Experimental Study of Vehicle Performance. TRRL Report 1056. Department of the Environment, Transport and Road Research Laboratory. Crowthorne, England, 1982.

Nordeen, D.L. and A.D. Cortese. Force and Moment Characteristics of Rolling Tires." Society of Automotive Engineers. Warrendale, Pennsylvania, 1964.

Oglesby, C.H. and R.G. Hicks. Highway Engineering, 4th ed., Wiley, New York, 1982.

Organization for Economic Cooperation and Development. Automobile Fuel Consumption in Actual Traffic Conditions. A report prepared by an OECD Research Group, Road Research, 1982.

Parsley, L. and R. Robinson. The TRRL Road Investment Model for Developing Countries (RTIM2). TRRL Report 1057. Department of the Environment, Transport and Road Research Laboratory. Crowthorne, England, 1982.

Paterson, W.D.O. Road Deterioration and Maintenance Effects: Models for Planning and Management. Transportation Department, World Bank. Washington, DC, 1987.

——————— . "Interim Report Reviewing Data Collection and Analysis in the Brazil PICR Project." Unpublished. December 1982.

Paterson, W.D.O. and T. Watanatada. "Relationships between vehicle Speed, Ride Quality, and Road Roughness." In T.D. Gillespie and M. Sayers (eds.), Measuring Road Roughness and Its Effect on User Cost and Comfort. ASTM STP 884. American Society for Testing and Materials. Philadelphia, Pennsylvania, 1985.

Rezende—Lima, P.R.S. "Analysis of Tire Wear Based on Principles of Pneumatic Tire Mechanics." Unpublished internal memorandum of the Highway Design and Maintenance Standards Study. Transportation Department. World Bank, Washington, DC, January 1984.

Robinson, R. and others. A Road Transport Investment Model for Developing Countries. TRRL Report LR 674. Department of the Environment, Transport and Road Research Laboratory. Crowthorne, England, 1975.

SAS Institute. SAS User's Guide. Raleigh, North Carolina, 1979.

Sayers, M.W., T.D. Gillespie and W.D.O. Paterson. Guidelines for Conducting and Calibrating Road Roughness Measurements. Technical Paper No. 46, World Bank. Washington, DC, 1986.

Schallamach, A. "Tire Traction and Wear." In Mechanics of Pneumatic Tires, edited by S.K. Clark. U.S. Department of Transportation, National Highway Traffic Safety Administration. Washington, DC, 1981.

Schallamach, A. and D.R. Turner. "The Wear of Slipping Wheels." Wear, vol. 3. 1960.

St. John, A.D. and D.R. Kobett. Grade Effects on Traffic Flow Stability and Capacity. National Cooperative Highway Research Program Report 185. Transportation Research Board, National Research Council. Washington, DC, 1978.

Sullivan, E.C. The Slip Energy Approach to Vehicle—Road Interactions: Background and Prospects. Institute of Transportation Studies Working Paper No.79-6, University of California. Berkeley, California: January 1979.

——————— . Vehicle Operating Cost Model - User's Guide. (2nd ed.) Institute of Transportation Studies Research Report (UCBITS-RR-77-3), University of California. Berkeley, California, 1977.

Taborek, J.J. "Mechanics of Vehicles." Machine Design. Towmotor Corporation. Cleveland, Ohio, 1957.

Taylor, C.F.   The Internal Combustion Engine in Theory and Practice. vol. I, MIT Press, Cambridge, Massachusetts, 1966.

Theil, H.   Linear Aggregation of Economic Relations. North-Holland Publishing Co., Amsterdam, Netherlands, 1955.

Thieme, H. van E. and A. Dijks.   "Measurement of Tire Properties." Mechanics of Pneumatic Tires.   National Highway Traffic Safety Administration, U.S. Department of Transportation. Washington, DC, 1981.

Veith, A.G.   "Tire Wear: Some Knowns and Unknowns." Paper presented at January 25, 1974 meeting of Akron Rubber Group. 1974.

Watanatada, T.   "Formulation of the Steady-State Speed Model." Unpublished working paper. Transportation and Water Department, World Bank. Washington, DC, April 1982.

———————— . Highway Design and Maintenance Standards Model (HDM-II): Model Description and User's Manual. Transportation and Water Department, World Bank. Washington, DC, December 1981.

Watanatada, T. and P.W. O'Keefe.   "Steady-State Speed Model Based on Probalistic Limiting Velocity Concept." Unpublished working paper. Transportation and Water Department, World Bank. Washington, DC, August 1982.

Watanatada, T. and others.   The Highway Design and Maintenance Standards Model: Volume 4a, HDM-III Model Description and Volume 4b, HDM-III User's Manual.   Transportation Department, World Bank. Washington, DC (forthcoming).

Williams, J.S.   Efficient Analysis of Weibull Survival Data from Experiments on Heterogeneous Patient Populations.   Biometrica (34), pp. 209-22, 1978.

Wong, J.Y.   Theory of Ground Vehicles.   Wiley, New York, 1978.

Wu, Shie-Shin and C.L. Heimbach.   Simulation of Highway Traffic on Two-lane Two-way Rural Highways.   North Carolina Department of Transportation. Raleigh, North Carolina.

Zaniewski, J. and others.   Vehicle Operating Costs, Fuel Consumption, and Pavement Type and Condition Factors.   Technical report prepared for U.S. Department of Transportation, Federal Highway Administration. Washington, DC, 1982.

Zaniewski, J. and others.   Research on the Interrelationships Between Costs of Highway Construction, Maintenance and Utilization Final Report IV: Road User Costs and Traffic Experiments.   Texas Research and Development Foundation. Austin, Texas, 1980.

List of Abbreviations

ARRB   – Australian Road Research Board
ASTM   – American Society for Testing and Measurement
CRRI   – Central Road Research Institute (India)
HDMS   – Highway Design and Maintenance Study
NCHRP   – National Cooperative Highway Research Program
GEIPOT – Brazilian Agency for Transportation Planning
TRRL   – Transport and Road Research Laboratory